# THE EARLY ANGLO-SAXON KINGDOMS OF SOUTHERN BRITAIN AD 450–650

*Beneath the Tribal Hidage*

Sue Harrington and †Martin Welch

Oxbow Books
Oxford & Philadelphia

First published in the United Kingdom in 2014. Reprinted in 2018 by
OXBOW BOOKS
The Old Music Hall, 106–108 Cowley Road, Oxford OX4 1JE

and in the United States by
OXBOW BOOKS
1950 Lawrence Road, Havertown, PA 19083

© Oxbow Books and the authors 2014

Paperback Edition: ISBN 978-178570-970-8

A CIP record for this book is available from the British Library

Library of Congress Cataloging-in-Publication Data

The early Anglo-Saxon kingdoms of southern Britain, AD 450-650 : beneath the Tribal Hidage / Sue Harrington and Martin Welch.
    pages cm
  Includes bibliographical references and index.
  ISBN 978-1-78297-612-7
  1. Anglo-Saxons--England--Antiquities. 2. Great Britain--History--Anglo-Saxon period, 449-1066. 3. Tribes--Great Britain--History--To 1500. 4. Hidage--History--To 1500. 5. Civilization, Anglo-Saxon. I. Welch, Martin G. II. Title.
  DA152.H274 2014
  942.01'4--dc23
                            2014015834

All rights reserved. No part of this book may be reproduced or transmitted in any form or by any means, electronic or mechanical including photocopying, recording or by any information storage and retrieval system, without permission from the publisher in writing.

For a complete list of Oxbow titles, please contact:

| UNITED KINGDOM | UNITED STATES OF AMERICA |
|---|---|
| Oxbow Books | Oxbow Books |
| Telephone (01865) 241249 | Telephone (800) 791-9354, Fax (610) 853-9146 |
| Email: oxbow@oxbowbooks.com | Email: queries@casemateacademic.com |
| www.oxbowbooks.com | www.casemateacademic.com/oxbow |

Oxbow Books is part of the Casemate group

Front cover:  South-easterly aspect from the Anglo-Saxon cemetery at Buckland Dinham, Somerset. Project boundary with major routeways.
Back cover:   Typical iron knives and shield boss.

Printed and bound in Great Britain by Marston Book Services Ltd, Oxfordshire

# Contents

List of Figures ............................................................................................................................. vii
List of Tables ............................................................................................................................... ix
List of Plates ................................................................................................................................. x
Preface ......................................................................................................................................... xi
Acknowledgements ................................................................................................................... xiii

1   The Early Anglo-Saxon Kingdoms of Southern Britain: evidence and questions ............ 1
    Introduction .......................................................................................................................... 1
    The kingdoms in the written sources *(text by Martin Welch, edited by Barbara Yorke)* ...... 3
    Research questions ............................................................................................................... 8
        What are the data? ......................................................................................................... 8
        What is the landscape context of that data? ................................................................. 8
        Why is the data located within this context – what were the criteria behind
            site location selection? .............................................................................................. 9
        How can this evidence be explained and interpreted – is this evidence of wealth creation
            and state formation? ................................................................................................. 9
    Methodology ...................................................................................................................... 10
    Overview of the contents of this volume .......................................................................... 11

2   The Early Anglo-Saxon Census ......................................................................................... 13
    Southern Britain south of the Thames and the archaeological data ................................. 13
    The database ...................................................................................................................... 14
        Data-quality assessment .............................................................................................. 14
        The dating framework ................................................................................................ 15
    The sites ............................................................................................................................. 19
    Populating the landscape .................................................................................................. 22
        These individuals and their graves .............................................................................. 26
        Phasing the burials ...................................................................................................... 28
    The artefacts ...................................................................................................................... 29
        Type ............................................................................................................................. 31
        Provenance ................................................................................................................. 31
            *Regional* ................................................................................................................ 32
            *Kentish; Saxon; Anglian; Wessex* ......................................................................... 32

|     | *Romano-British* | 32 |
|---|---|---|
|     | *British West* | 33 |
|     | *Curated/Roman; Curated/Jutlandic* | 33 |
|     | *Kentish/* | 33 |
|     | *Imported* | 33 |
|     | *Imported/* | 33 |
|     | Position in grave | 33 |
|     | Material component | 34 |
|     | Object weights | 34 |
| Findspots and their contents | | 36 |
| Other datasets used | | 39 |
|     | Late Roman sites | 39 |
|     | Place-name evidence | 40 |
| Concluding remarks | | 40 |

**3 The Environmental Context of Southern Britain** .......... 41
- Introduction .......... 41
- Mapping the evidence .......... 42
- The geology of southern Britain .......... 43
- Definitions of landscape units .......... 45
- Soil types and fertility: the mapping of land use potential .......... 48
- A new definition of landscape units in southern Britain .......... 50
- Climate .......... 52
- Rivers and floodplains .......... 53
- Palaeo-environmental evidence .......... 56
- Woodland .......... 56

**4 Travelling and Using the Land- and Sea-Scapes** .......... 58
- Coastal erosion and tide patterns .......... 58
- Changes to the southern coast of Britain .......... 60
- Roads, droveways and trackways south of the Thames .......... 63
- Agricultural practices .......... 66
- Pastoral practices .......... 69
- The environmental evidence from selected excavation reports for southern Britain .......... 70
  - The Upper Thames Valley and chalklands to the south .......... 70
  - Central chalk lands to the south coast .......... 71
  - The eastern area of the Thames, the Weald and the coast .......... 71
  - The western area .......... 73
- Conclusions .......... 73

**5 Sites, Locations and Soils** .......... 74
- Introduction .......... 74
- Theories of site location .......... 75
- Settlement and wealth in the three kingdoms .......... 78
  - Kent .......... 78
  - Wessex .......... 79

Sussex ....................................................................................................................................... 83
What was the spatial relationship between early cemeteries and their parent settlements? ............. 84
    Case study: The Lower Ouse Valley, East Sussex ...................................................................... 84
Where were the sites with the earliest artefactual evidence? ............................................................ 87
What are the spatial relationships of the cemeteries and settlements to routeways
    and other topographical features? ............................................................................................ 88
What kinds of soils do the cemetery/settlement communities occupy for their resource base
    and how does this compare with those occupied by the Later Roman sites? Were there
    spatial and temporal variations in site selection criteria? ....................................................... 90
    Roman sites .............................................................................................................................. 90
    Early Anglo-Saxon complexes .................................................................................................. 90
What relationships can be determined between the place-name data and the phase A
    and early phase B sites (AD 450–600)? ................................................................................... 91
Conclusions ...................................................................................................................................... 93

## 6 Surrey: A Case Study .................................................................................................................. 95
Surrey in the documentary sources .................................................................................................. 95
The archaeological evidence ............................................................................................................. 96
Conclusions .................................................................................................................................... 103

## 7 A Common Wealth in Iron? ..................................................................................................... 104
Introduction ................................................................................................................................... 104
Sources of iron ore .......................................................................................................................... 105
The regional settlement pattern and proximity to iron ore deposits ............................................... 105
The processes of iron working ........................................................................................................ 106
Iron working in Roman Britain ...................................................................................................... 107
Iron working in the Western Roman Empire .................................................................................. 109
Iron working in the northern European Barbaricum in the study period (AD 450–650) .............. 110
Iron working in southern Britain AD 450–650 and later ............................................................... 113
Discussion ...................................................................................................................................... 116

## 8 Community Wealth in Iron Compared .................................................................................... 122
Iron case study 1: shield bosses (AD 450–700) ............................................................................... 123
Iron case study 2: swords (AD 450–700) ........................................................................................ 124
Iron case study 3: knives (AD 450–700) ......................................................................................... 125
The iron-wealth over time and space (AD 450–700) ...................................................................... 126
    Phase A comparative study ..................................................................................................... 129
    Phase B comparative study ..................................................................................................... 132
    Phase C comparative study ..................................................................................................... 133
Conclusions on the value of iron in the study region and period ................................................... 135

## 9 A Restricted Wealth in Copper Alloys? .................................................................................... 137
European copper alloy production .................................................................................................. 138
Copper alloy production in Britain ................................................................................................. 138
Weights of copper alloy artefacts .................................................................................................... 140
Community access to copper alloy material over time and space ................................................... 141

|     |                                                                                  |     |
| --- | -------------------------------------------------------------------------------- | --- |
|     | Phase A comparative study                                                        | 142 |
|     | Phase B comparative study                                                        | 144 |
|     | Phase C comparative study                                                        | 144 |
|     | Copper alloy case study 1: buckle loops and plates                               | 145 |
|     | Copper alloy case study 2: bowls and escutcheons                                 | 148 |
|     | Phase A distribution of copper alloy bowls                                       | 149 |
|     | Phase B distribution of copper alloy bowls                                       | 150 |
|     | Phase C distribution of copper alloy bowls                                       | 150 |
|     | Sheet vessel fragments                                                           | 150 |
|     | Escutcheons                                                                      | 152 |
|     | Conclusions on copper alloy bowl distributions                                   | 154 |
| 10  | Esoteric Materials: Amber, Amethyst, Gold and Silver                             | 155 |
|     | Case study: amber beads                                                          | 155 |
|     | Case study: amethyst beads                                                       | 159 |
|     | Conclusions concerning amber and amethyst bead usage and distribution            | 161 |
|     | The role of precious metals: gold and silver                                     | 162 |
|     | Gold                                                                             | 164 |
|     | Phase A gold distribution                                                        | 167 |
|     | Phases B and C gold distribution                                                 | 168 |
|     | Silver                                                                           | 168 |
|     | Phase A silver distributions                                                     | 171 |
|     | Phase B silver distributions                                                     | 171 |
|     | Phase C silver distributions                                                     | 172 |
|     | Conclusions                                                                      | 173 |
| 11  | External Forces? A Review of the Frankish Influence within Southern Britain      | 174 |
| 12  | The Frankish Data Examined                                                       | 183 |
|     | Research questions                                                               | 183 |
|     | Phase A Frankish data                                                            | 184 |
|     | Frankish artefacts in Kent and Surrey                                            | 192 |
|     | Isle of Wight                                                                    | 192 |
|     | Westwards from the East Sussex coast                                             | 193 |
|     | Central Wiltshire and the Salisbury Plain                                        | 194 |
|     | Upper Thames Valley                                                              | 194 |
|     | Conclusions relating to Phase A                                                  | 195 |
|     | Phase B Frankish data                                                            | 196 |
|     | Phase C Frankish data                                                            | 197 |
|     | Frankish weapon burials                                                          | 201 |
|     | Conclusions                                                                      | 204 |
| 13  | Synthesis: Beneath the *Tribal Hidage*                                           | 206 |
| Bibliography                                                                           || 211 |
| Index                                                                                  || 227 |
| Plates                                                                                 || 235 |

# List of Figures

1. The study region with modern counties
2. The study region in the major Anglo-Saxon areas and the British West
3. View towards the south west from Camerton, Somerset, Anglo-Saxon cemetery: the Roman road from Bath to Radstock runs along the hedge line
4. View towards the south west from Kingston Down, Kent, Anglo-Saxon cemetery: the Roman road from Canterbury to Dover runs along the hedge line
5. The major geological features of the study region, together with the study region outline
6. The *pays* of Kent, from the work of Alan Everitt (1986)
7. The revised soil fertility map of the study region (level 5 is the greatest fertility)
8. The soil Ph values of the study region
9. The rivers and flood plains of the study region, with the rivers flowing either southwards into the sea or northwards into the River Thames
10. The site of the Cuxton, Kent, Anglo-Saxon cemetery from the River Medway
11. View north east from the plateau above Chatham Lines, Kent, Anglo-Saxon cemetery, towards the estuary of the River Medway and the Isle of Grain
12. The waves and tides of the North Sea and the English Channel (derived from Cresswell 1959)
13. View south west from Highdown, Sussex, Anglo-Saxon cemetery, towards the Channel and the Isle of Wight
14. Roman roads, with Margary numbers, and prehistoric trackways of the study region
15. View west up Saxton Road Abingdon, Berkshire (now Oxfordshire) from the River Thames: the site of the mixed rite cemetery
16. Case study area: the Lower Ouse Valley, Sussex, showing the floodplain, routeways, burial sites and find spots in Phase A
17. View north west from the lower slopes Chessell Down, Isle of Wight, Anglo-Saxon cemetery, overlooking the entrance to the Solent
18. The excavation at Apple Down, Sussex mixed rite cemetery (image courtesy The Welch Archive)
19. View south east from the Anglo-Saxon cemetery at Bradford Peverell, Dorset, towards the Roman road from Dorchester as it approaches the crossing point of the River Frome
20. Surrey case study area landscape block with Roman roads radiating out from the London River Thames crossing points
21. Surrey case study area soil fertility assessments with Roman villas and field systems
22. Surrey case study area earliest burial sites and settlements
23. View northwards towards the middle Thames basin from Guildown Anglo-Saxon cemetery, Surrey
24. Surrey case study area burial sites in Phases B and C
25. Surrey case study area with Portable Antiquity Scheme findspots and regional coin finds
26. Study region earliest burials in relation to iron ore deposits

## List of Figures

27. Undated and medieval bloomery sites on the Wealden iron deposits
28. An iron shield boss
29. An iron sword with pattern welding
30. Iron knives
31. Percentages of the study region population with iron, over all three phases
32. Inverse distance weightings of iron consumption in Phase A, showing eleven regional high spots
33. View south west towards Bitterne and the Channel coast from the Anglo-Saxon cemetery on St Giles Hill, Winchester, Hampshire
34. Phase A concentrations of iron consumption in relation to Late Roman sites, as potential sources of scrap iron for recycling
35. Inverse distance weightings of iron consumption in Phase B, showing ten regional high spots
36. Inverse distance weightings of iron consumption in Phase C, showing seven regional high spots
37. Inverse distance weightings of iron consumption in Phase C and Late Roman sites
38. A copper alloy great square headed brooch
39. Inverse distance weightings concentrations of copper alloy (white areas have the highest concentrations) in Phase A
40. Phase A copper alloy concentrations and Late Roman sites
41. Inverse distance weightings concentrations of copper alloy in Phase B
42. A copper alloy buckle loop
43. A copper alloy and garnet inlaid buckle loop and belt plate
44. The distribution of all copper alloy bowl types in three phases
45. The distribution of hanging bowl escutcheons in the study region
46. An example of a hanging bowl escutcheon
47. The distribution of amber beads in all phases
48. The distribution of amethyst beads in Phases B and C
49. The distribution of gold bracteates
50. The distribution of gold artefacts in Phase A
51. The distribution of silver artefacts all phases
52. Northern Europe around the North Sea
53. An overview of the distribution Frankish material in the study region
54. The distribution Frankish and Kentish finds in Phase A
55. An example of a francisca
56. The distribution of franciscas in the study region
57. Activity corridors through the study region
58. The Frankish and Kentish artefact distributions in Phase B
59. The Frankish and Kentish artefact distributions in Phase C
60. The distributions of imported and regional coins in Phase C
61. A comparison of Phase A Frankish and Kentish artefacts with Phase C coin distributions
62. The distribution of burials with spears in the reversed position in all phases

# List of Tables

1. Fully and partially datable sites within the study region
2. Compared dating schemes for the study period
3. Examples of site codes
4. Site types
5. Site types with qualitative grading
6. Percentages of sites by county (RT = Regional Total)
7. Numbers of individuals recorded by county
8. Overview of burial numbers by county
9. Median numbers of individuals in cemetery sites
10. Sites in Kent with more than 200 burials
11. Numbers of cremations present in mixed-rite cemeteries
12. Numbers of individuals in each age band at death
13. Numbers of burials by grave orientation
14. Grave orientation diversity by county
15. Numbers of individuals datable to each phase
16. Numbers of burials allocated to each phase
17. Numbers of artefacts on each category
18. Artefact provenance totals
19. Numbers of findspot artefacts by sub-type
20. Number by type of brooches present
21. Comparison of numbers of brooches by type from findspots with those from cemeteries
22. Numbers of Late Roman sites in the study region
23. Numbers of other potentially relevant Roman sites
24. Major soil types in the study region
25. Drainage and fertility combined
26. Soil preferences of arable crops
27. Cemetery and settlement proximities
28. Cemetery and settlement adjacencies to routeways
29. Percentage of sites by phase against soil type
30. Surrey people and their objects by phase
31. Numbers of shield bosses by type (main distribution area in bold)
32. Swords by phase and weight (number in sample in brackets)
33. Average and range of weights of knives (number in sample in brackets)
34. People and knives by phase
35. Knives per head of population
36. Phase A IDW areas
37. Phase B IDW areas
38. Phase C IDW areas
39. Numbers of copper alloy artefacts in phased burials
40. Numbers and weights of copper alloy objects by phase
41. Average community consumption of copper alloy by phase
42. Copper alloy buckle weights and provenances in Kent and the Saxon area by phase
43. Copper alloy buckles by percentage of population
44. Numbers of copper alloy buckles by provenance in Kent and elsewhere in Phase A
45. Numbers of copper alloy buckles by provenance in Kent and elsewhere in Phase B
46. Numbers of copper alloy buckles by provenance in Kent and the Saxon area in Phase C
47. Copper alloy fragments in burials
48. Percentage of graves in a county with the number of beads in that range
49. Number of personal artefacts and weapons from Frankia and Kent by phase

# List of Plates

1. The edaphic units of southern Britain, based on soil fertility and drainage
2. The earliest Anglo-Saxon sites set against the edaphic units, with the Roman roads and trackways
3. The Surrey parish boundaries set against the edaphic units
4. Apple Down to Isle of Wight
5. Market Lavington from the edge of the site towards Salisbury Plain
6. Annular Brooch from Hampshire
7. Apple Down grave 56
8. Selmeston to Caburn
9. The Kingdom of the South Saxons across the River Ouse at Lewes
10. Sibertswold to Barfreston

# Preface

This volume comprises the first and second elements of a tripartite publication arising from the *Beyond the Tribal Hidage* project (2006–9) funded by the Leverhulme Trust. It is not the complete work that we had hoped to present for publication as it consists only of the maps and the associated text discussing the research questions. Martin Welch's illness and untimely death at the age of 63 in February 2011 prevented full discussions between us of those issues that had arisen as a result of our work. We set out in 2006, with great expectations, to bring together into an accessible format all the available evidence for the Germanic presence in southern Britain from the fifth century onwards. Over the years Martin had compiled the precursor of his gazetteer project in the form of a meticulously assembled card catalogue in the knowledge that only the full deployment and accessibility of the data would allow the fundamental questions of the early Anglo-Saxon period to be addressed with clarity.

Our initial, ambitious research questions were a direct product of the doctoral thesis of Dr Stuart Brookes, my colleague at UCL Institute of Archaeology and a fellow student of Martin's courses in Early and Later Medieval Archaeology in the 1990s. However, given the state and scale of the archive, extensive work was required to bring it into a useful and accurate state in the first instance. What is presented here is only a fragment of the potential of that dataset. Aware of this from the outset, it was always the intention to make the project database available with the Archaeology Data Service (ADS), following the pilot project of the Anglo-Saxon Kent Electronic Database (ASKED) which was deposited in 2009. Thus, the third element of the publication is the Early Anglo-Saxon Census of Southern Britain: to be made public in the expectation that future researchers will be able to enhance and extend its content. The conclusions of this project could thus be tested, challenged, revised and extended as others see fit in the future, aware that what is presented here is but one assessment of the wonderfully complex and engaging material for this crucial period in Early Medieval studies.

Only a few chapters were completed jointly, several were still in my first draft stage and, crucially, there was no fully developed concluding chapter. There are variations in the authorial voice, hopefully it is clear where we are speaking as one and where I have taken the points forward alone. That is not to say that Martin and I were always in total agreement. Fundamentally we tussled over two areas; the role of gender in structuring social and political relations within emerging hierarchies and, secondly, the Germanic relationship to the surviving communities of the British West, a relationship that I saw increasingly as providing useful explanations for the distribution of cultural material in our study region. I suspect that eventually we may also have disagreed about the timing of the first appearance of the Anglo-Saxons in southern Britain, with Martin favouring a disjuncture with Late Roman Britain and dating the earliest material to the last quarter of the fifth century, whereas I would tend to see a continuity of landscape structures and viable productive entities throughout the fifth century.

It has therefore been decided to publish the work as it stands with a view to making the information available to future researchers who will be able to use it to further their own knowledge and work, something which Martin would have welcomed. This book is therefore dedicated to Martin's peers, colleagues and all who have drawn on his knowledge and experience in the past.

# Acknowledgements

Throughout the duration of the project we were fortunate to have on our steering group Catherine Hills, Leslie Webster, Barbara Yorke, Andy Bevan, Kris Lockyear and latterly John Baker. Their contributions and willingness to comment on draft texts were invaluable. In particular I am grateful to Barbara Yorke who was willing to edit Martin's text on the documentary sources to include the issue of the role of the British West, but likewise had no opportunity to debate this matter with him in full. Thanks too to John Hines for pre-publication discussions on the English Heritage chronology project. During the visits to museums in southern Britain I met with very many curators and volunteers and thanks go to them for their willingness to give me access to their archives and the many interesting conversations that ensued. These include Greg Chuter (East Sussex), Andrew Richardson (Canterbury Archaeological Trust), Sonja Marzinzik (British Museum), Bruce Eagles, Diana Peak (Worthing Museum), Frank Basford (Isle of Wight Finds Liaison Officer), Geoff Denford (Winchester Museum Service), Peter Woodward (Dorchester Museum), Duncan Brown and Sian Isles (Southampton Museums), Clare Pinder (Dorset Sites and Monuments Record), Kay Ainsworth (Hampshire Museums Service), Nick Stoodley, Paul Robinson (Wiltshire Heritage Museum, Devizes), Robert Symonds (Fishbourne Discovery Centre), Louise Rayner (Archaeology South East), Mary Alexander (Guildford) and Esther Cameron (Oxfordshire Museums Service). My apologies to those I have omitted from this list.

In the aftermath of Martin's death, I am extremely grateful to Alison Taylor, his literary executor, for her encouragement; to Stuart Brookes for producing the map illustrations; to Jessica Drewery for her help with copy editing; to the staff at the Institute of Archaeology, UCL for their many kindnesses in dealing with Martin's archive; to Andrew Reynolds for his continued support; and to Hazel Welch, without whom this would have been a very lonely task.

Finally, grateful thanks must go to the Marc Fitch Fund for their generous grant to enable this work to be brought to publication.

*Sue Harrington*
UCL Institute of Archaeology
31–34 Gordon Square
London
WC1H 0PY
s.harrington@ucl.ac.uk

# 1. The Early Anglo-Saxon Kingdoms of Southern Britain: Evidence and Questions

## Introduction

That there were Anglo-Saxon kingdoms in southern and eastern Britain by the end of the sixth century is taken generally as a given, but one that is, in the main, derived from readings of documentary sources. Named kings or regional overlords such as Ælle of the South Saxons, Æthelbert of Kent and Ine of Wessex, variously dated to the fifth, sixth and seventh centuries, hint at a hierarchical social structure, wherein the payment of tax or tribute to support a dynastic elite was long embedded. How kingdoms came into being, and what was their starting point before the advent of contemporary historic records, is within the province of archaeology to elucidate, given the frequency and wealth of the funerary material of the period. But, should, and can, archaeology embrace documentary sources to determine its research agenda for this period? As the *Tribal Hidage* document seems to offer, by the seventh century at least there were named groupings of peoples – the *Limenwara*, *Cantwarena*, *Supsexena*, *Meonware* and so on – who owed taxation to the, by then dominant, kingdom of Mercia. Thus each, one must suppose, was situated within a landscape with varying degrees of wealth-making potential that supported the payment of the tax. But what underlies this documentary inscription? Does the archaeological record chart in reality an organic growth of migrating Germanic peoples and Romano-British rural populations into fully-fledged kingdoms of bounded territories by the seventh century?

The narrative of bottom up settlement of a deserted landscape by Germanic migrants, making rational choices about optimal locations and subsequent expansion into more marginal lands, has had its followers in the past. The more vigorous, and romantic, top down replacement of local Roman elites by war bands of adventurers and mercenaries, inhabiting an ongoing and productive landscape structure, with communities re-using prehistoric monuments to legitimise their presence, too has many adherents. If we accept Gildas' narrative (Chapter 23) on the settlement of Saxons on the east side of the island of Britain and the hiring of Saxon mercenaries by British rulers to combat threat of Pictish raiders, then military sites should be the earliest visible. Interspersed these narratives with an acculturated Romano-British population continuing a subsistence lifestyle in rural locations, and the permutations become yet more intricate. Many other observations and sub-narratives have been woven into this framework, according, it might be said, to the prevailing contingent research agendas and need not be re-iterated in detail here.

Such is the history of much landscape archaeology in Britain that until recently it has not been the norm to extend researches beyond those of traditional county boundaries, each one producing its own narrative according to the material found within its borders. However, a region-wide analysis, such as that presented in this volume acknowledges the strong possibility of intra-regional dissimilarity in the rationales for and manifestations of the Germanic presence in southern Britain (see Figures 1 and 2 for an overview of the study region). This observation forces us to accept that local variations do not of necessity lend themselves to melding into an overarching and clearly definable regional framework of settlement and socio-economic patterning over time. At best we can search for common themes, if not the clear strategies knowingly derived from a particular cultural impetus, that any research programme might hope to elucidate. To this end, the focus in this volume is predominantly on the workings of the initial evidence for the Germanic presence in the fifth century and on to the end of the sixth century, with some venturings into the mid-seventh, thereafter transitional themes come to the fore. The Mid Saxon Shuffle – the shift in settlement patterning towards different topographical features noted elsewhere for the seventh century and later – may, from this basis, eventually become more explicable but is not dealt with here.

There are dangers, inherent in the research process, of falling into a pre-determined archaeological template for economic evolution and the seemingly inevitable trajectory towards hierarchical polities and kingship. In most general terms this narrative has been expressed as sequential phases, commencing with the Migration Period, noting the earliest presences of Germanic material, blending into the Frankish Phase, wherein material provenances from *Francia* is found in burial contexts, with the Final Phase of furnished burial denoting the waning of non-Christian burial customs and the transfer to more identifiable forms of Christian burial – with fuzzy chronological and spatial boundaries between each element. We must reflect on how we characterise and conceptualise the wealth of the Anglo-Saxon peoples and what we understand the archaeological record to represent (and ultimately electing not to refer explicitly to that sequential phasing as overtly meaningful). The methodological challenge, then, was one of paring down that record to its component parts and reconstituting it to allow us to interrogate it in a cross-comparable manner, in order to transcend the history of its generation through antiquarian to modern field unit excavations. It is fundamental that we should not engage with the archaeological record without making explicit the grounding principles on which the theory and research methods were based. Central was the assertion that state formation need not of necessity have come about through the top-down activities of elites imposing themselves onto a passive populace. Rather, it was proposed to explore the view that the processes evident by the late sixth century were ones resultant from the bottom-up activities of a populace forming itself into a series of hierarchical units, dependent on the economic attributes and potential of their settled landscapes. The findings of the Leverhulme Trust funded *Beyond the Tribal Hidage* project (2006–9), on which this text is based, support conclusions along a middle road between these two approaches.

*1. The Early Anglo-Saxon Kingdoms of Southern Britain*

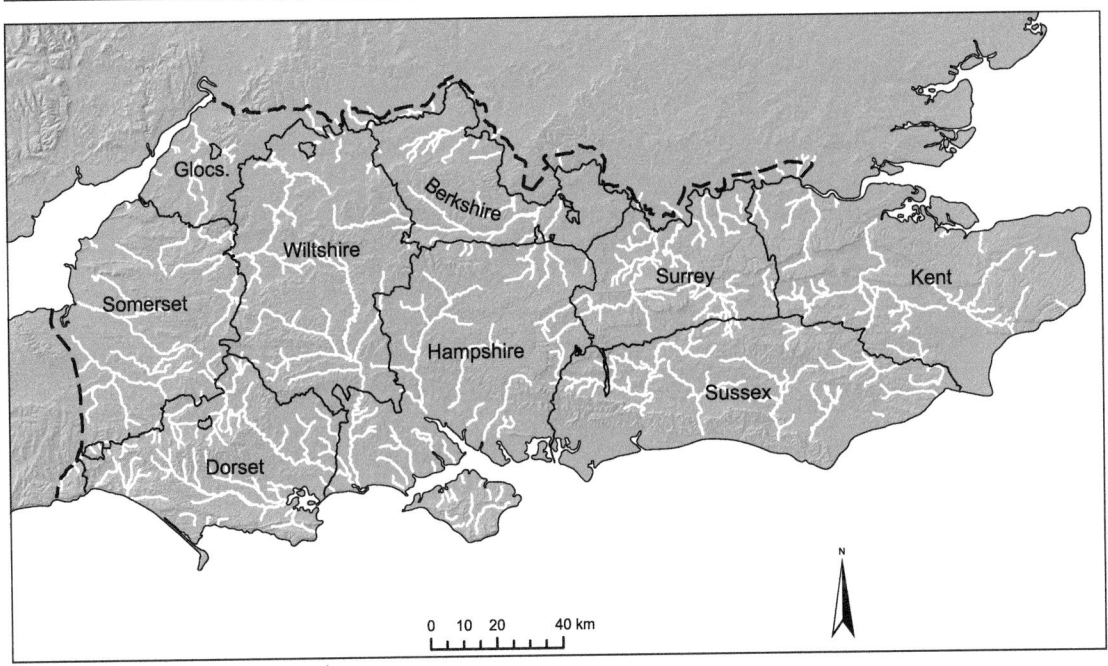

*Figure 1. The study region with modern counties*

## The kingdoms in the written sources *(text by Martin Welch, edited by Barbara Yorke)*

The three kingdoms selected for a detailed examination of their archaeological record appear to have contrasting characteristics when they emerge into the full historical record in the seventh century AD, yet they are within the same geographical region and are contiguous (see Figure 2). The kingdom of the South Saxons (Sussex) represents a standard, medium-sized political unit, which subsequently became a sub-unit (a shire or county) of a much larger kingdom during the eighth century. This was also the fate of Kent in the eighth century. Here, we begin with a small kingdom of similar size to Sussex centred on the east half of the present county of Kent, which had expanded to the west before the 590s. Finally, the kingdom of the West Saxons (Wessex) emerges as a large political entity by the 680s, as a result of the amalgamation and conquest of several smaller political units, such as the kingdom of the Jutes in Hampshire and the Isle of Wight. After 825, the West Saxon kingdom incorporated Sussex, Surrey and Kent into a still further enlarged kingdom. Also covered in the survey is the county of Surrey – a 'province' that falls between the West Saxon and Kentish spheres of influence in the seventh century, although coming under Mercian control for part of the seventh and most of the eighth century as well. It appears not to have achieved any independent status. Whilst the *Tribal Hidage* document provided some parameters and key questions for the research project, it is crucial to also take a critical appraisal of what the *range* of documentary sources have to offer on the issues that are explored primarily through the archaeological data.

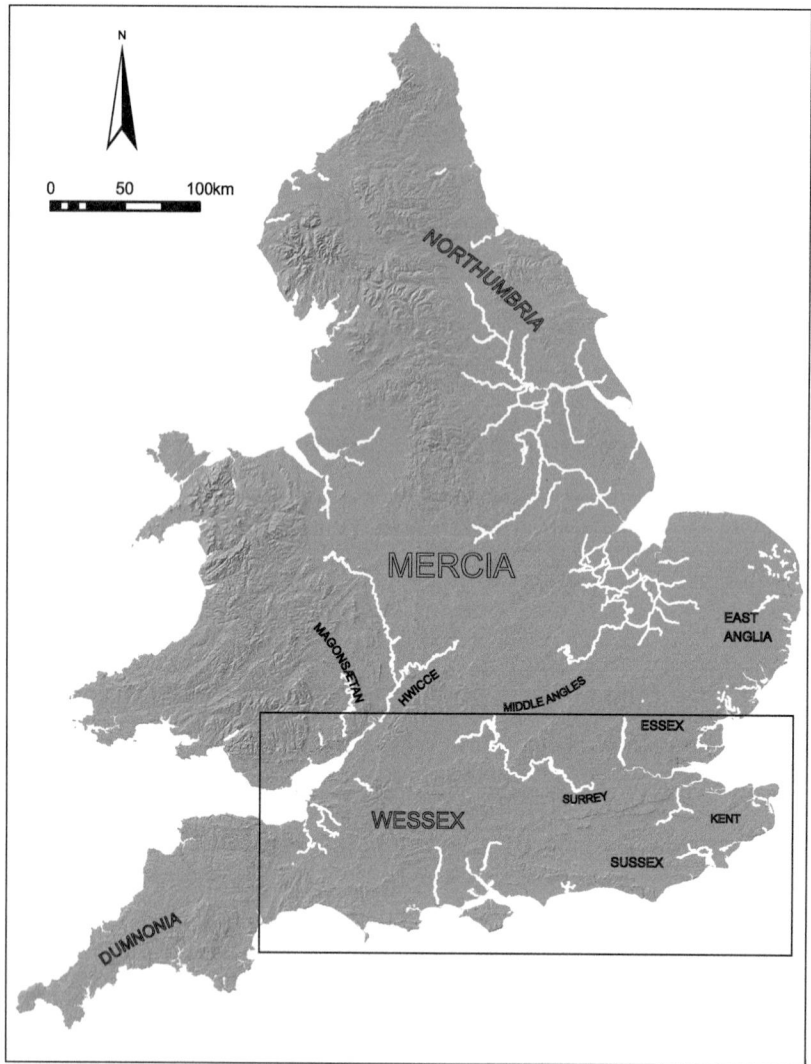

*Figure 2. The study region in the major Anglo-Saxon areas and the British West*

The written sources provide key information about the political situation in southern Britain from the seventh century onwards, but leave many questions unanswered, particularly concerning how that system came into existence and how its elites were supported. Written records were, of course, one consequence of the conversion of the Anglo-Saxon provinces that largely occurred in the seventh century. Records that purport to record earlier 'events' such as the fifth- and sixth-century annals of the *Anglo-Saxon Chronicle* are later constructs and rarely constitute reliable evidence. The *Chronicle* annals attempt to historicize West Saxon foundation legends, and the apparent arrival of their founders in the Solent in the fifth century contradicts the more reliable evidence in Bede's *Historia Ecclesiastica* that their royal house originated in the Gewissan province of the upper Thames valley (Sims-Williams 1983; Yorke 1989). Nevertheless some of the documents have implications that reach back into the sixth century and may help with the understanding of developments in that period.

The *Historica Ecclesiastica* of Bede, completed in 731, and the enigmatic *Tribal Hidage* (that may have had its origins in seventh-century tribute list of a Northumbrian or Mercian overlord) indicate that the major political units of the south-east by *c.*600 were Kent (15,000 hides), the East Saxons (7000 hides), the South Saxons (7000 hides), the West Saxons and (Isle of) Wight (600 hides), all of which are recorded by Bede or in early charters as being controlled by kings (Campbell 1986, 85–98; Dumville 1989). The earliest explicit reference to kingship in the region is from *The Ten Books of History* of Gregory of Tours (IX, 26) in the context of the marriage of Bertha, daughter of the Frankish king Charibert, 'to the son of a certain king in Kent'. We know from Bede that her husband was Æthelbert, son of Irminric, and can estimate that the marriage took place *c.*580 and that Æthelbert's accession had occurred by 593 at the latest (Brooks 1989). Bede (*HE* II, 5) also knew a tradition that Æthelbert was the third great overlord in southern England, his two predecessors being Ælle, king of the South Saxons and Ceawlin, king of the West Saxons (known until the late seventh century as the Gewisse). In the *Anglo-Saxon Chronicle* Ælle's activities are placed between 477 and 491, but these dates are not reliable, and likely to be ninth-century calculations. In reality Ælle is likely to have reigned closer to the time of Ceawlin whose reign is probably to be dated, on the evidence of West Saxon regnal lists, to either 571–88 or 581–88 (Dumville 1985; Yorke 2009). Kingdom formation in south-eastern England therefore appears to be a feature of the second half of the sixth century, but the written sources do not explain the circumstances in which it occurred.

They do, however, reveal that territorial organisation was in fact more complex and that any boundaries were subject to frequent revision. All the kingdoms can be shown to have had subdivisions within them, often referred to in Latin as *regiones*, and these have often been interpreted as being older than the kingdoms themselves and essential building-blocks in kingdom formation (Campbell 1986, 85–98; Bassett 1989). Particularly visible in the sources are such territories on the peripheries of kingdoms, which were liable to be transferred from one province to another in power struggles. For example, control of Surrey (*suðre ge* 'southern province') was contested between Kent, Mercia and Wessex for much of the seventh century (Blair 1989; Hines 2004). King Wulfhere of Mercia (658–675) placed the Isle of Wight and the district of the Meonware in Hampshire under the control of his ally Æthelwalh of the South Saxons (IV, 13), but they were subsequently incorporated into the expanding West Saxon kingdom by Caedwalla (685–88) (*HE* IV, 15–16). Kings, it would appear, were likely to have had core areas that were the centres of their power, and fluctuating overlordships of more peripheral areas that might in time become fully integrated parts of the kingdom. Sometimes it is possible to peer back from the seventh-century records to see comparable developments in the sixth century that may take us closer to the origins of kingdoms. A well-recorded subdivision into west and east Kent, with the latter the seat of a senior king and the former that of a junior partner, may well have had its origin in the annexation of a former separate territory in west Kent in the later sixth century (Yorke 1983; Brooks 1989).

How such core and peripheral areas appear in the archaeological record is obviously of great potential interest. As is well known, the division of southern England into Saxon and Jutish areas is recorded in Bede's history (*HE* I, 15) and seems to have had a corresponding archaeological signature in the late fifth and much of the sixth centuries (Hines 1994). On this basis, west Kent would appear to have been originally a Saxon cultural area and this gives valuable context to its incorporation into Kent that Bede describes as having a separate Jutish identity (Brookes and Harrington 2010). Also described as Jutish are the Isle of Wight and part of the area of mainland Hampshire immediately opposite (*HE* I, 15; IV, 16; Yorke 1989). Both these areas are given their own origin legends in the *Anglo-Saxon Chronicle*. The latter included the Meonware; the suffix -*ware* 'inhabitants' is found used for comparable subdivisions in Kent (Brooks 1989). Comparison of archaeological evidence from Kent and the Isle of Wight/Hampshire mainland may therefore tell us much about the reality behind a shared Jutish identity, and whether it was the result of movement of population or, as one might suspect, an alliance that had its in origin in the shadowy politics of the sixth century. Even less well understood is the implication of a Saxon confederation that might be presumed to lie behind the Saxon identity claimed in other areas of southern England, and whose reality appears to be supported by the early development of a distinctive Saxon dialect that implies frequent association (Hines 1994).

The written sources for the seventh century do highlight one factor to explain change in the sixth and seventh centuries, namely links with *Francia*. As Bede was primarily concerned with recording processes of conversion and church foundation that is the aspect of the Frankish connection to which he gives most attention. The first bishop he recorded working among the southern Anglo-Saxons was the Frank Liudhard who accompanied Bertha to the Kentish court (*HE* I, 25). Other Frankish clerics were active in southern England, including Agilbert and his nephew Leuthere who were both bishops of the West Saxons, whilst Wine, another West Saxon bishop but of Anglo-Saxon origin, had trained in *Francia* (Campbell 1986, 49–67; Blair 2005, 39–43). The many journeys between southern England and *Francia* recorded for church members can be taken as representative of a much broader and well-established traffic. In the same way emulation of Frankish family monasteries, and particularly the tendency for these to be run by princesses and other high status women, may be an indication of a wider and longer-rooted Frankish influence on elite life. The marriage of Æthelbert and Bertha not only helps to take such influences back into the sixth century, but suggests their political nature as well. Ian Wood has argued from a variety of Frankish and Anglo-Saxon sources for Frankish overlordship in parts of southern England in the sixth century, possibly stimulated by the desire to control land both sides of the English Channel and reduce the threat of piratical attacks (Wood 1990; 1992). It is possible that the first southern overlords in Bede's II, 5 list were Frankish agents – or, alternatively, rulers who led resistance to Frankish attempts at dominance (Yorke 2009). Another possible interpretation would be to see them as leaders of the Saxon confederation over which Æthelbert of Kent subsequently established control.

## 1. The Early Anglo-Saxon Kingdoms of Southern Britain

Unfortunately Bede is much less informative about Anglo-Saxon relations with another significant national group, namely the British. The impression he gives is that all inhabitants of the southern Anglo-Saxon kingdoms had a common identity by the seventh century. However, a goodly percentage, presumably a majority, must ultimately have been descended from the inhabitants of Roman Britain (Higham 2007). The earliest Kentish laws also assume a common identity, and so perhaps that was the reality by 600 in the southeast. However, further west, in the former province of Britannia Prima, lay areas still under British control in 600, but that by 700 had largely become part of a greatly expanded Wessex (White 2007). Written sources enable us to see something of how this was done, but do not explain everything. Narrative sources concentrate on military victories, while ecclesiastical sources imply large-scale appropriation of British assets, including land and churches, and redistribution to Anglo-Saxon elites. Of particular interest are clauses in the laws of King Ine of Wessex (688–725) recognising the rights of different British social classes, but in ways that made them inferior to their Anglo-Saxon equivalents (Attenborough 1922, 36–61). Such social apartheid may have provided a stimulus for the British to find ways of becoming Anglo-Saxons, or the means of further undermining their independence and separate identities (Woolf 2007).

One major question is whether the fate of the British in the south-west in the seventh century can provide a guide to what happened to their countrymen further east in the fifth and sixth centuries, or if the circumstances differed. Behind such concerns are also questions of the legacy from late Roman and British provinces to their Anglo-Saxon successors. The West Saxons may have carried out significant modifications, but these often seem to have taken place within a structure of estates and other territories they took over from British control in the seventh century (Hall 2000; Costen 2011). How much did the Anglo-Saxon polities of the fifth and sixth centuries inherit from the late Roman world in eastern England? Although many sources, particularly the ecclesiastical, from the time of Gildas onwards, stress the enmity between British and Anglo-Saxons, it does not necessarily mean that this was uniformly the case. The well-known incorporation of British-derived names in the Gewissan/West Saxon royal house, including that of their supposed founder Cerdic, may well indicate British as well as Anglo-Saxon contributions to Gewissan identity. Neither should it necessarily be assumed that there were only hostile interactions between British and Anglo-Saxon controlled areas in the south in the seventh century and earlier (Higham 2007).

The seventh-century laws of the Kentish kings and those of Ine of Wessex provide the best guide from the written sources to Anglo-Saxon social structures in the seventh century. Particularly important are those of Æthelbert of Kent that may date from the late sixth century or soon after (Oliver 2002). They reveal significant divisions between free and unfree, with several varying degrees of dependence in addition to the slavery that appears a common feature of that society. Æthelbert's laws also reveal something of kingship imposing itself on an older structure of assemblies where arbitration and compensation along agreed norms helped regulate relations in local communities and the escalation of feud. The early lawcodes also show an interest in supervising trade through royal officials as well as the results of Christianity becoming embedded more deeply in society.

The acceptance of Christianity was, of course, a major development in the seventh century.

Some commentators have suggested that the church, with its expectations of large, permanent grants of land to support their communities, was a major motor for the economic changes that are seen as a feature of 'the long eighth century' (Hansen and Wickham 2000; Blair 2005). But is such periodisation correct, and is there a danger that the advent of new types of information with the introduction of written sources makes the later seventh-century seem more different from the sixth century than was really the case? After all one of the apparent pre-conditions for the establishment of an organised church in Anglo-Saxon England, namely the development of kingdoms, had begun in the later sixth century. So a major issue is whether the sixth century itself should be seen as a period of continuity or change. Kingdoms could be seen as the gradual outcome of competition between elites who had never lost the military prowess that apparently had made them attractive as mercenaries to the British in the fifth century, if Gildas is to be believed. Competition could initially have been within the *regio*-sized territories, and then between them, leading to kingdom formation and the concentration of much greater wealth and power in the hands of the victorious families and their supporters (Scull 1999). On the other hand, it is possible to envisage much more sudden and fast-paced change as the result of war bands imposing themselves upon agricultural communities, for instance, if diverted from raiding in the Channel by Frankish intervention. Either way, the result is likely to have been a more unequal society with a greater need for the creation of surplus wealth to support rulers and their military elites in their aspirational lifestyles. Detailed analysis of the archaeological evidence provides the greatest hope of understanding more about this crucial period in the development of early medieval society in southern England.

## Research questions
### *What are the data?*
The initial task was to investigate the range of burial data available for the period AD 450–650 and to meld it into a coherent and cross-comparable format, without removing any elements of diversity that might be present. The methodological challenge was to produce a fine-grained and accurate tally of the material, with new data generated as required in order to address the research questions. How does the listing of raw materials and artefact type compare with that generated by Jeremy Huggett (1988)?

### *What is the landscape context of that data?*
The starting point for this research question was those issues raised by Hayo Vierck (Davies and Vierck 1974) in a review of the social aggregates and settlement patterns indicated by the *Tribal Hidage* document and place-names in relation to the then available archaeological evidence. One might be critical of some of the implicit assumptions presented regarding tribal units as discrete entities and this is by no means accepted unconditionally within this volume. There was a focus in that text on No-Man's Lands, characterising the separateness of tribal units in their territorial enclaves as the basis for further expansion and the impetus towards state formation. It is only

in recent years, however, with the advent of computer manipulable databases and geographical information systems, that the fundamental issues posed by that paper could now be explored fully. These key questions about the Germanic presence and their impact on the early kingdoms have resonated through subsequent research agendas and are, to paraphrase Vierck (*ibid.*, 249):

- What was the relationship of the areas of primary settlement to soil types – did this result in isolated areas of settlement?
- Did Anglo-Saxon people use 'uncongenial' environments to provide a strategic buffer zone around their territories – did these zones relate to tribal areas or to kingdoms?
- What was the environmental context of the early Anglo-Saxon period, particularly in relation to regenerated woodland and areas prone to flooding?
- Did the Germanic people take over existing favoured settlement areas and were these the areas reflected in the *Tribal Hidage* document? (A comparison with the settlement and burial patterns in the continental homelands was not attempted in this project)
- Does the distribution of the cemeteries represent the extent of the Anglo-Saxon settlement?
- Can we identify settlement areas, whether they are isolated or connected with each other by more or less broad corridors, and to locate their possible centres by the mapping of groups of cemeteries, and of single outstanding burials?
- How do the settlement areas so defined relate to the distribution of place-names?

*Why is the data located within this context*
  *– what were the criteria behind site location selection?*

Here we must introduce the issue of a continuation of Late Roman landscape structures – did they provide a template for fifth century settlement or were overtly Roman places avoided as alien? Key here are routeways, not only the major Roman roads but also the navigable rivers and coastal waters. Is an overall landscape structure discernible or is the patterning organic and opportunistic with regards to the spatial location of each community, however defined? At what point in the fifth and sixth centuries was a pattern established?

*How can this evidence be explained and interpreted*
  *– is this evidence of wealth creation and state formation?*

What is the evidence for wealth amongst burial groups? Is there evidence for unequal wealth distribution both within and between communities and does this change over time and space? Do theories of state formation account adequately for the data presented?

To these questions about the internal dynamics of the study region must be added the issue that arose most clearly from the above review of the written sources, specifically the role of external polities in the formation of kingdoms within the study region. Did interaction with *Francia*, on the periphery of its geographical sphere of influence, offer an impetus for political development? Did the presence of the British West provide a hindrance to or an opportunity for hierarchical expansion, one that was only addressed territorially in the seventh century?

## Methodology

The key component of the methodology was to use the weight of the raw material component of objects as shorthand for access to wealth and as a means of determining the relative wealth and status of communities. It is an area fraught with problems both methodological and epistemological, however. Alcock (1981) challenged the then prevailing view that areas scarce in burial data could not be adequately discussed, by countering that scarcity in numbers need not imply poverty and that those present may well be richly furnished. A small step towards inclusiveness perhaps, although he then chose to compare male weapon- and female jewellery-burials, within a grading scheme of alpha, beta and gamma designated graves associated with a three-fold social division into thegns, free warriors and the unfree, as indicated by documentary sources, following Veeck (1926). He did not consider it worth attempting to discuss the lowest grade, represented by unfurnished or meagrely furnished burials, perhaps containing only a knife. Whole cemeteries, he argued, could be graded along the same lines and compared geographically as a means of confirming the three-fold division and the historical narrative, although with a due note of caution that gamma might be under- and alpha might be over-represented in this schema. Loveluck (1996, 33), in his analysis of the cemeteries around Driffield, Yorkshire, sought to limit reliance on the tacit assumptions that burial ritual of necessity directly reflected wealth and social status in life and that this needed to have been a uniform process. His methodology compared the quantity, presence/absence and rarity of grave goods made from a range of raw materials, with the conclusion that control of access to iron was the key determinant in the ability to procure other raw materials and imported goods (*ibid.*, 42). Crucially, it is only by the seventh century that the possession of esoteric artefacts denote status within an elite, whilst the overall economic wealth of communities 'may be suggested more appropriately by the abundance of indigenous resources' (*ibid.*, 43).

Meanwhile Scandinavian scholars were taking a slightly different approach to similar concerns on how to characterise communities. Myhre (1987) used the grave finds from chieftains' graves to discuss changes in social and political organisation in the whole of southern Norway, a discussion again predicated on the richest finds of imported goods and rare raw materials, and as a means of locating political centres and their geographical and economic spheres of influence. The methodology here was based on the weight of gold distributed over space, together with counts of copper alloy and glass vessels. Mads Ravn (2003) criticised the circularity of the interpretative relationship between the historical and archaeological evidences, preferring the synthetic approach advocated by Härke (1992) that utilised qualitative, quantitative and anthropological methods in order to explicitly acknowledge the multi-dimensional nature of burials.

Stuart Brookes' (2007) stance in relation to these earlier approaches was based on a concern that the entirety of a community could not, and should not, be reduced to a partial examination of the upper echelons as a representative of the whole, as this serves to reinforce a top-down view of society. In addition, the issues of flows of wealth and the values attributed to goods can be masked unquestioningly. Although perhaps a function of the available techniques in the past, the need now therefore was for a maximising and inclusive methodology, both in scale and in content.

Focussing on weight of object was seen as an important methodological advance because it allowed one to assess the scarcity and diversity of raw materials across populations as an indicator of value, rather than the objects themselves.

Can it be assumed that the wealth of a community is self-generated, in terms of the manufacture of objects? Is part of their wealth then distributed to a central person and their immediate associates and beyond, according to the community's position within a regional hierarchy? Or is that wealth assembled by a central person from external sources and distributed down to the rest of the community according to local, cultural precepts? If internal differentiation within communities can be assumed in the early Anglo-Saxon period, and the general scheme of evidence suggests that this is a central social process of the period as a whole, it has yet to be demonstrated at what point in time these communities become so.

Also, if social differentiation is mediated through a range of personal attributes including age, ethnicity and gender, each of which is impacted by changing social norms and manifests itself accordingly, therefore to make a representative assessment for a community one is perhaps best served by choosing, averaging and comparing all adult men and women over time and space, as represented by their burial assemblages. By selecting as case studies ubiquitous object types, knives and spearheads for example, that fairly reflect access to raw material wealth at the base level meaningful comparisons can be made. Here one is obviously skirting round the issues of the meanings of burials, how they were performed and the intentionality of the depositions. One would not necessarily assume, however, that poor communities were making extravagant displays in the burial through the loss of wealth into the burial, in a sort of self-denying deposition, nor that wealthy communities were deliberately holding back their wealth in an orgy of ongoing consumption by the living. We must assume a level playing field of common cultural intentions regarding the composition of burial assemblages that changed on a broad front over time – unless it can be demonstrated otherwise, it is assumed that a common set of principles were current and that people used the best means available to them to illustrate these. The assumption made here in this methodology is that ascriptions of wealth to a community, as indicated by count, diversity and weight of raw material, are genuine reflections of their available, albeit variable, resources.

## Overview of the contents of this volume

The project datasets are presented in some detail, particularly the metadata for the Early Anglo-Saxon Census of burial records and associated artefacts, which form the main basis for the exploration of the research questions. The environmental context of southern Britain is discussed and the methods developed for re-defining the productive attributes of the landscape are outlined. Due reference is given to the contemporary climatic context, riverine and palaeo-environmental data and the evidence for woodlands. The methods and routes for travel over land and sea are considered together with agricultural and pastoral practices that may have required such routeways for the movement of surpluses and exchange. Included too is a review of the major environmental reports from excavations in the study region, each giving an insight into local conditions and practices.

Following a review of current theories about site location selection within the kingdoms of Kent, Wessex and Sussex, the locational evidence is assessed for the earliest sites, their relationships to routeways and the kinds of resource bases derived from the soil attributes that those sites could readily access. The Lower Ouse valley in East Sussex provides a brief case study, whilst the modern county of Surrey is used as a larger scale case study to test emerging analyses. In order to examine the issue of the distribution of wealth at the base layers of society and in relation to potential landscape hierarchies, the central part of the volume considers the manufacture and deployment of iron, iron artefacts, copper alloys and the more esoteric raw materials amber, amethyst, gold and silver. Each of these materials is charted over comparative phases and amply illustrates the shifting locations of relative material wealth over time. The final section deliberates over the Frankish presence in southern Britain and the potential impact on state formation in the fifth, sixth and seventh centuries. The distribution of Frankish material in relation to Kentish artefacts throughout the study region is mapped and conclusions drawn. The final chapter reviews the evidence collected together and reflects on the relationship between the archaeology and the *Tribal Hidage* document.

# 2. The Early Anglo-Saxon Census

### Southern Britain south of the Thames and the archaeological data

The geographical parameters of the region (see Figure 1) containing the early kingdoms of Kent, Sussex and Wessex were defined by the southern side of the Thames Estuary, clockwise around the North Foreland and along the Channel coast as far as the River Axe and including the Isle of Wight. The Axe through to the River Parrett into the Bristol Channel defined a broad western edge, with an arbitrary line across to Cirencester and back down the Thames to the estuary. However, the use of the Thames as a boundary was problematic in that it could appear to be more of a barrier than may have been the case. Therefore it was decided to include the parishes lining the northern bank, thus drawing in important sites such as Butler's Field, Lechlade and the Taplow burial. The Mucking cemetery (Hirst and Clark 2009) was studiously avoided, the collection point stopping short at the City of London, as to include it would have drawn in a potentially unbalancing dataset from the East Saxons, whose relationship to the West Saxons and Kent was not part of the intended discussions.

The decision to attempt total data retrieval rather than a regional sampling of the archaeology of the period AD 450–750 across southern Britain was one of taking up the challenge to determine whether it could be done and what the outcomes might be. Earlier surveys, principally Audrey Meaney's 1964 national gazetteer of early Anglo-Saxon cemetery sites, have had an enduring value as the only available comprehensive references. Other researchers have advanced the viewpoint that full data listing was actually necessary also in order to gain a full understanding of archaeology of a region. Here one can cite Tania Dickinson's unpublished but influential thesis on the sites of the Upper Thames Valley (1976) and Martin Welch's 1983 work on Sussex as the earliest main examples of this view, latterly followed by Andrew Richardson's Kent corpus (2005) and Simon Draper's work on Wiltshire (2006). The Anglo-Saxon Kent Electronic Database (ASKED), collaboratively assembled by the author and Stuart Brookes and made available with the Archaeology data Service had already demonstrated the value of such an approach (Brookes 2007; Harrington 2008).

## The database

The purpose of data collection was to produce a comprehensive list of every site, every stray find, every buried individual and every object associated with those individuals, with each entry recorded spatially as a 12-figure grid reference and placed within a clearly defined dating framework. No attempt was made to record in detail the objects from settlement sites. The national and county-based sources of information in many ways overlapped one another in their data collection policies, but by no means consistently replicated one another. At that time (2006–7) they varied a great deal in content. A major problem for a project concentrating on a restricted chronological period was the clumping together of data into a much broader period of 'Anglo-Saxon', framed as AD 410–1066 and was a particular problem when attempting to identify Late Roman sites that may have continued in use into the fifth century.

The process of data acquisition was thus one of desk-based assessment by county, followed by discrete searches for both published and unpublished grey literature and other archived material, held by county archaeological societies, research libraries, national and county journals, museum day books and accession registers as well as through various personal communications with local researchers. In general it was possible by this additional level of search to add 10% to the number of sites recorded by national and county resources. Next, discrete county site lists were assembled and museum and archive visits arranged to review the relevant objects from these initial listings. Data was collected geographically in county sets, working clockwise around the study region, beginning with East Sussex in November 2006 and finishing in Kent, Surrey and the relevant parts of Greater London in August 2008. Given the broad strategic approach to data gathering at the sites level, it is estimated that the final total of 3449 site entries probably represents the best that could be achieved in the available time. As an example of the growth in site numbers, Audrey Meaney (1964) recorded 47 locations for East and West Sussex combined, Martin Welch was able to extend this to 135 discrete sites, whilst the 2007 total was 338. Nevertheless, 3449 cannot be taken as a definitive number of sites. It was necessary to clump together some entries into a single site, particularly the settlements in and around *Lundenwic*, for which detailed data was not required by the project. Data provided by the Portable Antiquities Scheme (PAS) and the Early Medieval Coin Corpus (EMCC) has been incorporated in the assembled total of 3449 locations. 563 PAS finds accurate to 12 figure grid references and 816 coins finds accurate to 8 figure grid references contributed proportion of the locations.

### *Data-quality assessment*

The standard of recording and the accuracy of information available for the sites and finds varied considerably. The key required attributes for site level entry into the database were accuracy of location and clear identification of the site fitting within the project time frame of AD 400–750. In order to avoid presenting a deceptive level of accuracy, each site level entry was graded according to the following criteria:

Grade 1 – 1999 sites (58% of total)
Sites which were excavated and recorded by archaeologists, whether published or unpublished, and those where material has been deposited in a museum and verified as relevant to the project during fieldwork. All of these sites are recorded to 12 figure grid references.

Grade 2 – 1018 sites (30% of total)
Sites where some uncertainties remain over the accuracy of the record, for example, sites with 'numerous skeletons, swords and spears'. These are probably, but not certainly, early Anglo-Saxon and may have an accurate grid reference. Also sites may have a location to 8 figure grid reference or to parish level only, but are clearly relevant – 'unlocated' has been appended to their site name.

Grade 3 – 431 sites (12% of total)
Sites where it is uncertain whether the site is relevant to this project, although claimed as such by the excavator or a recorder. For example, a cemetery of unfurnished burials, which may be later or earlier than the time span of the project, or a secondary inhumation or cremation in a barrow with no diagnostic artefacts, for which 'Saxon' is a best guess. This grade includes sites identified only by sherds of Saxon pottery recorded in fieldwalking, but which are insufficiently diagnostic to verify their dating apart from belonging within the general Anglo-Saxon period. For some of these sites, the grid reference may only represent an approximation, as an interpretation of the location evidence provided. These sites were not used for analysis, but may prove to have relevance in future research.

*The dating framework*
Every site, findspot and individual for whom there are burial records was placed within the project-phasing scheme. Three phases were identified in a relative sequence and with notional absolute dates.

The three phases are:

A   Earliest finds up to AD 575
B   AD 575–650
C   AD 650–750

The three phases coincide broadly with already established qualitative terminology. Phase A is coincident with the Migration Period, the Frankish Phase of influence and the main period of furnished burial, whilst phases B and C cover the first impact of the re-Christianisation process, the Final Phase of furnished burial and the first documentation of fully-fledged Anglo-Saxon kingdoms. Helen Geake (1997, 129) notes 'a number of distinctive changes in the material culture of burial … first is the change from the migration-period to the Conversion period assemblage which takes place *c.*580 in Kent and *c.*600 elsewhere. Second is the change everywhere in *c.*650, which sees the introduction of a new range of material. Third is the change after *c.*720/30, which results in a sharp drop in the number of furnished graves'. The project has elected not to refer to these earlier devised terms, because of an ongoing perception of them as being too deterministic and restrictive, 'suggesting that it would be helpful to create a new terminology while investigating the character and appropriate definitions of phases for England without prejudice' (Hines and Nielsen 1999, 89, referring to comments by Martin Welch).

Clearly, in any given cemetery there were a number of closely datable graves, which might be placed into a relative scheme, but these formed a minority of the known burials from any site. The problems posed by an exercise that sought to give a date range to every element of the dataset were legion. They are framed by the requirement to include everything of the period, each item having the potential to inform, and the need for a sufficient number of correspondence analyses to have been carried out to begin to fix typologies into absolute date ranges. Through the process of building the database, dates were entered into the burial records of each individual as published in the excavation reports, with obvious anomalies, for example from antiquarian excavations, adjusted in the light of more recent work. A strategic approach established the framework as sufficiently robust to support the research questions of the project, but without compromising the potential for more refined dating as required in the longer term.

The template for the Tribal Hidage Project database was provided by ASKED. There, use was made of Vera Evison's key publication of the site at Buckland, Dover (1987) and Parfitt and Brugmann's report on Mill Hill, Deal (1997), both in effect acting as type sites for the range of antiquarian sites and unpublished excavations that had not been closely dated. For ASKED, where no clear dating evidence was available, graves were ascribed to the date range for the site as a whole – this inclusive strategy was sufficiently robust to facilitate statistical analyses, for example of the relative wealth per head of contemporary communities (Brookes 2007). Through a process of checking and comparing data from different Kentish sites, anomalies and inconsistencies became immediately evident and inevitably suggested the changing of some published dates. For example, Polhill in West Kent (Philp and Hawkes 1973) had been dated at AD 650–750, but in the light of balancing evidence from sites in East Kent, a revised date of 625–750 was proposed. In addition, it was argued that John Shephard's (1979) dating of the East Kentish upland sites might be a generation too late, commencing around the start of the seventh century rather than late in the first quarter of that century.

Problematically, the major unpublished sites, such as Broadstairs St Peter's Tip and Ozengell, both from Kent, under this treatment were not in a position to challenge or refine established chronologies, but are subordinate to them. If, by this cumulative method, the dates given throughout ASKED prove in the longer term to be in error by one or two generations (20–50 years) in either direction, the basic sequence has nevertheless been held to be generally coherent. Yet ASKED recorded a distinctively Kentish chronology. The dating of all these sites clearly has the potential for greater refinement and indeed Andrew Richardson (2005, 36–40) has proposed a nine-phase scheme for the period AD 395–750. This potential, though, is both a problem and a bonus. Kentish-derived chronologies are detailed, due to the sheer number and range of artefacts, the potential to link to Continental chronologies, and the large number of excavated cemeteries and located findspots, but they have an unproven chronological relationship to the whole zone of Anglo-Saxon settlement. There is a significant fall off in the range, type and quantity of material as one proceeds to the west of Kent. Here, there are two interlinked problems of contemporaneity – the pace of change across the study region – and regionality – the extent to which discrete areas are distinctive in the development of their material culture.

It was not possible to determine whether all material culture types are contemporary in all areas of the study region. The problem of curated items, with early dress fitments being kept and buried generations after they had fallen out of fashionable use, is more readily overcome by examination of the whole assemblage. But, it is obvious that the cultural activity in one location could impact on and in turn prompt change within adjacent locations. The degree of time lag in these processes may be relatively short or long and may in any case impact on only certain sections of a community. Nevertheless, by using broad time spans for phasing it is envisaged that the outcomes of such changes, rather than the processes themselves, will be detectable from one phase to another.

The second issue of regionality is linked to problems of contemporaneity, but presents the additional feature of differing material cultures in geographical locales. For example, did Saxon type saucer brooches run in exact chronological parallel with Kentish small square-headed brooches, or were they replaced by new styles at different times? There are obvious regional imbalances in the evidence. Thus Wessex and the Upper Thames Valley provided ample material for phase A, Kent was best for phase B and both had similar quantities, though of differing content, for phase C. The period AD 700–750 is dominated by coin finds. A noteworthy case in point, though, is that of the Sussex material.

A thorough review of the Sussex corpus did not shift the dating presented by Martin Welch in 1983, except in a few minor cases. The earliest material still could not be placed before the second half of the fifth century and that there was still a paucity of significant seventh century burials. It may be the case that some of the more poorly furnished burials of a site such as The Sanctuary, Alfriston may represent a tailing off of wealth in seventh-century Sussex, but there are no diagnostic artefacts, only those that could be placed to the period as a whole. There are poorly furnished (perhaps more correctly, poorly excavated and recorded) barrow burials, primary and secondary, that may represent fully the seventh-century corpus, but again these cannot be tied firmly into an absolute dating framework (see Plate 7). The issue of the longevity of the cremation rite also presents problems. Isolated cremations and those within cemeteries often have no distinguishing features that can delimit their date range and therefore must be placed as possibly occurring anywhere in the period AD 450–700, for lack of evidence to the contrary. The bulk of the site locations, objects and people could only be attributed to the whole period, however. Although a date range and phase entries are given for all sites, these were only used in conjunction with the data quality level. For example, a site could appear to have been active in all phases, but in reality its specific dates are unknown therefore it appears in all phases, but it is accorded a lower data-quality grading because of this uncertainty. The numbers of fully and partially datable sites within the study region as a whole are given below in Table 1.

The validity of the phase divisions for the project is reinforced, however, by comparison with the most recent work on providing dating schema for this period in a more coherent format.

Table 1. fully and partially datable sites within the study region

| Phase | Number of sites | % of total |
|---|---|---|
| Phase A | 575 | 17% |
| Phase B | 59 | 2% |
| Phase C | 912 | 26% |
| Phases A/B | 592 | 17% |
| Phases B/C | 326 | 9% |
| Phases A/B/C | 985 | 29% |
|  | 3449 | 100% |

Table 2. Compared dating schemes for the study period

| EH Male Phase | Date range to 1 and (2) sigma | EH Female Phase | Date range to 1 and (2) sigma | Bead phase | Date range |
|---|---|---|---|---|---|
| A | Pre-518 (pre-528) | P | 504–534 (511–528) | A1 | 450–530 |
| B | 518–548 (528–543) | P/Q | 519–541 (526–537) | A2 | 480–580 |
| C | 551–568 (554–565) |  |  | A2b B1 | 530–580 555–600 |
| D | 579–604 (584–599) | Q/R | 575–606 (582–599) | B2 | 580–650 |
| E | 615–647 (623–677) | R/S | 605–636 (612–629) |  |  |
| F | 662–681 (667–677) |  |  | C | 650– |
|  | 666–692 (670–683) | S ends | 675–699 (678–690) |  |  |

These are Birte Brugmann's study of glass beads from early Anglo-Saxon graves (2004) and the English Heritage-funded project combining seriation by correspondence analysis and radiocarbon dating for selected graves nationally for the period AD 450–720, although inevitably that project is dominated numerically by East Kentish graves. Two major points at present emerge from the English Heritage project: the decline in furnished burial before AD 700 rather than as late as AD 720, and the possibility of determining regional sequences. The dating schema used in ASKED, although pre-dating these researches followed much the same format and has not been compromised by these later works. The broad outline of both schemes is presented in Table 2 (the phase notation is arbitrary here).

In essence, the absolute dating and subsequent relative phasing scheme used by the Tribal Hidage Project here is an amalgamation of past work by the research community on burials, finds and settlements. Historic endeavours to date individuals in graves from the objects in their assemblages and current best practices that have deployed a range of sampling and scientific strategies to assess dates have been incorporated into the database. An enduring emphasis by the research community on typological work has produced a number of effective tools with which to work (for an overview see Nielsen 1997). These have been significantly added to in recent years (Marzinzik 2003; Brugmann 2004) together with identifications of Continental material in English contexts (Brugmann 1999). Whilst the data phasing parameters of the Tribal Hidage Project were applied consistently, it is a reflection of cumulative works to date and can claim no particular analytical advance as it currently stands. It is axiomatic that the dating parameters for any site may be revised in the light of further analysis (see Hills and O'Connell 2009). No attempt has been made to reconcile the dates used with Continental chronologies (Vierck 1977; Welch 1999), rather accepting implicitly the work of European colleagues (Legoux *et al.* 2004).

## The sites

A basic level of information is recorded for each of the 3449 sites. Twelve figure references are given for all sites, subject to the data quality assessment outlined above. The most common name for each site is also given. The PAS and EMCC sites are identified as such, without further place-name information. Each site has been ascribed a unique identifier consisting of a three-letter code denoting the pre-1964 county, followed by a three-letter code denoting the pre-1850 parish (its first consonant, the first consonant of final syllable and the final consonant, amended to avoid duplications as necessary), then a site type code and the sequential number of that site type within the parish. Examples are here given in Table 3.

*Table 3. Examples of site codes*

| Site Code | Components |
|---|---|
| BckTPW-FS1 | Buckinghamshire; Taplow; Findspot; 1 |
| BrkLTM-BC1 | Berkshire; Little Wittenham; Burial Cremation; 1 |
| DstDCR-FS9 | Dorset; Dorchester; Findspot; 9 |
| EsxBKG-SET1 | Essex; Barking; Settlement; 1 |
| GlsLLE-MC1 | Gloucestershire; Lechlade; Mixed Cemetery; 1 |
| HtsBSK-IC1 | Hampshire; Basingstoke; Inhumation Cemetery; 1 |
| IoWBST-LE1 | Isle of Wight; Binstead; Linear Earthwork; 1 |
| KntBLD-IC1 | Kent; Buckland; Inhumation Cemetery; 1 |
| MsxCOL-FS12 | Middlesex; City of London; Findspot; 12 |
| OxfOFD-BI3 | Oxfordshire; Oxford; Burial Inhumation; 3 |
| SmtQCL-IC1 | Somerset; Queen Camel; Inhumation Cemetery; 1 |
| SryHAM-SET1 | Surrey; Ham; Settlement; 1 |
| SsxCHC-FS18 | Sussex; Chichester; Findspot; 18 |
| WltEBW-BI1 | Wiltshire; Ebbsbourne Wake; Burial Inhumation; 1 |

In this scheme, the county and parish become the basic geographical units within which sites are clustered together. This is not to imply necessarily that the pre-1964 shire and pre-1850 parish boundaries relate directly to the landholdings of the people represented by the sites. Rather this system has been developed to facilitate the cross-referencing and checking of entries to ensure accuracy and consistency. Additionally, it allows for tentative groupings together of isolated finds from locations unfamiliar to the research team prior to mapping. It can be noted, however, that in certain areas it was difficult to establish a correct parish location for a site, as it was adjacent to, on, or bisected by the boundary. The use of pre-1964 shire boundaries entailed reconciling any sites found after that date back into the earlier counties. This was a problem in particular for the Vale of the White Horse, formerly in Berkshire, now Oxfordshire, as well as parts of Dorset and Hampshire and for South Gloucestershire. On the other hand, Sussex is treated as one county. The boundaries were traced and digitised from the early editions of the Ordnance Survey maps. For pre-1850 parish boundaries, the reference source used was the electronic map of the historic parishes of England and Wales with gazetteer (Kain and Oliver 2001). The primary publication for each site was consulted and used for data entry. County and sub-region wide gazetteers were also used as secondary sources (Welch 1983; Dickinson 1976).

The definitions of the major site types were devised particularly for this dataset. Easily searchable short descriptive text of a limited range of site types sufficed to underpin the requirements of the project. Eleven major site-types were defined and are given in Table 4.

The breakdown of the sites by major type and their grading for information quality is presented below in Table 5.

It has traditionally been the case that the archaeology of the early Anglo-Saxon period is dominated by cemetery and isolated burial sites. Here they comprise only 25% of total sites, although they make a major contribution to the grade 1 data. The relatively large number of settlements, now 9% of the site total, is mainly due to their excavation and identification by contractual field units and their publication in the 'grey literature'. Findspots now comprise over 66% of all sites and provide good quality data. These finds are derived equally from the PAS, the EMCC and earlier reported finds, and are now such a considerable resource that they cannot be treated as merely illustrative material to support excavated cemetery distributions (Harrington and Welch, 2010). Rather they have the potential to offer a different set of evidence on their own terms (Maclean and Richardson 2010).

Numbers of site types vary by county across the study region, as listed below in Table 6. As might be expected, those counties on the margins of the study region contribute the smallest proportions of sites to the total. Of the eight complete county contributions, Kent dominates with 31% of the total, while Hampshire and Wiltshire combined still only comprises 26%, with the remainder contributing less than 10% each to the total. As noted above, however, findspots contribute the greatest number of sites to the total and it could be queried whether they were contributing equally in proportion to the final total. For example, has particularly intensive metal-detecting activity and good local relations between the detectorists and PAS Finds Liaison Officers resulted in a skewed sample? From the data presented here, it can be observed that some counties

## 2. The Early Anglo-Saxon Census

*Table 4. site types*

| Site Type | Definition |
|---|---|
| BC<br>Burial Cremation | A single, isolated cremation burial event, containing the remains of one or more individuals, but not in association with any other contemporary burial events |
| BI<br>Burial Inhumation | A single, isolated inhumation burial event, containing the remains of one or more individuals, but not in association with any other contemporary burial events |
| CC<br>Cremation Cemetery | A cemetery consisting exclusively of cremation burials, comprising two or more spatially adjacent burial events |
| ECC<br>Ecclesiastical site | A church or monastic related site with a foundation date within the study period |
| FS<br>Findspot | A location-only site, where it is not recorded whether more material is in the immediate vicinity that might suggest another type of site. By implication, findspots are the locations of stray objects until determined otherwise. |
| IND Industrial | A site where industrial activity took place |
| IC<br>Inhumation Cemetery | A cemetery consisting exclusively of inhumation burials, comprising two or more spatially adjacent burial events |
| LE<br>Linear Earthwork | An extended earthwork defined as such by its NMR record |
| MC<br>Mixed Cemetery | A cemetery consisting of both inhumation and cremation burials, even if one rite is in a tiny minority, and comprising two or more spatially adjacent burial events |
| SET<br>Settlement | A site where there is evidence of human habitation, such as dwellings or workshops (typically SFBs) or evidence of and features likely to be associated with human habitation activities, such as ditches or pits |
| | Miscellaneous other sites were noted in publications, for example a shrine or a wreck, whose location might be relevant to the other sites listed |

*Table 5. Site types with qualitative grading*

| Site Type | Number | % of Total | Grade 1 | Grade 2 | Grade 3 |
|---|---|---|---|---|---|
| Burial Cremation (BC) | 23 | 1% | 20 | 1 | 2 |
| Burial Inhumation (BI) | 290 | 8% | 219 | 20 | 51 |
| Cremation Cemetery (CC) | 6 | <1% | 4 | 0 | 2 |
| Ecclesiastical site (ECC) | 8 | <1% | 8 | 0 | 0 |
| Findspot (FS) | 2262 | 66% | 1059 | 976 | 227 |
| Industrial (IND) | 13 | <1% | 7 | 1 | 5 |
| Inhumation Cemetery (IC) | 469 | 14% | 380 | 14 | 75 |
| Linear Earthwork (LE) | 15 | <1% | 6 | 3 | 6 |
| Mixed Cemetery (MC) | 53 | 2% | 50 | 2 | 1 |
| Settlement (SET) | 305 | 9% | 245 | 1 | 60 |
| Other | 5 | <1% | 1 | | 4 |
| Totals | 3349 | | 1998 | 1018 | 433 |

Table 6. Percentages of sites by county (RT = Regional Total)

| Shire Area | Burial Sites | % RT | Settlements | % RT | Findspots | % RT | Misc. | % RT | County Sites Total | % RT |
|---|---|---|---|---|---|---|---|---|---|---|
| *Major counties* | | | | | | | | | | |
| Kent | 247 | 29% | 79 | 25% | 733 | 32% | 7 | 14.63% | 1066 | 31% |
| Hampshire | 63 | 8% | 36 | 12% | 345 | 15% | 5 | 12.2% | 449 | 13% |
| Wiltshire | 109 | 13% | 29 | 9% | 306 | 14% | 1 | 2.44% | 445 | 13% |
| Sussex | 140 | 17% | 23 | 8% | 162 | 7% | 13 | 31.71% | 338 | 10% |
| Berkshire | 74 | 9% | 46 | 15% | 160 | 7% | 2 | 2.88% | 282 | 8% |
| Surrey | 70 | 8% | 28 | 9% | 156 | 7% | 2 | 4.88% | 256 | 7% |
| Isle of Wight | 20 | 2% | 1 | <1% | 118 | 5% | 2 | 7.32% | 141 | 4% |
| Dorset | 35 | 4% | 9 | 3% | 75 | 3% | 5 | 12.2% | 124 | 3% |
| *Marginal counties* | | | | | | | | | | |
| Middlesex | 3 | <1% | 15 | 5% | 65 | 3% | 1 | 2.44% | 84 | 2% |
| Oxfordshire | 29 | 3% | 18 | 6% | 35 | 2% | 0 | | 82 | 2% |
| Somerset | 26 | 3% | 8 | 3% | 30 | 1% | 4 | 7.32% | 68 | 2% |
| Essex | 0 | 0% | 3 | 1% | 52 | 2% | 0 | | 55 | 2% |
| Gloucestershire | 19 | 2% | 8 | 3% | 20 | 1% | 0 | | 47 | 1% |
| Buckinghamshire | 4 | <1% | 3 | <1% | 5 | <1% | 0 | | 12 | <1% |
| | | 100% | | 100% | | 100% | | 100% | | 100% |
| Totals | 839 | 24% | 306 | 8.7% | 2262 | 66% | 42 | 1.2% | 3449 | 100% |

are producing only marginally more findspots relative to other types of site, when compared with their total percentage contribution. This is the case for Hampshire and Wiltshire, though not to any significant degree. Local explanations here suffice in that these variations probably reflect the intensity of activity by local and county archaeological societies over time, particularly noticeable where thorough programmes of fieldwalking have generated a large number of findspots, primarily of potsherds that may be indicative of settlements and arable farming. As a result it appears that findspot location activity is reproducing a pattern of quantities of site per county, similar to that generated historically by excavation archaeology.

## Populating the landscape

It is difficult to arrive at an accurate total for the number of people whose burials have been chanced upon or excavated and for whom there are records, however brief and incomplete. It is more problematic still to estimate the numbers of individuals who were alive within the study region at any given point throughout the period AD 400–700. Expressed in simple terms, 839 burial sites were identified as relevant to the project. The majority of these are clearly identified as early Anglo-Saxon and the minority probably are so. Within this site total, 159 contained an unknown number of individuals, because they have not been excavated, perhaps being visible only as cropmarks, or else being encountered without proper excavation. Examples are sites revealed through nineteenth century gravel extraction, quarrying or railway cutting, from which artefacts

## 2. The Early Anglo-Saxon Census

*Table 7. Numbers of individuals recorded by county*

| County | No of burial sites | % of total burial sites | No. of individuals | % of total individuals | Sites with these individuals | Sites with unknown number of individuals |
| --- | --- | --- | --- | --- | --- | --- |
| Kent | 247 | 29% | 4993 | 41% | 194 | 53 |
| Sussex | 140 | 17% | 1418 | 12% | 112 | 28 |
| Wiltshire | 109 | 13% | 807 | 7% | 97 | 12 |
| Berkshire | 74 | 9% | 1162 | 10% | 63 | 11 |
| Surrey | 70 | 8% | 896 | 7% | 52 | 18 |
| Hampshire | 63 | 8% | 1029 | 8% | 54 | 9 |
| Dorset | 35 | 4% | 258 | 2% | 29 | 6 |
| Isle of Wight | 20 | 2% | 186 | 2% | 17 | 3 |
| Oxfordshire | 29 | 3% | 453 | 4% | 22 | 7 |
| Somerset | 26 | 3% | 416 | 3% | 21 | 5 |
| Gloucestershire | 19 | 2% | 511 | 3% | 14 | 5 |
| Essex | 0 | 0% | 0 | | 0 | 0 |
| Buckinghamshire | 4 | <1% | 3 | <1% | 3 | 1 |
| Middlesex | 3 | <1% | 9 | <1% | 2 | 1 |
| | | 100% | | 100% | | |
| Totals | 839 | | 12141 | | 680 | 159 |

have been retrieved to indicate their early Anglo-Saxon context. A further 315 sites are listed as isolated single and multiple burials. These contained perhaps 298 individuals, plus a further 44 individuals from multiple inhumations within a single grave (ten doubles, four triples and three quadruples). There is however, in Kent particularly, a steady conversion rate of these isolated burials into cemeteries, through later and more extensive area excavation. Sixteen of these isolated burial sites also have unassociated additional artefacts recorded, but in insufficient detail to identify full grave groups and thus verify the presence of a cemetery. The number of genuinely isolated burials might therefore be much smaller. From the remaining 365 cemetery sites we have burial records for 11,807 individuals with or without grave finds, making a total number of 12,141 people securely known within the study area, as shown in Table 7.

Once again the Kentish archive far outweighs that of other areas in terms of gross numbers of people, with over 40% of those recorded and more than its equitable share of burials, indicating a propensity for larger than average sized cemeteries. Sussex and Wiltshire have fewer people than might be expected, suggesting relatively small cemeteries, as recorded. For the remaining counties, site numbers and body counts run in parallel. Certain sites with a recent or extensive excavation history can be taken as indicators of the possible extents and potential community numbers for their respective localities. On the whole these indicate far greater numbers of people than simply those for whom there are records. Where extensive excavation has taken place, 160 of these 365 sites have also yielded unassociated material, probably residual material from disturbed or robbed burials, indicating that still greater numbers were buried there. Additionally, many of

23

Table 8. Overview of burial numbers by county

| County | No. of individuals | Sites in sample, excluding isolated burials | Range | Average number | Median | Potential additional individuals | No further record sites in county | Estimated total number of individuals by county |
|---|---|---|---|---|---|---|---|---|
| Kent | 4993 | 113 | 2–434 | 43 | 9 | 2279 | 53 | 7272 |
| Sussex | 1418 | 59 | 2–254 | 23 | 7 | 414 | 28 | 1832 |
| Wiltshire | 807 | 40 | 2–120 | 19 | 6 | 228 | 12 | 1035 |
| Berkshire | 1162 | 32 | 2–247 | 35 | 9 | 385 | 11 | 1547 |
| Surrey | 896 | 28 | 2–238 | 32 | 12 | 576 | 18 | 1472 |
| Hampshire | 1029 | 36 | 2–161 | 28 | 10 | 252 | 9 | 1281 |
| Dorset | 258 | 19 | 2–54 | 13 | 5 | 78 | 6 | 336 |
| Isle of Wight | 186 | 8 | 2–113 | 22 | 6 | 66 | 3 | 252 |
| Oxfordshire | 453 | 17 | 2–118 | 26 | 12 | 182 | 7 | 635 |
| Somerset | 416 | 18 | 5–116 | 23 | 10 | 115 | 5 | 531 |
| Gloucestershire | 511 | 11 | 2–254 | 36 | 8 | 180 | 5 | 691 |
| Essex | 0 | | | | | | 0 | |
| Buckinghamshire | 3 | | | | | | 1 | |
| Middlesex | 9 | | | | | | 1 | |
| **Totals** | 12141 | | | | | 4755 | 159 | 16884 |

the recorded cemetery sites have been only partially excavated, suggesting far higher numbers on each site over a wider area. An example here is the Wiltshire site at Collingbourne Ducis, which from its first excavation, on a small housing development in this country village, produced just 33 inhumations in 1974, ostensibly an average sized Anglo-Saxon rural community (Gingell 1978). Subsequent housing estate expansion in 2007 produced a further tranche of approximately 80 burials, probably including both unurned cremations and four-post grave structures. The plan layout of the site would indicate that still more burials lie outside of the excavated area, although perhaps not exceeding a total of 180 for the entire community. This remains, however, one of the largest recorded cemeteries in Wiltshire and would imply that others of the small average size might also be considerably larger, identifiable as such only if further comparable rural housing development were to take place. Here one must note that the 109 burials from Black Patch, Pewsey Wiltshire probably do represent the full extent of the site (pers. comm. Bruce Eagles; also Annable and Eagles 2010). These can all be dated within the period AD 475–550, leaving as a matter for speculation the whereabouts of burials from the subsequent occupation phases of this community within the landscape of the Vale of Pewsey. The second excavation in 1994 at Buckland Dover has doubled the number of people known from that site to 434. The site plan (Parfitt and Haith 1995; Welch 2007, 210) shows that the two excavated areas present different spatial patterning of the graves, and that a railway cutting and a quarry on either side truncate the newly revealed area of concentrated row-like graves. The true number of burials must have been substantial, perhaps over 600. The 159 sites without further records have the potential to add significantly to the total number of people indicated by the archaeology. By taking the average

## 2. The Early Anglo-Saxon Census

*Table 9. Median numbers of individuals in cemetery sites*

| Number of burials | Fewer than 10 | 11–50 | 51–100 | 101–200 | Over 201 |
|---|---|---|---|---|---|
| Number of sites | 214 | 108 | 23 | 23 | 13 |

number of individuals from each site in a county and multiplying by the number of no-further record sites, as shown above in Table 8, an additional 4755 people seem to be indicated. Thus for the entire study region there are, in probability over the period AD 400–750, burial traces of at least 17,000 people.

Although the average number of individuals recorded per cemetery in the study region is a mere 31, this is clearly not the average for every county dataset, as indicated in the table above. Kent has the highest average number per cemetery, but not the highest median placing, suggesting the presence of some very large, but also many smaller cemeteries. The counties of Hampshire, Berkshire and Surrey coalesce into a second tier grouping, with average numbers falling between 28 and 35, with a median of between nine and twelve. A third tier comprises Sussex, Wiltshire, the Isle of Wight and Dorset in which community groups may have been significantly smaller, also showing lower median placings. The greatest number of individuals from any one site, 434, has been recorded from the combined excavations at Buckland, Dover, Kent. Elsewhere, the greatest number from any single site does not generally exceed 260 people, with some counties containing sites that do not exceed 150 burials. As the Collingbourne Ducis example clearly illustrates, however, the excavation history of a site and changes to modern regional built environment programmes have the potential to skew all such results.

The median number of persons from all sites in the study area is eight, which reflects the very large number of sites with fewer than ten recorded people (excluding isolated burials), as indicated in Table 9 above.

It is debatable of course whether the 214 are really small community burial locations, or sites that only appear as such due to the nature of their piecemeal excavation histories. The top 13 sites with 201 or more burials contain 3633 people, or 30% of those represented here. Eight of these are in Kent, as listed in Table 10. Each one of these sites has an extensive excavation history and each may have had optimum recovery, although a substantial part of the Ozengell site was lost in nineteenth century railway cutting. Equally Mitcham, Surrey may spread well beyond the bounds of the housing estate that prompted its initial excavation and Butler's Field in Lechlade, Gloucestershire clearly extends well beyond the excavated area, with perhaps as many graves again as those already recorded through excavation.

A considerable number of these large total sites listed in Table 10 are mixed rite cemeteries, yet the database records only 53 of these sites, which form only 6% of the total burial sites and 14% of the cemeteries. The database holds records for approximately 800 cremation burials, both in mixed-rite cemeteries and as isolated burials, that is, 6% of the total burials. They range in number from 1 to 93 on a mixed-rite site, averaging 16% of the total burials (median at 18%). The average number is 16, with a median at 6. They occur in all sizes of mixed cemetery as shown

Table 10. Sites with more than 200 burials, the majority from Kent

| Site name | Site code | Number of burials |
|---|---|---|
| Eccles, Aylesford | KntAYF-IC1 | 203 |
| Saltwood, Stone Farm | KntSWD-IC1 | 220 |
| Saxton Road, Abingdon | BrkABD-MC1 | 228 |
| Ozengell, Ramsgate | KntRAM-IC1 | 232 |
| Mitcham, Surrey | SryMHM-IC1 | 238 |
| Long Wittenham | BrkLWM-MC1 | 247 |
| St Ann's Road, Eastbourne | SsxEAS-MC1 | 254 |
| Butler's Field, Lechlade | GlsLLE-MC1 | 254 |
| Finglesham (Northbourne) | KntNBN-IC1 | 257 |
| Sarre | KntSAR-IC1 | 319 |
| Kingston Down | KntKSN-IC1 | 321 |
| Broadstairs, St Peter's Tip | KntBRS-IC1 | 426 |
| Buckland, Dover | KntBLD-IC1 | 434 |

Table 11. Numbers of cremations present in mixed-rite cemeteries

| Number of cremations on mixed sites | Fewer than 10 | 11–50 | 51–100 | 101–200 | Over 201 |
|---|---|---|---|---|---|
| Number of sites | 5 | 16 | 5 | 13 | 4 |

in Table 11 (sample size: 44 sites with known numbers of inhumations and cremations), although they appear to be more common the larger the site and thus occur in higher numbers.

Those sites designated as solely cremation cemeteries are both very few in number and small in content. Just six sites account for a mere nine burials and with uncertain relevance to the overall time frame. Two at least of these are secondary insertions into earlier barrows. Cremation cemeteries, if they have any genuine presence as single-rite sites in the study region, have a distribution restricted to Sussex, Hampshire, Surrey and the Isle of Wight.

## *These individuals and their graves*
The pivotal aspect of the project database is the enumeration of individuals from their burial records. Each person has received a unique identifier, consisting of the site code and a grave number, to which associated artefacts are appended. For each individual there are thus potentially two datasets:

- Personal information regarding age at death placed within a banded group, sex, gender, burial position and grave orientation, date and phase, burial practice, burial structure
- Associated material described from the closed find context of the grave, essentially a listing of any grave finds, by type, provenance and raw material

Few individuals amongst the 12141 identified possess a complete personal record set. These are mainly those from recent excavations carried out by commercial field units, where full

## 2. The Early Anglo-Saxon Census

*Table 12. Numbers of individuals in each age band at death*

| Age band | Number present | As % of total |
| --- | --- | --- |
| Infant 0–2 | 190 | 3% |
| Child 3–6 | 651 | 11% |
| Juvenile 7–15 | 580 | 9% |
| Young adult 16–24 | 619 | 10% |
| Adult 25–44 | 3686 | 59% |
| Old adult 45+ | 493 | 8% |
| Total | 6219 | 100% |

*Table 13. Numbers of burials by grave orientation*

| Grave orientation | Number | % of sample |
| --- | --- | --- |
| W–E | 781 | 68% |
| S–N | 150 | 13% |
| NW–SE | 87 | 8% |
| SW–NE | 73 | 6% |
| N–S | 23 | 2% |
| SE–NW | 28 | 2% |
| E–W | 7 | 1% |

osteoarchaeological data is produced as a norm. For those individuals where biological sex has been recorded (3037), the relative numbers are female: 1429 (47%) and male: 1608 (53%). The most complete personal dataset is for age at death, with 6219 entries. The age range present spans from neonate to approximately 70. The ages at death as given in all reports have been placed into bands, in order to include those for which varying terminologies are used ('baby', 'young', 'elderly' 'adolescent' and 'youth' are some examples) and can be reconciled to a best fit, with the following numbers and proportions present.

As would be expected, the most common age at death was in adulthood, between 25 and 44, with only 8% of people living longer. Death before full maturity was the case for 33% of the population. Infants and children under six are probably under-represented, as recent intensive osteoarchaeological reporting has generated the majority of these entries, particularly for neonates and infants (Recent examples include Duhig unpublished; Harman 1990 and 1998; Marlow 1993; Anderson and Andrews 1997)

Grave orientations have been inconsistently recorded within data entry, due to historical variations in the recording notation that would have required a lengthy process to reconcile. Therefore only twenty-three of the more recently published sites have collated orientation data, but fortunately these provide for a good geographical spread, giving a sample of 1149 entries. These entries were adjusted to only eight compass points and are presented in Table 13 (above), with the head position given first.

Table 14. Grave orientation diversity by county

| County | Entries/sites | W–E | S–N | NW–SE | SW–NE | OTHER |
|---|---|---|---|---|---|---|
| Sussex | 184/7 | 102 | 50 | 1 | 14 | 17 |
| Hants | 167/4 | 92 | 65 | 0 | 8 | 2 |
| Wilts | 41/2 | 22 | 6 | 0 | 7 | 6 |
| Gloucs | 248/2 | 239 | 0 | 2 | 6 | 1 |
| Somerset | 130/3 | 120 | 0 | 6 | 3 | 1 |
| Dorset | 12/1 | 12 | 0 | 0 | 0 | 0 |
| Kent | 256/2 | 166 | 0 | 69 | 10 | 11 |
| Berks/Oxf | 118/2 | 28 | 29 | 9 | 25 | 27 |
| Total | 1149/23 | | | | | |

West-to-east orientations dominate throughout, but with a substantial number of south-to-north orientations, whilst a significant minority (19%) of the total consists of other variations. The geographical distribution of the various orientations is uneven. The sample is drawn from eight counties, and can be characterised as being divided between those counties with a relatively homogenous set of orientations and those exhibiting greater diversity, as shown in Table 14.

The absence from the sample of south-to-north burials in Kent is striking, with its principal alternative being a variant of the conventional west-to-east orientation, at northwest southeast. Similarly Gloucestershire, Somerset and Dorset, the far western parts of the study region, focus on the predominant alignment, suggesting a homogenous grouping. Wiltshire, Berkshire/Oxfordshire, Hampshire and Sussex, form a broad central band through the study region, and reveal a greater diversity containing most of the south-to-north burials sampled here. Whether this initial pattern can be interpreted as a cultural one remains as open to question as the meaning of grave orientation itself. The cemetery size patterning outlined above, being one of smaller sites in the central regions, set together with the diversity of community here, in terms of the range of cultural choices available in the burial rite, begins to identify regional difference in terms of characterisation, other than one based on artefact style and provenance alone.

## *Phasing the burials*

The dating and phasing parameters, as outlined above for the sites, were similarly applied to the individuals with burial records, primarily as a means of phasing the associated artefacts in order to calculate the relative wealth of communities over time. It was important to the principles of the project to include also those people from unfurnished and poorly furnished graves, for statistical and community profiling purposes. Only a minority of persons in the study period (25% of the total) could be placed directly into a phase as a result of the dating of associated artefacts, as in Table 15. These were not evenly distributed between phases and highlight the problem of phase B being particularly under-represented, although there is no external evidence to suggest an actual decrease in population numbers at that time and occurring before the widespread use of churchyard and unfurnished burial.

## 2. The Early Anglo-Saxon Census

*Table 15. Numbers of individuals datable to each phase*

| Phase | Number Datable to Phase | % of Individuals in Stusy Period |
|---|---|---|
| Phase A (450–575) | 1681 | 54% |
| Phase B (575–650) | 427 | 14% |
| Phase C (650–750) | 994 | 32% |

*Table 16. Numbers of burials allocated to each phase*

| Phase | Allocated To Phase | % Of Total |
|---|---|---|
| Phase A | 5295 | 44% |
| Phase B | 3656 | 30% |
| Phase C | 3082 | 26% |

For the majority of the people no such precise phasing could be applied, so instead they were allocated into phases based on the longevity of the site. For example, a site dated AD 500–700 with 100 unallocated people, covering 75 years of phase A, 75 years of phase B and 50 years of phase C, would have them randomly allocated to the phases in proportions of 3:3:2. Any remaining single burials were placed into a phase on the basis of the likelihood that they belonged there, for example a burial dated AD 500–600 would more likely fall within phase A (AD 450–575), whereas one dated AD 550–650 would more likely fall within phase B (AD 575–650). By this method less than 1% of burials were left unallocated. These comprise single burials with too wide a date range, equally possibly prehistoric or early Anglo-Saxon. After the allocation exercise the distribution by phase, as shown in Table 16, gave a more even proportional spread and perhaps one that is more representative of the population buried outside of minster churchyards in the seventh and early eighth centuries.

## The artefacts

The database records over 28,000 objects from burials and a further 2500 artefacts recorded from findspots. Each burial object is identified by its owner's unique grave ID or else, if unassociated, by a general site code and 'other artefact' (OA) designation. There are at least 220 different artefact types deposited in the burials, including organic objects. Due to historical variations in descriptions, levels of recording and the evolving identifications of objects, it was necessary to harmonise the terminology into a project thesaurus (to be published as metadata for the Early Anglo-Saxon Census online). Most objects have an individual entry, but in the case of beads, which might number up to 300 in any single inhumation, grouped entries were used, giving quantities for monochrome, polychrome and amber beads only. Unusual beads, for example barrel-shaped gold beads or melon beads, were tallied separately. Objects were placed into groups by type in an admittedly subjective yet functional manner, depending on their perceived usage in life. Should knives, for example, count as weapons, personal effects or tools? We opted for the latter. Some items could fall within several groups, depending on their use in the burial – a flint flake found in

*Table 17. Numbers of artefacts on each category*

| Category | Number of entries | % of total |
| --- | --- | --- |
| Personal effects | 12487 | 45% |
| Tools | 5211 | 19% |
| Weaponry | 4138 | 15% |
| Grave equipment | 3250 | 12% |
| Unknown | 1487 | 5% |
| Receptacles | 1429 | 5% |

the grave fill would be designated as grave equipment, whilst one from a bag assemblage would be interpreted as a personal effect. The *Personal Effects* category covers all of those objects associated with costume and also everyday objects on and with the body, including coins, toilet picks, amulets, organic bags, pouches and boxes. The *Weaponry* category covers all of those objects associated with armed combat, such as swords, axes, spears and shields, although shield grips are listed as separate objects within this category. Decorative features related to weapons such as scabbards, sword beads, pommels and pyramids are listed as *Personal Effects*, however. *Grave Equipment* covers coffins, nails and miscellaneous material inserted as part of the burial ritual including the placement of potsherds in the grave fill and animal bones. The *Tools* category covers productive and utilitarian objects, regardless of how they are used in the burial. Examples are awls, shears and horse harness, together with textile making and weaving equipment, such as spindle whorls and weaving beaters, although the so-called thread boxes are placed in *Personal Effects*. The *Tools* category also includes tube-like brush handles, often misleadingly named 'cosmetic brushes' in the earlier literature, but here designated as tools with an unknown function. The *Receptacles* category covers copper alloy bowls, wooden metal bound containers such as cups and buckets, drinking horns, glass vessels and complete pottery vessels other than cremation urns. Approximately 5% of all objects are regarded as unidentifiable artefacts and thus are placed into an *Unknown* category. The totals for each category are given in Table 17.

Although every recorded instance of an object has been entered into the database, many remain ambiguous as to their identification and usage in the burial ritual. What are noted, for example, as small copper alloy vessel repair clips may conceivably instead be evidence of clips to a veil around the head of a woman, although perhaps rather coarse for such a purpose. Miscellaneous rivets and studs could relate to shields, belts, bags or vessels. Various fitments relating to horse harness may account for the number of unidentified iron fragments. The project was not in a position to rectify all these levels of uncertainty, without further concentrated study of comparative grave plans and illustrations – it is adequate enough here only to note their presence and raw material content. The *Grave Equipment* category retains a level of ambiguity in its content. Reconstructions of the full complexity of the burial ritual and sequences of deposition to form the full burial tableau are rarely attempted. Potsherds, flints and charcoal in the fill of a grave are recorded in the database, as it is argued that these have not been proven to be residual in each and every context and require further investigation in the longer term. The presence of iron pyrites and slag iron in burials also require investigation, in the context of potential smelting activities in the vicinity and meanings associated with metalworking. This evidence may perhaps counter the rarity of metal working tools from burials. Perhaps the most problematic to encapsulate is the evidence of organic materials, other than those associated with clothing and personal effects. Here the database records 292 entries under the 'Other-organic' as a general artefact type. Where animal bone has been identified, it includes deer, sheep/goat, goose, whale, ox, lark, frog, lobster, dog, cattle, fish, fowl and pig. The majority of the entries, however, are for charcoal, for example charred logs lining a burial, or pieces of charcoal found on the skeleton, perhaps associated with burning rituals within the inhumation context. Also recorded are detached fragments of flaxen textile, cereals, grasses, seeds, nuts, fruits, rushes and a wreath of leaves. Some of these might be considered as foods, remaining from a burial feast, or for the afterlife of the individual in a new feasting environment, whilst others are clearly used to line the grave and perhaps garland it – impressions of grasses and rushes on the underside of copper alloy bowls is a consistently noted feature (Harrington, 2003). Marine resources are present in the form of seafood, for example shells, such as limpet, mussels and oysters, mainly from coastal cemeteries in Kent and Sussex, although the oyster shell from a burial at Purton in Wiltshire again highlights the coastal trading contacts of inland sites in that area. 'Other-organics' had a limited contribution to make to this project, but remain a much under-explored source of potential evidence. Similarly no attempt was made to reconcile the textiles data into the schema.

*Type*
Where typologies are known and have been used in excavation reports, this data has been accepted and entered directly. For unpublished material, standard typologies were followed, but these entries are provisional in advance of full site publication. Where possible, reference is made to the best-published sites in the region, in particular making full use of the works of Vera Evison and the late Sonia Chadwick Hawkes. Knives, where encountered without already having a type ascribed, have been classified according to Vera Evison's Kentish-based scheme (1987, 113–5), rather than that of the Continental scheme of Böhner (1958). Spearheads similarly encountered were ascribed a type following Swanton's 1974 scheme.

*Provenance*
For the purposes of comparing and quantifying the relative access that communities had to different objects over time and to elucidate exchange networks, it was necessary to identify the sources of those objects. A small number of artefacts have been shown to originate outside of Britain, others are the product of definable regional stylistic developments within Britain and still more artefacts have no particular distinguishing features to suggest their place of manufacture. To coalesce a range of attributes, comprising raw material content, stylistic and typological developments and function under discrete headings, loosely termed as a 'culture', is a speculative process at best. From this comprehensive distributional database it is now possible to re-assess regional distributions of

multiple object types. A pilot study is discussed below that subdivides spearheads and shield bosses entries by region. Nevertheless, out of necessity and in order to unify the data, a provenancing scheme with the following categories was applied.

*Regional*

Where little information is available regarding an object, the term *regional* is used as a default provenance. In more general terms it is applied to any artefact that could have been produced within a community, or else locally to the community or could have arrived via medium distance exchange within the region. It covers a wide range of artefact types, including weapons, tools and domestic objects, such as knives, hand-made pottery and dress fittings. It assumes that the manufacture and the deposition of the artefact were broadly contemporary processes taking place within a generation. The application of this term proposes that most of the ironwork and pottery were the result of localised production and exchange. Weapons could be the product of a local smithy, but equally well may have been in other cases status items given and received under particular circumstances, from a centralised source or central place, such as Faversham under the aegis of the Kentish king. Where regional provenances for particular artefact types have been suggested in publication, these have been used instead. The term is also used to cover more stylised material with very unclear provenances, but having a wide distribution and little regional variation, for example copper alloy buckles of the seventh century, lace tags and strap ends. It includes material requiring more detailed typological analysis. Particular artefacts in this category could be locally made, in imitation of others that were imported. Generally, there is insufficient information on which to base a more precise provenance.

*Kentish; Saxon; Anglian; Wessex*

These terms were applied to artefacts where discrete regions are known to be the principal area of distributions and possible manufacture. For example, we refer to Saxon saucer brooches, Kentish small square-headed brooches and Anglian girdle hangers. *Wessex* is applied exclusively to coins in the later phases. The use of such a term denotes artefacts of insular stylistic development, regardless of their material content, for example through the use of imported garnets on Kentish disc brooches or the gold used for gilding on brooches and buckles. Essentially, given the only sporadic occurrence of Anglian material, the major division within the study region is between Kentish and Saxon provenances. Where an object type clearly has only a minority presence in Kent, it is ascribed a provenance from the Saxon area and vice versa. Nevertheless these are isolated instances in the overall provenancing strategy. This strategy begins to illustrate cultural admixture across geographical space. Where objects have a distribution over all of the areas of lowland Britain outside Kent the term *Anglian/Saxon* is used.

*Romano-British*

This rarely used term denotes artefacts that were part of the indigenous culture of southern Britain in the Roman period and were still in active use at the time of deposition, for example, penannular brooches of the fifth or sixth centuries.

*British West*
A term primarily used for Late Celtic hanging bowls and their attachments, particularly those found in the seventh century, as referenced by Bruce-Mitford (2005; also Brenan 1991). A few other items, encountered during museum archive research, that appear to be copies of Anglo-Saxon material but probably produced in workshops in the British West have not been annotated as such at this point, as they would merit detailed further study to reach a more precise definition.

*Curated/Roman; Curated/Jutlandic*
The term *Curated* was applied to objects that were made significantly earlier than their period of deposition in the burial. Additionally, indicated by /, the period or geographical area from which an object originated is given. Examples are Roman shale spindle whorls such as occur at Stowting (KntSWT-IC1) and Jutlandic relief-decorated brooches, such as that from Gilton (KntASH-IC2) grave 48.

*Kentish/*
This term denotes artefacts found in both Kent and elsewhere in Europe, probably coming from the second named area into Kent. It suggests also that the artefact may have been made in Kent, as a stylistic development of Continental proto-types. An example is the shield-on-tongue buckle, which with its general distribution as a belt form throughout northern Europe hints at a much wider potential provenancing thus designated 'Kentish/Frankish'.

*Imported*
This term is used for artefacts that were probably neither made nor sourced by raw material in the Anglo-Saxon areas of southern Britain. Examples are rock crystal spindle whorls and glass beads. The term suggests that the artefacts may have arrived via trade, exchange or the movement of people through migration or exogamous marriage, without giving any indication or source.

*Imported/*
*Imported* followed by / indicates the best available estimate of a possible source, or at least the area within which objects are known to be principally deposited. An example is the Imported/Frankish radiate-headed brooch. This may be followed by a second / and a more specific source, if identified in a published text. The numbers of artefacts by provenance are given in Table 18.

The findspots dataset produces a disproportionate number of imported and regionally specific objects. As discussed further below, this bias in the dataset is a result of the numbers of finds of silver and copper alloy dress fittings generated by metal detecting.

**Position in grave**
The position of an object in relation to the buried individual was recorded in the ASKED series of cemeteries within Kent, but this data has not been extended much further for this project database, other than to note the location and orientation of spearheads, where given in the publication.

*Table 18. Artefact provenance totals*

| Provenance | From burials | From findspots | Total by provenance | % of total by provenance |
|---|---|---|---|---|
| Regional | 20694 | 1574 | 22268 | 73% |
| Imported | 3629 | 422 | 4051 | 13% |
| Curated | 717 | 17 | 734 | 2% |
| Kentish | 836 | 135 | 971 | 3% |
| Saxon | 1225 | 149 | 1374 | 5% |
| Anglian | 37 | 15 | 52 | >1% |
| Anglian/Saxon | 173 | 63 | 236 | 1% |
| Wessex (coins) | 0 | 83 | 83 | >1% |
| Kentish/other | 653 | 19 | 672 | 2% |
| Romano-British | 26 | 0 | 26 | >1% |
| British West | 39 | 21 | 60 | >1% |
| Total | 28029 (92%) | 2498 (8%) | 30527 (100%) | 100% |

## *Material component*

The primary raw material constituent of the artefact was recorded for 99% of the burial artefacts. The major constituents are iron (48% of recorded objects), copper alloy (21%), ceramic (7%, potsherds and whole vessels) and glass (7%, mainly beads), although more than 60 kinds of raw material are present overall (the full listing will be given with the online database). More than 6% of the objects were produced using two or more types of raw material, most commonly gilding applied to dress fittings of silver or copper alloy.

## *Object weights*

A principal objective of the project archive research programme was to record the weight of individual objects, although these are noted rarely in publications. The project database recorded actual weights for over 11,000 objects, including over 5000 objects already weighed for the ASKED project. Clearly Kent has the best data, but, once moving outside of Kent, there are considerably fewer objects representing a larger number of communities, thus offering a less precise basis for comparison. In any case the majority of objects recorded (73%) are designated with a 'regional' provenance, suggesting that an approach which selected assemblages skewed towards the esoteric objects and rarer raw materials of the remaining 27% were not reflective of the whole – again, the top-down/bottom-up dichotomy. To address these concerns, a strategy was adopted to assign weights to every object based on comparisons with contemporary and adjacent objects.

In practice, there was no single method that could be applied to all object types, apart from the use of median weights and working from the known to the unknown, in what was a lengthy but systematic process. Median rather than average weight was selected because of the extremes of variability, a problem encountered by Brookes (2007 113), associated with misidentifications and the differences between conserved, poorly conserved and unconserved objects – the latter especially pulling the average weights beyond the median in most cases. The weights listed in the archival research phase of the project included estimates of full weight based on the proportion of an object that survived, for example 75% of an object at 250 grams converted to 333 grams full weight. Any object with less than 20% of its substance remaining was not estimated.

It immediately became apparent that the weights of Kentish objects, even at the median level, were skewing the data in their favour when compared with the weights of the same type, but fewer in numbers, objects from elsewhere. To avoid making the non-Kentish material into a subset of the Kentish finds, and thus glossing over spatial differences, a division between Kentish and non-Kentish objects was interposed. The non-Kentish objects were considered separately by type and raw material (for example copper alloy and iron buckles), by phase, by site and by county and only on a whole region basis where no closer data could be established. The extant Kentish data was reviewed and adjusted as necessary. The study region was divided into 21 even grid square units and it was ensured that each grid square had weights recorded for a minimum of 28% of the objects within it, by major raw material type (iron, copper alloy, silver). Through this strategy, the unavailability of all the material in the Ashmolean Museum did not have a detrimental impact on the methodology, as its collection area could be covered from other sources.

Where object typologies have been devised, the same types were considered together in the same phase. Typologies also act as shorthand for weight when they have been determined by size. An example here is the H1 and H2 spearhead types which do show a shift in weight range from the smaller to the larger type, but not invariably so. Many smaller objects, particularly of copper alloy, weighed in at less than 5 grams. Variations within classes of objects were used to refine the data. For example, rather than give a median weight for all hand-thrown pottery vessels, cremation urns and ancillary vessels from burials were considered separately, so that a general weight difference between the two became evident – cremation urns being heavier. Again significant weight differences were determined between embossed rim bowls, Celtic hanging bowls and Gotland- and Vestland-kessels on the one hand and Mediterranean bowls on the other. A particular problem, however, is the presence of copper alloy objects signified by only a few grams of sheet material, leading one to question whether a whole or fragmentary object had been deposited originally.

Excluded from this exercise were all organic artefacts and inorganic elements such as flints and stone packing to burials. Beads, as a group of objects, were excluded from the final process because it was impossible to derive viable estimates of weight from the weighed sample primarily due to the absence of definable standardisation amongst them. High bead count burials might have examples ranging from only a fraction of a gram up to 50 grams, whilst a grave with only three glass beads might have more weight of glass than one with 150 glass beads. The tiniest beads could not be weighed, as this was impractical, although it is noted with some relief that the weighing of beads is now becoming a standard practice (pers. comm. Birte Brugmann). The presence of beads by raw material type was the preferred method of analysis and is discussed further below. Some classes of object where no weight data had been established, for example cremation urns in Dorset, were also omitted. In total 22,000 objects were available for the final analysis of raw material distributions over time and space, 10,000 with true weights and 12,000 with derived weights, including those objects that had not survived the excavation process.

## Findspots and their contents

The 2262 sites that are findspots consist of single finds, hoards, or collections of possibly associated material. The database holds object information for approximately 3466 artefacts from these sites. The latter number can really only be an estimate because some reports of sites only note the presence of 'weapons' or 'brooches' without giving precise numbers. The high proportions of sites with either coins or dress fittings are primarily due to the targeted recovery of non-ferrous materials by metal detectorists.

The central problem is how to interpret what the findspots actually represent in archaeological terms. They might be mainly casual losses along routeways contributing to general distribution patterns and regional artefact densities. Alternatively, they might be relics of burials and settlements disturbed by animal activity or modern agricultural activity such as ploughing. The sites were designated an intermediate classification within sub-types to provide a means of clustering similar object types together (major types only given in description) and are enumerated in Table 19.

Coins present the largest category of objects, but are not discussed in detail as they mostly date from phases B and C. They include 260 Early Continental examples and over 550 Early English sceattas. They are a particular form of artefact loss, most likely the result of casual loss or hoarding. The 'Mixed' category was adopted for findspots producing a diverse range of material, for example

*Table 19. Numbers of findspot artefacts by sub-type*

| Sub type | Description | Number of objects | Number of sites | % of total sites |
|---|---|---|---|---|
| Coin | All coin types | 1682 | 832 | 37% |
| Mixed | Associated objects from a shared context, mainly dress fittings and weaponry | 160 | 52 | 2% |
| Personal effects | Buckles, brooches, other dress fittings, knives | 939 | 821 | 36% |
| Pottery | Vessels and potsherds | 318 | 287 | 13% |
| Receptacle (non-ceramic, inorganic) | Copper alloy, glass, including vessel mounts | 34 | 34 | 2% |
| Tools (other) | Loomweights, horse harness, spindle whorls | 38 | 38 | 2% |
| Unclassified | Unknown artefacts | 16 | 16 | 1% |
| Weaponry | Swords, scabbards, axes, spearheads, ferrules shields | 279 | 263 | 12% |
| Totals | | 3466 | 2262 | |

beads and a spearhead, for which a cemetery would offer the most satisfactory explanation for their co-presence. The personal effects sub-type has the next greatest number of single objects (939). This is a group dominated by brooches with 523 recorded (brooches from the mixed category are excluded here). The numbers of the main types of brooches identified are given in Table 20.

Those brooch types with an established geographical spread across the study region derived from burials appear to have a similar frequency within findspots (Table 21). Small square headed brooches, a Kentish type, have a lower frequency, which is perhaps due to a more restricted distribution. Button brooches have a higher frequency than the other types, possibly because they are more easily identifiable, whilst numbers of the other types may be subsumed within the 52 unknown items. At present it is assumed that examples of the first five brooch types listed above are equally likely to be found within the study region.

It was necessary to consider whether the findspots of brooches were likely to indicate the locations of cemeteries, as has been assumed for those objects found in mixed assemblages. The six brooch types most commonly present in findspots were compared by number with those present within the burials over the same region and as proportions of their respective totals.

From the above proportions it remains unclear whether the brooch findspots are mirroring the distributions in burial assemblages. The most obvious anomalies are the very low numbers of cruciform brooches in burials, a point already raised by Maclean and Richardson (2010), and

*Table 20. Number by type of brooches present*

| Brooch type | Number present | % of identified total |
| --- | --- | --- |
| Button brooch | 74 | 15.71% |
| Saucer brooch | 62 | 13.16% |
| Cruciform brooch | 59 | 12.53% |
| Small long brooch | 58 | 12.31% |
| Disc brooch | 58 | 12.31% |
| Small square headed brooch | 44 | 9.34% |
| Other types | 116 | 24.63% |
| Total | 471 | 100% |

*Table 21. Comparison of numbers of brooches by type from findspots with those from cemeteries*

| Brooch type | From findspots | % of total | From burials | % of total |
| --- | --- | --- | --- | --- |
| Button brooch | 74 | 20.85% | 123 | 10.76% |
| Saucer brooch | 62 | 17.46% | 354 | 30.97% |
| Cruciform brooch | 59 | 16.62% | 32 | 2.8% |
| Small long brooch | 58 | 16.34% | 163 | 14.26% |
| Disc brooch | 58 | 16.34% | 349 | 30.53% |
| Small square headed brooch | 44 | 12.39% | 122 | 10.67% |
| Totals | 355 | 100% | 1143 | 100% |

the selection of saucer and disc brooches as preferred types for burial dress. Cruciform brooches have their highest frequencies amongst burials in Kent (16) and Berkshire (9), but are restricted to single occurrences in cemeteries elsewhere, with none in recorded Hampshire and Wiltshire. Their numbers might increase if more fifth century cemeteries are excavated in Kent.

Therefore it was deemed unsafe to regard these findspots of dress fittings as necessarily being indicators of cemeteries, and their use was restricted to locational activity mapping only. Whilst it is not yet clearly understood how findspot data can be best interpreted, it is possible to reflect on this data for specific comparisons. An example is the comparative numbers of objects recorded from cemeteries across East and West Sussex with those found by metal detectorists. There is a general parity in terms of the number of recorded individuals between East Sussex and West Sussex for the study period. But these comparable numbers of burials have produced almost three times as many artefacts in East Sussex as occur in West Sussex. Thus, analysis of the PAS findspots provided a mechanism for assessing whether this difference was authentic or a reflection of different histories of fieldwork. For the period AD 400–600 only five new finds from separate findspots had been recorded from West Sussex compared to 18 from East Sussex, accurately reflecting the imbalance in objects already noted and reinforcing the view that, for this period, the principal focus of early Anglo-Saxon activity was in East Sussex (Harrington and Welch, 2010).

The Pottery group of finds total of 289 entries includes 222 potsherds and at least 70 identifiable vessels, five of which are wheel-thrown examples. Given the known friability of early Anglo-Saxon handmade pottery, the identification of only a few sherds probably represents the most that might be expected from fieldwalking and is the result in the main of extremely diligent searching for such material by local societies. Unfortunately in most cases a refined dating of this material is not achievable, as much of it can only be attributed to all phases. Again, this data adds to locational mapping, but provides little beyond that.

For the weaponry, spearheads dominate with over 200 objects (approximately 75% of the total) amongst the 279 entries, which also include nine sword pyramid mounts, 16 swords and twelve each of seaxes, shields and axeheads. A substantial number of the weapon findspots, particularly spearheads, appear to be clustered at river crossing points. Although the possibility cannot be discounted that these particular findspots are the result of the location of cemeteries and isolated burials near the water's edge which were subsequently flooded or eroded, there is also the possibility that these are ritual deposits. Due to this ongoing uncertainty, and until more definitive work is presented, these occurrences of weapons are used for locations of activity only.

Various tools, including artefacts related to textile production, might be indicative of either burial or settlement, although loomweights do not appear in burial assemblages and so would appear to indicate settlement, as would the two quern stone fragments. The finds of non-ceramic receptacles, mainly copper alloy bowls and glass vessels are more difficult to interpret. As isolated finds, apparently unassociated with other funerary material, their deposition is anomalous. Some at least of the copper alloy bowls may represent high status cremation burials, comparable to those found throughout the study region and dating to the late sixth and early seventh centuries, for example at Coombe Woodnesborough (Davidson and Webster, 1967). However, it would be

## 2. The Early Anglo-Saxon Census

atypical if these were unaccompanied objects. Hanging bowl escutcheons, which may indicate casual losses from objects in transit or represent disturbed or robbed graves, represents a number of entries in this sub type. Again, they might be linked to ritual deposition.

## Other datasets used

### Late Roman sites

Information on sites from the Roman period was assembled from data supplied by the National Monuments Records, Swindon in 2007. The initial listing comprised over 15,000 sites from within the study region, but covering the period AD 43 to 410, prompting the selection of only those sites that could be adjudged to have relevance. All findspots of single objects were excluded, reducing the final total of sites to 2256. An assessment of data relevance has been made to enable the grouping of sites into an upper tier (data quality level 1), comprising all villas, temples and major and minor towns, together with other sites of whatever type, all having a stated endurance into the fourth century (some problems were encountered with NMR dating terminology and their use of inappropriate and unintentionally absolute dates). The second tier of sites comprised all of the villas, temples and major and minor towns which could not be dated other than to the whole period, together with other whole period site types that may have retained a landscape impact throughout the Roman period and were possibly visible as active occupied sites or inactive monuments into the fifth century. The landscape monuments categories selected were: field systems, barrows, settlements, cemeteries, forts, barns and a range of industrial sites, including pottery, lead, salt and iron workings. The sites data was organised to be on a level comparable with that for the early Anglo-Saxon sites in the Tribal Hidage database, with only a limited number of searchable fields, which included, however, accurate 12 figure grid references and minor site types, such as a granary or temple associated with a major site type. The 404 sites that can be designated as upper tier Late Roman are shown, by type, in Table 22.

A number of additional sites and monuments (1852) that may have had relevance to early Anglo-Saxon landscape structures, but cannot be firmly dated within the Roman period, were also considered. Their numbers by site type are given in Table 23.

*Table 22. Numbers of Late Roman sites in the study region (Data Quality 1)*

| Monument type | No. | % of total |
|---|---|---|
| Villas | 156 | 39% |
| Settlement | 75 | 19% |
| Cemeteries and burials | 57 | 14% |
| Other | 43 | 11% |
| Towns, Civitas capitals and Saxon Shore Forts | 29 | 7% |
| Pottery kilns | 25 | 6% |
| Temples | 19 | 5% |
| | 404 | |

Table 23. Numbers of other potentially relevant Roman sites

| Monument type | No. | % of total |
| --- | --- | --- |
| Villas | 863 | 47% |
| Field systems and earthwork features | 663 | 36% |
| Other | 132 | 7% |
| Cemeteries and burials, including barrows | 48 | 3% |
| Temples | 55 | 3% |
| Settlement | 44 | 2% |
| Forts | 30 | 2% |
| Towns | 17 | 1% |
| | 1852 | |

*Place-name evidence*

A database of relevant place-names, each given to a 12 figure grid reference, was compiled. The major source of information was the Cambridge Dictionary of English Place names (Watts, 2004), which was gleaned for the potentially early place name components of *-ham*, *-hamm*, *-ing*, *-tun*, *-walh* and *-wic* within the study area, producing 1777 entries. Other, earlier, listings of these place-name types were integrated, principally from the work of John McNeal Dodgson (1966; 1973) on the south eastern counties regarding *-ham*, *-hamm* and *-ing*, Kirk's analysis (1972) of Kentish *-ingas* distributions, Cameron (1980) on *-walh* names and Cox's important list (1976) of pre-AD 731 names.

## Concluding remarks

The foregoing is a statement of the scale and content of the available data at the end of 2007. The range of resources needed to build this complex association of data was variable in terms of their availability, accuracy and up-to-datedness. In the most general terms, for the purposes of comparison over time and space all of the material could be mapped with a good degree of confidence. Whilst caution was required when assembling data from outside of the specialisms of the research team, most of this material was in the public domain and was assumed to be accurate and valid unless proven otherwise. Sufficient cross-referencing was built in with regard to data quality to ensure that misleading results were not generated inadvertently.

# 3. The Environmental Context of Southern Britain

## Introduction

The research brief prompted, from 2006–8, a series of visits within the study area to investigate the excavation archives for additional data. Consequently, it was possible to experience a significant number of cemetery sites in their landscape settings and in a range of climatic and seasonal conditions. Time and again cemetery sites were found to occupy elevated land overlooking the junction of a Roman road or major ancient trackway with a river (as illustrated in Plates 4, 5, 8, 9 and 10). From such viewpoints in wintry wet weather, it was also possible to observe water catchment zones re-instating themselves as flooded areas across low-lying fields but not impinging on the cemetery sites. Awareness of site locations, even when travelling along modern routeways, helped to connect up the landscape in a multiplicity of ways. Thus, for example, the chalk ridge above the Polhill seventh-century cemetery site (Philp and Hawkes 1973), when travelling through the Holmesdale in an anti-clockwise direction around the M25 motorway, signalled an arrival back in Kent and access to the Darenth valley cutting through the North Downs to the Thames Estuary.

This experience can be characterised as a form of quasi-phenomenological research, albeit taking an unstructured format. Nevertheless it developed insights into the spatial syntax of early Anglo-Saxon period landscape structures. Further, it was instrumental in framing the selection of the environmental aspects for discussion further below and it certainly framed the process of building maps within a GIS environment. Additionally, early project steering-group discussions affirmed that a shift in focus from examining land-based to considering maritime-based communications networks might prove useful when ordering and analysing the data within mapping contexts. A recurrent insight was one of a reading of both coherent and incoherent landscapes, in terms of viewsheds from archaeological sites, the physical geography, routeways and dominance positioning. The homogeneity of the visible landscape as experienced typically from a cemetery site and its association with Roman components was a striking feature. By contrast zones that had no particular character or identifiable grain to them, in terms of their geology and topography appear to have been devoid of early Anglo-Saxon material and landscape culture. These zones are particularly found around the westernmost reaches of and in the very centre of the study area and this aspect will be explored further below. What follows here is a summary of evidence from a range of resources together with a literature review, including comments from published excavation environmental

*Figure 3. View towards the south west from Camerton, Somerset, Anglo-Saxon cemetery: the Roman road from Bath to Radstock runs along the hedge line*

reports, in order to reconstruct the physical context of the early Anglo-Saxon period in southern Britain as a whole, rather than describe discrete blocks identified by county-based studies. Within this exercise, there is a re-assessment of Alan Everitt's (1986) Kentish pays-mapping methodology and a fresh definition of landscape units, together with a review of topographical, climatic and agricultural issues relating to the period AD 400–750.

## Mapping the evidence

The project base map was compiled from a variety of sources, but the methodology adopted to draw these together was framed by the Cassini Old Series of Historical Maps at a scale 1:50000. These are derived from the Ordnance Survey One-Inch Old Series sheets, surveyed between 1791 and 1874 and published between 1805 and 1874. Whilst it is accepted that minor errors are introduced into the published map set by the stretching of some sheets to fit in with the modern OS grid, overall the use of these maps proved to be highly effective. This was due in particular to the absence of the modern urban development that now successfully masks many geographical features. The maps detail the extent of salt marsh and floodplain, facilitating a reconstruction of these features that may relate, in part at least, to earlier patterns. As detailed coastal reconstruction to the level carried out by Brookes (2007) for east Kent and by Gardiner *et al.* (2001) for the Lympne-Hythe coast is beyond the remit of this project, the use of early maps represented a

## 3. The Environmental Context of Southern Britain

*Figure 4. View towards the south west from Kingston Down, Kent, Anglo-Saxon cemetery: the Roman road from Canterbury to Dover runs along the hedge line*

compromise solution. The 25 Cassini sheets that cover the project study region were used both for annotating other information, such as the Roman roads and trackways, before digitising the maps and for providing outlines of the coast, the major rivers with their tributaries and floodplains and the pre-1964 shire boundaries.

## The geology of Southern Britain

The physical structure of the region south of the Thames comprises the major west to east elements of the coast, the Thames and the Chalk Downs, all running in general parallel to one another. The north-to-south features are primarily the rivers flowing either into the Thames or the sea. The geology consists primarily of chalk and to a secondary degree of Jurassic limestone located to the west of the chalklands (Figure 5). Both geological formations produce distinctive physical shapes and together with their associated soil types, fauna and flora, produce readily identifiable landscapes. The chalklands provide the dominant geomorphologic skeletal structure and also typically provide the location for much of the archaeological evidence for both prehistoric and later occupation. Chalk landscapes are typically gently rounded with scarp and vale topography, derived from the asymmetrical folding of the chalk. Their cuesta formation is characterised by a sharp escarpment and a dip slope on a gentler angle, classically represented by the inward-facing scarp profiles of the North and South Downs. They are subject to differential weathering and

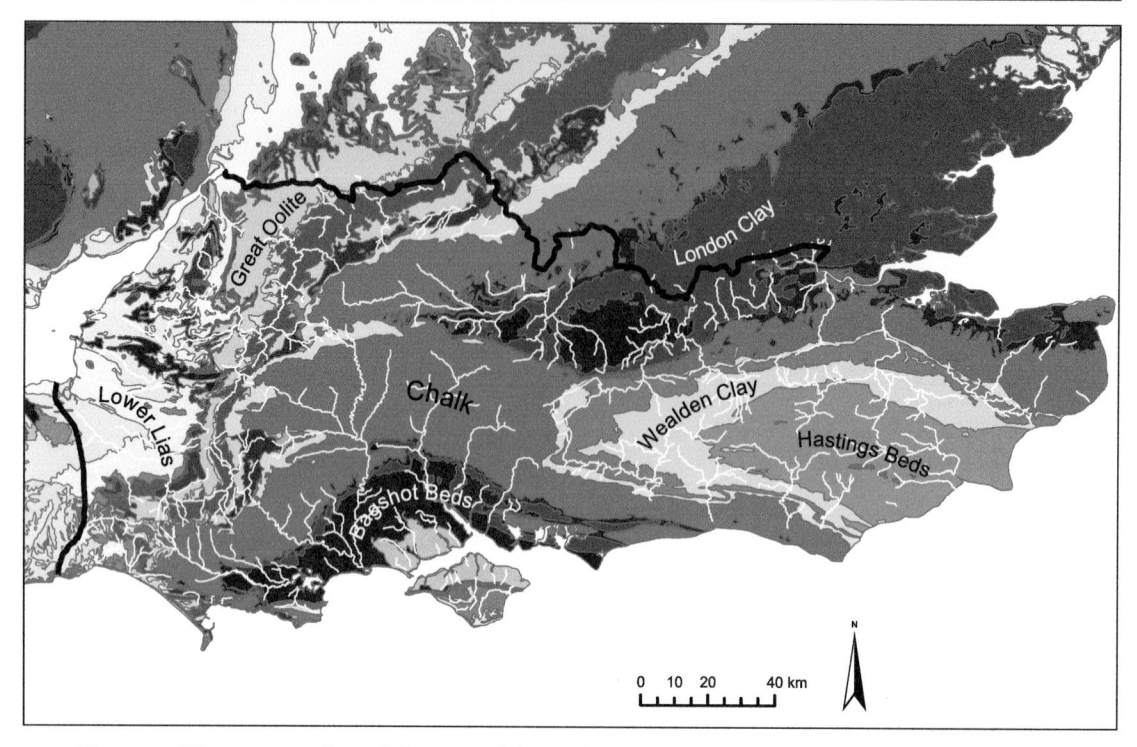

*Figure 5. The major geological features of the study region, together with the study region outline*

interspersed with dry valleys on the uplands and coombe hollows indenting the slopes. Their slopes are a combination of convex, straight and concave profiles, at varying angles, seeming to spring, throughout the study region, from the flood plains of a large number of river networks that drain either to the sea or into the River Thames.

The chalk landscapes are not uniformly shaped, however, as local variations in the thickness of the chalk beds have resulted in differential folding. Thus the Hog's Back above Guildford, Surrey with upstanding beds can be contrasted with Salisbury Plain, where the chalk layers are horizontal (Collard 1988, 62–4). The western limit of these landscapes is marked by a primary chalk escarpment extending from Chaldon Down on the Dorset coast to the north and subsequently to the northeast to terminate at the northern-most end of the Chilterns well beyond the study region. As Figure 5 shows, the chalklands are continuous throughout the greater part of the study region. The sea truncates them at three points and they also define the outer limits of significant sub-regions, notably the Weald, the London Basin and the Hampshire Basin (Short 2006, 26), as well as smaller distinctive areas such as the Vale of Pewsey in North Wiltshire.

The largest of these sub-regions, the Weald, is an unroofed anticline lifted up in late Cretaceous or Tertiary times. The original chalk cover over its rocks was uplifted and then removed by erosion, leaving just the remnants of the North and South Downs with their inward-facing scarps. At its centre are the Hastings Beds, which form an eroded landscape of east to west ridges and valleys, truncated by the coast. Surrounding the Hastings Beds and located between it and the chalk uplands are sequential geological zones consisting of Wealden Clay and both Lower and Upper Greensand and Gault Clay belts.

Similarly the London Basin is defined at its southern edges by the North Downs and to the north-west by the dipslopes of the chalk Chiltern Hills. For the greater part of the Basin there is an underlying chalk bedrock, but this is overlain by Tertiary river, estuarine and marine deposits and in particular by London Clay. The most recent of these Tertiary deposits are sands formed around the edge of the Basin and also occurring as outliers on the chalk dipslopes. The most extensive of these are the uplands that form prominent heathland plateau lands unsuited to agriculture. The Thames itself has long been a dominant feature here with extensive flood plains, and had achieved something close to its present form by the Late Bronze Age, being tidal at least as far west as Westminster in that period (Short 2006, 26–7, fig. 2.2), though its tidal reach in the early Anglo-Saxon period has yet to be established.

Finally, the Hampshire Basin is defined by the chalkland at its fringes, though these slope less steeply than is the case with the London Basin or the Weald. To the west are the North Dorset Downs and Cranbourne Chase, to the northwest the chalklands of Wiltshire and to the north the Hampshire Downs, while the Vale of Kingsclere links the Hampshire Basin to the western edge of the Weald. The Basin's rivers all run southwards, as do the Hampshire and Sussex rivers of the Meon, Arun, Adur, Ouse and Cuckmere (Short 2006, 31, fig. 2.4).

The second major geological element is provided by the limestones, which although characterised by scarps and low hills, achieve far greater altitude than found on the chalk and also a markedly less smooth appearance with rocky outcrops on their slopes. The distinctive Karst topography is produced by hard, grey stone that is jointed into massive blocks. Surface water can be totally absent here, due to subterranean drainage creating sinkholes and caves. The western chalk scarp from Dorset to the Chilterns is shadowed further to the west by Jurassic-period oolitic limestone formations that stretch north and then north-west to become the Cotswolds (Allen and Gardiner 2006, figs 2.1–2.2). West of the chalk there is a much wider range of geological formations, most of which, apart from the Upper Greensands, are not present in the chalk zone. Seven different landscape types have been defined to the west and north-west of the principal chalk scarp running north from Dorset (Allen and Gardiner 2006, 15–16; Bond 2006, fig. 7.1). These include the low-lying Somerset Plain, also known as the Somerset Levels. Each of these extensive wetlands has its own characteristics, but all originated as broad estuaries inundated by rising sea levels after the last Ice Age. The extensive Carboniferous Limestone outcrop of the Mendip Hills forms an open upland with almost level high plateau to the north of the Somerset Plain. The Cotswolds form an upland zone adjacent to the western reach of the Anglo-Saxon zone of settlement.

## Definitions of landscape units

It was necessary to divide the landscape of southern Britain into clearly defined units. Whilst it remains a methodological and historical necessity to sub-divide counties into units for local or county-based analysis, for example in Surrey (Central Weald, Low Weald, High Weald, North Downs, Eocene Basin: Macphail and Scaife 1987) and in Wiltshire (Cotswolds, Northern Clay Vale, Corallian-Gault-Greensand Belt, Marlborough Downs, Vale of Pewsey, South Wiltshire Downs, Vale of Wardour, Tertiary and Gravels: Draper 2006, 4), these are based on ranges of local names and attributes that cannot be extrapolated to fit an entire region, wherein the attributes usually transcend political boundaries. Within British archaeology, the term *pays* has been used to express a combination of a distinctive landscape with a type of human exploitation and the mode of settlement units. The concept of the *pays* 'emphasises the existence of each landscape as a distinctive and unique assemblage of facets or components' (Muir 2000, 7). A borrowing from French geographers of the Possibilist School, it has been used to assert that human impact on the landscape was independent of environmental controls, and that that human activity over time produced special locales with their own unique attributes. For a comparative study on a regional scale, it is not helpful to highlight the uniqueness of place. Rather the impetus here is to identify commonalities of physical form, in order to assess the early Anglo-Saxon usage of those forms.

The classic study of the historical geography of the *pays* of a county is that for Kent by the late Alan Everitt (Everitt 1986, 45–65, fig. 2). He combined the attributes of the physical geography of the eastern part of that county with understandings and interpretations of the phases of Anglo-Saxon settlement, lifestyle and landscape colonisation, all framed by an intimate and deep knowledge of the gradations of its countryside. Criticism of his approach might be made around issues of chronology, as there is certainly an implicit assumption of settlement movement away from the coast over time associated with the colonisation of new landscapes. Everitt identified six contrasting *pays* (Figure 6). These were based in part on interpretations of place-name sequences, which are yet to be tested against recent, chronologically refined, archaeological evidence.

To date there has been no comparable exercise carried out for the remainder of the study region. There are other resources that offer some guiding parameters, however, but no single dataset or methodology encompassed all of the particular requirements with regards to both scale and diversity. The formats rejected were:

- The 159 Countryside Character areas defined by the Countryside Commission, which in many respects resemble the Kentish pays (Countryside Agency 2000a; 2000b; Short 2006, 42,). A third of these (47) are within the study area, but such a large number obviates against creation of the more broad-reaching landscape designations ideally required here.
- Rackham (1995, 3) gives two divisions for the study region south of the Thames – an ancient countryside and a planned countryside of the Lowland Zone. This division was seen as a later outcome of the processes under discussion and too broad in scale. Of greater relevance is Joan Thirsk's mapping of early modern farming regions (Thirsk 1987, as discussed in Barnes and Williamson, 2006, 16). This charted units of forests and wood pastures, wolds and downland, marsh, heathland and arable vales.
- English Heritage's atlas of rural settlement diversity in England (Roberts and Wrathmell 2000) presents a more recent national-scale overview with a variety of mappable attributes. The physical regions map (*ibid*. 18, fig. 12) presents four grouped soil units: chalk; alluvium and gravel; sand, sandstone and gravel lands; and heavy clay. Whilst they each have varying and discrete

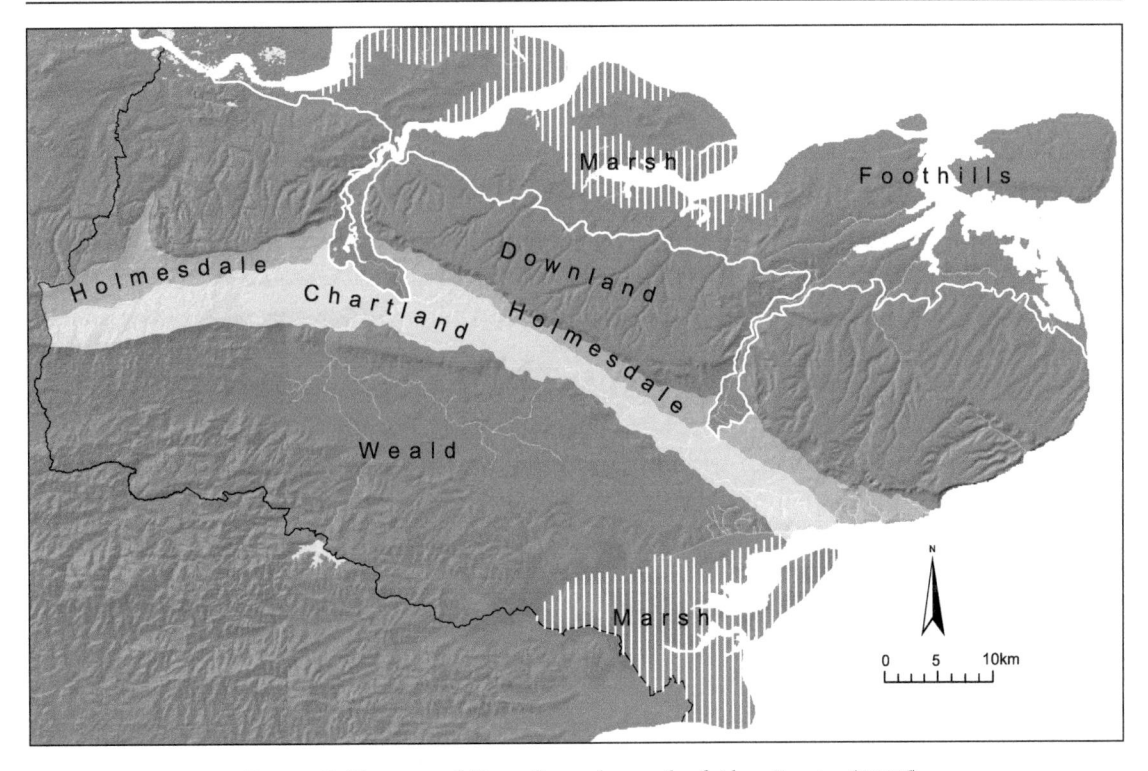

## 3. The Environmental Context of Southern Britain

*Figure 6. The pays of Kent, from the work of Alan Everitt (1986)*

properties, again they are presented on too coarse a scale to assist this project. Additionally, the sets of criteria used to define the spatial frameworks of sub-provinces and local regions (*ibid.*, 39–69), whilst sufficiently broad, are dependent on interpretations of later Medieval settlement patterns that do not necessarily relate to the early Anglo-Saxon period.
- Historic Landscape Characterisations. Delivered on a county-by-county basis, these utilised the Domesday Survey as a starting point to look at fields, settlement character and density, including the balance between open and enclosed land and variety of land use. The coverage was incomplete for the study region at the time of research. The reservations about this data set were that it was based on criteria subsequent to the period in question and would need to be demonstrated as being directly relational to the earliest Germanic presence.

The requirement of the project was to be able to identify tracts of land with similar properties, even if they formed discontinuous blocks, whose archaeological content could then be compared. This requirement was underpinned by the assumption that common landscape types would be equally attractive for settlement and exploitation, regardless of their location. The socio-economic decision-making processes and political context behind their occupation might then be examined. It was decided to focus on the lowest possible common denominator of soil attributes that would impact on the ability of communities to produce sufficient for subsistence and surpluses for tribute and tax.

## Soil types and fertility: the mapping of land use potential

Soil cover can mantle or modify the underlying solid geology, raising the need for caution when discussing, for example, the agrarian potential of chalk downlands in the early Anglo-Saxon period. The presence of clay-with-flint deposits on extensive areas of the North Downs of Kent appears to have inhibited early farming, which in this respect contrasts with the situation on the South Downs across much of Sussex, where this capping is largely absent. Soils occurring on river terraces appear to have been a preferred location for excavated early settlements, including early Anglo-Saxon sites, providing access to both arable and pasture, including water meadows. Yet, as Helena Hamerow (1992, 39–46) has observed, the amount of modern gravel extraction that has taken place and the suitability of air photography for revealing sites over gravels is responsible for the large number of sites recorded here. It may have given us a distorted of site location choices in the early Anglo-Saxon period, but within this scheme the gravels are subsumed within the larger soil units. The ability to exploit soils depends on the technology available, as with the replacement of the ard by a plough with mould-turning board. More problematically, the attributes associated with modern soils in their present state cannot necessarily be ascribed to those on the same locations in the first millennium AD. This is because the soils will have been subjected to a wide range of agricultural practices in the interim, such as drainage control, improvement, near-continuous ploughing and modern deep ploughing and subsoiling, together with the effects of climatic change and soil erosion. Nevertheless, by taking a broad approach to soil characteristics, it is suggested that the temporal differences can be ameliorated, although not fully resolved.

The Soilscapes dataset from the National Soil Resources Institute, Cranfield University was used (https://www.landis.org.uk/soilscapes/). This is a simplified version of the National Soil Map for England and Wales at 1:250,000, which describes 300 soil associations, whereas Soilscapes defines 30 units, 27 of which are found in the study area. These are assessed in terms of their texture, drainage potential, acidity/alkalinity (pH value), fertility and the habitat that they naturally support. The revised Soilscapes format permitted broad characterisations of the soil types using basic attribute combinations. The study region is dominated by five soil types of varying characteristics, listed and described in Table 24, in descending order of land area and highlighting the basic split between alkaline soils on chalk and other limestone geologies and the slightly to very acidic soils found elsewhere.

Soilscapes provides the resources for further characterisation in terms of fertility, as each soil unit is ascribed a further attribute within a range from 1 (very poor) to 5 (very good). Therefore, all soil units with the same level of fertility were clumped together, re-mapped and re-digitised (see Figure 7). The most fertile soils occur mainly in four locations. These are:

1. in the west of the study region within the area of Jurassic limestone (parts of Gloucestershire, Somerset and West Wiltshire);
2. in the north around the Upper and Middle Thames;
3. in the Lower Darenth valley of Kent and extending westwards along the dip-slope along the northern edge of the North Downs;
4. in the Holmesdale in East Kent.

## 3. The Environmental Context of Southern Britain

Table 24. Major soil types in the study region

| Area ranking | Description | Soilscapes ID |
|---|---|---|
| 1 | Shallow lime-rich soils over chalk or limestone, loamy, freely draining | 3 |
| 2 | Slightly acid but base-rich loamy and clayey soils, impeded drainage | 18 |
| 3 | Slightly acid and clayey soils, loamy, slightly impeded drainage | 8 |
| 4 | Slightly acid soils, loamy, freely draining | 6 |
| 5 | Very acid sandy and loamy soils, freely draining | 14 |

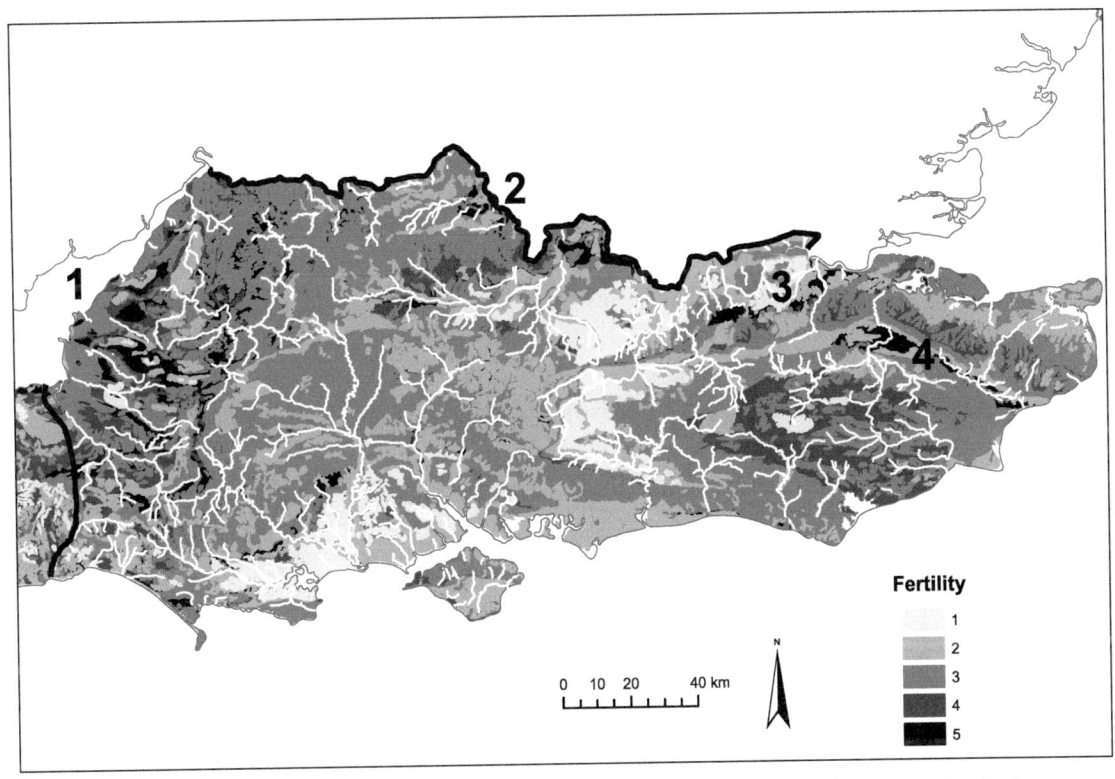

Figure 7. The revised soil fertility map of the study region (level 5 is the greatest fertility)

Minor outcrops of fertile soil also occur around the rim of the Hampshire basin, along the coast of Dorset to the River Axe and around the upper reaches of the rivers in the central chalklands Berkshire and Wiltshire.

The drainage potential of each soil unit was been assigned into one of the following three categories and mapped against the major and minor rivers as **freely draining** or with **impeded drainage** or **naturally wet**. Next the habitat descriptions within Soilscapes have been grouped under the rudimentary headings of **pasture and woodland** or **wet meadow** or **heath and moor**. Areas of pasture and woodland are deemed to be particularly significant in that they would require a modest labour input to render them usable for animal husbandry or arable farming. Wet or water

49

meadow would have seasonal usability, but would require substantial drainage to make it viable for the full annual agricultural cycle. Heath and moor would require substantial soil improvement regimes to make them viable for agriculture, beyond use as rough pasture.

## A new definition of landscape units in southern Britain

In order to identify simple land units by type, the three levels of drainage were combined with the five levels of fertility offered by the Soilscapes data and are shown in Plate 1. They are defined in Table 25.

Now reduced to fourteen separately described units, this method of categorisation produced several advantages over the methods described above. The fourteen units allow for nuanced mapping and more refined description of areas of agricultural potential within which archaeological sites were located. By stepping beyond gross categorisations of fertility, contrasts between fertile areas can be shown. For example, the level 5 fertility soils of the Jurassic limestone area to the west of the study region can now be seen as possessing impeded drainage. These contrast to other level 5 soils in the centre and east of the region that had free drainage. Nevertheless, the western sector has a greater area of good soils, albeit of various types, than elsewhere within the region. The contrast between soils on the various chalk Downlands is also highlighted. Thus the central chalklands of the South Downs and Salisbury Plain have free draining soils of moderate fertility, whereas the clay-with-flint cappings of the North Downs and the Wealden clays have impeded drainage with level 4 fertility.

To what extent has this approach altered the characterisation of the Kentish pays defined by Everitt? Kent has eight of the newly designated units and a minor presence for two more. The only areas with top-quality, fertile, free-draining soils are bundled together along the Holmesdale and

*Table 25. Drainage and fertility combined*

| Fertility | Drainage | SS ID | Description |
|---|---|---|---|
| 5 | Free draining | 7 | F5FD |
|   | Impeded drainage | 9 | F5ID |
|   | Naturally wet | 1 | F5NW |
| 4 | Free draining | 12 | F4FD |
|   | Impeded drainage | 8 | F4ID |
|   | Naturally wet | 27 | F4NW |
| 3 | Free draining | 3, 5 | F3FD |
|   | Impeded drainage | 18 | F3ID |
|   | Naturally wet | 20, 21, 23 | F3NW |
| 2 | Free draining | 4, 6, 10, 13 | F2FD |
|   | Impeded drainage | 17, 19 | F2ID |
|   | Naturally wet | 22 | F2NW |
| 1 | Free draining | 14 | F1FD |
|   | Impeded drainage | None | na |
|   | Naturally wet | 15, 16, 25, 26 | F1NW |

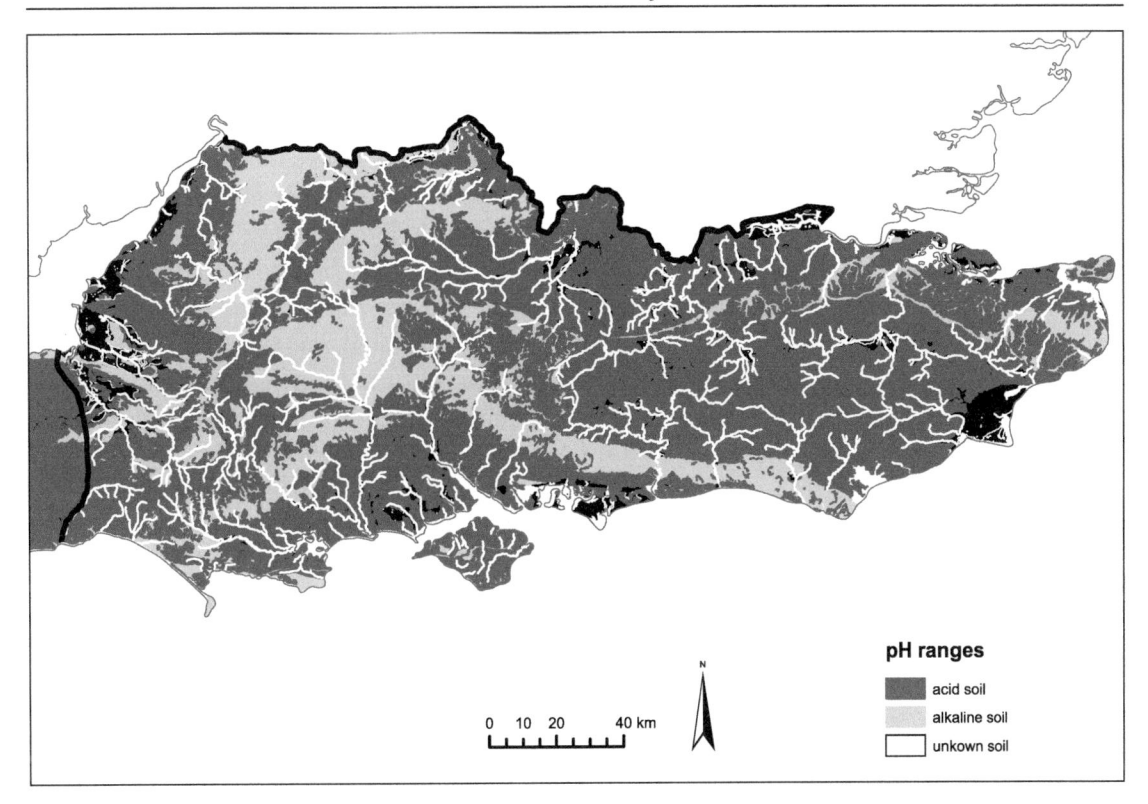

*Figure 8. The soil Ph values of the study region*

Chart and also around the lower reaches of the River Darenth. The fertile clays of the Weald and the North Downs overlie poorer-quality soils, while coastal areas are dominated by soils of fertility level three and below, much of which has impeded drainage or else is naturally wet. From the map (Figure 6) of Kent pays it can be observed that none of Everitt's pays are coherent in terms of their soil capabilities. It was felt that the continued use of the term pays was inappropriate – the term 'edaphic unit' is preferred here, being both descriptive of soil and indicating environment, but without locating these zones within any cultural or geographical region. In this context, the term 'edaphic' is defined as meaning 'influenced by conditions of soil or substratum' (Lawrence 1995, 169).

Clearly, the capabilities of past societies to manage these edaphic units will have varied and developed over time, particularly with regard to the available technology, the range of subsistence practices, the ability to drain accessible, but seasonally wet, fertile soils and the prevailing climatic conditions. Habitat analysis has not played a part in the process of edaphic unit definition, given that the range of categories available is limited. Yet the survival of ancient woodland is noted, although such have been the fluctuations in its management and location (Rackham 1993) that only the obvious major tracts have been mapped here. From the available data, an outline map of soil ph value was established (Figure 8) but gives only a basic contrast between acid and alkaline soils.

## Climate

Climate change is an omni-present feature impacting on human activities over time. Archaeologists have enthusiastically adopted it as a valid causative factor in explaining changes in the archaeological record (Harding 1982, 2), most pertinently here to explain the apparent abandonment of the Anglian homelands in the fifth century. Uncritical adoption of climate change as a primary factor in migration, however, negates consideration of how societies might be pro-active in responding to the conditions that developed. For a period as short as between AD 400 and 750, the impacts may be subtle, sporadic and difficult to characterise within a restricted geographical region. Indeed they may perhaps only appear as localised effects. Nevertheless it is clearly useful to consider the impact of climate change and certain general climatic trajectories have been identified for southern Britain, with a basic contrast noted either side of AD 400 (Lamb 1981, 56; Jones 1996, 188). The climate from AD 250 was characterised as 'a fairly steady climate, somewhat warmer and drier than now' (although the 'now' is of *c*.1980 and may itself be contrasted with the present climate of 2012). Lamb noted that the period up to AD 400 was one in which riverside land and marshes could be drained and managed, although thereafter they became untenable for agriculture (*ibid.*, 60). The Thames was embanked to give flood protection for Londinium in the third century AD (Devoy 1980, 145). The Romano-British Transgression (RBT) of sea onto the land causing flooding was the result of a warm period that had commenced probably up to a century earlier (Cracknell 2005, 2) causing ice cap and glacial melting, the full effects of which were still continuing up to two centuries later. Cracknell suggests therefore that the RBT should be dated to AD 300–600, being followed by a Middle-Saxon Warm Period Transgression, involving another phase of land inundation, datable to around AD 750–850. Correlated data demonstrates peaks of temperature around AD 600 and again between AD 700–800 (Cracknell 2005, 6). As an example of the impact of fluctuating sea levels, that of the shingle beach that formed below the late Roman coastal fort at Lympne in Kent is prime (Cunliffe 1980, 45). This was breached in the late Roman or early Anglo-Saxon period, either by the force of rising sea levels or by the dynamics of shingle movement that was removing material to create the headland at Dungeness. By the eighth century, however, this area had become dry land available for human exploitation. A period of cooler weather was experienced after AD 400, with wetter summers and colder winters. Climatic conditions seem to have improved somewhat with a relatively dry period until *c*.650–700, although a greater frequency of severe winters was indicated for the period AD 600–800 within northwest Europe (Parry 1978, 65). However, Gregory of Tours, a contemporary written source, suggests climatic instability in northern Europe during the sixth century.

While it is not necessary here to delve into the causes of these climatic events, the major effect was a rise in sea level of varying and contested orders of magnitude, although possibly one to two metres in some places, although negligible elsewhere (Cresswell 1959, 101; Everard 1980, 21). The impact of rising sea levels on low-lying continental coastal areas across the North Sea was rather more intense during the fourth century. The coastal zone between Dunkirk and the mouth of the Rhine was submerged, as was the area further north around the present-day Zuider

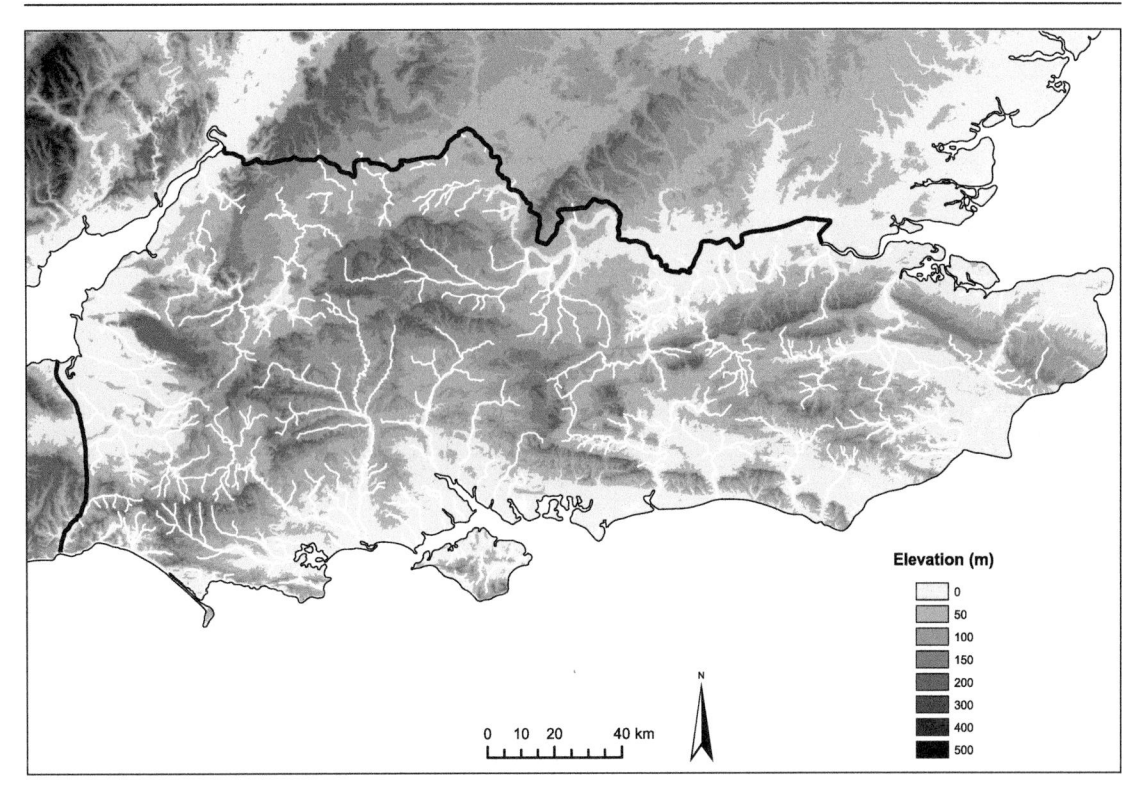

## 3. The Environmental Context of Southern Britain

*Figure 9. The rivers and flood plains of the study region, with the rivers flowing either southwards into the sea or northwards into the River Thames*

Zee and the Frisian islands (Cracknell 2005, 10) with evidence of depopulation of the coastal areas. From the examples cited above, definitive statements about temperature and rainfall in this period remain elusive, beyond there being evidence for short-term fluctuations within longer-term trends (Rippon 2000, 145). What is agreed on, however, is the impact of rising sea levels on coastal formation and erosion.

### Rivers and floodplains

The study region encompasses a complex network of major rivers and minor tributaries (Figure 9). The rivers split the geological landscape into substantial blocks. The Weald is a particularly important watershed region with rivers running either north or south from its central upland (the High Weald) cutting deep valleys through the chalk uplands of the North and South Downs. Similar networks run north and south from the central chalk uplands of southern England to the west of the Weald. The extent to which any of these rivers was either navigable in the early Anglo-Saxon period or formed a substantial impediment to cross-country overland movement is not determinable in the majority of cases. Hill (1981, 10) suggests that the following major rivers were possibly navigable in

*Figure 10. The site of the Cuxton, Kent, Anglo-Saxon cemetery from the River Medway*

the Later Anglo-Saxon period: the Stour to Wimborne, the Wiltshire Avon to Salisbury, the Itchen as far as Winchester, the Medway, but not beyond Maidstone, the Wey tributary of the Thames as far as Guildford, the Kennet to Newbury and the Thames to Cricklade, while Bath could be reached by the Bristol Avon. Studies relating to the Later Medieval period, although not directly relevant, also indicate the possibility of earlier navigability for the Wiltshire Avon up to Salisbury, the Test to Romsey, the Itchen beyond Winchester to New Alresford, the Rother to Etchingham, the Medway to Tonbridge, the Thames at least as far as Lechlade and those rivers flowing into the Severn Estuary reaching back far into the Somerset Levels and as far east as Bath, with the Parrett being still navigable to Taunton and Langport (Edwards and Hindle 1991, 130, though critiqued by Jones 2000, who suggests that river navigability was declining in this period). Many of these navigable locations are known as the sites of Early Anglo-Saxon cemeteries.

The issue of tidal reach is key to understanding the potential for navigability and prompted the second project team research exercise. A boat of 2-metre draft was taken from Rochester to Aylesford on the Medway tide on a single day in August 2008. A non-raising bridge prevented further travel on the tide to Maidstone and a similar return flow carried the boat back out into the Medway estuary. The undulating riverbed offered a hindrance to the boat in places, but also opened up the possibility of intermittent crossing points. The visibility from the river to known cemetery sites was noted. Clearly locatable were Holborough (Evison, 1956) on the chalk scarp adjacent to the North Downs trackway; Cuxton, immediately above the riverbank; and Chatham Lines on the

## 3. The Environmental Context of Southern Britain

*Figure 11. View north east from the plateau above Chatham Lines, Kent, Anglo-Saxon cemetery, towards the estuary of the River Medway and the Isle of Grain*

headland above Rochester. It was possible to suggest the locations of the landing sites that related to them. In particular, this research exercise highlighted the intersection of river, floodplain and slope as important features for travel, transportation and possible habitation locations.

Tidal floodplains have already been noted above, but the boating exercises highlighted the importance of riverine floodplains. These operate both as potential catchments of floodwater and also as habitation environments in their own right. Floodplains, which are the flat areas adjacent to rivers that are liable to flooding (Brown 1997, 17), might be completely re-worked over a 500-year period, as the course of the river can change channels and form meanders and oxbow lakes. Brown (*ibid.*, 227) comments though that 'the majority of lowland floodplains in Britain show remarkably little channel change during Roman and Medieval times', and in particular notes the Thames and Severn rivers and estuaries in this respect.

Pollen analyses from inorganic alluvial sediments from the floodplains of the Ouse, Cuckmere and Rother rivers in East Sussex, all rising in the Weald, indicate that there was possibly a gradual penetration of Neolithic exploitation of the Weald (Scaife and Burrin 1992, 75–91). Therefore that it is not necessary to regard it as an inhospitable tract throughout prehistory, although certain areas and features such as the narrow ghylls would have remained densely wooded into the medieval period. Parts of the Ouse valley and the Rother valley have Roman features, roads and occupation horizons, buried under later periods of sedimentation (*ibid.*, 89). Lambrick (1992, 209–226) in discussing the Upper Thames Basin considered that changes to the hydrology and alluviation on the floodplain could be adequately explained by changing human settlement and land use patterns in the catchment area, rather than by climatic changes. The depth of alluvium in any case rarely exceeds one metre there (Robinson 1992, 201). In the Early to Middle Anglo-Saxon periods, Robinson noted continued flooding and a slowing down of rates of alluviation (*ibid.*, 206). He attributed this as a by-product of agricultural collapse at the end of the Roman period. The tendency for carbonised crop remains to be less common on Anglo-Saxon settlements on the gravels than on sites of earlier periods could be attributed to a level of reversion to pastoralism, with floodplain grasslands becoming a key resource for labour-intensive hay-making (Lambrick 1992, 222).

## Palaeo-environmental evidence

The environmental evidence available for the study region and its time frame remains limited. Turner (1981, 67–73) noted just a few pollen-bearing deposits that had been core-sampled in the south east of England. A regional literature on soil-pollen analysis and plant macrofossils (Scaife 1987, 158–9, 170–1) and faunal evidence from animal bone (Coy and Maltby 1987, 216–7, 229–31) does exist, but any attempt at a national overview (*e.g.* Dark and Dark 1997; Dark 2000) of necessity depended on a few key sites. Examples are the Amberley Brooks in West Sussex and Epping Forest in south-west Essex for pollen cores and excavations at *Hamwic* (Saxon Southampton) for faunal remains. It is not necessarily realistic to extrapolate from these to the wider rural landscape, nor determine long-term trends on a regional basis. Nevertheless, Dark concluded that any deterioration in the climate was not sufficient to have been destructive of agriculture across all regions. Rather those sites located above 150m OD will have become marginalised, whilst those at lower levels have demonstrated continuity or even increased activity (Dark 2000, 152).

## Woodland

Although it is no longer tenable to propose widespread woodland regeneration as resulting from a wholesale abandonment of agricultural land in the early fifth century, as propounded by earlier researchers (discussed by Rackham 1995), a clear-cut alternative narrative has yet to replace that concept. Pollen evidence, although sparse for the study period, does not indicate widespread, as opposed to localised, reforestation (De la Bédoyère 1993, 129). Rather, as Jones comments (1996, 227), "the absence of a massive return to secondary forest (in either the uplands or the lowlands) invading long-cleared arable or pasture probably implies at least a significant degree of rural population and economy". Again the evidence suggests localised developments and conditions. At Barton Court Farm, near Abingdon in Berkshire, pollen data does not indicate any major regeneration of woodland (Miles 1986, 23), though sites from other areas do. Thus pollen analyses show land abandonment and woodland regeneration in a few areas, *e.g.* Snelsmore, Berkshire and Amberley, Sussex, but this can be set against evidence for continuity elsewhere, *e.g.* Sidlings

Copse, Oxfordshire (Dark, 2000, 152). On the other hand, there are dendrochronologically-dated timbers from Middle Saxon settlement sites that indicate the widespread use of trees that had begun to grow in the first decades of the fifth century (Tyers *et al.* 1994, 20). Explanations for this phenomenon vary between the regeneration of woodland on abandoned land and the growing-out of Roman short-cycle coppice material. The survival into the modern era of such ancient woodlands as occur at Blean in east Kent, Selwood in Somerset and the Forest of Savernake in Wiltshire, shows the potential for the curation of large woodland tracts on poorer soils. Place-name formations for habitations that include elements relating to woodland clearance also have a distinctive distribution, particularly in the Weald. While it might be expected that they would be evenly spread if encountering 'boundless woodland', it has been argued that there was no radical reorganisation of the woodland in the post-Roman period (Rackham 1995, 84). Indeed, as Grocock has observed (2010, 37) much of what has been identified in archaeological research as 'scrub' may well have been areas of long-standing coppice, regularly harvested to supply the fundamental needs of a community.

Recent work on pollen profiles from around Rye, Sussex, (Waller and Schofield 2007) again shows that the eastern Weald would not have been an impenetrable tract in the Bronze Age and that the Wealden transhumance system originated in the Iron Age. Even the development of the Roman iron industry would probably not have destroyed the woodland further. It has particularly been noted that "in terms of the extent of woodland cover and continuation of cultivation, the early Anglo-Saxon period in the Rye area appears to have been a time of continuity" (*ibid.*, 382). A regional rise in beech (Fagus) pollen in this period will have resulted from the increased use of Wealden woods for swine pannage, as reflected in the place-name evidence (Everitt 1986; Witney 1976).

# 4. Travelling and Using the Land- and Sea-Scapes

**Coastal erosion and tide patterns**

In the context of the environmental circumstances of the period AD 450–700, it is important to delineate the potentialities of coastal routeways as they impacted on Early Anglo-Saxon site location and landscape syntax. The coastline of southern England as it exists today was probably broadly in place 3000 years ago (*c*.1000 BC) with localised variations thereafter caused by erosion and deposition related to tide and weather patterns. Where different geological formations form the coast, they erode at different rates. Modern estimates suggest that, for the study region's south coast, the erosion rate will have varied between 28 metres and 108 metres per hundred years. Thus, for example, between Selsey Bill and the mouth of the Cuckmere in East Sussex, the coastline in AD 400 may have been over 1700 metres further out (Goudie and Brunsden 1994, 48, fig. 33). The coast of the Isle of Thanet and north Kent has lost land to a similar extent with estimates of up to 4.8 kilometres for the same period (Brookes 2007, 44). Between Folkestone and Dungeness in southeast Kent, however, the loss seems to have been far less, estimated at approximately 400 metres.

There are two consistent factors in coastal formation (Cresswell 1959): tide rotation and wave fetch. Wave fetch refers to the distance a wave travels before it hits the shoreline and, as Figure 12 (derived from Cresswell 1959, 21) shows, the greatest impact is of the Atlantic Ocean onto the west coast of the British Isles. Correspondingly, the shortest fetches occur across the Irish Sea and along the English Channel. The North Sea is an area of medium fetch, with the break point between this and the short-fetch waves of the English Channel found around the North Foreland in Kent, indicating contrasting maritime conditions along each of these coasts. Tidal rotation (derived from Cresswell 1959, 113–5) refers here to the cyclical anti-clockwise movements of tides around the North Sea. Between the coast of East Anglia and the mouth of the Rhine, there is a relatively small, localised system, with its amphidromic point (a centre of spin with no tide) located between Lowestoft in Suffolk and Egmond aan Zee, on the Dutch coast. Points furthest away from the centre have higher tides and Dover and Calais have tidal ranges in the order of about 14 feet, whereas that for the North Foreland of Kent is nearer 12 feet. It has long been noted that the discrete systems of the Channel and the North Sea merge to form a combined

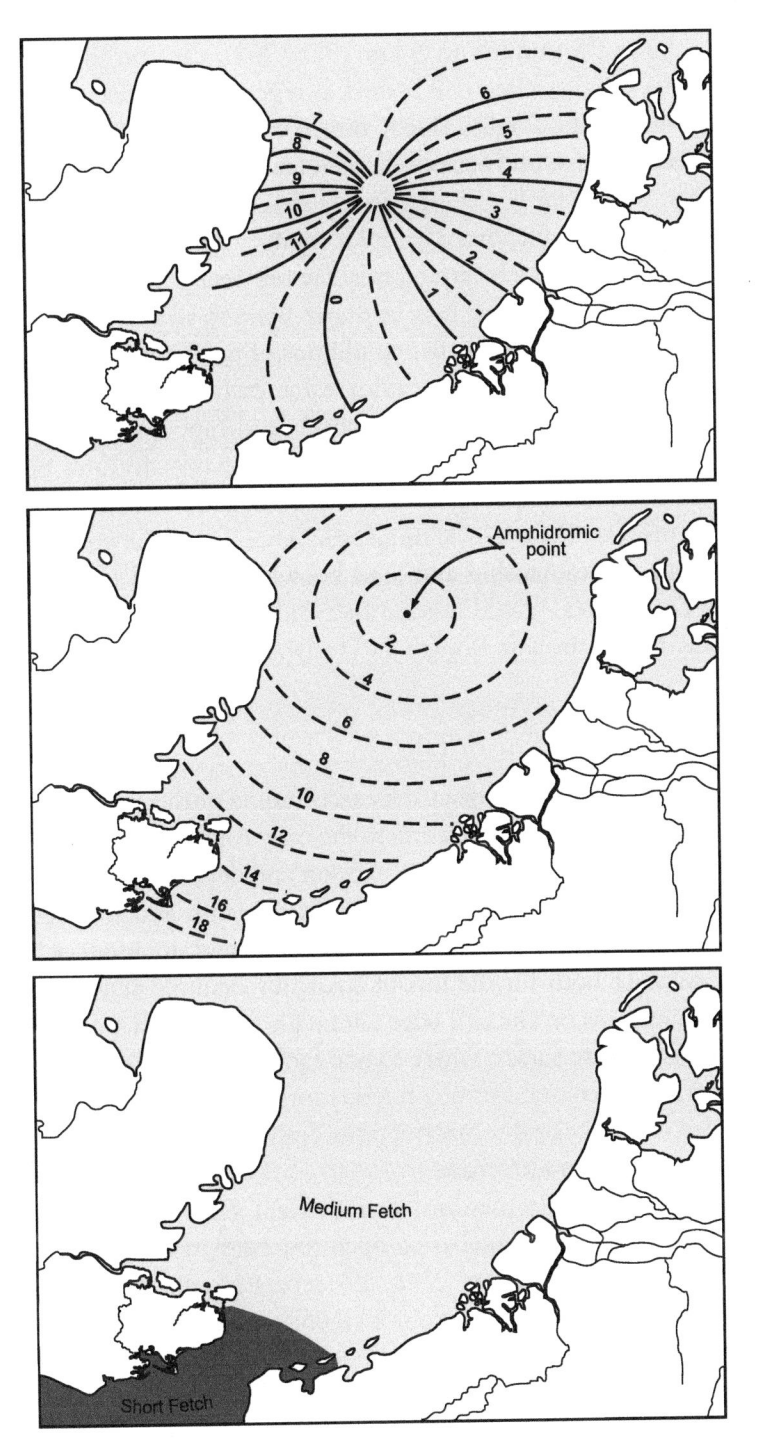

*Figure 12. The waves and tides of the North Sea and the English Channel (derived from Cresswell 1959)*

wave at the Straits of Dover (Beechey 1850). A tide, which can be characterised as a 'long wave' with a period of 12 hours 25 minutes (Sandon 1975, 262), can run differently, depending on the configuration of the coast and depth of seabed. It is generally higher and faster up the French side of the Channel, but on the English side it runs relatively fast between Plymouth and Lyme Regis, slows between Lyme Regis and Selsey Bill, then picks up speed again to the Straits of Dover. Additionally, however, the Solent is a comparatively shallow stretch of water sheltered from the Channel by the Isle of Wight, which has a complex double tidal pattern, with strong movements and quickly changing sea states. Such varying tidal factors clearly have the potential to assist and impede movement around the coast and may be drawn upon to account for the locational choices exhibited in the study period. The particular conditions of the Thames Estuary between Tilbury and Whitstable were the subject of an empirical research exercise in June 2008. To summarise, a radical re-appraisal of perceptual understandings of the landscape from the seascape came about. Knowing the positions of certain Roman and early Anglo-Saxon features prompted the rapid identification of probable trans-shipment points and areas difficult to access. These perceptions fed into the mapping process. The overwhelming experience was of the power of the tidal Thames through its estuary and the seamanship and local knowledge needed to navigate this routeway. It became clear that certain areas would need to be avoided at all costs and these marginal places proved to be similarly lacking in Late Roman and early Anglo-Saxon settlement archaeology.

## Changes to the southern coast of Britain

It is particularly problematic to reconstruct the exact outline of the ancient coast. This is due in part to an under-representation of data relating to the early Anglo-Saxon period in recent studies. In addition, the problem of differential rates of erosion and deposition hamper reconstruction of coastlines, although the earliest published maps of the sixteenth and seventeenth centuries and other topographical records provide some indications. The current situations of Late Roman 'Saxon Shore' forts reveal evidence both for the loss of coast, for example at Reculver in Kent, where only a part of the site remains on the cliff edge, although now inland, and infilling of the coast, for example at Pevensey in East Sussex, where coastal sand or shingle barriers helped to create the Pevensey Levels, turning the coastal fort of Anderida into a land-locked anachronism. Piecemeal work has been carried out on coastal reconstructions, findings from which are reviewed here in a clockwise direction around the south coast.

A detailed reconstruction of the coastline for East Kent was carried out by Brookes (2007), clearly delineating the Wantsum channel as an open routeway in the early Anglo-Saxon period, 'a safe and navigable short-cut and haven' (*ibid.*, 39), separating the chalk upfold of Thanet from the mainland. If the current two-metre contour is taken as the earlier extent of the channel (*ibid.*, 41), it would have been approximately 1000m wide between Wall End on the north coast and Sarre at its mid point and up to four kilometres wide on its eastern edge. The processes of shingle migration that formed the Stonar Bank gradually cut off the entrance to the Wantsum from the English Channel. The extensive area of marsh and inlets to the south of the Wantsum Channel

*Figure 13. View south west from Highdown, Sussex, Anglo-Saxon cemetery, towards the Channel and the Isle of Wight*

is to be noted, the rim of which is known as the location of richly-furnished early Anglo-Saxon cemeteries (See Richardson 2005 for a detailed list).

Romney Marsh has been the subject of a long-term research programme to determine the sequences of marshland formation and usage (Cunliffe 1980; Long *et al.* 2002). Major causes of change appear to have been sedimentation, the deviating courses of major waterways and movements of shingle. Excavations at Sandtun, near Lympne have demonstrated that the site was occupied from *c.*AD 700 and may have been used as a landing place for coastal shipping and also operating as a saltworks (Gardiner *et al.* 2001). The former beach harbour had silted over again by the mid-ninth century and the marshlands had dried out, to be used as pasture.

Further west along the Channel, the Sussex coast has altered considerably since the early Anglo-Saxon period, with significant erosion of the chalk headlands, the formation of shingle spits and the reclamation of land that was previously inundated. From the second century onwards, Roman villas sited on tidal inlets went out of use progressively, including the palace at Fishbourne, quite possibly because rising sea levels destroyed local land drainage systems (Cracknell 2005, 131). Additionally, tidal inlets and estuaries expanded inland, although many of these were later important for the location of salt-making industries. Roman communities may therefore have deserted the coastal plain for sites further up the slopes. Lengthy sections of the coast and its hinterland are still prone to flooding, both from seaward inundation and from the build-up of water in the river catchment areas (most recently the River Ouse flooding around Lewes in 2000).

Roman fords, ostensibly located inland, as at Glynde near Lewes, became impassable even at low tide, whilst other roads were re-aligned to avoid such obstacles (*ibid.*, 131). The precise position of the coast c.400–750 is undetermined, although the headland to the west of Eastbourne towards Beachy Head is likely to have extended much further out than at present. A series of coastal settlements, now only represented by that at Rookery Hill, Bishopstone, Sussex on the headland above the entrance to the River Ouse, may have been lost in the intervening years. A change further along the coast on the coastal plain has been the infilling of the tidal inlet below the Iron Age enclosure housing the Highdown early Anglo-Saxon cemetery, otherwise leaving it in an anachronistic position.

The section of coast around Selsey Bill has been reconstructed (Cracknell 2005, 146) to show phases of erosion and deposition, for which the Roman coastline was postulated to be several miles to the south of its modern alignment. Selsey has, over time, been both separate from and attached to the mainland and is described by Bede as a peninsular joined by a narrow strip to the mainland (HE IV.16). Langstone harbour was a marine rather than a terrestrial environment, with extensive salt marsh (Allen and Gardiner 2000, 217). The 'Saxon Shore' fort at Portchester, built towards the latter part of the third century, occupies a low promontory within a sheltered harbour and was abandoned in the late fourth century, possibly due to rising sea levels. It has been suggested (Brooks and Glasspoole 1928) that the entire coastline of Hampshire was flooded in AD 419, when storms caused the Goodwin Sands to be formed, following the submersion of part of a former island. The remaining stretches of coast through to Poole, including the Isle of Wight, had limited impact from sea-level changes, apart from the flooding of estuaries, but were subject to erosion at various points. Brading harbour on the Isle of Wight was much more extensive than the modern silted up estuary (Cracknell 2005, 150).

Poole Harbour similarly has provided evidence of rising sea levels after AD 300, although it was probably much smaller in overall area than at present. Further west, the coastal geology is much more resistant to erosive forces. The project study region boundary re-emerges on the north coast of Somerset at the River Parrett, which forms the southern edge of the Somerset Levels. The landscape from here to the Mendips was consistently marshy and liable to flood, making it unsuitable for habitation unless extensive drainage could be carried out. To the north of the Mendips, the North Somerset Levels coastline was protected by a low embankment from the mid-third century, to retain an area used for pasture and in various places for cereal crops, as shown by excavation of Roman period corn driers here (Cracknell 2005, 188). After the mid fourth century, however, there was a dramatic change from a freshwater drained marsh to a salt-marsh environment. For the area of the levels and the Severn Estuary region as a whole, it is unclear whether the rises in sea level represented a steady increase or were subject to fluctuations. Nevertheless, this region was abandoned in the later Roman period and not fully reclaimed again until the eleventh century (Rippon 2006, 80–1).

Overall, the evidence from which to reconstruct the coastline of southern Britain in the early Anglo-Saxon period is fragmentary and in many places dependent on Late Roman evidence. Present-day coastal inlets may have been longer and suitable beaching places on river estuaries may well have been further inland from the sea 1500 years ago. Salt marshes and wetland areas in general appear as key zones with potential for resource expansion and exploitation (Rippon 2000). There is only clear evidence of their use in the later Roman period, although this declines before the end of the fourth century. There is then an upsurge in coastal activity in the Middle Saxon period, from *c*.AD 700 onwards, evidenced by the construction of massive fish traps (Murphy 2007) and of settlements at the waters edge, as at Medmerry, West Sussex (White 1934).

The possibilities of navigating around this particular coast using wooden craft, whether rowed, paddled or with a rudimentary form of sail, have yet to be fully investigated. Of the known, archaeologically recovered examples, shallow boats, typically dugouts with or without planked additional strakes, that might have been paddled or propelled by punting, would have been suitable for use on rivers. An example is the Walthamstow dugout with dendrodates of AD 675–80 and AD 650–85. Larger, easily-beached, sea-going, clinker-built, planked ships of the Sutton Hoo type would have been more suited to estuaries and other sheltered coastal shipping routes, as well as short open-sea crossings (Haywood 1991; Milne 2003, 37–8).

It is possible to conceive of the southern coast of the study region as presenting a series of navigational challenges that demanded detailed local knowledge of tides and sandbanks. The story of Bishop Wilfrid's ship being blown off course and stranded off the Sussex coast in AD 666 and threatened by pagan wreckers until rescued by the tide illustrates this point. Coastal headlands that are demanding to negotiate now in engine propelled craft cannot have been less so in the past. Suitable landing places and beaches today may well have been inaccessible in the past due to extensive salt marshes. Coastal routes of the English Channel in the early Anglo-Saxon period should be seen, therefore, as discontinuous and patched into a web of different transportation possibilities to form a continuous network, facilitating access to the whole of the study region.

## Roads, droveways and trackways south of the Thames

If the coast and rivers of southern Britain offered opportunities and obstacles to movement, what then of the land-based routeways? The surviving roads and trackways of the study region represent a composite of past practices inscribed onto the landscape. As corridors of linear movement, they are generally directional rather than rigidly prescribed and it is difficult to differentiate between land routes developed in the Anglo-Saxon, Roman and prehistoric periods, even when named are attached to them. Whilst the precise dating of the origins of the majority of extant routeways cannot be assessed, three particular types can be suggested as being locally or regionally in use in the first millennium AD. These are Roman roads, long-distance high-level trackways and droveways. Much research is devoted to reconstructing the precise positions of Roman roads and sections of known roads are regularly re-discovered (Whaley 2007). New paved roads are revealed through excavation from time to time, such as that on the west bank of the river Ouse above Lewes, on the opposite bank to Margary's (1973) proposed line for the London to Lewes road. Of course, the identification of a road through excavation does not confirm that it remained a viable and used route into the early Anglo-Saxon period. Margary (1973, 23) suggested that in the period following the demise of Roman authority in Britain, long stretches of substantial metalled and ditched roadways would have fallen into disrepair or be converted into green lanes or transformed into the boundary banks between later land holdings. Sections may have become subsumed subsequently into parish, hundred or shire boundaries. Note should be taken, however, of the substantial cross-sectional structure of the major Roman roads, with between 56 and 81 cm of metalling on those in southern Britain, as well as paved sections and other hard surfaces designed to prevent rutting (Davies 2002, 56–66). In certain locations, it is clear that field-boundary layouts respect a Roman road, for example at Cudham on the North Downs, where the road marks the county boundary between Surrey and Kent and was used as the Episcopal boundary of the see of Rochester established in the early seventh century (Harrington 2004, 43). This certainly suggests continuous use into the medieval period for that particular section of the road. Nevertheless a basic structure of major routes, typically linking Roman towns, with those in the southeast radiating from Roman London, together with trans-Wealden tracks, has been established and is shown on Figure 14, derived from Margary (1965; 1973) and more recent updates.

More open to differences of interpretation are the ancient trackways, commonly assumed to date back into the prehistoric landscapes, yet with continuous use ever since. While a few major prehistoric trackways can be clearly defined, the reconstruction of others is much more speculative. An example is provided by the Pilgrim's Way in Kent, existing today as a long-distance chalkland footpath, the North Downs Way, that continues beyond Kent towards Winchester in Hampshire. Where identified, and fixed in the modern landscape, this can appear as two parallel routeways, for alternate use in winter or summer, depending on the prevailing weather conditions. In use they may have represented only very broad directional lines, up to two miles wide, along which each traveller or drover picked their own appropriate path (Hindle 1993, 20). Any grounds for claiming an origin in distant antiquity must be regarded with caution, as current knowledge of them may be the result of imaginative and speculative fieldwork. Nevertheless, high-level routes across free-draining chalk uplands in any pre-modern era would represent a viable means of cross-country travel, although one dependent on factors of the terrain, soils and slopes. The routes are those described by Hippisley Cox (1973) and are also depicted on Figure 14.

A degree of networking between the Roman roads and the presumed prehistoric trackways is evident, with some sections of the latter used as components of the principal road system. Finally some medieval routeways named as 'Port Ways' are taken to indicate the re-use of such earlier roads (Hindle 1993, 50). Both Roman roads and earlier trackways could have operated with multiple uses. They could provide long-distance routes as well as being maintained for local, short-distance movement of livestock as part of a transhumance system. Many of the droveways are documented as being exploited for medieval transhumance practices utilising Wealden pastures. This is particularly the case in Kent (Witney 1976) and a significant number of the Kentish droveways share a demonstrable relationship with early Anglo-Saxon cemeteries (Brookes 2007, 61), although they may only have developed as actual roads in the later Saxon periods. County-focused studies elsewhere in the Wealden region have identified comparable links between settlements and outlier holdings that were utilised as pasture or woodland resources (Gardiner 1984). These have been

## 4. Travelling and Using the Land- and Sea-Scapes

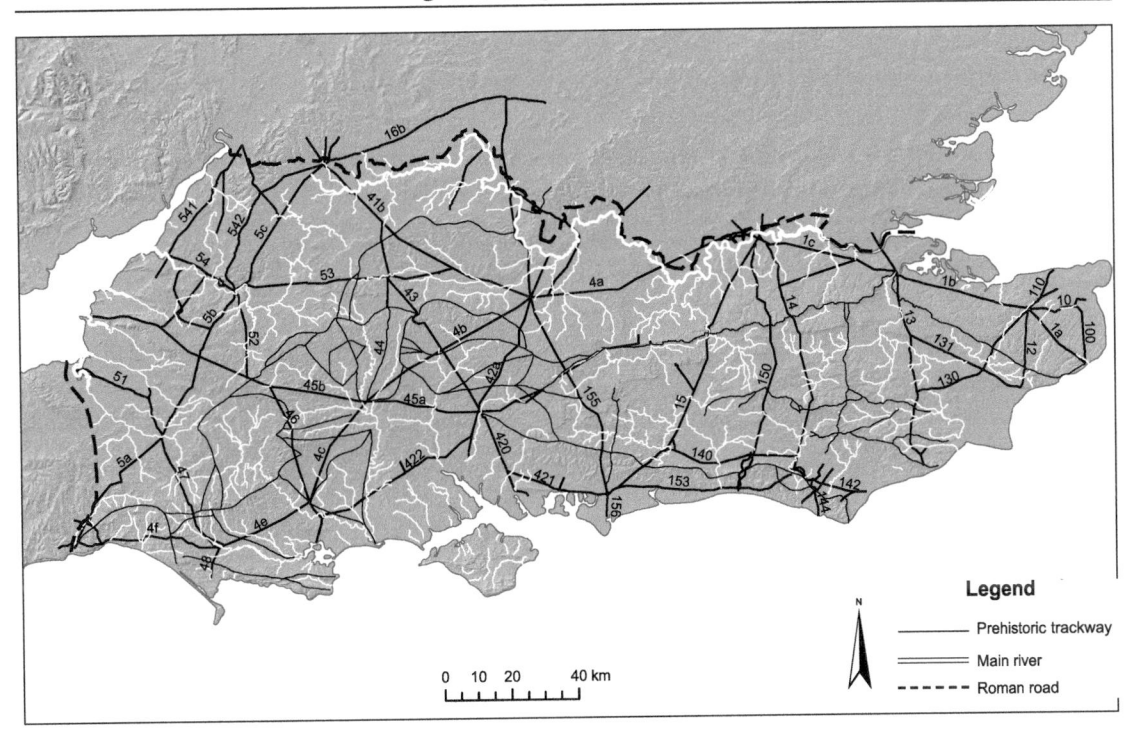

*Figure 14. Roman roads, with Margary numbers, and prehistoric trackways of the study region*

identified primarily through mapping both place-name and documentary sources. The north-south linearity of routeways in western Sussex have attracted comment as they appear to align with the Roman Stane Street as it crosses the Weald (Chatwin and Gardiner 2005, 39, fig. 6).

By common consent the networks of tracks and roads in use in the early Anglo-Saxon period are among the most difficult for landscape geographers and archaeologists to re-construct (Taylor 1979, 84). The settlement pattern, especially in the wooded regions of southern Britain, may have been dispersed (Williamson 1988), without any evidence for nucleation until much later if at all. These need not be seen as isolated settlements, rather placed within a diffuse network of contacts maintaining local routeways. Further broader patterns of social linkages would have incorporated opportunities for exploitation of the resources provided by river and coastal environments. The assumption that the Roman roads went out of use because they could not be maintained requires consideration and is best considered on a broader regional basis rather than on a county-by-county survey, as clearly some did survive in certain sections into the modern era. As the mapping of these myriad routeways can now demonstrate, there is convincing evidence that they provided the optimum routeways between distant places in the early Anglo-Saxon period across the study region. The extent to which people in the period AD 400–750 instituted new trackways, cutting new routes across the landscape, presents a further conundrum, however. Hoskins (1955, 66–70) suggested that Anglo-Saxon estate boundaries, sinuous in layout and with high banking to form

65

hollow ways or sunken lanes, were newly-created features. In his opinion, they dated from the seventh century onwards and probably used slave-labour to construct, though labour services might also be owed by free peasants to their overlord. Convincing evidence for the institution of new, major routeways linking newly-founded settlements during the study period has not been found, rather a reliance on existing, long-established routes is proposed.

## Agricultural practices

The impact of climatic change on agriculture is difficult to assess with respect to local regimes, though some general observations can be made regarding likely outcomes. The influence of colder weather on crop yields may have the most impact on marginal landscapes, particularly uplands where there is a greater decrease in average temperature and the length of the growing season. This lessens the potential to accumulate surpluses and seed stores for the following season (Parry 1978, 70–3). In the island of Britain, 27% of the land area falls within the category of climatically marginal land (that is land particularly sensitive to climatic change), though by location all of this land category is to the north and west and none of it occurs within the study area (*ibid.*, 85, fig. 20). The landscapes of areas adjacent to the coast are differentially affected by climatic changes with any rise in spring temperatures being offset by having a lower summer maximum. When altitude is put into the equation, there is a shorter growing season in coastal highlands (ibid., 78). Further annual fluctuations in climate could have produced catastrophic results, should the agriculturalists not have the capacity to bridge over them in the short term.

The extent to which agricultural activities were already in terminal decline in the Late Roman period is a subject for debate that cannot be resolved here. A review of the relevant literature implies a decline in the large villa estates, although their associated land holdings may have continued to be worked (De la Bédoyère 1993, 122–3). Medium-sized farms and landholdings, large enough for a degree of self-sufficiency, may well have continued in use (Millett 1990, 186; Lewit 1991, 33) with relatively high levels of occupancy and prosperity. The apparent absence of evidence for continuity into the fifth century here may well be a function of the inability of archaeology to detect this, given the general absence of datable pottery and coinage extending beyond the first decade of that century, although there are occasional finds that might suggest otherwise. A mass locational shift from low-lying locations to higher ground is also indicated (Lewit 1991, 43). Major changes to regional rural economies in fourth-century Britain are evidenced, in which large areas of the southeast region, mainly Surrey in the study area, "perhaps underwent large-scale transformations from a predominately arable economy into a mixed or even largely stock-raising economy" (Jones 1996, 171–2).

The expansion of arable production has been interpreted as a response to a Roman tax levy (Applebaum 1972, 223–49), the pressure of which had the ultimate effect of destroying the native rural economy (Jones 1996, 206). The grain yields of Romano-British agriculture cannot be assessed with any degree of accuracy, particularly when relating this to estimates of the grain demands of the Roman army, both for food rations and for military animals, in addition to local subsistence and other taxation requirements. When discussing the area supporting the civitas capital at Silchester, Boon (1974, 247) suggested a low yield for its soils of only 2.8 hundred-weight per acre, whilst by contrast Applebaum (1975, 121–30), assessed the very fertile soils around Bignor Roman villa in Sussex as capable of producing 11.2 hundred-weight per acre. Thus there does not seem to be a reason to propose adjacency in the production and consumption of bulk quantities of cereals – a trade in this staple over distance might be proposed for the Roman period.

Dense clay soils with poor drainage, although fertile for cereal production when worked with a true plough with a coulter and mould board (Hill 2000), would probably have been adversely affected by changing climatic conditions, in that increased rainfall would have degraded their structure and hastened the processes of erosion (Jones 1996, 220). Lighter and thin soils would have been impacted on by increased rainfall through the acceleration of the processes of leaching out of minerals and nutrients. Problematically, the expansion onto both of these soil types was a characteristic of late Romano-British agriculture (*ibid.*, 221). Changes to the types of pasture available would have affected regimes of animal husbandry, perhaps reducing the density of livestock, although in a period of climatic change pastoralism may have represented a more secure option than cereal production with the prospect of reduced harvests and crop failure (*ibid.*, 224). Nevertheless, climatic changes eventually rendered millions of hectares of upland areas and marginal lands unsustainable for arable agriculture.

The enviro-archaeological evidence from Barton Court Farm near Abingdon illustrates adaptive strategies to the new climatic conditions. Here, less intensive land use has been identified for the fifth-century occupation of the site. Decline in grazing was mirrored by an increase in the numbers of sheep, in contrast to falling numbers of cattle and horses (Jones 1996, 228). Spelt-wheat ceased to be grown, although both barley and flax production continued, the latter being well suited to damp land (Miles 1986, 25). An increase in the presence of oil- and fibre producing plants is also noted throughout the study period (Dark 2000, 131). More recently Fowler (2000, 228) has commented on the intensification of settlement and agricultural activity on the Wessex chalklands in the fourth century, with a network of villa estates and hinterland settlements exploiting the full agrarian potential of the landscape. A central role is envisaged for sheep rearing here, to meet external demands for wool production, with cultivation only supporting local needs (*ibid.*, 229). This pattern is also replicated on the Berkshire Downs (*ibid.*, 229 with reference to the work of Gaffney and Tingle 1989).

Pervasive trends in the form and content of Anglo-Saxon agricultural practices have been well established through historical and archaeological researches. The association of open fields, ploughlands, ridge and furrow and the mould board plough with the later Anglo-Saxon period are well known (Hill 2000). Finberg (1972, 398) could find no evidence that Anglo-Saxon immigrants had knowledge of better ploughs or more advanced agricultural techniques than the ones already in use by the native population (also Wilson 1962). The recent find of an iron coulter from a secure seventh century context at the Mid Saxon settlement at Lyminge, Kent may well prompt revision to the chronology and impact of these changes however (pers. comm. Gabor Thomas). In the main, the evidence for the period AD 400–750 is more thinly scattered. Clearly, regional

*Table 26. Soil preferences of arable crops*

| Crop | Preferred soil type |
| --- | --- |
| Emmer | Light and dry soils. Spring sown |
| Spelt | Heavy and light soils. Hardy |
| Bread wheat | Heavy soils – silts and clays, deep loams. Winter hardy. High yield, but requires greater soil fertility than other wheats and more prone to depredation by insects, birds and fungi. Easily threshed |
| Barley | Heavy and light soils, but not in poorly drained or with Ph value below 6. Winter or spring sown |
| Oats | Deep loams and clays, requires water, used on acid and infertile soils in Romano-British period |
| Rye | Not heavy soils. Copes with poor quality soils. Harvested in August. Probably used for fodder and thatching. |
| Flax | Deep retentive loams, heavy low-lying ground, not tolerant of frost or heavy rain. Probably not used for oil, but for textile production. Only survives on waterlogged sites |

and local agricultural traditions must have related to working the available soil types and in many respects these must have dictated settlement patterns and preferences. The overall scale of variation between areas was perhaps one of degree, however, rather than wholesale differences. The range of habitat resources available to each community would have been mediated through proximity, rights of access and the ability to move through the landscape to more distant environmental niches. Whilst subsistence farming underpinned the cycle of working the land, acquisition of imported goods, the need to supply food rents as tribute to a lord and later incentives to supply a market economy probably impacted on these practices over time.

Cereal assemblages exhibit patterns of change, although archaeologically recovered remains demonstrate both variations between similar and approximately contemporary sites and greater variation over time than has been suggested previously (Green 1994, 85). In the light of a developing body of evidence for variability, one cannot assert with confidence that different soil types can necessarily be equated with specific crops (*ibid.*, 84). Site function as much as site location might account for recorded variations, so, for example, a royal estate centre might produce evidence for specialised production. Nevertheless different crops have different soil preferences, as shown in Table 26 (derived from Jones 1981).

Barley (*Hordeum vulgare*) is the most commonly represented cereal remain on early Anglo-Saxon settlement sites, with fewer occurrences of bread wheat (*Triticum aestivum*), rye (*Secale cereale*) and oats (*Avena sativa*) and more rarely spelt (*Triticum spelta*) and emmer (*Triticum dicoccum*). There are, however, regional variations with, for example rye more prominent in the areas of drier, sandy soils (Dark 2000, 131) but rare in Hampshire (Pelling 2003, 103). Taking West Stow, Suffolk, as the main example, continuity in the usage of spelt (the hulled wheat) was identified from the Roman period into the mid fifth century, but a change occurred thereafter wherein this cereal had disappeared from use by the late seventh century, a pattern replicated over the lowland area (Fowler

2002, 213). In urban contexts after AD 700, the naked bread wheat is the most common type, a cereal that is more easily threshed and suitable for cultivation on heavy soils (Arnold 1997, 37), although any causal relationship between a shift in types of cereal and the emergence of urban and trading communities must remain speculative (contra Moreland 2000, 97; also with respect to estate reorganisation and agricultural intensification that develops after the establishment of emporia – pers. comm. Andrew Reynolds). Debbie Banham (2010, 176–8) robustly propounds the importance of 'foodways', in this case a change in dietary preference towards wheat bread for quality, religious, social or status reasons. Concomitant changes in farming practice may have been in place by AD 700 – the Lyminge coulter may well add to this argument, particularly if it is eventually identified as a Merovingian-type artefact as seems indicated. Overall, beyond a perceived gross trend towards bread wheat production through the whole of the Anglo-Saxon period, the data remains ambiguous and perhaps currently resists geographical and temporal patterning.

Pelling (2003, 106), however, discussing finds of emmer wheat in early Anglo-Saxon contexts in the Thames valley suggests that, although the evidence is rather limited, there may be a case for considering its use there as a cultural preference exercised by incoming Germanic settlers. She notes its contemporary cultivation in the region between the Ems and the Elbe in northern Germany, although it had disappeared from use elsewhere in mainland Europe. One might suggest, however, that emmer cultivation may have been a continuation of Romano-British practices, as evidenced by waste from crop processing in a corn drier (2465) at Alington Avenue, Dorchester, Dorset, early in the Post-Roman phases of the site (Jones and Straker 2002, 118–121). Emmer has also been recovered from the site at Bath Road, Harmondsworth, London (Cowie and Blackmore 2008, 159).

## Pastoral practices

The evidence from the settlement at West Stow, Suffolk (Crabtree 1989), demonstrated that wild animals formed only a very small part of that communities' diet, a point possibly reinforced by the absence of specific hunting equipment from furnished burials of the period (Arnold 1997, 35–6). Butchery techniques and kill-patterns practised on domesticated animals at West Stow showed no change from those of the local Romano-British samples. Taken together with the lack of evidence for the introduction of new breeds, though limited importation of livestock cannot be ruled out entirely, this would indicate continuity of local traditions catering for local needs (*ibid.*, 35). Comparison of the faunal assemblages of rural settlements with those of early urban centres of the Middle Anglo-Saxon period, however, has suggested that 'the early Anglo-Saxon countryside was managed differently, or not as efficiently, as in the following centuries' (*ibid.*). The major livestock types of cattle, sheep and pigs, where recovered archaeologically, do not exhibit any significant changes in either type or size throughout the study period, although there are clear variations over time and space in the proportions of species present on any given site (Fowler 2002, 223). In contrast, Coy and Maltby (1987, 189) noted an increase in the average size of sheep in the Romano-British and Anglo-Saxon periods, with regional variations. Sheep in the southwest may have continued to be smaller than elsewhere in the study period (*ibid.*, 224). Further, the variety of fleece types found had a range similar to that of the Romano-British period (Ryder 1981, 226).

Systems of transhumance were important throughout the study period and livestock would be moved from settlements to summer pastures between May and September, utilising uplands, marginal lands or woodland dens. This would allow the spring-grazing land to recover and provide a winter hay crop to be harvested over the summer. It is assumed that the main pasture would be in proximity to the settlements, whilst the summer grazing might be some distance away, hence producing a long lasting system of droveways across the landscape.

Reviewing the evidence from settlement sites in Sussex, Gardiner (2003, 152) asserts that, in a situation of declining population numbers, the agricultural economy of the Sussex Downs changed at the end of the Roman period. It was then that arable cultivation ceased and the settlements were withdrawn from the hilltops and slopes of the Downs into the more fertile valleys, although an accurate distribution pattern of these later sites has yet to be established. Environmental evidence from the fifth- and sixth-century buildings at Bishopstone in East Sussex overlooking the Ouse estuary illustrates the wide range of resources that the community was able to access. These included arable crops, livestock (indicating access to pasture and grazing), foreshore and maritime foods and wild animals, a pattern replicated at the contemporary site at Botolphs in the Adur valley (*ibid.*, 153–4). The establishment of temporary sites for the procurement of resources for return to the home settlement is also indicated. By contrast, excavations at Bullock Down above Eastbourne in East Sussex identified that it was deserted from the early fifth century until 700 years later. In the interim it may have been used as pasture (grazing rights were in place in the eleventh century) or it may have reverted to scrub (Drewett 1982, 213). Evidence from other chalkland sites and areas, at Chalton, Hampshire and the Vale of the White Horse in old Berkshire, suggests that this was a pattern replicated across this landscape type in the Post-Roman period (Gardiner 2003, 152).

## The environmental evidence from selected excavation reports for southern Britain

### The Upper Thames Valley and chalklands to the south

It is noted by Booth *et al.* (2007) that for the Upper Thames Valley there were average accumulations of alluvium of about 0.5mm per annum as at Drayton, near Abingdon, formerly in Berkshire, between AD 1 and AD 400. Such accumulations occurred again between AD 800 and AD 1100, whereas the rate had decreased to 0.2mm or less between AD 400 and AD 800. It is not inconceivable that alluviation caused by agricultural activity had virtually ceased between the fifth and seventh centuries and only picked up between the seventh and eighth centuries. Certainly such a slowing down is confirmed in a sequence at a palaeochannel at Yarnton again in the Upper Thames floodplain (*ibid.*, 18–20). A change of emphasis from cereal and other arable production to pastoral exploitation seems to be implied here. There was no evidence for systematic abandonment into neither scrub, however, nor woodland regeneration of the floodplain and terraces in the early Anglo-Saxon period. There may have been a reduction in grazing activity, but the insects present in the archaeological record typify open landscape with grassland. Woodland regeneration on Roman sites in the Cotswolds may have contributed to the reduced level of alluviation in this period (*ibid.*, 29–30). The faunal remains at the fourth- to early seventh-century settlement at Barrow Hills, Radley (Barnetson 2007, 289–290) showed healthy livestock, implying that beef may have played a significant part in the meat diet of the community, whereas sheep were probably exploited primarily for their milk and fleeces.

The palaeochannel adjacent to the settlement at Grove Farm, Market Lavington Wiltshire was surrounded by open herb-rich meadow, damp grassland, pasture and poor fen. The range of grasses (*poaceae*) present in the pollen spectrum indicated that there was grazing and a low level of grassland management in the area. Also present was evidence in the vicinity for low-level arable agriculture and heathland. No evidence for Post-Roman woodland regeneration was identified (Wiltshire 2006, 122–3). The evidence implies that the conditions on the floor of the Easterton valley were locally wet, producing sedges for roofing or flooring material. It also indicates that arable fields contained wheat, rye and barley, and the presence of horticultural plots producing a variety of foods including brassicas that were located elsewhere. Although arable agriculture continued from the sixth century onwards, it appears to become more extensive only in the Later Saxon period (*ibid.*, 135). The wheat grains have been tentatively identified as a free-threshing form (Straker 2006, 138). Meanwhile the diet indicated by the faunal remains from the whole of the excavated area included salt-water fish, a few wild animals and birds, poultry, good-sized cattle and sheep, many of which were kept to maturity, but pigs were poorly represented. Perhaps this reflects on the absence of available woodland for pannage (Bourdillon 2006, 168).

*Central chalk lands to the south coast*
The spectrum of cereals present at Abbots Worthy, Hampshire reflects the overall pattern for Hampshire sites, with an order of importance of barley, wheat, oats and rye. The range of soils in the vicinity of the site would have been suitable for both barley (calcareous) and wheat (heavier, colluvial soils on the valley floor). Seeds present in the samples indicated the use of both damp and dry grasslands (Carruthers 1991, 74). It has been suggested that the Itchen Valley was systematically drained for meadow by the eighth century (*ibid.* discussing Tubbs 1978).

*The eastern area of the Thames, the Weald and the coast*
The environmental data from settlement excavations in east Kent has been summarised by Martin Welch (2007, 205–8). The downland site at Church Whitfield produced SFBs with evidence for the herding, butchery and consumption of cattle, sheep and pigs – a diet diversified by the hunting of roe deer and by fishing. The Manston site at Ramsgate in Kent, similarly datable to the late sixth/early seventh centuries, had more sheep/goat remains than other hoofed animals, but in ratios similar to those from West Stow (Welch, 2007, 207). The fish types present (ray, herring and flatfish) would probably be the result of inshore fishing, with shellfish collected from the foreshore to extend the dietary range. The plant-based diet present included free-threshing wheats, hulled barley, rye, oats, peas and hazelnuts. The charcoal remains showed access to exploitable

stands of deciduous trees such as oak and maple, with the presence of scrubland indicated by dogwood, blackthorn and hazel. The mollusc remains indicated an open countryside. Despite the diversity of resources, the community was in all probability a marginal one, subsidiary to a more substantial settlement.

The Anglo-Saxon finds within an early to mid Saxon SFB from the West Malling and Leybourne bypass excavation, at the western end of the Holmesdale in Kent (Andrews *et al.* 2009, 54) produced inconclusive evidence for the contemporary growing of emmer and spelt. Charcoal from this site was dominated by fruit species and hazelnuts, interpreted as reflecting an open landscape with few choices of material for fuel, although hazel might equally be a coppice product. In the same volume (133–4) the environmental evidence from a seventh century SFB at Cottington, on a small promontory at the southeast end of the Wantsum Channel, included hulled barley and wheats (emmer), but no bread wheat (*T. aestivum*). The use of the adjacent wetlands is hinted at by a single capsule fragment of rush.

In central London, pollen analysis from an extensive layer of 'dirty brickearth' at the Royal Opera House site indicates that the local environment at the beginning of the *Lundenwic* settlement in the period *c.*600–675 was one of open grassland, with some oak and hazel trees present (Malcolm *et al.* 2003, 19). Although it is not known where the crops consumed in *Lundenwic* were grown, the presence of damp-ground species amongst the arable weed seeds indicated access to river-valley fields and damp meadows. The presence of coppiced products indicates access to managed woodland (*ibid.*, 184–5). A recent survey of early and middle Anglo-Saxon evidence from the London region highlighted the possible regrowth of forest and colonisation of heathland in the vicinity of New Palace Yard, Westminster. Further east, on the bank of the Thames tributary, the River Ravensbourne at Ladywell, Lewisham, the early Saxon sediment showed that 'the local flood-plain mainly comprised grass-sedge fen, with some alder growing on wetland margins. At a regional level pollen from this site suggests that the landscape was largely deforested, but with some oak and hazel woodland' (Cowie and Blackmore 2008, 135).

Martin Bell's studies of the South Down chalks and associated river valleys (1981 and 1983) focused particularly on alluvial and colluvial sediment, the latter accumulating at boundaries of cultivation, for example at plateau edges and as lynchets. He argued (1981, 84–5) for significant erosion of the chalkland soils and the removal of fertile loess horizons occurring during and since prehistory. He noted that this would have impacted on land use both on the chalk and in surrounding areas, with a long-term pattern of agricultural reorientation away from the chalk. Only those areas on the South Downs that had surviving superficial pockets of fertile loess, as at Kiln Combe, Eastbourne, East Sussex and Chalton in east Hampshire, would have been able to support long-term intensive land use.

The environmental background to the settlement at Friar's Oak, Hassocks, Sussex (Somerville 2000, 47), a site located at the foot of the South Downs, was one that was locally open, indicating that cereals were grown. The weed seeds present in the plant macro-remains indicated that the cereal was autumn sown. The diversity of woodland species represented implied the exploitation of managed woodland resources both on the Downs scarp and on the local sandy soils. Palaeo-environmental examination of dry valleys on the Downs above Brighton (Wilkinson *et al.* 2002, 203–238) showed that arable agriculture did continue on the higher ground, but at a reduced scale and as a localised activity.

### *The western area*

The corn drying ovens dating to the late seventh or early eighth centuries at Chantry Fields, Gillingham, Dorset had carbonised plant macrofossils present, suggesting that the ovens were located in already cleared woodland, but still with access to supplies of partially-coppiced timber, principally oak. From here one can infer that woodland-management regimes were already well established, though as there were no pig bones in the samples, it would seem this area was not used for pannage (Heaton 1993, 125).

## Conclusions

The climatic context of worsening conditions and rising sea levels from the fourth century onwards is amply demonstrated, most likely prompting a range of strategic responses from the rural communities so affected. A withdrawal from upland sites and from the floodplains as places of settlement appears to be indicated, although more localised responses are difficult to categorise. Yet, the environmental evidence from settlements throughout the study region demonstrates the exploitation of diverse environmental resources. There is no particular evidence for agricultural specialisation, although the long-term change to the production of bread-wheat is a consistent feature. A striking element is the lack of evidence for woodland regeneration and the strength of evidence for both continuities of woodland management and the presence of open grasslands, scrublands and meadows. Problematically, environmental reports on early Anglo-Saxon sites struggle against historically derived parameters and explanations of culture-history change in the period. These are the breakdown of Roman material culture, the end of Roman administration, the migration of Germanic peoples and so on. All too frequently such parameters become the explanation for the evidence, when it is possible that the environmental evidence is presenting a rather more nuanced and far less cataclysmic picture. There is no conclusive evidence of a hiatus in the exploitation of the landscape, rather indications of changes of scale and intensity. The basic structure of the topography of the landscape, apart from those areas of water ingress, in terms of viable routeways, view sheds and environmental potential remained constant and open to similar locational choices as those taken up in earlier epochs. What is to be noted, however, is the infrequency of the representation of these agricultural subsistence tasks in the burial assemblages of the study period.

# 5. Sites, Locations and Soils

## Introduction

The research questions central to this chapter are predicated on the relationships between cemeteries and settlements (whether one can be used spatially to denote the proximity of the other), the topographies of site location and the environmental context of site location selection. From this point the continuity or discontinuity with late Roman landscape structures can be assessed and differential use of the environmental resources unevenly spread within the study region can be examined – the elements that may have structured the precursor polities of the early Anglo-Saxon kingdoms. Given that the extent of the earliest settlements' territories is unknown, with a distinctly unclear relationship to the *Tribal Hidage* document, it is difficult to establish whether models of community self-sufficiency should be sought. Rather strategic drives to derive community wealth from the activities of others in the vicinity, essentially the exploitation of a rural underclass of the Romano-British, may have been the case. For example, was Kent wealthy primarily because of its environmental resource base or because of a monopoly of Continental trading routes? Indeed, Brookes (2007, 54) comments that, although ecological and topographical factors are important in spatial analysis, 'the spatial characteristics of settlement … are resolutely related to the nature of social relations' and as these changed, so did the ordering of the landscape.

In the fifth and sixth the concept of land as a commodity may not have been strongly developed, with the landscape having cultural rather than overtly economic meaning. Archaeological interpretations of the re-use of prehistoric monuments in the landscape as signifiers of longevity of association and ownership (Semple 1998, 2003, 2009) perhaps preclude overtly economic explanations for the distribution patterns. Nevertheless, network utility and the parcelling of the landscape into economic units was an important feature of the evolving institutions of kingship in Anglo-Saxon society. Thus, an assertion of federated settlements of Germanic people to secure against piratical incursions in the coastal regions carries an implication of land allotments of sufficient resources to support a unit of associated persons given over by treaty. Unless a random selection is implied, this must mean an awareness of land units that could be so allocated. Therefore, it is entirely reasonable to suggest that the concepts underlying the distribution patterns of the Germanic settlement can be determined, rather than suspecting *a priori* a random and organic migration/colonisation process.

Researchers have consistently proposed that there is a genuine spatial proximity between early Anglo-Saxon cemeteries and their associated settlements (summarised by Chester-Kadwell 2009). Bonney (1976), for example, theorised that settlements were on the best land and cemeteries were on the poorest (contested by Arnold and Wardle 1981) but this makes an unwarranted assumption of uniformity about where sites were located – clearly the sites could be differentiated further by examining their perceived functions within their socio-economic context. Whilst earlier discussions have of necessity been based on only a few, though striking, examples (most notably Rookery Hill, Bishopstone, East Sussex, (Bell 1977)), the study region now offers a more extensive list of settlement/cemetery combinations for discussion. But, how physically close might they have been to each other and what implications are there for the density of both settlements and populations within a landscape? This chapter argues that a cemetery or settlement location can be used as an interchangeable notation for the presence of a community. If the proposed 150m interval distance is accepted, the spatial relationships between these two societal elements may allow us to tease out some inferences about how communities may have lived amongst their dead and how they presented their communities to the outside world, especially to those passing amongst them. In any case, it is evident that earlier received opinions about settlement and cemetery relationships, for example Bonney's assertion (1976) that cemeteries occupied marginal land in contrast to settlements placed on the optimum soils, while demonstrable in some cases, may not have a general applicability and indeed the relationship may not necessarily be predicated on soil type to any strong degree.

## Theories of site location

What decision-making processes were involved in the patterning of the early Anglo-Saxon settlement? General settlement behaviour theory in archaeology suggests that either of two predispositions would be at work: a community might establish a territory in order to keep other groups at a distance, or a community might minimalise the distance from other groups if there was a mutual bond. Thus, a pattern that identified isolated and non-adjacent territories would run counter to these models. Rational action would produce settlement clusters, with regularly spaced nuclei, rendered mappable through the use of Thiessen polygons. The processes of infilling, reacting to the pressure of increased population, would lead to a halving and then quartering of the distances between nuclei, and would also produce pressure to exploit new, possibly marginal, areas (Heidinga 1987, 157–8). Although the initial territories might be more or less of an equal size, the processes of internal expansion could result in unequally sized units (Hamerow 2002, 101)

Clearly these models work best in an idealised landscape – a blank canvas with an initially simple settlement pattern. However, if there are extant groups, that is surviving and economically active Romano-British communities, then the incomers might have several choices – to co-exist in adjacent communities, with the incomers acting as infill; to move the indigenous population to marginal areas, or to excise the native presence altogether, in order to occupy the prime environmental niches; or to overwrite this continued presence through the use of top-down elite structures that exploited the economic activity of an in-situ lower tier of society. The certainty expressed by Shepherd Frere in 1966 that 'the real process of Saxon settlement was a slow, gradual penetration into areas of the countryside where the breakdown of the RB economic system had left a solitude' must now appear as overly simplistic, if elegiac. As Heidinga comments (*ibid.*, 158) 'where continuity of occupation was established, the territorial division that had been inherited from the past thus formed no hindrance for an optimal organisation of these territories'. Furthermore, as long as the earlier regional structures, such as roads and routeways were still viable and there was no wholesale change to the methods of landscape exploitation, then a new territorial organisation could be developed approximately along the same lines (Heidinga *ibid.*, 166). However, one might observe that these optimising models of migrant activity are based on an inference of landscape exploitation through agrarian production, rather than non-agrarian usage. Archaeological evidence of specialised communities could mount a challenge to this model, particularly if, for example, coastal communities appear to have little direct engagement with the exploitation of maritime resources or the agrarian potential of their immediate hinterlands, leading one to categorise them as primarily trading places. Müller-Wille (1999, 205–11), discussing the landing places around Roskilde Fjord in the period AD 200–1100, identified two types of trading site:

- Landing places of agrarian character, that is rural settlements which had an additional function as a landing place
- Specialised landing places, that is settlements without any signs of agrarian economy, but which had other primary functions focussing on trade and exchange (and possibly raw material conversion)

On a broader front, Ellison and Harriss (1972) hypothesised those research agendas that emphasise cultural continuity mask underlying social trends and changes to internal economic organisation. Using the methodology now adopted by this project, they mapped sites distributions against landscapes of differing economic potentials over time. In their Wiltshire case study they determined that two thirds of Roman villa sites were oriented towards high quality arable in valleys, whilst the native settlements were more likely to be on Downlands. In their Sussex case study of the area between the rivers Adur and Ouse, based on place-name evidence of *-ingas* to define the early sites, they determined that settlements expanded into 2km intervals to give the optimum polygon of resources for each community from what was available. These communities would coalesce to form parishes. In any case, in most periods, the preferred site location would be at the junction between two sorts of land categories. The use of *-ingas* as an indicator of the earliest sites could be questioned however, as this component could be seen as later rather than earlier in the Anglo-Saxon place-naming process.

Studies of, and explanations for, settlement patterning in the early Medieval period are problematised by the diversity of landscape and the eventual notional division of the island of Britain into Upland and Lowland zones, and Champion and Ancient landscapes (Rackham 1995) as a means of introducing generalities into the discussion. Somewhat awkwardly, all of these geological and topographical elements are present in the study region, but the specific landscape outcomes are seen as the result of different trajectories of colonisation and exploitation. Williamson

(2007, 104) proposes that there may have been a congruence between high watersheds and cultural boundaries, for example in the Chilterns and the Quantocks and also that they may have marked the boundaries between woodland areas of dispersed settlement and champion landscapes of nucleated villages, where the constraints of the soil types may have led to communal forms of agriculture. The Wessex downlands, for example, were key areas of sheep/corn farming in the Planned Countryside, but were flanked by areas of Ancient countryside. The location of settlements might be determined by a number of factors. As a more generalising statement, Williamson asserts (ibid) that "this essential contrast between the more densely settled valleys and the less intensively occupied interfluves underlies much of the early landscape development of southern Britain. And it explains, in part, the long-term sustainability of many 'large terrains'". If the watersheds define neighbouring territories, then the territorial centres were in the drainage basins. Taking the area of Lindsey and the East Riding of Yorkshire, broadly comparable to the southern Britain study region with its variety of landscape components, Bruce Eagles (1979, 240–3) assessed the evidence for the presence of Germanic troops and their families, located to meet the needs of Roman military strategy in the fourth century. Cremation cemeteries were in use in the fifth century in the East Riding, their material culture indicating origins in Frisia, North West Germany and perhaps Jutland. The survival of Romano-British farms as self-sufficient units away from major routes and towns is assumed. These co-existent communities that made up Early Anglo-Saxon society provided resources on one side and a market on the other, with the Anglo-Saxons 'providing new outlets for the produce from former Romano-British estates, by now integrated into a new system of taxation supporting the thegns and itinerant Royal courts' (*ibid.*, 242). Taylor (1974) also questioned the proposal of total discontinuity between the late Roman settlement pattern and that of the Anglo-Saxons, suggesting two options for the incomers: occupy existing Roman sites or occupy remote or marginal land. Thus, in that scenario, many cemeteries would relate to Romano-British settlements, but those on marginal land, such as Chalton, Hampshire, would not, a point presumably only now demonstrable through DNA and Strontium Isotope analyses (see Thomas *et al.* 2006 for analysis of this evidence; see Hills 2009 for a critique of the interpretations). If the actual numbers of migrants were few, but comprised of a particular elite rather than merely small numbers of relocating farming communities, then tenurial or indeed political control over the existing people may have occurred. The basic system of land units may have been taken over and only modified slightly.

The comprehensive network of parish boundaries offers a deceptively straightforward inroad into the issue of the organisation of the landscape on which the earliest Anglo-Saxon kingdoms were based. John Blair (2005, 154) argues that the establishment of territorial parishes from the seventh century onwards was facilitated by the prior existence of 'earlier demarcated landholdings'. Hundred-type sized 'provinces' or *'regios'*, assessed in multiples of hides, whether or not in actuality the earlier independent kingdoms, were the basis for royal resource collection in later seventh century, providing food renders for the itinerant courts. The groups of hides that formed the early monastic estates were derived from the hide assessments of the *regiones*, therefore, Blair argues, the extents and productive capacities of these estates must have been known already and could be fairly precisely calculated. It is from this basis of quantifiable and productive landscapes that 'extensive lordship' had the means to create parochial territories and to assess for taxation the far larger groupings denoted in the *Tribal Hidage* document.

Therefore, it had been assumed that there could be a relationship between parish boundaries and pagan burials that was statistically verifiable (Goodier 1984), as it had been noted that some burial sites were close to these boundaries. Such an association was identified for the seventh century, but not for the fifth century, leading to the assertion that it was unlikely that 'pre-existing land-units dictated the boundaries of Anglo-Saxon estates' and that the location of burials was more random. The boundaries seem to have become increasingly stable during the study period, thus explaining why more seventh than sixth century burials are on or close to them (see Brookes *et al.*, forthcoming). However, these developments were not uniform spatially. Now, one might question why there should necessarily be any relationship between burials and boundaries. As Martin Welch noted (1985, 12), in some districts barrows were raised as territorial markers and they do have a statistically significant relationship to parish boundaries, thus implying continuity from early in the study period. But, if they were centrally placed in a territory, this would imply that a major reorganisation of territorial units had occurred since the early Anglo-Saxon period and prior to the earliest documentary record for those boundaries. Yet, if the parish boundaries are indeed earlier than their juridical function, we must ask what their original function might have been in the context of the fifth and sixth centuries. They delineate space and landscape and can be placed to regulate movement, thus they may coincide with sections of live routeways, as Della Hooke determined for the kingdom of the *Hwicce* (1985), where they are most common along water courses and for short distances along roads. Whether medieval parish boundaries were a continuation of Roman period bounded entities remains undemonstrated for the study region as a whole in this research project, although local associations can be suggested. A case study of the inter-relationships of Roman sites, early Anglo-Saxon material and parish boundaries in Surrey is presented below. The issue of site locations within the three kingdoms of the study region have been subject to differing research agendas.

## Settlement and wealth in the three kingdoms

### Kent

From his investigation of the physical patterning of settlement, drawing on archaeological, place-name and documentary sources, Stuart Brookes (2007, 100–101) broadly confirmed Everitt's model of Kentish settlement colonisation, that of movement over time away from the Original Lands of the Foothills and Holmesdale, although these areas were subject to subsequent phases of infilling settlements, particularly in the marshes and woodlands. The primary colonisation was along established corridors of movement, coastal inlets and the Holmesdale, including transhumance routes to the south and west to Wealden denns. Beyond these routes, further colonisation – the secondary settlement infilling as evidenced by place-names, suggests the creation of a marginal hinterland, although with a capacity to generate wealth in excess of their resource base – here one must point to the upland barrow cemeteries of the seventh century with particularly rich female inhumations such as Kingston Down grave 205. He identified that primary settlements had a clear link to Roman precedents, although this was not the case for secondary infilling. A model of settlement parcelisation was proposed, with the site location giving access to a requisite range of resources. In the marginal zones a more developed strategy was evident, with a preference for location between environmental zones. Brookes (2007, 94–97) drew on evidence from both the Early Anglo-Saxon and Middle Saxon periods to identify four types of settlement in Kent:

1. Settlements with
   a. Romano-British or Early Anglo-Saxon evidence
   b. Early minster/nunnery/church
   c. Within the Foothills or close to the sea (within 5km)

2. Settlements with:
   a. No Romano-British precedent but with Early Anglo-Saxon evidence
   b. In the Foothills
   c. No particular association with an early church foundation
   d. Primary or secondary phase of settlement

3. Settlements with:
   a. Neither Romano-British nor Early Anglo-Saxon evidence
   b. Possible early ecclesiastical evidence
   c. More than 10km from the sea
   d. Location in Holmesdale or margins of the Downland
   e. Secondary phase of settlement

4. Settlements with:
   a. No Early Anglo-Saxon evidence, although Romano-British may be present
   b. Possible early ecclesiastical presence or Middle Saxon material
   c. In areas of possible secondary infilling

*Wessex*
This rather diffuse geographical sub-region, that only has a clear political identity from the seventh century, eludes definitive statements about its earliest format and settlement pattern. Integral researches have concentrated on three major themes: the interaction of the Anglo-Saxon settlement with the British West; the continuity of landscape usage from the Roman period and earlier, providing a template for Later Saxon bounded estates and parishes; and the role of prehistoric monument re-use in legitimising the control of the landscape. The narratives for the settlement of those areas that later became the kingdom of Wessex give a much higher profile to remnant populations of Sub Roman Britons and the remaining British kingdoms to the west of the Anglo-Saxon zone of settlement than is generally the case for the rest of the study region. As Barry Cunliffe characterised it (1993, 289) 'the large number of cemeteries scattered across

the face of Wessex implies a widely dispersed rural population made up of Sub Roman Britons, immigrant Saxons and communities of mixed ethnic antecedents'. The less than robust evidence of grass-tempered-pottery scatters and isolated sherds in the region of Late Roman settlements at Portchester, Downton, Round Hill Down and Wellhead, is used to propose continuity of occupation. He suggests (*ibid.*, 291) a linear model of adjacent Anglo-Saxon sites across the Southern Downlands, very much in the mode of that seen in East Sussex. Bruce Eagles proposed (2001, 199; also 2004) that the initial Germanic immigration may have taken place within the framework of the former Romano-British civitates, with the north west, west and possibly north east corner and extreme south west of Wiltshire remaining in British hands until the seventh century conquest by the expansionist Saxons (see also James 2010 for comments on the boundaries and settlements in this area). Supporting data comes in the form of place-name evidence for Britons, groups of which, together with river names, recur throughout the county. The recently excavated cemetery and settlement site of Market Lavington in Wiltshire is near to the shared boundary of the tribes of the Belgarum and the Dubonnorum, prompting an interpretation of this community as a planted group far to the west of the other Anglo-Saxon sites on west side of Salisbury Plain. It perhaps marks the limit of a newly acquired territory in the early sixth century – the absence of a concentration of weapon burials on that site would indicate an absence of overt conflict with a native population. The burial assemblages thus do not have the hallmarks of a frontier community. Other sites to the western edges of Wessex in Dorset and Somerset have been similarly interpreted, for example Hardown Hill (Evison 1968) and also Beckford, Hereford and Worcester (1996), begging the question as to the locations of the power bases in this area if these are indeed satellite communities. The documentary sources indicate that the late fifth and early sixth centuries were periods of relative peace in this area (Härke 1990, 28). By the last quarter of the seventh century there is charter evidence for Anglo-Saxon control of northwest Wiltshire and north Somerset, with archaeological evidence of the Anglo-Saxon presence from cemeteries at Buckland Dinham and Keynsham. By then, the frontier of Wessex had moved westwards into Devon. Taylor (1997, 12), reflecting on the complex arrangement of estates and land units which covered the county by the ninth century, proposed that the relatively late arrival of the Saxons in Dorset could not have created these, rather that they were more directly linked to the Roman period, which laid the outlines for the later combination of settlements and land units into parishes. Yet, as Bruce Eagles has discussed, there was a Germanic presence in the Dorset/Wiltshire area in the fifth century, evidenced by a number of widely distributed finds, for example at Spetisbury and Badbury (Eagles 1994, 2001) with the earliest perhaps at Hod Hill. That presence was not necessarily one of settlement, rather one of Germanic mercenaries working for a British local ruler and owing allegiance to that polity. Wiltshire had parts of four or five civitates within its modern confines, although the landscape structure of these has not been determined to any great degree – did elements of their structure survive, with strong centres and defended edges, or with strong perimeters guarding tribal homelands, into which the Anglo-Saxons were interposed?

In Somerset, the historical evidence suggests that there was an interim in the Saxon advance that allowed for the consolidation of a territory with a difficult terrain. As there were few major

## 5. Sites, Locations and Soils

*Figure 15. View west up Saxton Road Abingdon, Berkshire (now Oxfordshire) from the River Thames: the site of the mixed rite cemetery*

Roman roads, the main routeways were riverine and coastal, with the forest of Selwood forming a natural barrier to advancement. The major economic resources that made the settlement of Somerset valuable were dairy produce and minerals (Rahtz and Fowler 1972). Rippon (2007, 117) notes a significant change in the landscape of SW England around the seventh and eighth centuries, with the creation of villages in Somerset, evidenced by their location and the forms of their place-names.

The Upper Thames Valley was extensively farmed in the Late Roman period, to an extent that any fifth or sixth century settlement would inevitably be located on Roman farmland (Booth *et al.* 2007, 80–98). In the area around Abingdon, the Saxon settlement has been characterised as having an 'intimate connection' with both Roman and earlier patterns, given the re-use of prehistoric complexes that gave easy access to Romano-British fields (Miles 1974), although there is little evidence for upstanding field boundaries on the gravel terraces and no estate boundaries identified (Miles 1978). Yet, there are very obvious tracts of landscape, in Berkshire particularly, without evidence of Anglo-Saxon material culture – J. N. L. Myres (1969) suggested the presence of a British enclave centred on Silchester in this period.

Early Anglo-Saxon sites in Wessex tended to be located in river valleys and on the first floodplain gravel terraces, with concentrations on the confluences (see Figure 15), although it is noted that there may be a bias in the data recovery as most sites have been found as a result of modern gravel working. Clearly there is evidence, both from aerial survey, excavation and examination of later charters, of substantial royal estates, as at Sutton Courtenay and timber-halled settlements, as at Long Wittenham, that speaks to the high agrarian economic value of this area. The Vale of the White Horse and the Wylye valley both show patterns of parallel elongated estates that run from the river floodplain up onto the chalk downlands (Hooke 1988) – a pattern of this configuration of resources is replicated reasonably frequently elsewhere, for example in Surrey and Sussex. Intensive investigation of field patterns have demonstrated a correlation between Anglo-Saxon and medieval cultivated land in the Vale of White Horse, but there is insufficient evidence to argue for direct villa/estate continuity (Hooke 1988, 138), although clearly there was deliberate planning of boundaries to include all resource types. Such a strategy is optimising and the various regional economic regimes may have accessed the potential resources of the natural environment in such a way.

During the Roman period Wiltshire was extensively occupied, but with only marginal evidence of extended occupation into the early fifth century. Overton Down XII does provide evidence of a settled agricultural life on the Marlborough Downs after AD 350. Most settlements that have been excavated were on the chalk, although again this may represent an excavation bias. Draper (2006) raises the possibility that some villas may have lain at the head of extensive grain producing estates, whilst Cirencester was a focal point for the whole of the West Country in the fourth century for grain and wool production. Analyses and counts of faunal assemblages also indicate surplus production of pigs, cattle and sheep, but no local evidence of villa involvement with iron production. However, small non-villa type settlements were the norm in the rural landscape, with evidence of continuity from those of the Iron Age. In the non-chalk areas there was a widespread pattern of cattle farming having a greater dominance, although the use of pigs and sheep continued. Draper comments (*ibid.*, 31) that 'the most stable settlements in Wiltshire post AD 350 were undoubtedly those non-villa farming communities'. Given that the western counties of Wiltshire, Somerset and Gloucestershire were at heart of wealthiest area of Late Roman Britain, the absence of evidence for a sudden collapse, rather actual evidence for the terminal decline of the villas, continuity of economic activity, albeit at a lower level of intensity, can be suggested. Indeed Fowler (2000, 228–9) describes an intensification of settlement and agriculture on Wessex chalk in the fourth century. He notes a strong external demand for wool as part of a cash economy, in contrast to the cashless demands made by the requirement to supply the army and to pay tax. Later Roman small towns such as Cunetio, functioned, he argues, precisely to secure tax revenues and to collect raw materials. A similar situation existed on the Berkshire Downs, with the economy based on sheep. The existence of silver and gold coin hoards, such as that from Bishops Canning – possibly deposited as late as AD 420–30, suggests activite wealth creation ongoing beyond the formal end of Roman Britain.

Sarah Semple (2003) noted the fifth and sixth century concentration of sites in South Wiltshire, but with changing locational preferences thereafter on into the ninth century. In the early period, although single funerary events might have variable amounts of wealth within their assemblages, a comparability of location was noted, primarily as secondary burial within certain prehistoric monuments, but not within others, suggesting that monument form was not the determining criteria for their selection. This evidence strengthens the view that location was the key criteria. Julian Richards (1978, 51–55) noted the largely hypothetical issue of possible settlement plantation into vacated areas during the sub-Roman period and this issue of the strategic placement of communities merits much further exploration. The Berkshire Downs is one district where the presence of Saxon cemetery material at East Shefford suggests a planted settlement in a vacant area of light, well drained soils, with subsequent settlements in the sixth and seventh century around East Garston and Lambourn, as the result of westwards expansion from East Shefford, or eastwards expansion from earlier foci in Wiltshire.

*Sussex*
Despite the use of the example of the Malling Estate, near Lewes in East Sussex, by Jones (1976) to illustrate the landscape structures of Middle Saxon multiple estates, the settlement pattern of the South Saxon kingdom and its antecedents is imprecisely determined. Clearly at some point in time the unification of different land parcels into a common structure with labour obligations to the central power, be they present or absent, or to a king or landholder, is the later medieval outcome of very unclear processes in the early medieval period. Mark Gardiner (2003) argues that the post Roman land divisions became formalised as Rapes by the Normans. Martin Welch has suggested (1985) that the Downland settlements of Early Anglo-Saxon Sussex and East Hampshire were the final phase of exploitation of the chalk as prime arable land, congruent with prehistoric and Roman usage. These people settled in the middle of existing field systems that may have been in continual usage since before the Roman period. Certainly, this is the interpretation of the field systems on Bullock Down above Eastbourne (Drewett 1978). More difficult to determine is any continuity of usage of the centuriated fields around Ripe and Laughton in East Sussex to the north of the Downs – a tract of good soils with a still surviving grid of roads. However, there is little evidence for settlement on the Sussex coastal plain before the Middle Saxon period, by which time the chalklands soil had become degraded. The lower water table may have opened up previously unworkable floodplains for exploitation at this time. Sarah Semple (2008) has identified distinctive topographic traits in cemetery and burial placements, to the point where it is possible to indicate putative early micro-kingdom structures. These polities were, she argues, echoing Cunliffe's discussion (1993), centred on rivers, with burials on estuary headlands, as at Lancing and Slonk Hill above the river Adur, that were highly visible from coastal routes. Certainly, some of the early Anglo-Saxon sites exhibit a preference for exposed hilltops and hill slopes (Welch 1983, 31), although many were low-lying.

All of the above examples that have discussed the patterning of the early Anglo-Saxon settlements have worked from an intimate knowledge of specific localities, up to the scale of counties. Taking a study region wide view of the basic issues now allows us to present a rather different narrative, constructed though the exploration of a series of issues.

## What was the spatial relationship between early cemeteries and their parent settlements?

By concentrating on burial evidence to elucidate issues of wealth and spatial context, the first potential stumbling block is whether cemeteries and settlements actually share the same space and whether the one can be taken to signify the presence of the other. There is an implicit assumption that a cemetery community of a certain relative wealth would have had a settlement with components that were of a similar status. From what has been identified from settlement excavations, a typology has been proposed (Welch 1985; Hamerow 2002). Essentially the types are: single isolated farm units (New Wintles Farm, Oxfordshire); small hamlets (Chalton, Hampshire); larger settlements (Sutton Courtenay, Berkshire; Mucking, Essex); areas with only SFBs, that may be craft industrial complexes (Flögeln, Lower Saxony, Germany); settlements with great halls with dimensions in excess of 23m × 7m (74ft × 23ft), often with enclosures – possibly royal/aristocratic estate centres (Yeavering, Northumberland; also Long Wittenham (Hamerow, pers. comm.)). Martin Welch's suggestion of 150m as the probable distance between a settlement and its attendant cemetery merited testing across the project dataset, although it is acknowledged, from the example of Mucking (Hamerow 1993) that both components might drift across space over time. The number of genuinely early (phase A with a start date before AD 550) paired sites recorded for this discussion, due to the exigencies of excavation, focuses inevitably on a rather restricted set, listed in Table 27, and of necessity is rather speculative in the precise dating of settlement foundation. The criterion for inclusion is a recorded proximity limit of 1000m between site centroids. In practice however, there were very few other candidate sites available to include in the discussion, as the distances between the remainder were much greater and pointed to no practical or genuine spatial association. An upper limit of 700 to 1000m distance between contemporary settlement and cemetery during phase A is therefore asserted.

It is noted that a disproportionate number of these adjacencies involve mixed rite cemeteries, where the number of individuals buried is above the norm for the immediate region. As Table 27 illustrates, 150m to 250m is a not unreasonable estimate for the probable proximity of the outer edges of adjacent contemporary features.

### Case Study: The Lower Ouse Valley, East Sussex

A range of factors appear to have been taken into consideration when laying out the relative locations of settlements and cemeteries, as shown on Figure 16, rather than an absolute desire to live cheek-by-jowl with the immediate ancestors. Sites might be more spread out spatially beyond 250m in order to adapt to the terrain, although the reverse may also hold good – the Rookery Hill complex of cemetery and settlement (SsxBPS), with a Roman precursor settlement (Bell 1977), may be an example of this, given the restricted nature of the slope on which it is sited and the requirement for arable and pasturing opportunities, producing adjacency as the optimum relationship in order to maximise the use of space. Additionally, the complex, together with the Bronze Age barrows on the skyline, would have acted as highly visible markers for coastal traffic,

## 5. Sites, Locations and Soils

*Table 27. Cemetery and settlement proximities*

| | Settlement site | Code | Cemetery site | Code | Distance between centroids | Distance to nearest major routeway |
|---|---|---|---|---|---|---|
| 1 | Rookery Hill | SsxBPS-SET1 | Rookery Hill | SsxBPS-MC1 | 100m | 2km+ |
| 2 | Eynsham | OxfEHM-SET1 | Wytham View | OxfEHM-MC1 | 270m | 1km+ |
| 3 | Barton Court Farm | BrkABD-SET1 | Barton Court Farm | BrkABD-IC7 | Adjacent | 600m |
| 4 | Barrow Hills | BrkRLY-SET1 | Barrow Hills | BrkRLY-MC1 | 220m | 1km+ |
| 5 | Amphitheatre | GlsCCR-SET1 | Barton Roman Villa | GlsCCR-BI1 | 1000m | 400m |
| 6 | Bickton | HtsFDB-SET1 | Huckles Bridge | HtsHYD-BC1 | 150m | 1km+ |
| 7 | Northbrook | HtsMDV-SET2 | Weston Colley | HtsMDV-IC1 | 1000m | 2km+ |
| 8 | 10–20 Kent Road | KntOPN-SET1 | Poverest Road | KntOPN-MC1 | 400m | 50m |
| 9 | Highdown Hill | SsxFRG-SET1 | Highdown | SsxFRG-MC1 | Adjacent | 1km+ |
| 10 | Sherbourne House | GlsLLE-SET2 | Butler's Field | GlsLLE-MC1 | 500m | 350m |
| 11 | Springhead | KntNFT-SET1 | Southfleet | KntSFT-MC1 | 80m | 200m |
| 12 | Coln House School | GlsFFD-SET2 | Tanner's Field | GlsFFD-MC1 | 700m | 4km |
| 13 | Brighthampton | OxfSLK-SET1 | Brighthampton | OxfSLK-MC1 | 170m | 1km+ |
| 14 | New Wintles Farm | OxfEHM-SET2 | New Wintles Farm | OxfEHM-IC2 | 130m | 2km+ |
| 15 | Abbots Worthy | HtsICH-SET1 | Worthy Park | HtsKWY-MC1 | 550m | 750m |
| 16 | Collingbourne Ducis | WltCBD-SET1 | Collingbourne Ducis | WltCBD-IC1 | 600 | 1km+ |
| 17 | Dolland's Moor | KntNNH-SET1 | Dolland's Moor | KntNNH-IC2 | 400m | 1km+ |
| 18 | Saltwood | KntSWD-SET3 | Stone Farm Bridleway | KntSWD-IC1 | 200–400m | 2km+ |
| 19 | Middle Street Meadow | WltNSM-SET1 | Low Field | WltNSM-IC2 | 300–700m | 150m |
| 20 | Shavard's Farm | HtsCAM-SET1 | Shavard's Farm | HtsCAM-IC1 | 350 | 800m |
| 21 | Chalton | HtsCLF-SET1 | Chalton Peak | HtsCLF-IC1 | 280m | 4km |
| 22 | Purwell Farm | OxfCSN-SET4 | Purwell Farm | OxfCSN-IC5 | 670m | 1km+ |
| 23 | Cassington Enclosure | OxfCSN-SET2 | Smith's Pit II | OxfCSN-IC5 | 500m | 650m |
| 24 | Grove Farm | WltMLV-SET1 | Grove Farm | WltMLV-IC1 | Adjacent | 1.1km |
| 25 | Corporation Farm | BrkABD-SET5 | Saxton Road | BrkABD-MC1 | 550m | 400m |

indicating the location of the Ouse river valley through the Downs. The actual entrance to the river was further to the east at Seaford. Other communities, as yet only indicated by unassociated finds and metal detected material, appear to be strung out along the east side of the river Ouse within a coherent ribbon of settlement, thus limiting the spatial spread of any one group. The nearest

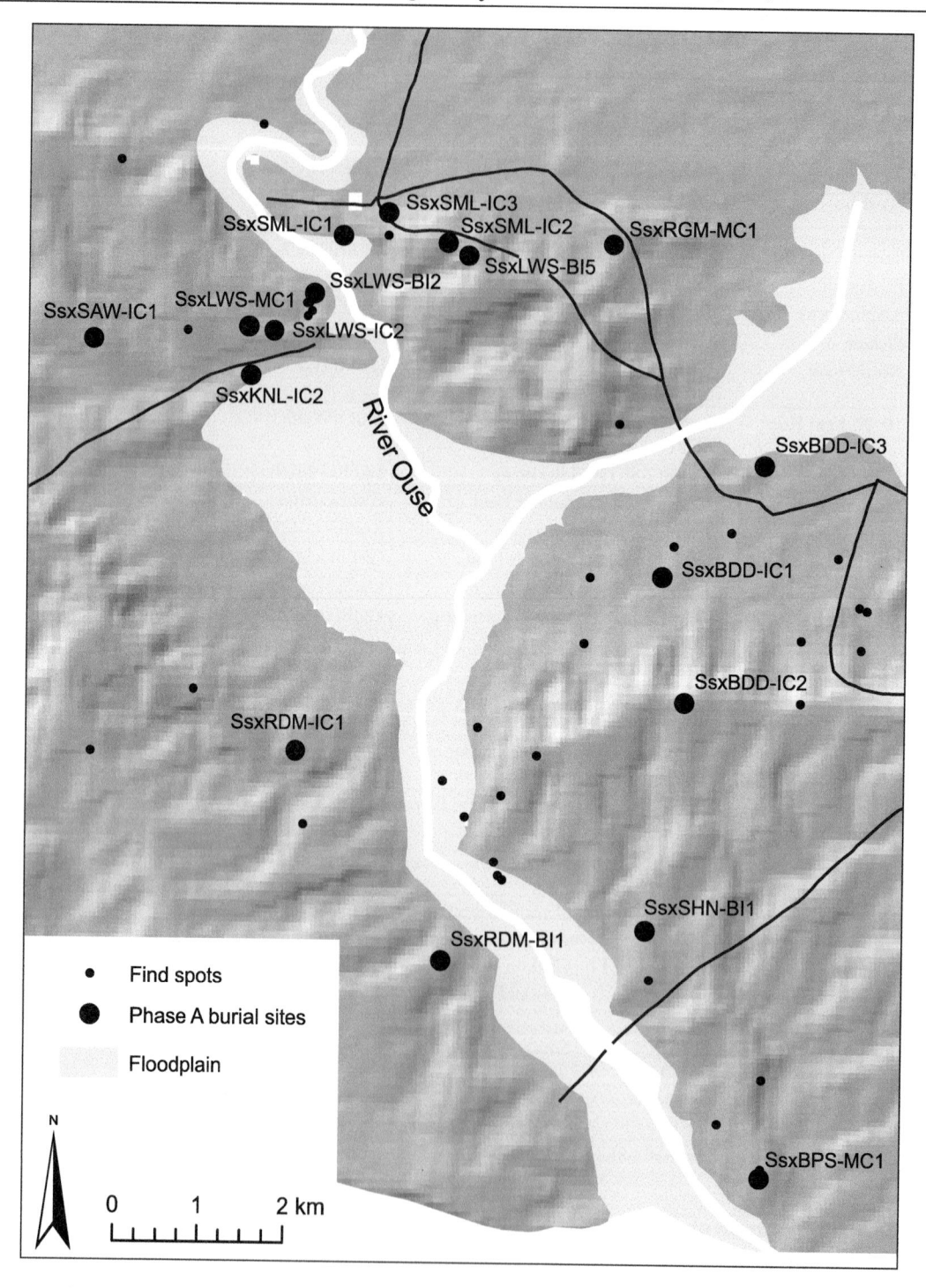

*Figure 16. Case study area: the Lower Ouse Valley, Sussex, showing the floodplain, routeways, burial sites and find spots in Phase A*

*Figure 17. View north west from the lower slopes Chessell Down, Isle of Wight, Anglo-Saxon cemetery, overlooking the entrance to the Solent*

community may yet prove to be in the vicinity of the crossing point of the Roman road/trackway across the Ouse some 2.2km to the northwest, perhaps analogous to the location of the Malling cemeteries on the same river above Lewes. The next community to this may be indicated by an imprecisely dated isolated weapon burial a further 1km along the Downland scarp from the river crossing, located above the river valley.

## Where were the sites with the earliest artefactual evidence?

Plate 2 shows those cemetery sites with artefactual material most probably deposited in the fifth century. The string of sites marks a broad swathe across and around the study area, with seven distinct clusters:

- The Upper Thames Valley (beyond the Goring Gap);
- From the River Medway west to Guildford, that is West Kent and Surrey;
- East Kent between Canterbury and the coast to the east of there;
- East Sussex between Eastbourne and Brighton, possibly extending westwards towards Hampshire;
- The Isle of Wight;
- Around Salisbury and the confluence of the main tributaries of the River Avon;
- Around the upper reaches of the rivers Itchen and Test.

Each of these areas exhibits similarities to the others, apart from the Upper Thames Valley. The sites focus on Roman roads, major trackways and/or major river crossing points throughout the study region. Very few sites appear as isolated entities. The Upper Thames Valley group, whilst clearly dependent on the river as the major artery, deploy onto the arterial rivers and the terraces above the flood plain – together they form a more coherent and interconnected grouping. Whether these were discrete clusters of settlement or were contiguous, the gaps eventually to be filled through further excavation, is open to debate. There are clearly defined empty zones in the fifth century, primarily the Weald and the area to the west of a line from Cirencester to the River Avon. But it is the interstices which attract attention. The clear gap between East Kent and the west Kent/Surrey cluster, known to be filled in from the sixth century onwards with sites such as Faversham and Milton Regis, may be actual, given the absence of genuinely early artefacts amongst the archives of these nineteenth century railway-cut cemeteries. The gap between East Kent and East Sussex, also appears actual in the fifth century. A clear divide between East and West Sussex is proposed, given the ongoing paucity of sites either side of the river Adur from Brighton to Highdown. The line of the South Downs west of Highdown presents a conundrum. Highdown itself has an impressive range of early material (Welch, 1983 and unpublished notes) enhanced by the rare find, two kilometres to the north-west, of a fifth century hoard, at Patching (White *et al.* 1999), although this latter assemblage should perhaps be characterised as indicative of flight and abandonment rather than progressive settlement. The locations of other early sites may not yet have been subject to archaeological investigation – the one site that has been excavated at Apple Down was the result of a metal detectorist find (Down and Welch 1990). The site at Droxford, Hampshire is plausibly late fifth century in origin, but on current evidence appears isolated – its location does fit, however, with the scheme proposed below in terms of its relationship to a river crossing point and a Roman road and as such has similarities to another seemingly isolated site at Guildown, Surrey. Taken as a regional whole, it now appears that the extent of the early Anglo-Saxon presence framed the entire study region in the fifth century and was not a progressive movement westwards, rather a one-off claiming of space.

## What are the spatial relationships of the cemeteries and settlements to routeways and other topographical features?

An assessment of the relationships of the component parts of the 25 identified linked cemetery/settlement sites to major routeways, including Roman roads, prehistoric trackways and substantial rivers, flood plains and their relative elevations addresses the issue of which of the sites would be encountered first by travellers through the landscape. The results are presented in Table 28.

For those complexes with the cemetery nearest to the routeway, few lie directly on the Roman road, prehistoric trackway or by the riverside. The presence of minor routes, such as droveways and local, short distance tracks leading from the main routes are inferred in these cases, although more detailed proofs are required through case studies. The distance from the nearest major routeway varies between 50m and up to 4km, but the intervening terrain does not appear to impede access to the routeway. Indeed, in some cases, the cemetery may serve to mark the presence of a settlement from a range of adjacent routeways, regardless of its greater proximity to one. For

## 5. Sites, Locations and Soils

*Table 28. Cemetery and settlement adjacencies to routeways*

| Cemetery nearest to routeway | Settlement nearest to routeway | Equally distant from nearest routeway |
|---|---|---|
| 4, 7, 8, 13, 14, 15, 16, 18, 20, 21, 22, 23 | 2, 10, 12, 19 | 1, 3, 5, 6, 9, 11, 17, 24, 25 |
| Total 12 | Total 4 | Total 9 |

those four complexes where the settlement is closest to the nearest main routeway, in all cases here the river Thames, the cemetery is situated on higher ground above the settlement and thus would have been more visible from a distance, although with some variation in the visibility when travelling either up or down stream. The locations of the group of nine where the cemetery and settlement are equidistant from the main routeways tend to support the proposition of cemetery visibility as an indicator of settlement. Four examples are adjacent to one another, as at Rookery Hill (SsxBPS). The cemetery and settlement at Highdown, West Sussex (SsxFRG) are located within and around an Iron Age enclosure at a visible high point along the coast. However, the enclosure is roughly equidistant between the Lewes to Chichester Roman road along the Downs and a tidal inlet (now infilled) at Hangleton, thus offering a visible indicator of a trans-shipment point for coastal traffic. Similarly the mixed rite cemetery at Saxton Road, Abingdon, Berkshire (BrkABD) is situated on rising ground above the Thames flood plain, at the confluence with the River Ock, again marking a possible trans-shipment point.

As a control exercise, the locations of phase A cemeteries were mapped against 78 recorded examples of unassociated potsherds and ceramic vessels from findspots dated to the period AD 450–600, taken to be potential indicators of settlement activity. The friable nature of this material and its similarity to Iron Age pottery that can preclude secure identification must be acknowledged. Nevertheless, the examples were mostly found through county archaeological society fieldwalking projects, where local knowledge for identification must be accepted. These societies, particularly in Hampshire and Wiltshire have been particularly assiduous in their hunt for this material, given the paucity of recognised early settlements in these areas. Only eight examples could be generated where the cemetery had relevant pottery located in the vicinity – that is within 1km. It is noted that both site types always had the same parish code.

One early dated settlement with no contemporary cemetery is at Lower Warbank, Keston, Kent (Philp 1973). A later, unfurnished cemetery of five burials was found 500m to the east in the churchyard situated above but overlooking the low lying valley route through to the London to Lewes Roman road traversing the North Downs. Following the assessment of the locational attributes of the early cemeteries, it can now be suggested that a likely optimum location for an early cemetery here would be above the settlement and within view of movement along the routeway, possibly between the settlement and the later cemetery and approaching the 150m proximity proposed above. The settlement itself is in the vicinity of a Roman mausoleum, although no continuity of use has been indicated archaeologically.

## What kinds of soils do the cemetery/settlement communities occupy for their resource base and how does this compare with those occupied by the Later Roman sites? Were there spatial and temporal variations in site selection criteria?

If the above analysis points to a strategic reasoning for site location underpinning the early Germanic presence, their resource base must also be drawn into consideration. Do their choices reflect the Roman use of the landscape, replicating their use of environmental resources? Do rivers and routeways inevitably draw new populations to the best resource base? This issue was addressed by considering the location of sites in relation to the productive potential of the soils, as identified using the re-worked Soil Scapes data.

### Roman sites

There is significant patterning evident in the soil-based location of Roman archaeological complexes, in nearly all phases of the first to fourth centuries AD, even though the very large number of sites meant that all soils saw some form of settlement. When all site types are mapped against the Soil Scapes data, it is shown that they significantly favour alkaline soils throughout and avoid acidic soils. There is a general avoidance of poor fertility soils (1 and 2 in the classification) and those with impeded drainage. Their favoured soil types were the free-draining, good-quality ones with fertility 3 and 5 (in particular 3, 5, 7), a preference that is marked in all phases.

### Early Anglo-Saxon complexes

There is a trend of favouring soils of fertility 3 evident throughout the study period into phase C. Whilst this is not evident in relation to the cemeteries of phase A, it becomes increasingly important during phase AB and ABC, and BC; that is to say for the most long-lived cemeteries. This pattern can be refined to particular edaphic units. During phase A there is a trend towards F5FD and F3FD soils (F4FD are inconsequential in overall size and all exist in Devon outside the study area). From the point of view of individual soil types this trend for good quality free draining soils is all the more evident: phase A cemeteries are correlated with SS7 (*i.e.* F5FD), with colonisation of next-best free-draining soils taking place in following phases (*i.e.* F3FD soils of SS3 and SS5, during phase AB, ABC, and BC). There are fewer correlations evident in short-lived cemeteries of phase B and C, which are still correlated with good quality soils or free-draining fertile areas. The implication of this finding is that long-lived cemeteries occupy the best soils, and had done so since their inception, whilst those that do not are more short lived. It is possible that short-lived cemeteries and their living communities were located for network utility rather than soils. Table 29 shows the percentage of sites in each phase, and ones spread over several phases, against their contextual soil type.

There is significant patterning evident in the cemetery locations, in nearly all phases. Taken together there is a general avoidance of poor fertility soils (1) and a disposition for good quality soils (3 and 5), where 620 of 805 are located. However, it appears as if free-drainage was more important that fertility, with some numbers of cemeteries located on F2FD. They also significantly

*Table 29. Percentage of sites by phase against soil type*

| Phase | Fertility 1–2 free draining | Fertility 3–5 free draining |
|-------|------------------------------|------------------------------|
| A     | 14.6%                        | 77.1%                        |
| AB    | 21.3%                        | 66.2%                        |
| ABC   | 17.8%                        | 73.2%                        |
| B     | 36.4%                        | 60.6%                        |
| BC    | 8.8%                         | 76.8%                        |
| C     | 26.2%                        | 59.5%                        |

favour alkaline soils in all phases and avoid acid and unknown soils. This pattern is broadly similar to that of the Roman period.

The issue raised in earlier researches, alluded to above, was for there to be a separation of cemetery and settlement by soil type. As a test of this the settlement site data was mapped independently of that for the cemeteries. Again, there is a general disposition for free-draining soils, including F2FD, F3FD and F5FD, although with the exception of the latter this is not statistically significant. They also significantly favour alkaline soils in all phases, and avoid acidic soils. There is a statistically significant correlation with F5FD pays, particularly of soil type 7 but also soils type 5. This is a pattern comparable with that from cemeteries. It is therefore likely that cemeteries are found in the same locations as settlements, as they both display a similar preference for soils types.

The environmental characteristics of those areas excluded from settlement during the study period are ones of poor drainage and/or low fertility. Whilst these areas may have had Roman settlements, they did not come into play again until much later in the Anglo-Saxon and Later Medieval periods, although their usage for seasonal pasturage and ore mining is not excluded, given the routeways crossing them, for example the Weald and the West Surrey/East Berkshire heaths.

## What relationships can be determined between the place-name data and the phase A and early phase B sites (AD 450–600)?

The potentially early place name components of -*ham*, -*hamm*, -*ing*, -*tun*, -*walh* and -*wic* were mapped against the various soil types to investigate whether they related to a definable site selection strategy. It was found that all of the components taken together demonstrated some patterning relative to soils fertility: they significantly avoid soils of quality 1 and 2, and favoured high fertility quality 5. However, this pattern is not generally supported by examination of individual place-name elements.

It was found that -*hamm* are correlated with soil fertility 4, but this could not be refined to individual soils. In general they avoid alkaline soils. Place-names in -*ing* avoid quality 1 and 2, and favour fertility 4. Although there was no statistical significance with F3FD -*ing* are closely correlated in particular with soil type 5 (Herb-rich chalk and limestone pastures; lime-rich deciduous woodlands suitable for Pasture-Woodland). These correlations are particularly evident in Sussex and East Kent.

*Figure 18. The excavation at Apple Down, Sussex mixed rite cemetery (image courtesy The Welch Archive)*

Place-names in -tun avoid quality 1 and 2, and favour fertility 3 and 5; in particular F3FD and F5ID. The latter correlation is not matched by any other place-name element or archaeological complexes, and must reflect a 'late' phenomenon (*i.e.* the naming of *tuns*) in the Somerset levels and Dorset, where the majority of these correlations occur. There are no -*tuns* correlated with these 'poor' soils east of Stanton Fitzwarren, Wiltshire. They avoid acid, but favour alkaline soils. There are no significant correlations between soil fertility and the elements -*walh*, -*wic*, and -*ham*. However, the former two appear to be incomplete data sets, derived as they were from publications and would profit from checking against the more detailed University of Nottingham Place-Name database in the longer term. Of the pre-731 place-names, the only significant correlation was between these places and F2NW soils, (in particular those of soil type 22); a correlation which is not paralleled by other place-name elements or archaeological complexes. These correlations are particularly evident in two locations: around Selsey Bill and in the Thames estuary near Dartford. It may be significant that the 33 of 63 pre-731 place-names are located on 'poor' quality soils (*i.e.* Fertility 1 and 2), with only 11 of 63 on free-draining soils of Fertility 3–5; especially given that these latter two soil types are where the majority of archaeological complexes are located in both the Roman and Anglo-Saxon periods. There is no significant trend with soils acidity/alkalinity, but a strong preference for unknown soils. Although it is difficult to generalise about these findings, they would seem to indicate that the names are later than the earliest of the Anglo-Saxon archaeology and may reflect an in-filling of the landscape after the first phases of settlement.

*Figure 19. View south east from the Anglo-Saxon cemetery at Bradford Peverell, Dorset, towards the Roman road from Dorchester as it approaches the crossing point of the River Frome*

## Conclusions

From the above deployments of the data, mapped within its environmental and productive context, it is now proposed that the locations of the earliest Germanic presence conformed to a pre-determined cultural and strategic guideline, one that took as its template the Roman usage of the landscape, but without direct replication. The Early Anglo-Saxon guideline required the presence of a community to be signalled from afar to those approaching by the visual marker of the cemetery, particularly if indicated by burial mounds, either new or reused prehistoric features, or by the presence of post structures, such as found at Apple Down over cremations.

Here one must consider the function of a cemetery both as a repository of community heritage and memory and also as a spatial marker for the living. The same factor, that is the need to identify the presence of a community, both of the living and the dead, could have resulted in a close proximity between settlement and cemetery as much as a slightly more distant one, dependent on the kinds of routeways used and the sight lines dictated by the terrain. The conjunction of living and dead, particularly if the traveller was routed to pass or go through the cemetery in order to access the settlement, would only confirm the weight of presence in the landscape of these communities and asserted their control and domination and right to be there. The environmental resource base is in many senses pre-determined, but the site locations vary between those with a clear strategic impact on routeways and trans-shipment points and those with a clearer intent on occupying the most fertile and workable soils. That they were able to do so indicates that the indigenous population did not have a strong hold over these aspects in the study region as a whole, although localised variations are to be expected. It now appears that the wealth of the kingdom of East Kent was built on control of trade and not to a greater extent on the agricultural capacity of its hinterland. Access to better soils may have prompted its expansion into West Kent and Surrey in the sixth century.

However, is this pattern restricted to the particular topographic and cultural circumstances of the study region, or can it be extrapolated to the areas beyond? Here the work of Mary Chester-Kadwell (2009) on early Anglo-Saxon Norfolk offers the most recent comparable research material, with parallel results. For example, intervisibility of burial site and settlement is demonstrated statistically (*ibid.*, 144), with a similar spatial relationship and range of distances identified for southern Britain. The encounter of early Anglo-Saxon complexes with earlier features is seen as incidental, given that valley sides were 'the most commonly settled locations' (*ibid.*, 144). In Norfolk too there was a close relationship with the location of Roman sites, a 'common co-location'.

# 6. Surrey: A Case Study

## Surrey in the documentary sources

The landscape of the modern county of Surrey includes many of the environmental and cultural attributes of the study region as a whole and therefore presents itself as a case study to investigate in more detail the issues raised. Of particular interest is whether the Germanic presence of the fifth and sixth centuries relates to earlier and later administrative boundaries, particularly civitates and parish boundaries. Particular reference can now be made to the *Tribal Hidage* document of tax assessments.

Much of what became the historic county of Surrey should probably be seen as sharing the same political structure as west Kent had before it was annexed into Kent in the late sixth century. In terms of its archaeology, the material culture of its cemeteries in the fifth to sixth centuries, the majority of which occur within the southern half of Greater London, shares a great deal in common with those of west Kent and south-west Essex. Cemetery sites such as those at Orpington and several in the Dartford and Northfleet area in Kent as well as the pair of cemeteries across the Thames at Mucking are relevant here. Kings and kingdoms are not necessary elements of Anglo-Saxon political organisation and looser structures in which freemen met periodically in assemblies and elected war leaders when required, as existed in Old Saxony in continental Germany (approximating to modern Niedersachsen), may have been used by Saxon communities in the Lower Thames region. Bede uses the Latin term *provincia* (or province) as the equivalent to a kingdom with its own people, its own ruler and once Christian also its own bishop. A sub-unit of a province is referred to as a *regio* (or region).

Surrey takes its name from such a small political unit – a *regio*. Bede mentions the original 'southern region' in the context of the foundation of a monastery at Chertsey (Cerotaesi) by Eorcenwald, who was to become bishop of London, as being located 'in regione Sudergeona'. John Blair (1991) has argued that this 'region' was probably that of the *Woccingas* centred on modern Woking and may well have been related to a matching territory south of the Hog's Back centred on Godalming. It lay south of a territory to the north of the Thames. This was presumably centred on the Staines area (Roman Pontibus) and perhaps called the region of the '*Stæningas*'.

In the charter issued in the name of Frithuwold dated to 672 x 674 granting further landed

95

estates to the Chertsey monastery the name of the 'southern region' has been extended to a province extending from the boundary of the Chertsey territory with the *Sunningas* in Berkshire eastwards to the south bank of the Thames opposite *Lundenwic* on the Strand and the walled Roman city of London. Thereafter Surrey seems to have taken broadly the format it retained as a historical county until recently. The Mercians had taken over the Thames region and exercised overlordship over much of southern England in the 670s and Frithuwold was a Mercian nobleman in the service of King Wulfhere who governed Surrey as a 'subregulus' and probably also neighbouring regions on behalf of his king. In the 680s Surrey came under West Saxon rule, but within a few decades Mercian supremacy was reasserted and this remained the case until the 820s when the West Saxons liberated south-east England from Mercian control. So, Surrey was a region that became a province apparently without ever having its own king or royal dynasty by a series of ad hoc decisions and survived as a Late Saxon shire of Wessex, as did the formerly independent kingdoms of Sussex (the South Saxons) and Kent (the Cantwarena).

In the *Tribal Hidage* manuscripts, which seem to describe an earlier, seventh-century situation, a province-sized unit valued at seven thousand hides of land, which might fit either in northern Hampshire (the Basingas) together with Surrey or else in Berkshire (the Sunningas) together with Surrey, is represented by combining the Nox gaga and the Oht gaga (a north and east people). Another alternative is that the names of the Hendrica (3500 hides) and the Unecunga (1200 hides) could represent scribal alterations for the Sudrica (Surrey) and the Sunninga (Sunningas of Berkshire). As the historical evidence amply illustrates, we seem to be witnessing a situation of flux regarding territorial ownership. There were only a few fixed points and continually shifting allegiances amongst the upper orders of society.

### The archaeological evidence

For Surrey the project has recorded over 250 early Anglo-Saxon sites, 7% of the total for southern England. These consist of 70 burial sites of various types, 28 settlements and a further 158 findspots (at 2007). The number and range of sites is comparable with that for the neighbouring county of Berkshire (including modern south Oxfordshire). There are individual records for over 900 people in Surrey and a further 600 can be inferred, which suggests 1500 as a working figure for the county or 8% of the total for the whole study region. Yet, these 900 people are accompanied by only 784 objects or 3% of the regional number for grave finds. By phase, we can observe that there is

*Table 30. Surrey people and their objects by phase*

|  | Surrey people (% in each phase) | Their objects (% in each phase) | Regional people (% in each phase) | Regional objects (% in each phase) |
| --- | --- | --- | --- | --- |
| Phase A | 48% | 66% | 44% | 49% |
| Phase B | 31% | 26% | 30% | 30% |
| Phase C | 22% | 8% | 26% | 21% |

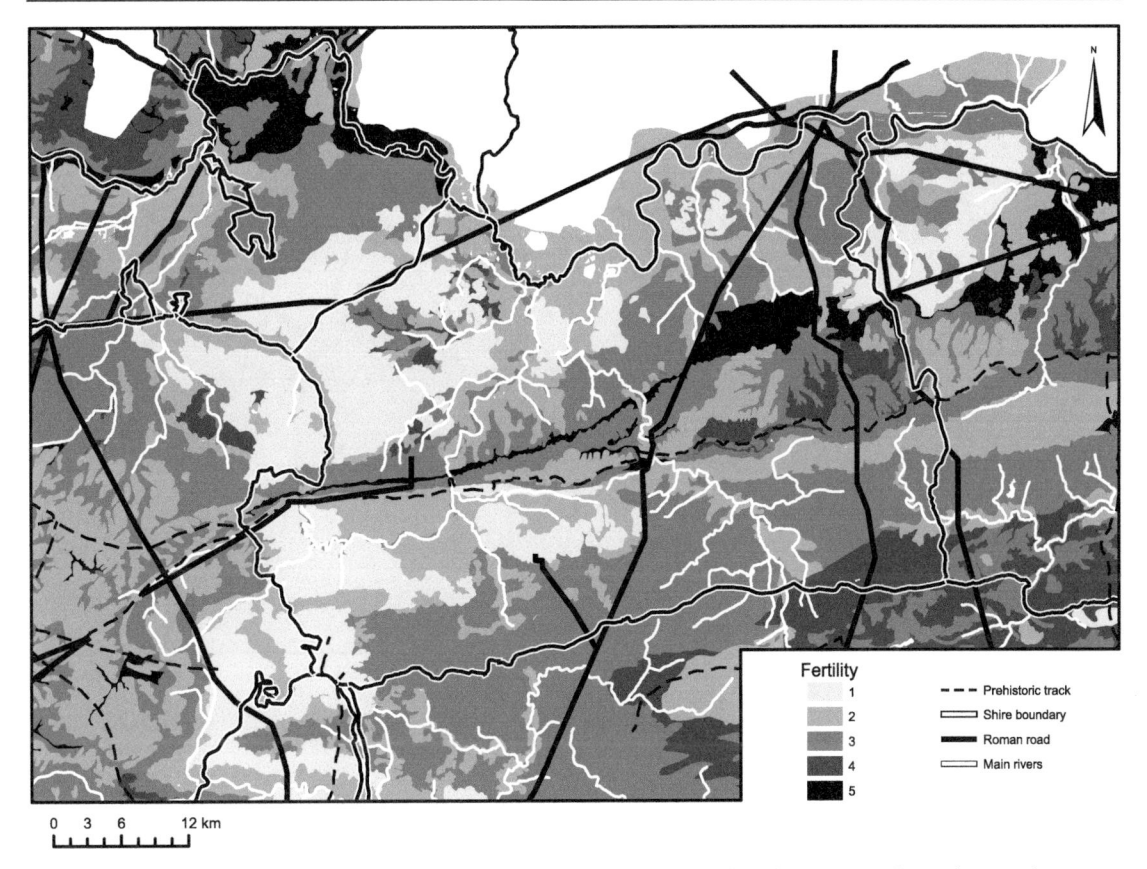

*Figure 20. Surrey case study area landscape block with Roman roads radiating out from the London River Thames crossing points*

a dramatic fall-off from phases A to C in terms of the numbers of objects that these people have, when looked at in the wider context of the regional picture. So, the Surrey area appears to begin like many others within the study region in the fifth and sixth centuries in terms of its burial wealth and yet becomes markedly poorer by the second half of the seventh century by comparison with elsewhere. It should be noted that Sussex follows a very similar pattern to Surrey in this respect.

As John Hines observed in his 2004 review of the foundations of Surrey, a cemetery site such as Mitcham with 238 individuals, by far the largest in Surrey, probably represents a community of only 25–30 adults at any given moment in time over a 150–200 year period of use. In the main, early Anglo-Saxon cemeteries appear to represent smallish communities, but it could be argued that they are not representative of the whole population within the landscape, in particular of any pre-Saxon native population. Thus, only the middle and upper echelons of society might be visible archaeologically.

The block of landscape, containing modern Surrey, is bounded by 460,000 west to 550,000 east and 30,000 south to 180,000 north. The north-eastwards flow of the major rivers into the

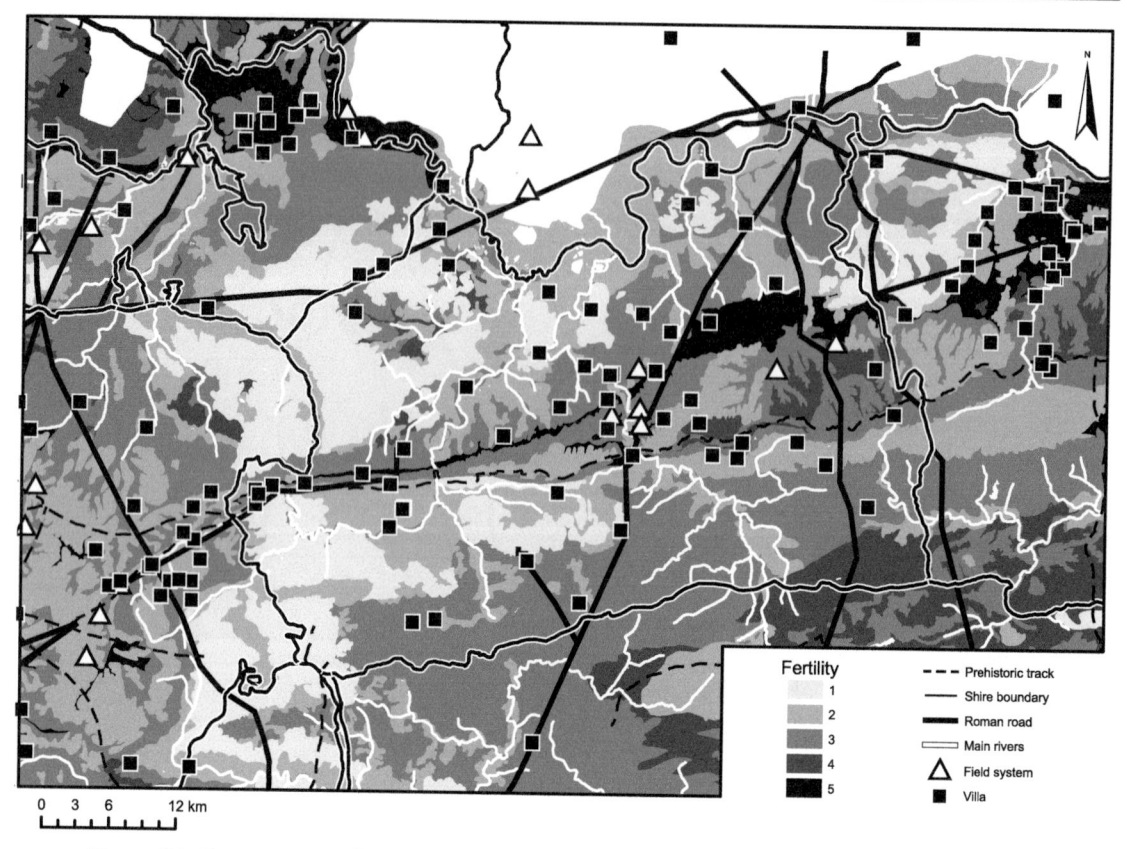

*Figure 21. Surrey case study area soil fertility assessments with Roman villas and field systems*

Thames is matched by the direction of the Roman roads traversing the block towards the focal point of London (Figure 20). The navigability of these rivers is unknown, although ostensibly viable with the use of small shallow-draughted craft such as dugouts. The case study follows a series of maps for this tranche of landscape, superimposing the various elements in a chronological sequence. Plate 3 shows the soil fertility, defined to five levels. The eastern sector has the best soils, primarily on the dip-slopes of the North Downs, with greatest areas of such soils located between the major Roman roads. These soils are also present in the north west part of the block on the Thames floodplains either side of Taplow, between Henley and Windsor. There is also a great deal of poor quality soil suitable only for rough pasture at best and the western sector possesses most of this.

The first question is the extent to which soil fertility affected the Romans' choice of sites for villas and field systems. Such sites, indicated on Figure 21, are strung out along the major roads or at least positioned within a reasonably short distance of them. The other structuring feature is the river valleys, with clusters of field systems recorded to the east of Winchester along the river Itchen, and along the Darenth Valley on the eastern edge of the block. The very poor soils with the lowest fertility levels were ignored, both for field systems and villas. The tendency is for the field systems to be on the better soils, of fertility 3 and above, in the east and north-west parts of

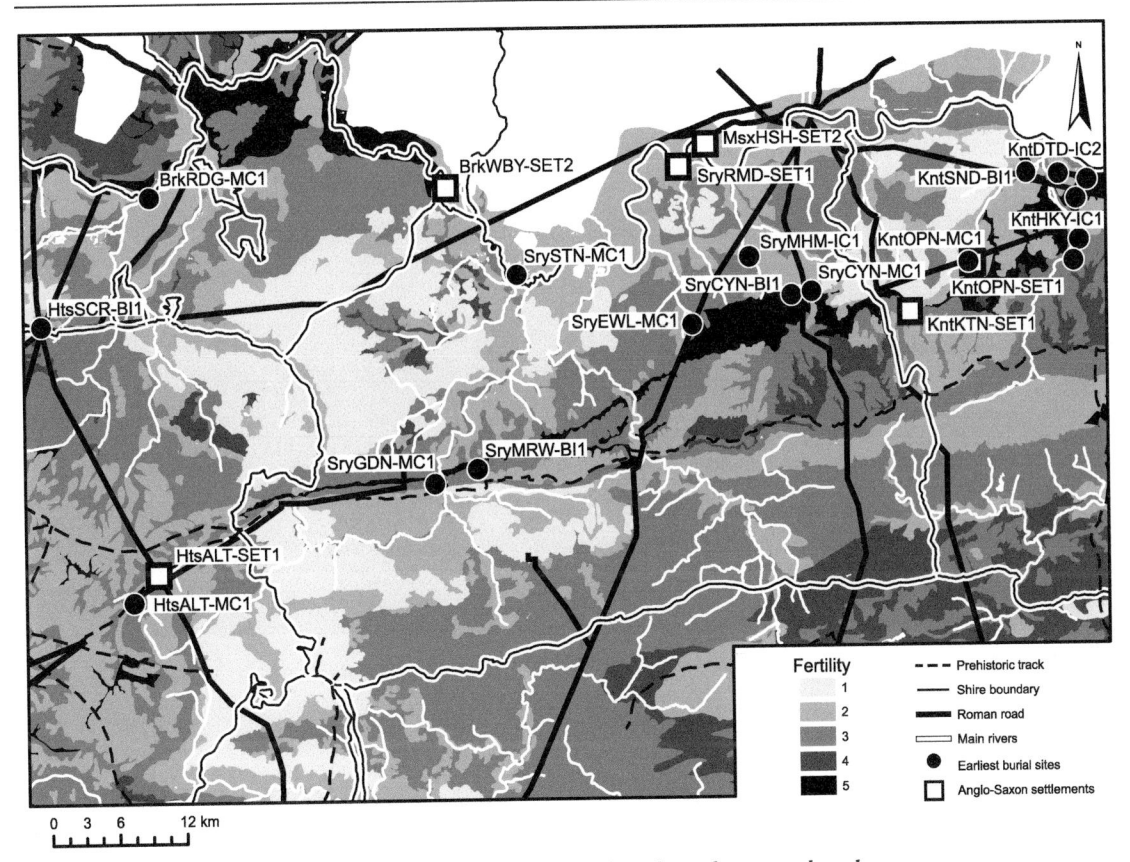

*Figure 22. Surrey case study area earliest burial sites and settlements*

the block. The level of inundation may have precluded the use of parts of the Henley to Windsor sector for farming, other than as water meadows, and it is noticeable that the Roman field systems, whilst still accessing this high fertility soil, are not located near to the river. However, there are plenty of villas on this soil, which is in contrast to the area between the Roman small town of Ewell to the west and Fordcroft Roman villa at Orpington to the east. The absence of villas and field systems there is marked, although this must be explained by the excavation history of the area and the interpretation of the sites found. For example, the 'temple' site at Carshalton has the local hallmarks of a villa, with stone/flint foundations, and the roadside settlements at Croydon and West Wickham may have developed into villa complexes. The bathhouse at Baston Manor, Hayes also suggests a villa, as does the Keston Mausoleum site, all neatly extending the line between Ewell and Fordcroft. Urban expansion in the nineteenth century, primarily through the railway network, may have discovered certain features such as burials but would not have recorded field systems, had they survived, as they were built over. This part of the landscape, as the most valuable agriculturally, could have been worked over many times in the intervening years.

Where is Anglo-Saxon material culture first visible? The earliest burial and settlement sites – those cemetery sites with sufficient evidence to indicate an inception in the fifth century – are

*Figure 23. View northwards towards the middle Thames basin from Guildown Anglo-Saxon cemetery, Surrey*

shown on Figure 22. This block has markedly few early sites in comparison to the Kent and Sussex coasts and the Upper Thames Valley. They all lie to the north of the Weald and their location appears predicated on the major routeways of the Roman roads, probably conjoined with the level trackway along the North Downs. Already there appears to be a divide, with those sites to the east of Ewell over to Orpington along the north side of the Downs in a continuous line from those in west Kent. This leaves Guildown, above modern Guildford, in an isolated and anomalous position. Yet it was so placed to overlook a crossing point of the River Wey and to be encountered by any movement along the high level route. The find of a Late Roman military belt fitting in grave 78 may be pertinent here. The isolated burial from Levylsdene, Merrow further to the east supports the view that this routeway extended to join Stane Street as it passed through the Dorking area. Given the similar topographies of Guildford and Dorking, with a high level routeway, a river crossing point and the addition at Dorking of a major Roman road, the presence of an early cemetery there may be indicated. This proposal is supported by the Portable Antiquity Scheme finds of small long brooches at Leatherhead and Dorking – although these are generally more indicative of casual losses along routeways rather than burials (Maclean and Richardson 2010).

The earliest cemetery/settlement complexes seem to be targeting the best soils to the east of the block, rather as an extension of the early settlement pattern of West Kent. The conjunction of good soils and routeways appears to underpin the pattern in the eastern part of the block. For example the settlement at Lower Warbank, Keston (Philp 1973) is located adjacent to a routeway through the North Downs, linking low level routes through to access the Roman road and an

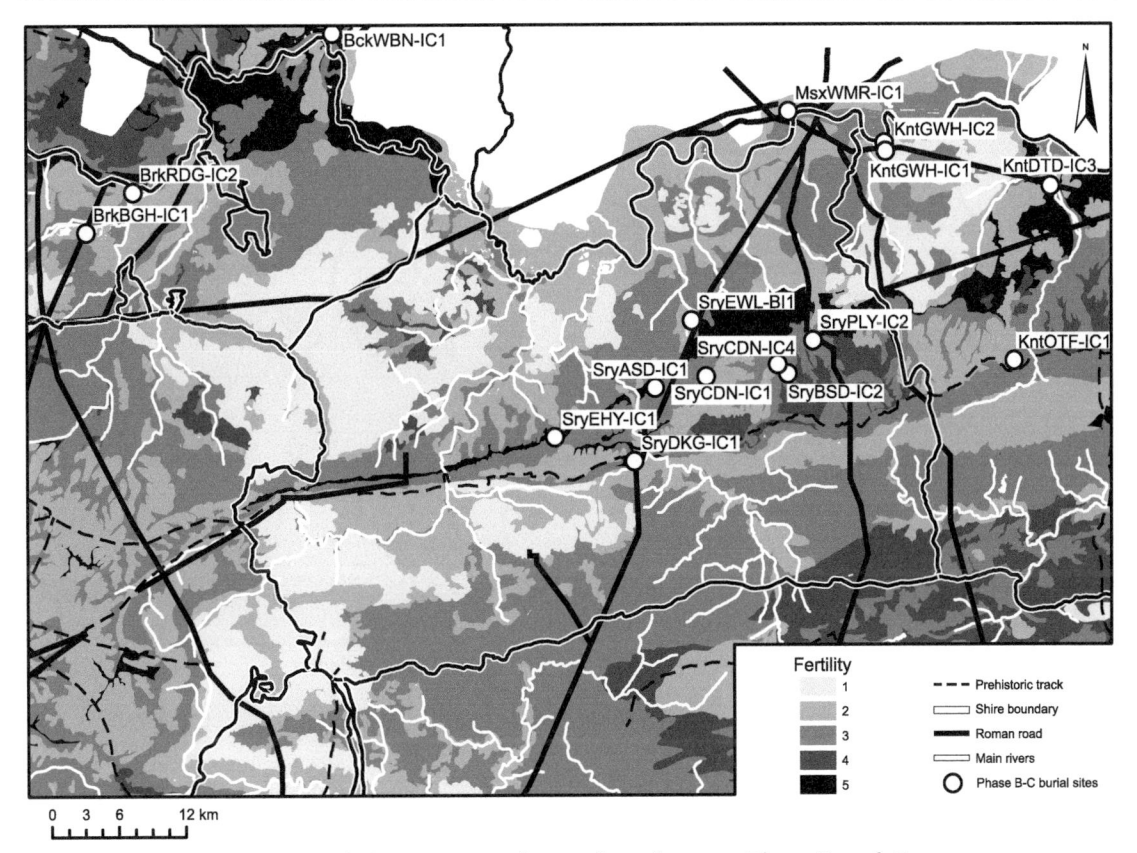

*Figure 24. Surrey case study area burial sites in Phases B and C*

east-west routeway. Similarly, the emerging body of evidence from the area around Croydon and Wallington, which might also include the Mitcham cemetery, points to a densely occupied tract, linking good soils with ongoing access to the North Downs and the Weald, later marked by the high status seventh century barrow cemetery at Farthingdown.

Yet, the pattern of sites also shows an early occupation of the Holmesdale Vale on the south side of the North Downs, between Stane Street and the London to Lewes road to match the Roman villa locations in this area. These are all isolated burials, however, with two inhumations to the west at West Dorking and the Old Vicarage at Reigate and two cremations to the east at Tilburstow Hill Common and at West Heath near Limpsfield. Isolated cremations are rare and cremation appears to be a minority practice across the study region of southern England as a whole, so a certain caution must be employed in ascribing a genuinely early date to these burials.

A Saxon presence is also highly visible in the Middle Thames area adjacent to this major river routeway at Shepperton, where the site appears to represent a community controlling traffic on the river. The preponderance of weapon evidence from the few excavated burials here – a sword and two early spear types – taken together with a buckelurn, indicate an early appropriation of

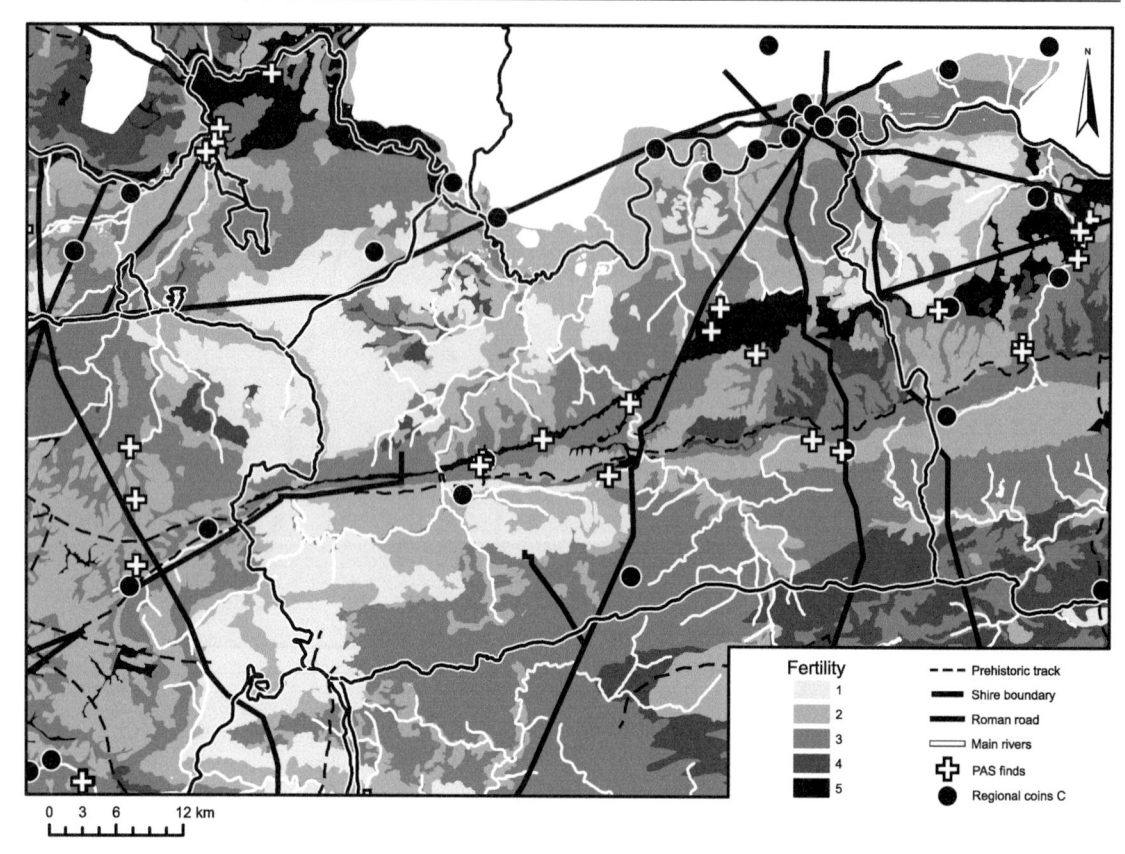

*Figure 25. Surrey case study area with Portable Antiquity Scheme findspots and regional coin finds*

this location, with only relatively poor soils in the vicinity. The remainder of the block to the west is once again a zone devoid of a Saxon presence, on present evidence.

Figure 24 shows project phases B and C, covering the period from 575 to *c*.700 and shows a reduction of activity and a concentration in the core area of the best soils in the vicinity of the major Roman roads. We can point particularly to the downland barrow burials at Gally Hills near Banstead and on Farthingdown, together with a few, rather poorly furnished cemeteries. In particular Farthingdown seems to dominate the perhaps strategic route through the North Downs linking the main settlement zones to the Weald. Yet again there is no cemetery presence in the western sector. The mapping of the parish boundaries (Plate 3) confirms this perception of a significant difference between the eastern and western parts of the block. The pattern of parallel parishes, laid out in order to access a range of environmental resources up the dip-slope of the North Downs, is visible elsewhere, particularly in Sussex for the South Downs and in the Berkshire chalklands. The pattern peters out to the west of Ewell and Stane Street, where the parishes are far more unevenly sized and shaped and occupy only a single soil fertility type. Here then is the edge of the earliest phase of Germanic settlement for agrarian exploitation.

One must ask, however, whether the history of archaeological investigation in Surrey is skewing our perceptions. By turning to the litmus test that is provided by the Portable Antiquities Scheme data these reservations can be resolved, as shown on Figure 25. The pattern already noted is essentially reproduced by this data for the eastern sector. More excitingly, however, there are some tantalising new locations to the south west, associated with the Roman road linking Chichester to Silchester (a sixth-century brooch and a pin of the seventh century or later), and to the north west at the crossing of the Thames at Wargrave by the Roman road from Silchester (cruciform brooch, mount, disc brooch). This might be associated with a detached part of Wiltshire that exists between Wargrave and Wokingham.

Finally, we can look at coins of the seventh to eighth centuries that form the latest datable material in the project data collection, also shown on Figure 25. Here finally is some substantial evidence beyond the restricted eastern sector. The coin evidence from south of the North Downs extends into the Weald along the main Roman roads. The best soils are still in evidence as a continuing preferred location for occupation, but we can observe the beginnings of expansion into the western sector and along the Thames producing a more coherent and in filled settlement pattern.

## Conclusions

To conclude, it appears that the greater part of Surrey, as defined by its current boundary, was an extension of west Kent in terms of its settlement pattern, with cultural affiliations that included the Thames Estuary and areas of East Saxon control. Certainly, the preference for access to good soils is demonstrated, although any exact relationship to Roman precursors, apart from within the key area between the Roman roads striking south west from London, cannot be demonstrated. In any case, the overlap is general rather than precise in this location, but is a significant conjunction of agricultural potential and domination of routeways to and from the south and the Weald. The westward reach of the early settlement appears to be concerned in the main with control of routeways, particularly the westward high level route towards Winchester and the settlements in Hampshire – a rather extended and vulnerable route if the intervening territory were occupied by other, extant communities.

The fact of large tracts of landscape of low obvious fertility would lead one to suggest that these would represent those areas with the lowest hidation value in the *Tribal Hidage* document. However, the settlement of this western area appears to be later, perhaps from the seventh century only, although ownership of it – as detached estates or used for seasonal pasturage – cannot be discounted. In essence, by examining the earliest data for this area, it has not been possible to state with any firm conviction the political and economic situation for this tract in the fifth and sixth centuries as an independent and coherent unit.

# 7. A Common Wealth in Iron?

## Introduction

How important was iron to the economies of the early Anglo-Saxon kingdoms? A concentration of research into the esoteric and ascribed high-status materials, such as gold, silver, garnet, amethyst and glass, has probably served to gloss over the centrality of iron to everyday social life and cultural reproduction. In what ways did iron contribute to changing community profiles of wealth over time? Was it base-line components of a single over-arching exchange system, albeit one exhibiting increasing complexity over time or does it underpin economic change through relative scarcity and changing perceptions of its value?

Metalwork falls in the middle of the order of hierarchical complexity through which peasant or native populations might acquire goods through trade and exchange (Wickham, 2005, 699). This hierarchical structure places goods that could be made in the domestic sphere at its base, such as textiles and clothing, capable of being processed at the household level. This is much less the case for metalwork, for which it is proposed that goods can be exchanged or purchased from part-time or full-time specialist producers in the locality. Articles that were only available to be acquired from peripatetic traders, at seasonal markets or from itinerants, occur at the higher end of the hierarchy. Large-scale exchange networks are usually dependent on goods that can be produced relatively easily, both in terms of labour and raw material inputs, in relatively large quantities, and can be transported without difficulty, thus offering the opportunity of a profit for the producer. Cloth, iron and ceramics can be viewed as the key goods of bulk exchange in past societies, rather than the luxury items that have tended to be the main focus in both historical and archaeological studies. Chris Wickham (2005, 700) has characterised these key staples as the principal markers of the scale and complexity of any economic system, particularly as it moves from one mode of production to another through the dynamic processes of social change. Where archaeological evidence of bulk production and movement of these goods cannot be determined, it is reasonable to assume that that the needs of a household were met by local-scale production activities, unless proved otherwise. One might argue however that an assumption of domestic production regimes within a context of an undifferentiated social structure is an assumption on both counts for the fifth and sixth centuries and requires rigorous investigation. Early Anglo-

Saxon burial communities are iron-rich to varying degrees, as iron was the single most frequently deposited inorganic raw material, providing 48% of all burial finds. In considering the wealth of the Early to Middle Saxon communities in the Driffield region of the East Yorkshire Wolds, Chris Loveluck (1996, 27) observed that the "material prosperity of the inhabitants of the area … seems to reflect an 'economic' inheritance from the Late Roman period, manifested in the production and working of iron, possibly for exchange", although the scale of the iron-ore deposits in the Driffield region are negligible in comparison to those of the study region as a whole (Geological Survey of Great Britain 1935).

## Sources of iron ore

The best-quality iron ores in Britain, in terms of the purity of their iron content, all occur outside of our study region in the north and west of the island. For example, haematites found in Cumberland and South Wales possess a content of 50–80% iron, while those occurring in the Jurassic ridge running from north Oxfordshire through Northamptonshire to Lincolnshire have a significantly lower iron content of 20–30%. Within the study region (see Figure 26), West Somerset has haematite deposits of 27–34% purity (Cleere 1981, quoting Kendall 1893). There are also hydrated ores or 'bog ores', which are uncomplicated to exploit in simple bloomery furnaces. These occur in an outcrop in the Oldhaven Beds between Faversham and Canterbury in Kent, around Broughton-under-Blean and Harbledown. Other relevant deposits exist in the Weald, also at Westbury in Wiltshire, at Dover in Kent; Seend near Devizes in Wiltshire, at Hengistbury Head in Hampshire (now Dorset) and on the Isle of Wight between Hamstead and Yarmouth Lodge. There is also a thick band of iron sand at 23% purity near the base of the Sandgate Beds, which run to the north of Midhurst in West Sussex, with outcrops at Petersfield in south-east Hampshire and at Albury in Surrey (*ibid.*, 56–61). As Figure 26 showing the locations of the regional iron ore deposits clearly illustrates, these are unevenly spread, although with the exception of Berkshire, most of the study region's constituent modern counties encompass some deposits within their boundaries.

## The regional settlement pattern and proximity to iron ore deposits

The question arises as to whether the regional pattern of iron deposits in any way impacted on the choice of site location for the earliest communities (those with a proposed foundation date in the fifth century). When the iron ore deposits are plotted against the earliest burial sites in the study region (Figure 26) no close physical proximity can be established overall. In the light of North European models, discussed below, a direct location of settlements on top of or directly adjacent iron deposits is not necessarily to be expected. Certainly the absence of settled communities, represented by cemeteries, in the vicinity of the Wealden deposits can be noted. Again, the central tracts covering the later heartlands of the West Saxon kingdom are completely devoid of iron deposits. This iron-poor region covers most of Hampshire, central and eastern Wiltshire, that

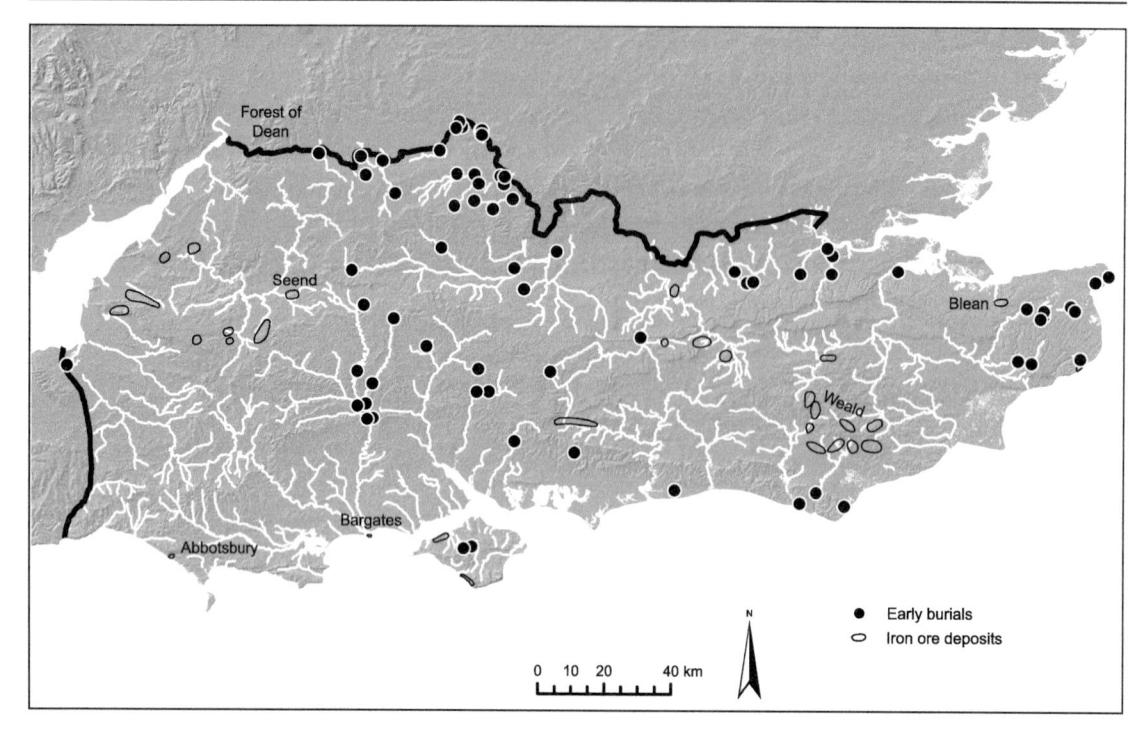

*Figure 26. Study region earliest burials in relation to iron ore deposits*

part of Gloucestershire within the study region, all of Berkshire and the westernmost sector of Surrey. The early burials located furthest to the west in the study area are all isolated and poorly dated inhumations and these suggest that the deposits at Seend, Bargates and Abbotsbury were not within the ambit of early settled communities. By contrast, the Isle of Wight appears to be well resourced for iron, particularly in its western half, which is also the focus of the major cemeteries in phase A (Figure 26). Only in Kent does there appear to be any physical overlap between known cemetery sites and iron deposits, at Dover and the area peripheral to Blean. The degree to which any of these deposits may have been worked is undetermined. In general there is no archaeological evidence for geographical movement towards the iron-ore deposits over time, although access to them might be assumed to support later expansions of iron-working activity, as identified on Middle-Saxon settlements and trading *wics*.

## The processes of iron working

Iron-bearing deposits are excavated by hand for their ores. The ores, especially if the iron content is low, would then be cleaned to remove extraneous material or *gangue*, such as clay, sand or limestone. This process would typically entail pounding the ore to reduce the particle size, then washing it, preferably in running water, before roasting it to drive out the water and make the ore porous. The refined ore would then be smelted in a furnace usually constructed of clay or sand. A spongy mass of bloom and a residue of slag would be produced. Roasting and smelting of the ore might be achieved, however, in a single firing. The recovered bloom would then be converted into worked iron in a forge removing any remaining slag and consolidating the metal (Hodges 1989, 81–2).

The archaeological signatures of each component process vary in kind and visibility. A simple pit for ore extraction, a slagheap, or a whole complex of associated structures might be located. Given the various material requirements at each stage in the process, such as running water, the production of charcoal, clay and sand to build a furnace, then the selection of a site to carry out all of these processes in the same place would suggest a considerable investment in time and infrastructure to produce an industrialised mode of production, as was built up in the Roman complexes in the eastern Weald (Cleere and Crossley 1985). The component processes need have not been carried out in one place, however, but could be separated at the completion of any or every one of the stages. Such a working method would be dependent on the available natural resources, access to human labour and a working knowledge of the requisite technologies.

## Iron working in Roman Britain

The trade in iron was a "significant, if not determining, element in the economy of the ancient world" (Cleere 1984, 3), which, when considered in the context of Roman Britain where the range and depth of evidence is exceptional, assists in determining the overall economic patterns of the region. Cleere proposed a model for the iron industry in Britain wherein minor production sites fed finished products into minor urban centres and then on in turn to major urban centres. Each had reciprocal relations facilitating the circulation of goods, with ports for the export of iron goods at the apex of the system (*ibid.*, fig. 3). Each area, though, probably had a defined geographical range for the supply of iron goods along the Roman road network. The major exit routes for ironwork in southern Britain were by ship via the Thames Estuary and via Dover (*ibid.*, fig. 4).

Roman Britain possessed three primary iron-producing areas (Cleere 1984, 3; fig. 1):

- the Weald in the southeast and within the study region;
- the Forest of Dean just outside, operating on a large scale
- the Jurassic Limestone belt across the east Midlands, operating as a seasonal activity, interspersed with the farming year and pottery manufacture producing on a domestic basis. This area remained as a minor producer throughout the Roman period. (*ibid.*, 3).

This is not an exhaustive list, however, as there is evidence from later prehistory indicating iron-goods production in a variety of locations across Britain. Thus Schubert (1957, 15–17) noted that iron working was evident from the Iron Age contexts on Mount Caburn in East Sussex, in the Mendip Hills of Somerset and on the Lower Greensand in Wiltshire at both All Cannings and Swallowcliffe Down. In late prehistoric contexts, given the outcropping of ore deposits on or near the surface, it would have sufficed to use opencast methods of ore extraction, or within the Weald the digging of round pits (*ibid.*, 17). The Roman iron industry in the Weald was based around several convergent factors. The iron-bearing deposits were of both good and variable qualities, but were fairly small in overall area. They occurred in bands of up to 150 mm in thickness (Hodgkinson 2008, 10) and thus would be quickly exhausted, necessitating a constant search for replacement sources. The complex geology of the Weald offered both easily accessible and disjointed deposits, usually found at the junction of the Wadhurst Clay and the Ashdown Sand (Cleere 1975, 176–7).

The archaeological signature of an iron working site would be a mined source of ore, a working area and a slag heap. A typical bloomery site in the High Weald, combining ore mining and smelting would be located on the banks of a small stream that had cut a channel through the base of the Wadhurst Clay, thus exposing the ore. The resources needed for the smelting process included the iron ore, clay and charcoal, whilst the surface of the Ashdown Sand provided a silty clay-like surface suitable for furnace construction. There were also pockets of derived ore in pure Ashdown Sand layers (Tebbutt, 1981, 281). Hard, steely iron could be produced from good ores, such as those found at Petley Wood, East Sussex (Davidson 1962, 16). The supply of charcoal required to fuel the furnaces was derived from immediately adjacent sources, although whether the industry exploited managed woodlands in the form of regenerating coppice or from the clearance of primary woodland is not readily determinable. The wide range of woody species present in the surviving charcoals suggests little selection was required to achieve the best results (Cleere and Crossley 1985, 37). Oliver Rackham (1995, 75) has calculated that the military ironworks alone, involving a rate of production at 550 tons a year for 120 years, would have required coppiced charcoal from 23,000 acres. Tylecote (1987, 17) commented on the lowly status of the Roman smith, who in general produced only low-grade edge tools, although there are some notable exceptions (see also Tylecote and Gilmour 1986, 99). The Latin term *faber*, found in the later context of the Old English place-name for Faversham in Kent, did not denote uniquely a blacksmith producing artefacts, rather a worker who was equally capable of reducing iron from its ores (Cleere 1975, 174).

The labour requirements to operate a smelting furnace were modest with perhaps only three people needed to supervise, use the bellows and feed the furnace. The preparatory tasks involving ore mining, timber accumulation, charcoal making and furnace building, would have required far greater numbers. It would also demand access to very large quantities of timber for reduction to charcoal, if the smelting were to be carried out repeatedly throughout the year with production simultaneously operated in several furnaces, rather than as a simple one-off event. The ratio of ore required to produce one unit of iron has been estimated at 6:1 (Cleere and Crossley 1985, 78). Variable numbers of people might have been designated to the individual tasks, however, in order to stockpile the necessary materials in advance. The iron output of a single furnace over a year might be in the order of 6 tons (*ibid.*, 79). The forging of the bloom into usable products did not necessarily take place at the bloomery site (Hodgkinson 2008, 24), as the reduction in volume inherent in the process and the small sizes of the furnaces rendered the bloom output into a transportable weight. The size range of blooms in the Early Medieval period was probably smaller than the estimated Roman 8kg maximum (Tylecote 1992, 75). The consumption of iron by the population on an annual basis cannot be calculated meaningfully, but it has been estimated, for example, that a Roman boat might require more than 50kg of iron, mainly in the form of nails, in its construction. Given the presence of such substantial volumes of iron produced in the Roman period, scrapping and recycling iron from various resources would have been worthwhile in the longer term.

The proximity of Roman iron sites within two miles of the major north to south road system crossing the Weald from London has been noted for the western or mid-Wealden group of excavated sites on the High Weald. It has been argued that these sites were operated by private entrepreneurs under licence from the imperial authorities (Cleere 1984, 3), as their end-users were not linked into the military infrastructure. It seems more likely that their customers were civilians and the open urban market (Cleere and Crossley 1985, 61). The very process of road construction across the High Weald may have led military engineers to encounter viable bodies of ore as they progressed, and to exploit these for road metalling. The industrial-scale settlements in the High Weald may have been operating continuously since the pre-Roman Iron Age, as the ore deposits here were less fragmented than elsewhere and were not locally exhausted (Gibson-Hill and Worssam 1976, 251).

The eastern or coastal group of Wealden sites are located in relation to the minor roads and tracks of south-east Sussex, with outlets for their products via the Roman road north to Rochester and thus on to Watling Street and the coast, but also with possible outlets by ship at the estuaries of the eastern Rother and Brede, formerly the river Limen. The northernmost Wealden sites may have supplied London with iron via the major trans-Wealden roads (Cleere 1975, 177–9). The *Classis Britannica*, the Roman fleet operating out of Dover, probably exercised control from the mid-second century AD over the eastern group of sites, which included the major production site at Beauport Park in East Sussex, where the slag extended over more than 8ha. Large-scale iron making ceased for the eastern group for a number of possible reasons. Cleere (1975, 189) has suggested that over-exploitation of local natural resources and the silting up of the river estuaries had restricted access, but the abandonment of its Dover base by the *Classis Britannica* may have increased the vulnerability of these coastal sites to raids by Frankish and Saxon pirates. Major production had ceased completely in both the eastern and western areas by the end of the third century. Only a few sites still functioned into the fourth century and none at all continued into the fifth century (Jeremy Hodgkinson, pers. comm.).

## Iron working in the Western Roman Empire

The main centres of large-scale, government-controlled iron production in mainland Europe within the Roman Empire were in the province of Noricum by the Danube (modern Hungary), the Sana valley in Bosnia, Carinthia in Spain and Aude in Gaul (Davidson 1962, 17). The documented rate of iron production from Wealden sources in Britain would indicate a comparable importance for this particular source in the western half of the Empire. There was a widespread pattern of disintegration of these industries throughout the Later Roman period, which occurred not only in the Britain, but also in Gaul and Switzerland (Helvetia), to be replaced, at least in these two latter regions, by decentralised and localised activities. Without access to high-quality ores, smiths would have become dependent on surface ores and material from old workings (*ibid.*). Continuity of production within the former Roman provinces, albeit on a more moderate scale, is also observed during the fifth to seventh centuries in northern France (Gaul), however (Pleiner 2000, 275) – all of the above offer templates for any continuity of production in Britain in the post-Roman era.

Throughout the Later Roman Empire, organised industries for metal extraction were already in decline before individual provinces were lost to Imperial control (McCormick 2001, 45). Where they survived as continuing activities, the mode of production was far more restricted, fragmented and operated on a smaller scale, producing significantly less in terms of annual tonnage. A regional survey of the production sites in central Gaul around Autun (discussed by McCormick 2001, 45), identifies the area as an industrial zone, with a relatively high density of smelting sites, yet with no integrated settlements. Instead the settlements and villas were located on the periphery of the industrial region, which is analogous to the Weald in certain respects. Industrial activity had ended at Autun by *c.*400, however.

In the western Roman Empire, the division of mining activities into two different modes of production had varying impacts on the local and regional economies (Edmondson 1989, 98–102). Where state-run, it tended to be divorced from the local economy, given that its output was directed towards the needs of the state, in particular meeting military or naval requirements. The subsistence needs of the industrial workers for food and housing would have stimulated regional economic growth overall to some extent. The smaller-scale independent mining works were probably organised in part at least under the aegis of estate landowners. These were more likely to have operated on a seasonal basis and might well be integrated into the rural patterns of agricultural production and the products of such metal extraction could be used to meet Imperial tax demands. The labour needs to operate the various metal extraction activities may have been supplied by semi-autonomous individuals or small groups of freemen. On the other hand, the workforce may well have consisted of estate slaves, especially if there was any shortage of labour to carry out these tasks, although Cleere and Crossley argued that slaves were never involved in the Wealden industries (1985, 75). The involvement of some female as well as child labour cannot necessarily be excluded, particularly for the ancillary tasks. The decline in state-run industries may well have seen an exodus of labour to participate in agriculture and the rural economy.

## Iron working in the northern European Barbaricum in the study period (AD 450–650)

Within Schleswig-Holstein (Germany), iron production in the fourth and fifth centuries was based at individual farms, where groups of furnaces, perhaps with only one-off use, were located adjacent to small deposits of bog ore near streams, practices indicative of small-scale, localised activities (Pleiner 2000, 47). Even at its best, it was not a kind of production that could match that of the Roman industry, working at an estimated 10% of its output level (*ibid.*, 47). By contrast, there is archaeological evidence of concentrations of iron working production further north in

Scandinavia at this time, in particular in central and northern Norway and in adjacent regions in Sweden. Both regions used slag-pit or bowl furnaces to generate thousands of tons of iron (*ibid.*, 48). The peak of production here appears to have been between AD 100–300. In the Norwegian region of central Trøndelag, it has been estimated that every farm must have been involved in the production, with a regional output in excess of ten tons per annum and far beyond the domestic needs of the producer communities. Coastal populations probably imported iron from the central region of Trøndelag, as did settlements located further to the north towards the Arctic Circle, in exchange for animal-derived resources such as fur and whalebone. The centrality of iron to trade and exchange mechanisms in Norway, taking full advantage of its sheltered north to south seaways offers an explanation for the concentration of imported Roman objects in Trøndelag. It hints at a centrally organised system of production to mobilise adequate resources to carry out surplus production. Iron production collapsed here in the sixth century, however, and did not recover until the eighth century, when a new technology in the form of a low-shaft furnace with slag-tapping holes at the bottom was introduced to the region (Stenvik 1997, 258).

Strategic control over the rich outcrops of bog iron that occurred in Jutland was likely to have been an essential element in the political control of territories in the Later Roman Iron Age in Denmark (Hedeager 1992a, 172, 246). The raw material would have had importance as a tribute or taxation good in its own right, but it was also the means to equip an armed force composed of local chieftains and their retainers (*ibid.*, 247). It has been noted that the areas of bog-iron deposits in the western and central parts of Jutland rarely match the locations of weapon burials (*ibid.* fig. 3.47). The raw material source for the weapons and war equipment deposited at Illerup Ådal in the third and fourth centuries AD was Scandinavian, probably Norwegian (Ilkjær 2001). Conjecturally, these could have been from the remnants of a defeated invading army from the north. Alternatively they might represent weapons in more local use, but sourced through trade with Norway (Stenvik 1997, 259). The pattern of iron working in Denmark over millennia had been one of a seasonal activity by farming communities in possession of easy access to bog iron ore and plentiful fuel supplies. Changes to this pattern have been identified from the sixth century AD, when a separation of tasks took place, splitting local and specialist production and appears to be concurrent with the emergence of full-time smiths (Lyngstrøm 2003).

In northwest Europe, smiths of the fifth century were generally dependent on impure bog ores. These, while workable at relatively low temperatures, produced soft, impure iron. The use of pattern-welding techniques in a process of twisting, hammering and welding strips of iron, to some extent mitigated the difficulties of producing a strong blade from iron with unreliable carbon content, in that a blade could be built up from variable-quality iron. The Early Medieval smith, in contrast to Roman craftsmen, was conversant with the techniques of carburising and quenching, which improved the edge hardness of tools (McDonnell 1989, 378). Such specialist knowledge could have been acquired beyond the bounds of the Roman Empire and developed within Germanic traditions of metalworking. The dissemination of such skills proceeded rapidly throughout northern Europe, most likely through migrating and itinerant crafts persons (Davidson 1962, 17), although these persons have a very limited archaeological presence in the burial record.

The trading settlement at Dorestad in the Netherlands, which was established by the 630s, but did not begin to expand before *c.*720, also produced metal amongst its range of activities (Wickham 2005, 682–4). As such it reflects similar activities that have been recorded by excavation at *Hamwic* (Saxon Southampton). The Veluwe region of the central Netherlands formed a hinterland for Dorestad and appears to have been the largest iron-producing region in Western Europe between the seventh and ninth centuries, with an estimated total output of 55,000 tons. It exhibits a complex range of iron-working activities throughout the 250 years of its exploitation. But, examination of the ore composition from the site at Braamberg dated to the seventh century, established that its slags bore no chemical relationship to local iron deposits. Rather the bog iron used had been imported onto the site in the form of blooms. It appears that the blooms had been traded to Dorestad and elsewhere within the Veluwe for smelting rather than being worked *in-situ* close to the ore deposits. Only in the later phases were the local ores exploited for large-scale production in the Veluwe (Joosten 2004, 71).

A simple bowl-shaped furnace from Millbrook in the Ashdown Forest dated to the ninth century displays technical similarities (Hodgkinson 2008, 35) to a much earlier site excavated at Heeten, a Germanic settlement to the east of the Veluwe, between the Rhine and the river Vecht in a densely-wooded area just to the north of the old Roman frontier. Other settlements in the Vecht area were ironmaking for their own needs, but the short-lived Heeten community produced in excess of 0.5 metric tons per annum from bog-iron ore, well beyond their immediate needs, in the period AD 300–350. An explanation for overproduction and a longer-term move to large-scale production in this region has been postulated as resulting from the demands of the Salian Franks for military and other equipment following their settlement within the Roman Empire (Joosten 2004, 62).

The areas of northern Europe that are the designated homelands of Germanic migrants exhibit particular patterns of iron working that may be replicated evidentially in the study region of southern Britain. The Schleswig-Holstein area between Jutland and Hamburg has 200 iron working sites dated from the pre-Roman Iron Age to the Middle Ages. Here is an iron working region which contrasts with the relative absence of such sites elsewhere. Sites producing slags are closely associated here with small bog-ore deposits adjacent to streams – slag has also been found in contemporary graves. In the fourth to fifth centuries, furnace groups are associated with individual farms, suggesting a small-scale, local production. In Jutland, the largest area of iron working was in the region of Snorup, near Varde, located near the western coast to the north of Esbjerg. Over 3000 furnaces have been recorded here between the first and seventh centuries AD, although the majority date from the second to fourth centuries (Pleiner 2000, 46–7). Despite the intensity of activity here, the rate of iron production has been estimated as only a tenth of that achieved within the Roman Empire. Yet, as the Roman iron-working industries declined, Scandinavia began to exploit its iron resources, particularly those in Central Norway and Central Sweden, and produced significant tonnages, far in excess of domestic needs (Pleiner 2000, 48).

A recent study of Langobardic (or Lombardic) iron working in Italy (La Salvia 2007) identified a radical re-organisation of metallurgical production, one that restructured iron production cycles as collateral to agricultural activity, whilst also spreading iron working amongst territorially-based production centres, embedded within the dynamics of local economic regimes and markets (*ibid.*, 74). La Salvia has characterised production as extensive, rather than redolent of the intensive production found in Late Antiquity, but one clearly linked to regional exchange-mechanisms. Technologically, he identified a fusion of Germanic and Late Roman traditions (*ibid.*, 42). In considering the numbers of iron artefacts deposited in Langobardic cemeteries, La Salvia suggested that the recycling of scrap material does not offer a plausible explanation for such volume. Rather there is sufficient evidence, at least for this region, of continuous metal production from ores. Indeed the capabilities and market-led demands of the Langobards may have been integral to the processes of a re-structuring of iron production cycles (*ibid.*, 46). Efficient organisation of craftsmen from the mid-sixth century would have enabled the supply of standardised products, with a sufficient volume to make the trade in their products an important component of all commercial exchanges within the Italian peninsula, despite the competition from and penetration into its markets by eastern Roman (Byzantine) products (*ibid.*, 72). The latter are not seen as the staples of exchange, however, but rather as elements of a less extensive luxury trade.

## Iron working in southern Britain AD 450–650 and later

Evidence for iron working on any scale for the period AD 450–650 is scant and can only be inferred indirectly from later finds and technical practices. The only securely datable Wealden site that offers evidence of iron working in the Anglo-Saxon period is that at Millbrook on Ashdown Forest in East Sussex, dated by radiocarbon and archaeomagnetic samples to AD 800–835. The site was only in use over a limited period, but unusually produced intrusive material, in the form of pottery and a sandstone hone, indicating domestic and maintenance activities contemporary with the use of the furnace (Tebbutt 1982). The primitive furnace type and technology found there demonstrated affinities with the non-slag-tapping furnace tradition of Germanic northern Europe as found in southern Denmark and Schleswig-Holstein (Cleere and Crossley 1985, 85). The evidence supports the view that the technology was imported from those homeland regions to the eastern seaboard of Britain (McDonnell 1989, 374) and presents a hiatus in techniques from the Roman period in Britain. Nevertheless, the contemporaneous usage of two broad metalworking traditions is evidenced, characterised as indigenous smelting technologies and an intrusive technology associated with slag blocks (*ibid.*, 380). Another bloomery furnace, at Long Gill, Mayfield, Sussex has very broad radiocarbon dating extending from AD 315 to 785 (Hodgkinson 2008, 36).

Only just outside the study region, the same furnace type has been identified from dumped iron working residues in sunken-featured buildings (SFBs) at Mucking, Essex (McDonnell 1993, 82–3). The presence of slag cakes gives an indication of the type of furnace, although in this particular instance the evidence suggests small-scale activities of both smelting and smithing in the sixth and seventh centuries. The working of just one or two small production units is implied. By extension, we can infer that knowledge of this particular technology for smelting had been successfully preserved or curated and utilised throughout the whole study period, although its date of adoption in Britain is unknown. Slag-block melting technology has been identified additionally from the thick slag deposits at the Market Place, Romsey, Hampshire, a site provisionally dated to the sixth and seventh centuries (Russel 2002, 23). Significantly for discussions of the organisation of iron working activities within the study period, sites with such evidence rarely occur in the vicinity of any major iron-ore deposits.

The non-slag-tapping furnace found in the earliest phase at the Ramsbury settlement in Wiltshire, has been dated to the late eighth century using iron ore that had been transported to the site from a distance (Haslam 1980). Analyses of the ironstones indicated that their sources may have been a concretionary iron ore from the Savernake Forest, 7km to the southwest of Ramsbury as well as from the Lower Greensand outcrop at Seend, 30km to the west (Fells 1980). Savernake Forest does not appear as a location for major iron-ore deposits within the geological listings consulted (Geological Survey of Great Britain 1935) and the evidence for Roman industrial activity there is for pottery production. The identification of such an iron-ore source highlights the application of detailed local knowledge by ironworkers operating in the Anglo-Saxon period, who were able to locate and work the Savernake source. It also shows the value to them of such minor and marginal, yet still accessible, resources. In a later phase of the site, in the early ninth century, the type of furnace used shared similarities with the more efficient slag-tapping methods used by the Romans, suggesting a re-emergence of still earlier traditions (Tebbutt 1982, 33).

There is also evidence of iron blooms being forged on settlement sites along the southern and western edges of the Weald. At Friar's Oak near Hassocks in Sussex, bloom consolidation or forging is the only part of the iron working process that is present. It can be inferred that smelting must have taken place in the vicinity, rather than at the source of the ore itself (Hodgkinson 2000, 41). It has been suggested that these activities were intended to produce iron in a form that could be traded on, while the presence of a grindstone there suggests the manufacture of finished iron artefacts for market (Butler 2000, 73). The Friar's Oak site has been dated to the Middle Saxon period. A Mid to Late Saxon date has also been assigned to a site at Buriton, near Petersfield in Hampshire, although the presence of scatters of grass-tempered pottery here might suggest an earlier date. The iron working activity involved re-heating blooms produced from smelting furnaces in the vicinity (Tebbutt 1980, 16).

There are over 450 undated and undatable bloomery sites in the Weald (Figure 27; Jeremy Hodgkinson, pers. comm.). Whilst the majority may well represent Roman workings, a proportion may equally belong to the Anglo-Saxon period, although none have produced any artefactual evidence to confirm such a date. Tebbutt (1973, 8–10) in a discussion of a site at Turner's Hill in Sussex offered the negative proposition that a bloomery with no pottery is likely to be either Anglo-Saxon or post-Conquest Medieval in origin. Unfortunately, there is no direct evidence for continuity of iron-production activities in the Weald within the study period, problematising any attempt to identify the potential sources of this key raw material for the early Anglo-Saxon population in southern Britain. However, it is possible to conjecture about how iron ore extraction and smelting may have been embedded into the activities of early Anglo-Saxon communities.

## 7. A Common Wealth in Iron?

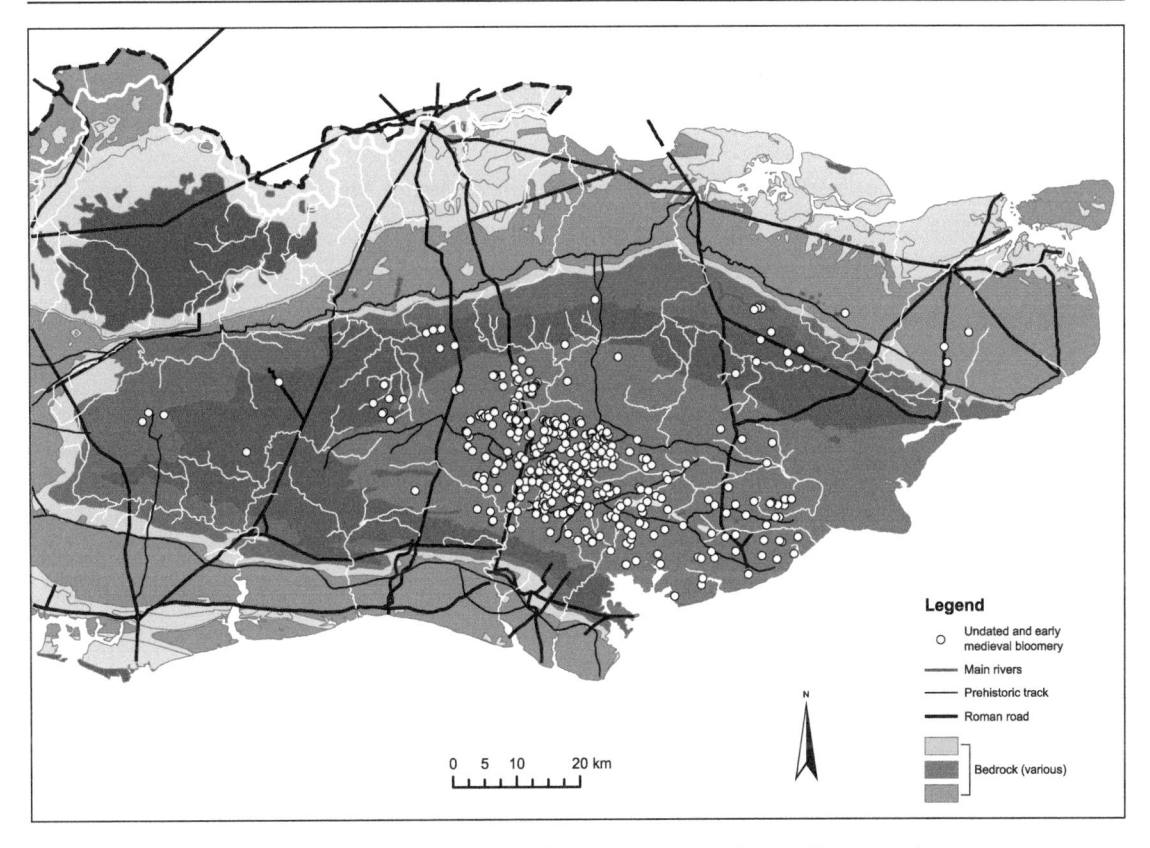

*Figure 27. Undated and medieval bloomery sites on the Wealden iron deposits*

Transhumant herding of animals, particularly swine, into the Wealden denns, using still-extant routes, be they drove-ways or sections of Roman roads, would have provided access to the ore deposits for people living in the eastern part of Sussex, to the east of the London to Brighton road (Margary Roman Road 150). It would have been well within the technical and physical capabilities of early Anglo-Saxon herders to dig out ore, roast the ore or perhaps produce raw blooms, to take back with them on pack animals for seasonal work at the forge in the settlement. The seasonal movement of members of a community with the herds would have presented opportunities to exploit a range of different resources, such as plants for dyeing or wild animal pelts, for return to the home domicile, as can be inferred from the activities discovered at the ninth-century Millbrook site (see above). The possibility that these resource-gathering practices were continuous from the Roman period cannot be discounted with any certainty (Hodgkinson 2000, 36). Accumulation of material at the settlement, albeit of variable quality, together with access to sufficient timber resources for furnaces and forges, would have facilitated the work of peripatetic but specialist metalworkers. Ore accumulation and smelting may not have been a very precise activity, leading on occasion to the generation of surplus bloom material. Taxation or tribute submitted to a central authority could have been offered in the forms of iron artefacts, or else bloom worked into bars, or un-worked bloom or even the constituent ore, whether in bulk or roasted form. It may have possessed a relatively high weight-to-value ratio and may have been able to function as a form of currency in other exchange/value transactions.

The importance of ownership of ore deposits is demonstrated in the charter S12 (Sawyer 1968) which states that:

> AD 689 (July). Oswine, king of Kent, to St Peter's Minster (St Augustine's, Canterbury) and Abbot Hadrian; grant of 1 sulung (*aratrum*) of iron-bearing land, formerly belonging to the royal vill at Lyminge, Kent.

The entry is unusual in the context of charters of the study period in specifically naming the resource that is being granted. John Blair (2005, 258) has interpreted the reference as relating to a Wealden mine (or ore deposit), but this need not be the case as a more local source within the *regio* of Lyminge might be plausible. There are undated bloomeries in the vicinity of Westwood near Lyminge, although these are associated with the sparse ores of the Greensand (Spurrell 1883, 292). Undated iron clinkers have also been found at Stowting Roughs and at Westwell above Charing, again indicating the presence of workable, if poor quality, deposits along the scarp edge of the North Downs (Bradshaw 1970, 179–80).

## Discussion

Several factors can be used to argue against the importation of raw iron ore into southern Britain early in the study period. One is clearly the fact that large and more accessible deposits existed in the Weald. Another is the issue as to whether types and sizes of sea-going vessels available in the fifth and sixth centuries would have been adequate for cross-channel exchange of heavy goods. Certainly a relatively light, but bulky staple such as cloth or wool would have been a more obvious and viable proposition. As for the widespread use of scrap, Cleere has claimed that iron metallurgy "did not achieve a technological level … that would permit the recycling of scrap material" in contrast to the situation for copper and copper alloys (Cleere 1984, 6). The assertion might be challenged, however, in the light of developing understandings of iron working techniques in other periods (pers. comm. John Merkel). The metallurgically identified variability in the quality of the iron within composite objects may have been the result of variable ore qualities, however, rather than be a function of re-used scrap from diverse sources.

The issue of the wholesale importation of iron objects in the earliest phases of the study period would be best examined through analysis of extensive and comparative metallurgical investigations. Unfortunately relatively little research has been carried out in this area beyond the study by Tylecote and Gilmour (1986) into Anglo-Saxon edged tools and weapons and, as a result, definitive statements cannot be provided. To take just the example of double-edged long swords (*spathæ*), Tylecote and Gilmour found that the majority of the relevant examples for the study period were pattern-welded using low-carbon iron with butt-welded edges. Their quality was variable and they would have been only barely adequate in use as weapons, as opposed to their symbolic display value- improvements in standards were not apparent until the seventh century (*ibid.*, 249). Single-bladed seaxes, although probably only regularly in use as part of a weapon kit from the seventh century onwards, exhibit a different type of manufacturing technique. They possessed an iron core in a steel jacket and were not pattern-welded (*ibid.*, 243). Knives of the period were generally of a much greater hardness by a factor of three than any of their Roman predecessors (*ibid.*, 99). In contrast, certain spearheads found in association with Late Roman military equipment, probably acquired by federate troops, were observed by Swanton (1973, 140) to be technically similar to those found in the votive bog deposits of the Jutland peninsula (Continental Anglia). These spears may have arrived as personal imports with their owners or else have been the products of first-generation migrant-smiths from Anglia. Swanton proposed a mode of iron working that would provide for the needs of isolated communities, thus leading to local and regional individual forms of spearhead types (*ibid.*, 141).

The extent to which iron objects deposited in Anglo-Saxon burials had been manufactured in and curated from the Roman period and kept in active use for the interim needs to be considered next. Clearly, certain kinds of copper alloy artefact had a long-use life from the Late Roman period. The project database records nearly 500 entries under the 'Curated/Roman Ae' category. The most numerous of these are perforated coins, but there are also brooches, bracelets, tweezers and keys. Yet, for iron objects entered in the database as 'Curated/Roman', there are a mere 22 items, with a similar range of object types as those in copper alloys, together with an occasional spearhead and a chatelaine chain. Significantly these Roman iron artefacts are evenly distributed geographically throughout the study region. The range of Roman tools, fittings and weapons collated by Manning (1985) from the British Museum's collections, indicate that a further modest advance on the total of 22 might be achieved through further identification exercises on archived material. Candidates for objects that may also appear as one-off inclusions in early Anglo-Saxon burials (identified by Manning corpus type number) include:

- In-shaves (B18),
- Saws (B21), shears (D4 and D7, which are similar to seventh-century versions in Kent: Harrington 2003, fig. 42),
- Various components from snaffle-bits (H13–H17 as discussed by Fern 2005),
- Certain types of key (O23–O27, although Anglo-Saxon examples usually operate on only one lock lever rather than on multiples),
- Box-lock components,
- Iron bucket fittings (P11–P20),
- Loop-headed spikes and double-spiked loops (R34–50),
- Various nails (R74–103) and chain links and loops (S6–S17), the latter used as components in chatelaine assemblages in feminine-gendered graves.

The restricted range of these items and their minimal frequency in early Anglo-Saxon burials does little to suggest a wholesale subsistence reliance on curated Roman ironwork. The major type finds of early Anglo-Saxon spearheads and knives are distinctly different as a comparison of Swanton's spear typology and Evison's knife typology (1987, 113–5) with Manning's Q30–Q60 and V25–V139 makes clear. The Anglo-Saxon versions must have been manufactured later. It should be noted, however, that both tools and everyday items are more conspicuous by their absence than by their presence in Anglo-Saxon burial assemblages (Harrington 2003, 306–8). Comparisons with finds recovered from settlement sites might achieve more to clarify the issue of the longevity of Roman iron artefacts. Nevertheless, it is safe to assert that the vast majority of iron objects used in the burials at least were not of Roman manufacture.

The absence of metalworking tools from burial assemblages prior to the middle of the seventh century or later further obscures any discussion of the earliest phases of iron working. Birch (2011; also Wright 2010) argues that this absence may relate to the liminal position of smelting and smithing in the Anglo-Saxon psyche – between the living and the dead, an argument that further underlines why evidence for smelting is rarely found on settlement sites. Within the study region, the single example of a related tool is a pair of pincers or tongs, now known by published illustration only (Faussett 1856) from grave 115/6 at Sibertswold in Kent (KntSIB-IC1). The tool occurred in what was otherwise an ordinary spear-and-shield-boss grave. Elsewhere in Britain, the only other relevant burial is an isolated grave near Tattershall Thorpe in Lincolnshire, whose assemblage indicates an itinerant smith. The tong types are similar in both cases, but in the Lincolnshire context the tool kit included an anvil, snips, files, punches and a hammer. The associated collection of scrap iron with the smith is interpreted as waiting recycling and as emphasising the value of scrap as a source of metal (Hinton 2000, 105). Metal workers of the study period appear to have been adept at using different qualities of iron and combining them to produce a single object of aesthetic value (*e.g.* Leahy 2003, 127 considering a polished spearhead from Bedfordshire).

Iron slag occurs occasionally in burials, but the database records only 17 instances from just eight sites and is perhaps insufficient evidence to point to its use within a ritualistic deposition (Haaland 2004, 15). There are both inhumations and cremations here, mostly dating prior to 600, but also occurring as late as the eighth century. The majority are recorded from modern excavations conducted by contract field units, with seven coming from the inhumation cemetery at Market Lavington in Wiltshire. There the slag fragments amount to 10kg in total and are scattered over the whole settlement and cemetery site. It would seem that they indicate nothing more than seasonal smithing activity (Montague 2006, 83). The slag material is found in both male and female graves and is distributed throughout the study region, although no examples occur in either Berkshire or Sussex. The presence of slag is interpreted typically as residual material from a settlement in the vicinity or as residual relating to earlier phases of the site. It can be noted that none of these sites (GlsFFD, GlsLLE, HtsALT, HtsSTN, HtsTFD, KntRAM, SryCYN and WltMLV) is located in particularly close proximity to iron-ore deposits.

Whilst a close comparison of all settlements in the study region for evidence of iron working residues is beyond the scope of the project datasets, consultation of some of the most recently published site reports highlights the potential for such an exercise to expand the inferences that might be made about iron working. A review of the data from 26 occupation sites in the London region, which are on or beyond the margins of the study region, prepared by Cowie and Blackmore (2008) has produced metalworking evidence from only three of them. These have been interpreted by their excavators as probably only residual material from Roman activities and as in no way comparable to the scale of activities evidenced at Mucking in Essex. Access to metal goods in the Lower Thames area in the Middle Saxon period would therefore most likely have been mediated through the trading *emporium* of *Lundenwic* (*ibid.*, 150–1). Metalworking residue evidence from the Royal Opera House, Covent Garden site, however, only provided evidence of smithing and recycling rather than smelting. Concentrations of scrap iron and strips of iron bar probably indicate stock for future use, with other supplies notionally present in the form of blooms. The source of any iron ore used here has not been established, although conjecturally by the eighth century it might be from the Weald (Malcolm *et al.* 2003, 175–6).

For the Upper Thames Valley during the early Anglo-Saxon period there is little evidence for iron working, beyond traces of smithing within what were primarily agricultural communities. The main craft activities in evidence here are textile production and ceramic production (Booth *et al.* 2007, 322–4). It is only in the Middle and Later Saxon periods that iron-working debris becomes a consistent find on its settlement sites, including a rare instance of the smelting of local bog ore at Wraysbury in Berkshire (*ibid.*, 347). The settlement at Barrow Hills near Radley in Berkshire (now Oxfordshire) has been dated between the fifth and seventh centuries and also presents limited evidence for iron working, with between two and ten kg of metal used for the manufacture and repair of domestic artefacts. More than one source of iron was used here, presumably transported to the site in the form of blooms (Salter 2007, 259–262). Again these Thames Valley sites are not within easy reach of large iron-ore deposits. Thus for the Upper Thames communities located between Reading and Lechlade, the nearest source of quality ores would have been further north in the Midlands around Banbury in north Oxfordshire, although the presence of small, locally outcropping deposits cannot be discounted. Finally, at Bishopstone in East Sussex, the late fifth to early seventh-century settlement on Rookery Hill similarly has produced no evidence of iron working on the excavated site. Its main economic activities focused on exploiting livestock, probably within a mixed farming regime. Nevertheless, it is the closest excavated settlement to the iron-ore deposits of the western Weald, located approximately fifteen miles to the north. Although residual Roman iron artefacts are present here, the morphology of a group of door nails does suggest manufacture contemporary with its Anglo-Saxon community (Bell 1977, 237).

To conclude, there is no uncontested evidence of primary iron working in the study region, in terms of ore mining and smelting and roasting. Indeed it is not clear how such a site might present itself within the early Anglo-Saxon period. A mine-pit or shallow diggings into a deposit might belong to any date and such obscure man-made features are plentiful enough throughout the study region. Nevertheless, the available settlement evidence indicates a separation of the component processes. Several specific questions still need to be addressed, however. Kentish burials appear to be iron-rich, with a wide range of object-types deposited in large numbers. Yet the main centres of settlement in east Kent are distant from Wealden ore-sources, although east Kent does contain the iron deposits at Blean near Canterbury, which had been worked and smelted in the Roman period until the late fourth century. It also encompasses the outcrops at Dover. Whether these two sources, together with other marginal outcrops, were sufficient to supply domestic and surplus requirements cannot be established.

The mechanisms for the social replication of mining and metalworking skills are unknown to us, although it could be argued that the mere presence of itinerant smiths would be insufficient to explain the levels of skill deployed or the separation of tasks and hence a full working knowledge of all the processes involved. Clearly there was an inheritance of techniques and methods from the North European *Barbaricum*, but did this necessarily negate the continuity of Romano-British iron-production traditions and the locations of iron working sites? The evidence of iron-making and iron working at Silchester (Hampshire) Insula IX poses a conundrum within the discussion as the activity potentially belongs in the post-Roman period. It may thus represent a continuation of the Late Roman iron working and manufacturing activities previously noted from excavations of the Basilica site here, albeit on a fairly small-scale though steady rate spread over 150 years (Fulford and Timby 2000, 72–4). Fulford (2006, 278) has argued for widespread occupation within Silchester between the fifth and seventh centuries, although the iron working did not occur at any point in sufficient quantity to suggest a large-scale metalworking industry *per se* (Tootell 2006, 159). Rather the evidence of slag indicates small-scale activities, perhaps recycling scrap iron from derelict buildings elsewhere. On the other hand, the excavator is firmly of the opinion that iron smelting also took place here using what have been interpreted as simple bowl furnaces (Michael Fulford, pers.comm.). Metallurgical analyses indicate that the source of the ore was the Forest of Dean. The excavation of two iron hoards in the vicinity of Insula IX, each containing a wide variety of tools, together with some copper alloy [bronze?] objects indicates the scale of available material from the site. These have been dated to the late fourth century and were probably votive deposits. Yet, Silchester is located within an extensive territorial zone devoid of most early Anglo-Saxon activity. The only contemporary evidence comes from an apparently isolated burial in the North Gate of this *civitas* capital, which has been radiocarbon-dated to the fifth century, and a handful of artefacts of uncertain provenance (Boon 1974, 76).

The main points that emerge from the above review of literature and recent evidence are that:

- Few settlements exhibit iron-working activity and most of those that do were probably not working beyond meeting their immediate needs in the production of domestic artefacts. There may be regional differences in the presence or absence of iron-working activity.
- The movement of blooms and iron bars to settlements is strongly inferred as is movement of them between settlements.
- Certain areas appear to experience iron as a scarce resource, although other raw materials and products obtainable from an agrarian base are more plentiful. An exchange network must be inferred in order to meet subsistence needs, implying the production of surpluses elsewhere.
- Whatever the North European point of origin of migrant communities, their collective experience of iron working was based on small-scale, localised production. Included was the movement of component raw materials and semi-finished products within regional and specialised trading networks. A central coordination or the provision of a market place for exchange may have facilitated production. Some community specialisation is noted in the activities of some North European sites.

- The seasonality of metalworking tasks is consistently interpreted as the result of the movement of and the need to await the arrival of peripatetic smiths, as indicated by written sources, rather than as an activity integrated into the work cycles of rural communities relying on their own labour and expertise.
- Iron may have been a valuable component of a taxation and tribute system.
- Central places for the conversion of iron into artefacts other than those required for domestic use can be inferred, through the accumulation of the necessary resources.
- Iron objects were probably made from raw materials supplied from a variety of sources, including new blooms, iron bars or blanks and recycled objects, again suggesting centralised accumulation of resources.
- The value of very local deposits to fulfil community needs is demonstrated throughout. Full-scale exploitation of large deposits, such as occur in the Weald, may not have been necessary during the study period. If these deposits were not exploited, then perhaps iron had a high value due to its scarcity and its distribution may have been strictly controlled. However, the same argument may apply if there was ongoing exploitation of Wealden deposits by vested interests.

# 8. Community Wealth in Iron Compared

Decision-making processes would have been necessary concerning the conversion of a scarce raw material into objects that consumed a large proportion of the available store. The primary artefacts are spearheads, swords and shield bosses, which were the heaviest iron objects recorded. Can the mapped distribution of these items provide an indication of the territorial reach of those persons central to iron conversion and distribution? Or, should we envisage instead extremely localised production regimes? For example, might each weapon-bearing male be responsible for the manufacture of his own equipment? Such a suggestion would characterise him as a multi-tasking militia-man as well as a farmer and blacksmith. An alternative model might see weapon provision as a household responsibility, with the militia member a representative of the activities and skills of the entire household. Would a complete weapon set have come from a single source or did each component have a different sourcing framework? To investigate these issues, case studies of these artefact types are presented below.

If there was unequal access to iron resources over space and over time, then it might be expected that these artefacts would mirror this in terms of their weight (used here as a short-hand for volume of iron) and in terms of counts of artefacts. This was clearly the case, as Kent has by far the largest number of iron objects and the greatest number of people buried when compared to the rest of the study region. There are also spatial differences in the quantities of iron (relating to weight) used to manufacture similar objects throughout the study region. The data was split between that from Kent and that from the remainder of the study region. For this purpose, west Kent was included in the Kent figures, as although clearly it was a culturally Saxon area, it derived benefit from its relationship to the 'original' kingdom of Kent to the east of the Medway. The rest of the study region was considered together as broadly Saxon in cultural terms and more distant from the east Kent nexus. The date range is extended in the following case studies to AD 700 to highlight the broad trends, the detail of which will require further investigation in the future.

## 8. Community Wealth in Iron Compared

| Type | Region | No. from that area | Average weight in grams |
|---|---|---|---|
| Group 1 | **Saxon** | 106 | 390g |
| | Kentish | 7 | 364g |
| Group 2 | **Saxon** | 22 | 344g |
| | Kentish | 3 | 364g |
| Group 3 | **Saxon** | 53 | 322g |
| | Kentish | 54 | 310g |
| Group 4 | **Saxon** | 31 | 328g |
| | Kentish | 0 | - |
| Group 5 | **Saxon** | 8 | 374g |
| | Kentish | 0 | - |
| Group 6 | **Saxon** | 22 | 239g |
| | Kentish | 14 | 253g |
| Group 7 | **Saxon** | 23 | 348g |
| | Kentish | 23 | 345g |

*Figure 28. An iron shield boss*

*Table 31. Numbers of shield bosses by type (main distribution area in bold)*

### Iron case study 1: shield bosses (AD 450–700)

Using the well-established typology of Dickinson and Härke (1992) the constituent groups were compared by weight and cultural geographical distribution (further refinements to the typology are forthcoming, John Hines pers. comm. It is unknown at the time of publication whether they will impact on this assessment).

Over 700 shield bosses are recorded in the project database, but only 378 (52%) of these have been assigned to a type. Kent accounts for 306 of the total number of bosses (42%) but only 116 of these (38%) have a defined type. The average weights for each type are derived using the weighting methodology adopted and outlined in the Database Metadata chapter. The regional preferences for shield-boss type as identified in the table run broadly in step with those identified by Tania Dickinson (1992, table 2). There appear to be no exclusively Kentish shield-boss types, although there is a preference towards groups 3 and 7, which are the most numerous finds here. The sheer number of Kentish bosses that cannot be assigned to a group would have the potential, however, to vary this tentative conclusion. There is a definite bias towards bosses of groups 1, 2, 4 and 5 within the Saxon areas, with groups 4 and 5 apparently absent in Kent. Dickinson's own distributions provide more fine-grained information than is presented here and further divisions may well be present within the Saxon zone. There is no substantial variation between the weights of the same-group shield bosses found in Kent and elsewhere. An overall difference occurs within Group 6 (low-cone) bosses, which are generally lighter and less substantial than the other types. The Group 6 type occurs from Phase B onwards (after c.575) and might suggest a restriction in the amount of iron available for shield-fitting manufacture at that time.

123

*Figure 29. An iron sword with pattern welding*

*Table 32. Swords by phase and weight (number in sample in brackets)*

| Phase | Average weight in grams (all) | Saxon average weight in grams | Kentish average weight in grams |
|---|---|---|---|
| A | 893g (139) | 925g (87) | 839g (52) |
| B | 720g (118) | 558g (27) | 768g (91) |
| C | 913g (22) | 817g (5) | 942g (17) |

## Iron case study 2: swords (AD 450–700)

In order to highlight the overall trends, the study period is extended here to AD 700, until the demise of furnished burial. A decreasing number of sword burials appear between Phase A and Phase C for the study region as a whole, although in Kent the numbers relative to those from the Saxon area to the west actually increase over time. The Phase A average weight of a sword in the study region drops significantly in Phase B, but increases again in Phase C. Comparing the two sectors of the study region, a rather different picture emerges from what might be expected given the frequency of sword burials in Kent. Thus in Phase A, Kentish swords are lighter than those in the Saxon areas, while in Phase B both sectors are investing less iron in swords than hitherto, based on weight, though Kent sees an increase in the number deposited, perhaps stretching its resources to do so. Finally Phase C sees a recovery in the quantity of iron deposited for each individual sword, but the quantity is focused on significantly fewer items with still fewer within the Saxon areas. Although there are fewer swords, a greater amount of iron than before is invested in each, suggesting again a restructuring of the iron supply through phase B.

## 8. Community Wealth in Iron Compared

*Figure 30. Iron knives*

*Table 33. Average and range of weights of knives (number in sample in brackets)*

| Phase | Saxon average weight in grams | Saxon range of weights | Number of knives in Saxon area | Kentish average weight in grams | Kent range of weights | Number of knives In Kent |
|---|---|---|---|---|---|---|
| A | 24g (559) | 4g–100g | 986 | 22g (229) | 3g–73g | 491 |
| B | 28g (213) | 6g–184g | 409 | 22g (349) | 2g–170g | 846 |
| C | 24g (109) | 5g–114g | 241 | 20g (312) | 2g–170g | 740 |

## Iron case study 3: knives (AD 450–700)

A knife is the most common artefact to be deposited with an inhumation of either gender in all three phases. It might be expected to reflect rather better than any weaponry the underlying patterns for access to iron for the population as a whole. Using only the accurately-weighed examples, rather than the average-weighted data, differences in the patterns of iron consumption over time have been identified as shown in Table 33 (the total number of knives found in burials is also given). Although there can be confusion in some publications when separating single-edged blades between the categories of a knife or a seax, the items included here have been filtered to exclude overly-large artefacts that could fall into the seax-weapon category.

In this analysis, the Saxon area knives are consistently slightly heavier than those recorded in Kent. There is an apparent upward movement in both the range of weight and the average weight of knives in Phase B, reverting to the earlier norms by Phase C. Their weight is maintained then, although there are far fewer knives in circulation successively in phases B and C. Kent is more consistent in the amount of iron used per knife over time, although it has produced proportionately many more in phases B and C than has the Saxon area. The Kent and Saxon knives also dramatically increase the upper end of their weight range in Phase B, but this is only maintained in Phase C in Kent. These features occur in parallel with a significant increase in the total number of knives in circulation in Kent.

*Table 34. People and knives by phase*

| Phase | Total People | Kent | Saxon | Total knives | Kent % of knives | Saxon % of knives |
|---|---|---|---|---|---|---|
| A | 4989 | 26% | 74% | 1079 | 45% | 55% |
| B | 3419 | 52% | 48% | 1257 | 67% | 33% |
| C | 2965 | 60% | 40% | 994 | 75% | 25% |

*Table 35. Knives per head of population*

| Phase | Total knives | Total People | Kent knives to people ratio | Saxon knives to people ratio |
|---|---|---|---|---|
| A | 1079 | 4989 | 1:1.7 | 1:3.7 |
| B | 1257 | 3419 | 1:1.3 | 1:4 |
| C | 994 | 2965 | 1.1.25 | 1:4.7 |

These results may merely reflect the demographics of the study period, in that we have many more burial records for Kent than elsewhere. In order to dig deeper into the data, Tables 34 and 35 are based on all those individuals for whom we have burial records and the counts of their associated knives. The data is split again in order to compare Kent with the remainder of the study region.

Kent is well furnished with knives throughout the study period and is always within the parameter of one knife per one-to-two people. The ratio actually improves over time, so that by Phase C, although we have fewer burial records and fewer knives, a greater proportion of the Kent population is buried with a knife than before. This intensification occurs at a time when other materials and quantities of goods were being less frequently deposited in burial assemblages. Perhaps what is implied is that possession of an iron knife in a burial had become a status-marker by Phase C in Kent, but also demonstrates the Kentish grip on this raw material.

The reverse situation applies outside of Kent with the ratio actually worsening, so that whilst in Phase A a single knife was deposited for approximately every four persons, by Phase C, there were fewer knives in each cemetery and the ratio had increased to one knife for every five individuals. The Saxon data set includes barely-furnished burial communities, such as occurred at Ulwell near Swanage in Dorset (DstSWG-IC1), which had only one knife amongst its 54 seventh-century burials although by then within the ambit of the kingdom of Wessex, and the contemporary site at Farthingdown in Surrey (SryCDN-IC1) which produced 15 knives amongst 30 burials, with high-status artefacts in other materials also present. This evidence suggests that the regional variation in access to iron knives was dependent on a community's status.

## The iron-wealth over time and space (AD 450–700)

Although we can highlight differences in the wealth of iron on the regional scale, this evidence does not point to the internal dynamics of differential access to this material on the locale and community scales. Although the gross number and types of artefact of varying raw materials diminished amongst burials between phases B and C, iron retained a constant presence throughout. The range of iron objects is large, extending from a simple small iron dress pin or a nail through to a prestigious two-edged sword of the *spatha* tradition. If iron was a readily available material, then it can be hypothesised that the greater proportion of the community would have access to it for deposition in a grave or a cremation deposit. Even if iron were not present in great quantities, the available amount might have been distributed within the community, according to the tenets of its social organisation. We might expect to see either a generalised spread of iron throughout a community or else a differential distribution with only a limited number of persons accessing it as an exclusive material. In order to explore these issues, the percentages of each cemetery population with iron present in their burial assemblage, regardless of artefact type, were traced through the three phases and are presented in a map format (Figure 31).

In Phase A there is a broad picture of both very evenly and also some unevenly spread iron resources, with some indications of core and peripheral areas of iron deposition. Those communities closest to the coast include a higher number of sites in which over 75% of the population was buried with iron. There is a fall off amongst the more inland sites both on either side of the North Downs in Kent and westwards along the South Downs from the Ouse-Cuckmere block in East Sussex. Central Wiltshire produces the most even spread of sites with the majority of them accessing iron, although the western-most sites in Dorset and Somerset have fewer than 13% of their populations accompanied by an iron artefact. The West Kent-Surrey area and the Upper Thames Valley have no sites in which more than 75% of their populations possessed iron artefacts, and mostly they fall below the 50% range.

For Phase B a common pattern occurs throughout the study region that sees an increase in the number of sites in which a smaller proportion of the population is buried with iron artefacts. The new communities on the uplands of the North Downs in east Kent are not accessing as much iron per head of population as occurs for the older communities on the coast, which maintained their spread of iron throughout the whole of each community. East Sussex begins to reveal a greater degree of differentiation, with the extremes of either whole communities or minorities within communities being buried with iron artefacts.

The Phase C pattern is broadly contiguous with the known boundaries of the seventh-century Anglo-Saxon kingdoms, defined by the large geographical blank spaces between contemporary communities. The wealth and distribution of iron still continues amongst Kentish early coastal communities and iron wealthy communities developed along Watling Street, though not extending into London (then *Lundenburh* or *Lundenwic*). The Surrey area between two Roman roads (Margary numbers 15 and 150) has a collection of communities with little wealth in iron. The Upper Thames Valley again has a central core of iron wealth and iron-poor peripheral sites. Wessex, extending through Sussex, Hampshire to the east and through Dorset and Somerset to the west, spreads its iron wealth equitably amongst the communities at either end of the South Downs. There are noticeably fewer people buried with iron to the immediate west and north of Salisbury.

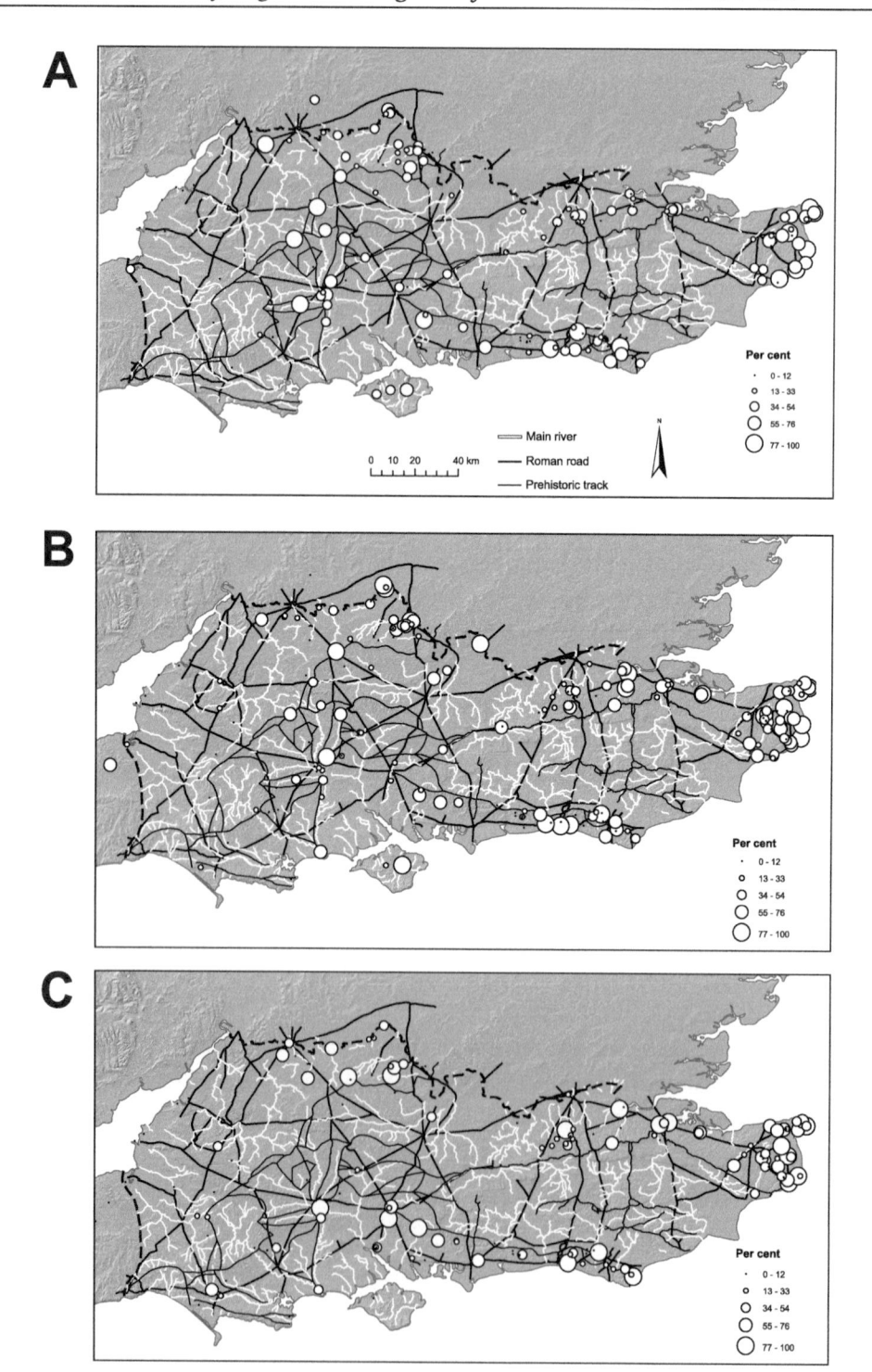

*Figure 31. Percentages of the study region population with iron, over all three phases*

*8. Community Wealth in Iron Compared*

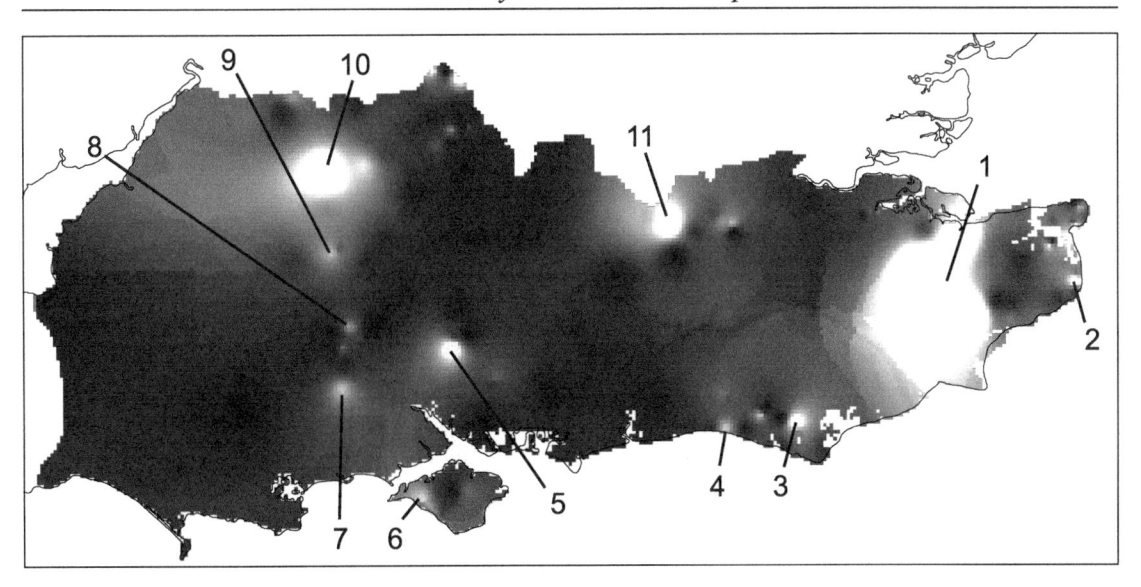

*Figure 32. Inverse distance weightings of iron consumption in Phase A, showing eleven regional high spots*

## Phase A comparative study

Through this examination of the relative numbers of people in communities with iron, we can begin to suggest that the material held a relatively high value for inclusion in the burial assemblages and that further there was a distinctive spatial pattern to its distribution and usage over time. Nevertheless, the methodology does not take into account the volume of iron actually used, as it equates a small pin with a sword at the most basic level of analysis. Therefore, we have followed the methodology adopted by Brookes (2007, 144–150) to map spatial patterns of wealth in East Kent, using Inverse-Distance-Weightings (IDW) by 12 nearest neighbours. These were generated for each phase for the entire study region. The purpose here was to identify trends of iron consumption, using all iron artefacts, over space and time. The output calculation was based on the amount of iron per individual (termed here as Gross Domestic Consumption or GDC). This is the total weight of iron present per site divided by the number of individuals in each phase to provide a community-by-phase average. The dataset deliberately excluded isolated iron-rich weapon burials as these could skew the surface patterns. On the maps, areas with the highest predicted presence of worked iron are represented in white.

The Phase A IDW (Figure 32) highlights specific areas with a probable dense presence of worked iron in the burial. Area A1 covers a substantial tranche of landscape through East Kent. It extends from the mouth of the Swale centred on Faversham, including the Blean iron-ore deposits, over the North Downs with their poorer deposits on the southern scarp near Lyminge, encloses the Roman road network linking through to Hastings, but well to the west of Canterbury and includes much of the Vale of Holmesdale. A much smaller area density occurs around the Dover ore deposits (A2). The communities in both these areas in Kent appear to be accessing directly their local ore deposits.

A similar case can be made in East Sussex, with cemeteries in Eastbourne extending through

*Table 36. Phase A IDW areas*

| Area | Description |
|---|---|
| A1 | Central East Kent |
| A2 | Dover |
| A3 | East Sussex |
| A4 | Brighton (Stafford Road) |
| A5 | Itchen Valley |
| A6 | West side of Isle of Wight |
| A7 | West Hampshire |
| A8 | Winterbourne Gunner |
| A9 | Vale of Pewsey |
| A10 | Central North Wiltshire |
| A11 | Western Surrey by Thames |

to Lewes and Keymer on the South Downs (A3). These communities could have accessed the southernmost Wealden deposits, perhaps utilising the now-truncated Roman road system north from Selmeston and Glynde. Brighton and the partially-investigated cemetery at Stafford Road is nearby by the coast (A4). To the west is a hot-spot in central east Hampshire (A5), which is centred on the cemetery at St Giles Hill above Winchester, with sites at Worthy Park and Itchen Abbas as its satellites. Once again the Isle of Wight (A6) demonstrates a high concentration of ironwork at its western end, principally associated with the Chessell Down cemetery, which is located close to its coastal iron-ore deposits. The West Hampshire area is based on the recently-excavated cemetery at Breamore by the Avon (A7). Directly north again, there is a further concentration, now in Wiltshire, at the Winterbourne Gunner cemetery near Salisbury (A8). The latter is comparable in having a lesser density of iron to the area around the Black Patch, Pewsey cemetery and the site at Woodbridge Inn in North Newnton (A9). A much larger zone in northern Wiltshire is centred on Bassett Down, with satellites at Wanborough and Overton Hill (A10) and is comparable to the iron density found in Central East Kent (A1). Much further to the east and the only area to be located beside the Thames is another density of sites located in close proximity to a known ore deposit (A11). The zone is centred on the cemetery at Sandown Park in Esher, Surrey together with satellites at Shepperton to its west and Ewell to the east, while a further slightly less dense area is located further east again in Surrey (now Greater London) around the cemeteries at Beddington and Croydon.

The two densest concentrations of iron in Phase A do exhibit a spatial proximity to major iron-ore deposits in the study region. Nevertheless, there is an underlying issue regarding the practicality of intensive re-use of iron scrap from adjacent Roman sites in this first phase. As Figure 34 demonstrates, a proximity to Late Roman sites of any type may offer an explanation in certain cases, but again some spatial differences emerge. In fact the densest areas of Phase A iron use do not cluster amongst the Roman sites anywhere with the obvious exceptions of Area A5 surrounding around the former *civitas* capital at Winchester (*Venta Belgarum*) and Area A7 around Breamore. Obviously the Winchester sites are distant from any ore deposits in the Weald while Breamore is well upstream from the Hengistbury Head ores. The concentration of iron found in northern Wiltshire (A10) is therefore rather anomalous, being distant from both iron-ore deposits and from known Late Roman sites. Nevertheless, it is ringed by a heavy concentration of Roman sites, particularly to the south and east, although the majority of these can only be dated to the Roman period as a whole. Therefore we cannot necessarily claim that many of these sites had any influence on the development of early Anglo-Saxon communities here.

## 8. Community Wealth in Iron Compared

*Figure 33. View south west towards Bitterne and the Channel coast from the Anglo-Saxon cemetery on St Giles Hill, Winchester, Hampshire*

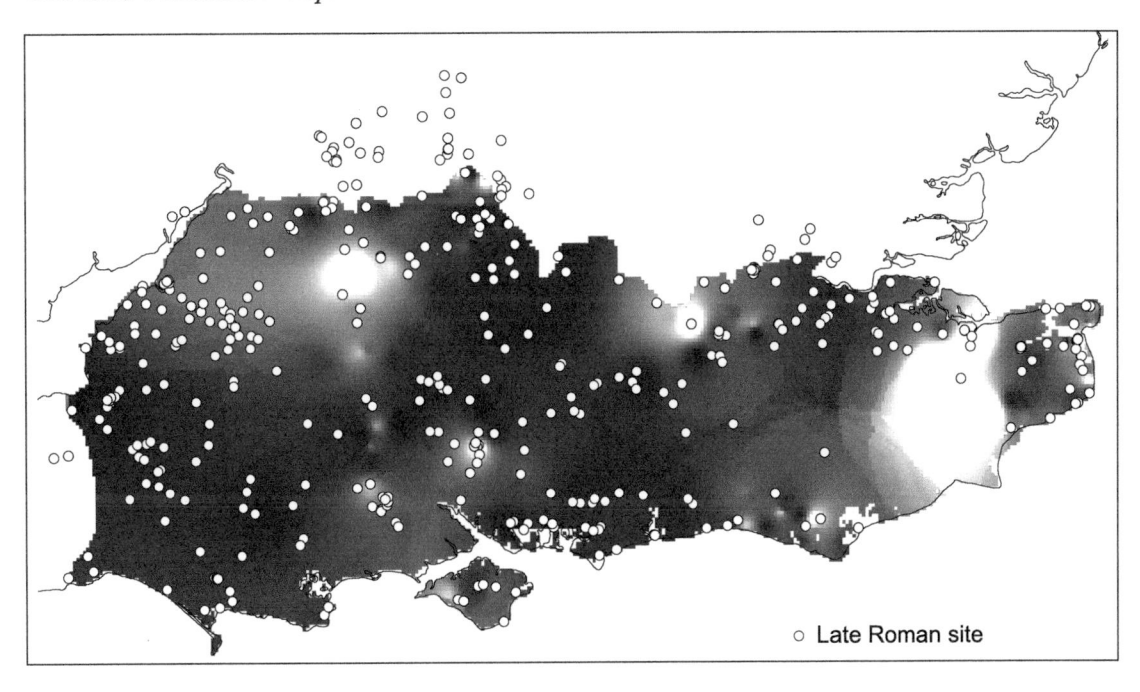

*Figure 34. Phase A concentrations of iron consumption in relation to Late Roman sites, as potential sources of scrap iron for recycling*

## Phase B comparative study

The pattern for Phase B shows spatial shifts in iron consumption across the region as a whole and also within the known kingdoms of Kent, Sussex and Wessex from Phase A. Within Kent the focus is now on the area between the Wantsum Channel and Canterbury (B1) with a marked increase in consumption on the coastlands north of Folkestone and Dover (B1a). The Faversham/Hastings tranche has become diminished in terms of iron wealth, but a new area of intense consumption appears on the junction of the Upper Medway and the western Holmesdale around Aylesford and Holborough (B2). The new zone possessed a particularly dense and rather isolated concentration of undated Roman sites. A similar, although less iron-rich area (B10) appears just to the west along the Darenth Valley, a part of west Kent that was well furnished with Roman remains including several villas. The riverside community near Northfleet set above the Ebbsfleet near its confluence with the Thames begins to develop an iron-rich presence in Phase B.

On the south coastal region of Sussex (B3), communities located to the south of the Wealden deposits and to the north of the South Downs centred on the Cuckmere Valley continue to display more iron than their neighbours. In Phase B their iron wealth appears to have been surpassed, however, by communities above the coastline around Hove and occupying the southern ridges of the Downs. Then, although a series of poorer communities are present along the line of the South Downs in Phase B, as for example at Horndean and Apple Down near Compton, none are particularly iron rich. The next area that is highlighted on the map to the west along the coast is located at Bargates in Christchurch (B4) by the mouth of the river Avon. Once again Breamore to the north on the same river maintains its elevated iron profile (B5).

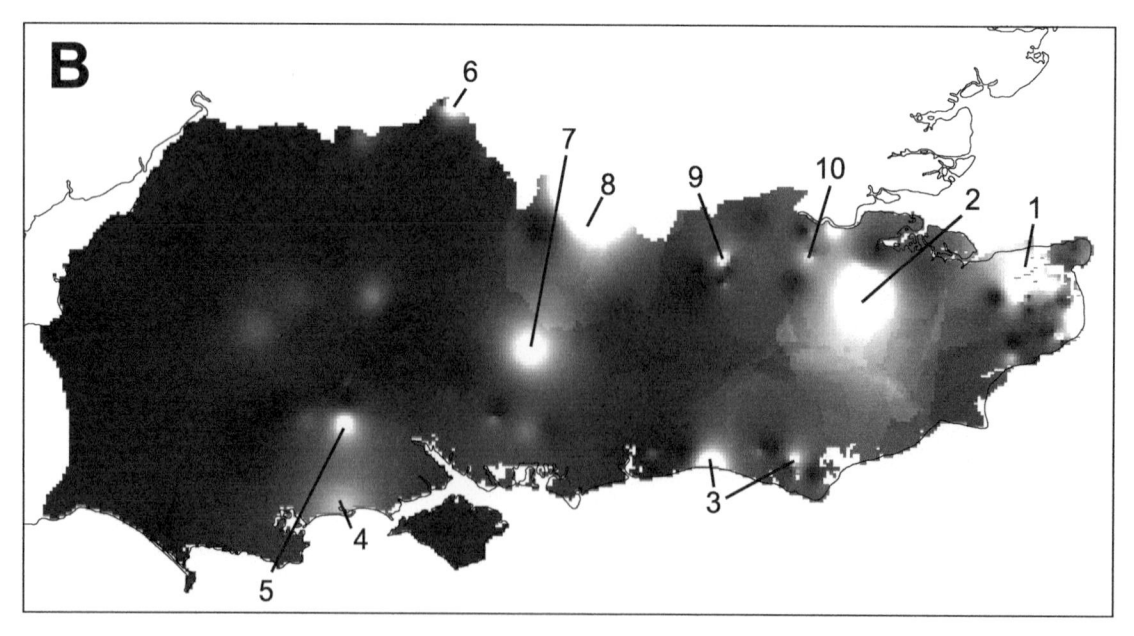

*Figure 35. Inverse distance weightings of iron consumption in Phase B, showing ten regional high spots*

Table 37. Phase B IDW (Map 6) areas

| Area | Description |
|---|---|
| B1 | Wantsum Channel and Dover |
| B2 | Upper Medway/West Holmesdale |
| B3 | Sussex |
| B4 | Coastal Hampshire and Dorset |
| B5 | Breamore |
| B6 | Upper Thames Valley near Oxford |
| B7 | Northeast Hampshire |
| B8 | Middle Thames near Cookham |
| B9 | Beddington and Croydon |
| B10 | Darent Valley and Northfleet (Ebbsfleet) |

Table 38. Phase C IDW areas

| Area | Description |
|---|---|
| C1 | East Kent to the Medway |
| C2 | Southeast Hampshire |
| C3 | Bargates |
| C4 | Central Somerset |
| C5 | North Wiltshire |
| C6 | West Berkshire |
| C7 | Central Surrey |

On the other hand, the dominant area for Wessex in Phase A of northern Wiltshire has all but disappeared in Phase B, despite the continuing presence of numerous cemeteries in the area. The Upper and Middle Thames Valley (B6 and B8 respectively) now make a first showing as zones of relatively high wealth in iron. This result may be a factor of edge effects, however, occurring as they do on the northern borders of the study region. Centrally inland is the cemetery at Alton in Hampshire (A7), which once again is a location surrounded by a dense concentration of poorly-dated Roman sites, as indeed is the Middle Thames area B8. In Surrey the main area of iron consumption (B9) has now shifted eastwards to the previously more marginal location of Beddington with satellite cemeteries at Mitcham and Croydon.

*Phase C comparative study*

Further shifts in the relative consumption of iron are evident within Phase C, with both localised changes and expansion into new areas. East Kent (C1) has three higher zones of consumption involving the coastal region from Folkestone up to and through the Wantsum seaway, next a clutch of sites along Watling Street around Faversham, Sittingbourne and Milton Regis, and finally the Roman bridge crossing of the Medway adjacent to Rochester with the recently excavated cemetery near Cuxton a short distance to the south. The seventh-century foundation sites on the North Downs nearest to the coast also benefit from the general wealth in iron exhibited in the area. Sussex has virtually disappeared in terms of relative wealth, however, though there is a discernable geographical shift away from the Cuckmere valley towards the site at Saxonbury in Southover below Lewes in the Ouse valley. The Meon valley sites at Shavard's Farm near Corhampton and Meonstoke represent a new centre of relative iron wealth in southeast Hampshire (C2). Further west along the coast the Bargates cemetery (C3) retains a presence, while a completely new zone opens up to the west in Somerset (C4), which is focused on cemeteries at Queen Camel and Hicknell Slait.

Interestingly, communities in north Wiltshire (C5) make a fresh appearance after a gap in Phase B, although this area's centre has shifted to the north of the previous Phase A iron-rich communities. The principal sites here are The Fox at Purton and Blunsdon St Andrew, which at first glance appear to be poorly-furnished cemeteries with only a few iron artefacts. Relatively assessed, however, these prove to possess a greater weight than that from surrounding communities. For example, the well-known cemetery at Butler's Field near Lechlade in Gloucestershire by the Thames (Boyle *et al.* 1998), despite having large numbers of iron artefacts in all three phases, only makes an appearance on the periphery of Area C4 in Phase C (and this is equally true in phases A and B). The average weight of the iron at Butler's Field proves unremarkable when spread across its whole community and when considered in the context of its nearest neighbours. Another new area for iron wealth is based on the eight-grave cemetery at East Ilsley (C6). The single furnished burial here has a shield boss, two spearheads, a seax and a knife, which is sufficient in weight to raise the community average above that of the surrounding cemeteries. Finally a cluster of potentially higher-status cemeteries in Surrey is represented by the Gally Hills near Banstead, Lion Green at Purley and the Farthingdown site (C7). They barely stand out locally, however, and are located within a largely blank tract of landscape between the Thames and the south coast in this period.

Throughout Phase C there appears to be a continuing relationship with the large numbers of undated Roman sites (Figure 37). This relationship is particularly apparent in Kent with the shift from Area B2 in the Upper Medway to Area C1 centred on the Swale. There is also a dense concentration of Roman sites running directly across Area C5 in Berkshire, whilst clusters of Roman sites appear on the periphery of C3 in Somerset, C4 in north Wiltshire and C2 in southeast Hampshire.

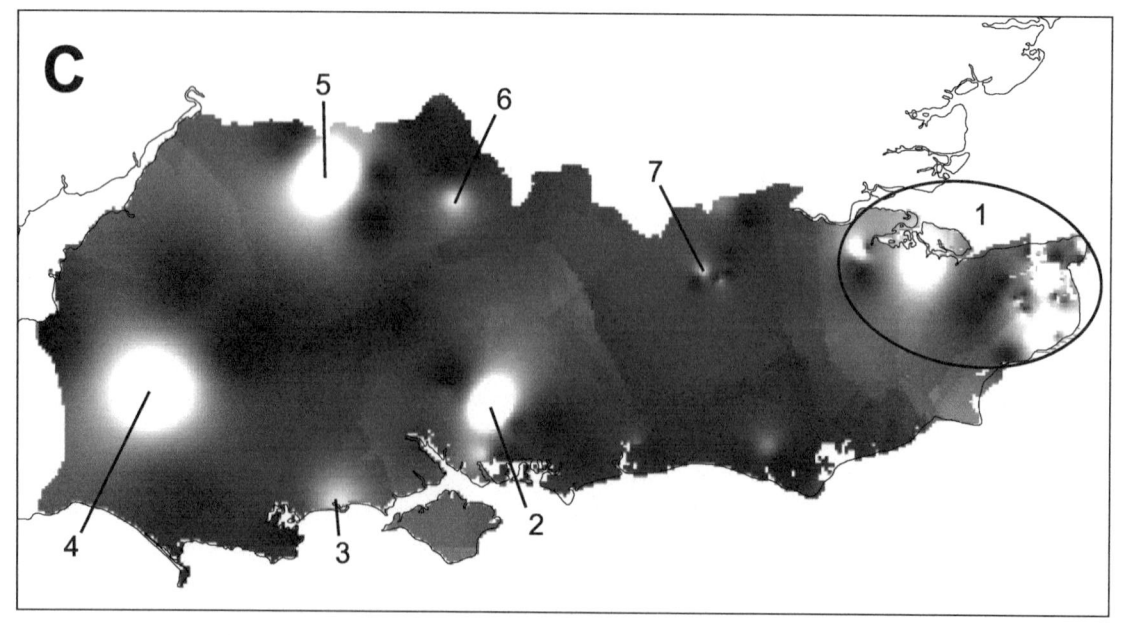

*Figure 36. Inverse distance weightings of iron consumption in Phase C, showing seven regional high spots*

## 8. Community Wealth in Iron Compared

### Conclusions on the value of iron in the study region and period

The procurement strategies, modes of production and differential usage for iron artefacts throughout the study period all exhibit spatial shifts over time. In particular Phase B appears to represent a transition period, perhaps indicating a hiatus in supply for a variety of purposes, above all for deposition with the deceased. The apparent relationship with many poorly-dated Roman sites requires some explanation and it might be reasonable to suppose that intensive re-use of iron scrap could and did fulfil the domestic and military requirements of a broadly-spread population. This would explain the apparent constant search for replacement sources, as scrap iron from known deserted sites became exhausted. The new Silchester evidence is particularly relevant in this context, further supporting the view that the sourcing, manufacture and distribution of iron ranged over geographical space and was not exclusively bound into local networks. It would appear that there may have been competition for access to these specific resources, rather than a wholesale exploitation of iron-ore deposits that had been previously worked within the Roman period. Ore resources do not seem to have been key to the location of the earliest communities with origins in the fifth century, however. The evidence suggests instead that these ore sources need not have been fully accessed until Phase C at the earliest. This is a statement that seems anomalous in relation to East Sussex downland settlements with their proximity to the largest ore deposits available in Phase C, yet with only minimal iron wealth exhibited in that period. It is tempting to suggest instead that any iron wealth derived from the Sussex Weald may have gone elsewhere as tribute to overlords.

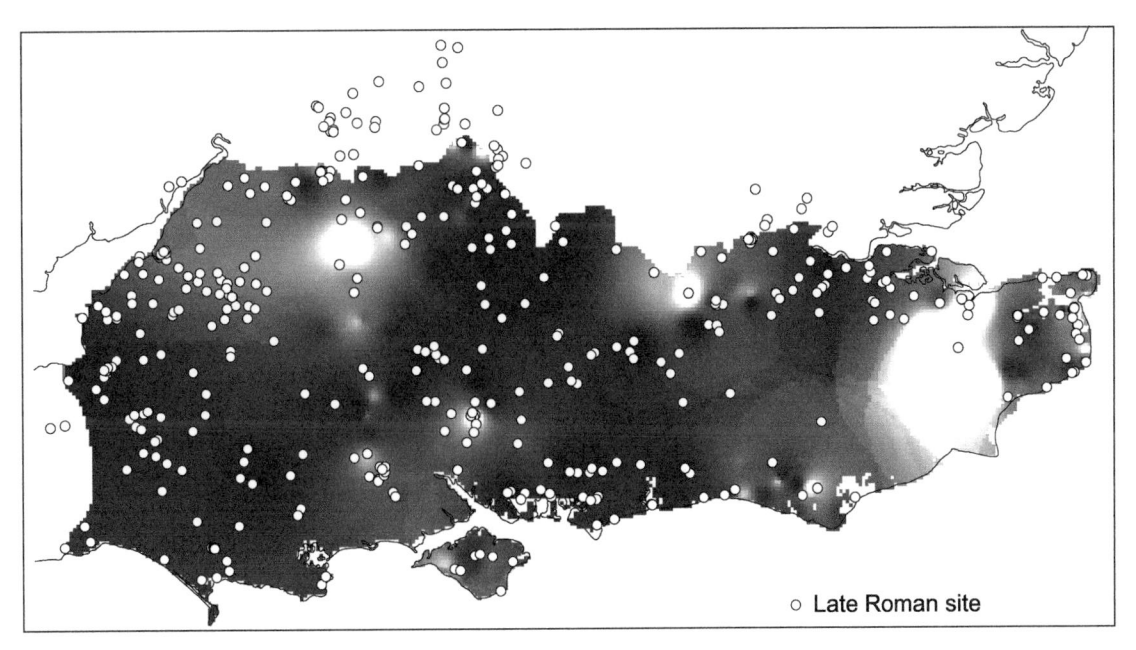

*Figure 37. Inverse distance weightings of iron consumption in Phase C and Late Roman sites*

The enduring central position of east Kent with regards the volume of iron usage in its cemeteries, particularly in its coastal areas, and a demonstrable ability to spread iron wealth across the population over time raises the need for a coherent explanation. Certainly there is no obvious reason why the population of Kent should be better placed than the rest of southern Britain to monopolise available iron supplies. Nor does its immediate environment appear to provide a landscape with a particularly dense population of Roman sites, in comparison to Sussex or Dorset for example.

East Kent did possess one obvious and enduring advantage, however, in its proximity to the Frankish realms across the Dover Straits. There does seem to be a case for considering the importation of iron from continental Europe as a basis for its iron wealth. Certainly there is plenty of evidence to suggest that documented trading contacts with the Frisians in particular could have engaged Kent with continental networks of iron production and trade in northwest Europe. Additionally such an explanation might account for the fall-off rate of iron consumption as we move further away from east Kent across southern Britain.

Alternatively and secondly, we might suggest that sufficient scrap material remained from the Roman coastal infrastructure in Kent from forts, ports and their wharves and derelict craft, to support its population's needs throughout Phase A and indeed beyond. A third possibility is that scrap material from the hinterland of Kent, perhaps including partially-worked ore from the Weald and other more marginal resources, was funnelled to the Kent coast, where effective exchange mechanisms utilised iron as a rudimentary currency by weight or volume. The hinterland of Kent was perhaps as extensive as that for the whole of the rest of southern Britain and might have taken in territory between the outlier communities on the Isle of Wight to the south and Surrey to the north.

If Fulford is correct, however, a major Roman site such as Silchester or Canterbury could provide enough scrap to support recycling for more than a century. The conjunction of high Anglo-Saxon iron consumption in certain communities and the availability in adjacent territories of abandoned Roman sites in the two later phases (B and C) may well prove to be a function of their strategic location within continuing landscape structures. The drawing-in of iron resources to central places seems to be demonstrated in Phase C, with high consumption points surrounded by potential resource bases represented by Roman sites. The glaring spatial gaps in the visible consumption patterns, albeit with swathes of potentially exploitable Roman artefacts, would further support this view.

For Kent, access to iron is excellent in all three phases, yet it seems unlikely that Wealden mined sources are being exploited at this time, although the more marginal resources of the North Downs, Blean and Dover may have been in use, although perhaps not to an extent that would necessarily explain Kentish wealth in iron. Instead a more probable explanation lies in the proximity of east Kent by sea to large-scale iron working centres such as the Veluwe region in the Netherlands and beyond that could have been accessed through the Frisian trading network. Such ironwork may have been traded on into other areas of Kentish influence as an exchange good. More concerted exploitation of iron ore deposits, however, may well stem from the seventh century, when a dip in the consumption pattern is noted, requiring a restructuring of the resource base and concentration of control within the upper echelons of society.

# 9. A Restricted Wealth in Copper Alloys?

If iron had common currency, then what can the changing patterns of use of more esoteric materials tell us about relative community wealth? Key elements here are copper alloy, silver, gold, amber and amethysts which are explored through a series of case studies and are compared with the evidence from Jeremy Huggett's seminal article on imported Anglo-Saxon grave goods (Huggett 1988).

Copper alloy artefacts in general have limited relationship to the everyday tasks of social replication that are more readily associated with items made in iron. Rather, their forms are such as to highlight display, cultural allegiance and the personal adornment of women at the time of marriage and throughout their life courses (Harrington 2011), They might be considered to have a higher value related to the esoteric and brighter nature of the finished articles, particularly if they were also gilded, silvered or tinned, relative to the overt functionality of iron artefacts, although on occasion used to embellish them. The project database records 21% of all objects in burial assemblages for the study period as being made of copper alloy, both as sheet metal and cast objects. Their distribution on phased burials is given in Table 39 (see Plate 6 for an *in situ* example).

Copper alloy artefacts are thus relatively common in Phase A and become much rarer thereafter, as a proportion of the total number of objects deposited. The evidence would suggest that either the types of artefacts for which copper alloy was the major component were no longer being buried, or that there was a reduction in the supply of the component raw materials at the interface between phases A and B. That interface was essentially contemporary with the transition from Style I to Style II in Kent, possibly a little later elsewhere within the study region. The fall-off in the real number of copper alloy artefacts deposited in Phase C is also noticeable. However, the relative number of curated Roman copper alloy artefacts deposited throughout the three phases

*Table 39. Numbers of copper alloy artefacts in phased burials*

| Phase | Ae objects | Total objects | Ae as % of total | Curated Roman artefacts | As % of Ae total |
|-------|------------|---------------|------------------|-------------------------|------------------|
| A     | 3573       | 12455         | 29%              | 316                     | 1%               |
| B     | 1069       | 7684          | 14%              | 71                      | 0.06%            |
| C     | 677        | 5331          | 13%              | 38                      | 0.06%            |

mirrors that of the early Anglo-Saxon manufactured copper alloy objects. This again highlights a cultural change that was taking place towards the end of the sixth century. How then might we explain these very broad shifts in the deposition of copper alloy through the study period? Firstly the potential sources of material and methods of manufacture require investigation.

## European copper alloy production

The main areas of copper production in the Roman world had been in Spain, central Europe and Cyprus. Although in the Roman period there was centralised production of types of object, or central sources of raw material, by the later stages of the Empire there is increasing evidence for mixed alloys. This suggests an increase in recycling or conversely some stress on raw-material mined sources, a situation which continued into the early Anglo-Saxon period (Bayley 1998, 167). The eastern Mediterranean mine workings in Cyprus may have re-opened from the late sixth century, but documentary sources indicate a widespread shortage of alloyed copper for the Eastern Empire in the seventh century (McCormick 2001, 52). The extent to which people and exchange systems were dependent on scrap for the manufacture of copper alloy artefacts in the post-Roman period is a consistent feature of interpretations presented on a Europe-wide basis dealing with the period through to the eighth century. In northern Europe excavation evidence from a range of elite settlement sites illustrates that non-ferrous metalworking was closely linked to the upper strata of society between the fifth and seventh centuries and this elite achieved a near monopoly over the manufacture and distribution of fine metalwork. The finished products of cast copper alloy ornamented metalwork indicate that larger scale centralised production was certainly in place by the sixth century (Hamerow 2002, 117). The sources of raw materials for the alloys in this manufacturing model was again scrap, as evidenced, for example, by cut-up brooches, ingots and possibly coins at the fifth-century craft working site at Gennep on the river Maas in the Netherlands (*ibid.*).

## Copper alloy production in Britain

While mineral deposits are present within the British Isles, in Shropshire, North Wales and Anglesey, published metallurgical studies have determined that the raw-material content of early Anglo-Saxon copper alloy artefacts was generally derived from recycled material (Mortimer 1991, 162). Metallurgical comparisons of the northern European corpus of cruciform brooches have shown that, whilst the chemical composition was similar throughout in the earliest phases of their production, a decline in the quality of metal used was apparent from the late fifth century onwards, identifiable through the presence of more impurities in the alloy. The evidence would suggest a problem with the supply of metal, rather than ineptitude on the part of the Anglo-Saxon metal-workers (*ibid.*, 167). More recent work has highlighted that such an early shift in metal content might only relate to cruciform brooches and that shifts in the content of other brooch forms may more likely relate to the early sixth century (Mortimer 2007). Metallurgical analyses of the corpus of great square-headed brooches illustrate the point that the alloy compositions were randomly constructed. Apparently the brooch-casters exercised little or no precise control, regardless of whether the brooch was to be gilded or not (Hines 1997, 211–3; Mortimer 1993, 30, who considered a wider range of brooch forms). Brownsword and Hines (1993) established that great square-headed brooches might share a similar metallurgical composition to one another, yet be stylistically different and vice-versa. Halliwell (1997a, 261–6) carried out metallurgical analyses of the copper alloy buckles from the late fifth to sixth-century cemetery at Mill Hill, Deal, Kent (KntGMM-IC1). The results raised doubts about the received opinion that Anglo-Saxon copper alloys were essentially the same as those of the Late Roman period and were produced from vast quantities of low value copper alloy coinage. Instead, it appeared that a decrease in the copper content occurred over time, suggesting that, at this Kentish site at least, there was a gradual change in the supply of scrap or the use of more from one particular source than another. Nevertheless, here the manufacturing source of the cast buckles may have been in *Francia*, as their composition was broadly similar to those from the cemetery at Saint-Sulpice VD near Paris (*ibid.*, 265).

Mortimer (1999, 88–9) in her discussion of cruciform brooches identified that the earlier types had a purer alloy composition than the later types, which were more frequently of mixed alloys. Again, the absence of fresh sources of metal, until the Middle Saxon period, is a causal explanation for the need of craft metalworkers to re-cast previously-alloyed materials. No regional variations in the alloy composition were detected, although a wide range of construction techniques can be demonstrated in this particular brooch form. Intensive and enforced recycling appears to have been the norm (*ibid.*, 89), though she did tentatively note (Mortimer 1990, 393) that Kent may have received a limited supply of copper alloy from Frisia, identified by a small corpus of zinc-rich alloys among its cruciform brooches. Nevertheless, metalworkers had the capability to produce alloys with predictable qualities even when assembling batches of disparate raw materials. The final appearance of the metal may well have been a primary consideration here (Mortimer 1988, 233).

The tinning on brooch and buckle surfaces and on other fitted mounts was probably carried out to simulate the appearance of silver in the early Anglo-Saxon period. This typically used the application of molten tin to a copper alloy object, but the selective use of the technique suggests a limited availability of tin in a raw state, while of insufficient quantity to be a component of the copper alloys themselves. The technique used for gilding has proved to be invariably that of mercury-gilding or fire-gilding, in which an amalgam of mercury and gold could be rubbed onto the surface and then heated. As the gold was applied as a paste, there was little difficulty in using it on uneven and angular (chip-carved) cast surfaces. Alternatively, and more rarely, the surface of an object was amalgamated using clean mercury, after which layers of gold leaf could be added, then finally it was heat-treated to drive off the remaining mercury ready for burnishing. Both techniques give virtually indistinguishable results on the finished item (Oddy 1980, 131). Clearly, gilding was a ubiquitous technique in the production of early Anglo-Saxon ornamented artefacts throughout the study region, but it was one that required access to a reasonably wide range of raw materials. The source of tin would most probably be in Cornwall (Mortimer 1988, 229), although there is no direct evidence for continuing production there after the Roman period other

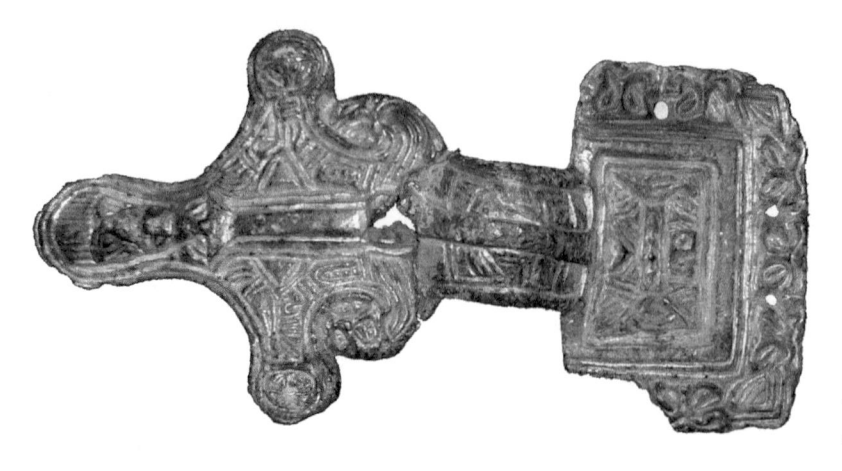

*Figure 38. A copper alloy great square headed brooch*

than from indications from written sources (Gerrard 2000, 23). Mercury may have been sourced from Spain, where there are suitable deposits. Alternatively, one might also suggest the substantial deposits in Carinthia, southern Austria as a possible source, perhaps arriving via the trading networks through the Rhineland (Bowie *et al.* 1978, 37). Mercury was found in a glass phial in a contemporary metalworker's toolkit in Grave 10 at Hérouvillette in Lower Normandy and also later in the study period from the Six Dials site at *Hamwic* (Oddy 1996, 82), thus demonstrating its circulation as a material over a long period. It must, however, always have been the province of the specialist craftsperson in its acquisition, curation and usage.

A detailed consideration of the copper alloy brooches and other personal artefacts from the cemetery at Butler's Field, Lechlade (GlsLLE-MC1) (Mortimer 1988, 230–233) concluded that different alloys were chosen for different object types. The disc brooches may have shared a single point of origin, as they have compositional similarities. Then the cast saucer brooches exhibit a compositional change over time, with purer alloys in the earlier examples and higher levels of zinc in the later forms (Dickinson 1993, 34). Pairs of saucer brooches with the same design have been identified within this research rarely to share the same weight, with a variation usually within three grams. Given the similarities in the alloy compositions of matched pairs, it is therefore implied that they were produced unevenly from the same batch of scrap metal in each case. Non-identical brooch pairs tend to have different alloy compositions, although there are even variations within this scenario (Dickinson 1993, 34).

## Weights of copper alloy artefacts

The metallurgical and other analyses of copper alloys discussed above suggest a hiatus in the supply of the raw material by the late sixth century, a point also established by Brookes (2007) for the consumption patterns in East Kent at that time. This interpretation of the evidence can

## 9. A Restricted Wealth in Copper Alloys?

*Table 40. Numbers and weights copper alloy objects by phase*

| Phase | Ae objects | Total weight of Ae | Average weight of object | Weight range of objects | Median weight |
|---|---|---|---|---|---|
| A | 3573 | 53741g | 15.04g | 1–647g | 8g |
| B | 1069 | 39869g | 37.00g | 1–2550g | 6g |
| C | 677 | 7157g | 10.6g | 1–218g (2000g) | 3g |

be deconstructed further through a review of the weights of copper alloy artefacts over the three phases, as delineated in Table 40.

For each phase the heaviest object present is a copper alloy bowl. In Phase A this vessel is a bossed-rim bowl, an unusually heavy example with a foot ring presumably from the Rhineland, in Phase B it is an eastern Mediterranean 'Coptic' cast bowl and in Phase C it is a 'Celtic' hanging-bowl weighing in at 218g. Admittedly Phase C also contains an anomalously heavy bowl at 2000g from Buckland, Dover, grave 137, although this may represent a repaired and curated Roman object (Evison 1987, 103). Away from these extremes, the median weights, representing the most common everyday finds such as buckles and pins, reveal a diminishing copper alloy content by weight over time. The sudden leap in the average weight of objects in Phase B is entirely attributable to the presence of the particularly heavy imported eastern Mediterranean cast bowls, within a context of far fewer objects being in circulation. The distribution of copper alloy bowls will be discussed separately as a case study below.

## Community access to copper alloy material over time and space

If it is accepted that the accumulation of scrap copper alloy was the main source of raw material for the range of artefacts deposited in burial assemblages, then it might be argued that those areas and communities with the greatest average weight of copper alloy present would share a locational relationship to the Late Roman sites from which the material might have been scavenged. This would be to present just one model of procurement, however, assuming a range of abandoned sites from which the material might be readily picked up or excavated. It might be suggested that portable valuables such as dress fittings and even statuary, would be transported away at the time of site abandonment by their owners, unless the occupants were forcibly and violently removed and unable to return. The discard pattern for copper alloy seems likely to have been very different to that from iron, based on size, weight and purpose, although both materials could and did occur in hoard contexts. An alternative model would be to suggest the exchange (voluntary or otherwise) of copper alloy by a post-Roman population in return for other goods or services from migrant north Europeans (the first Anglo-Saxons), over whom the latter may have exercised dominance or had some other form of control.

As Table 41 illustrates, the average consumption of copper alloy varied greatly between contemporary communities. The drastic reduction in the average by Phase B in terms of the

*Table 41. Average community consumption of copper alloy by phase*

| Phase | Lowest average per community | Highest average per community | Median per community |
|-------|------------------------------|-------------------------------|----------------------|
| A     | 0.24g                        | 95.67g                        | 8.22g                |
| B     | 0.11g                        | 2020g                         | 4g                   |
| C     | 0.13g                        | 33.43g                        | 1g                   |

lowest amount and diminished median is partly off-set by the huge increase from the copper alloy bowls. In itself, however, this last factor was insufficient to reverse a region-wide trend of lower availability for this particular material.

In order to investigate this trend further, both chronologically and spatially, Inverse-Distance-Weightings (IDW) were plotted for the Gross Domestic Consumption (GDC) recorded by phase for copper alloys, for all those communities with two or more burials, in order to illustrate the spread of access to artefacts manufactured in this material. The weight of copper alloy for a phase was divided by the number of people in that phase on a site and sites with no copper alloy present were included in the analysis. The data has been ranged equally about the median GDC in each case, in order to aid visual comparisons on the maps.

## Phase A comparative study

The map for Phase A (Figure 39) shows that there are five main concentrations of copper alloy, each set within a concentric ring of diminishing usage over space. As might be expected, the concentrations are centred on east Kent in the southern hinterland to the Wantsum Channel, with high points at Beakesbourne (KntBKB-IC2), Mill Hill, Deal (KntGMM-ICF1) and Finglesham (KntNBN-IC1). Next is East Sussex between Pevensey and the River Adur, with high points at Alfriston and Brighton. There is a more diffuse area consisting of southern Hampshire and the Isle of Wight, possibly extending westwards, with an uncertain northern limit around Laverstock and Old Sarum (WltLVK-IC2). Then a polyfocal area of north Wiltshire and Berkshire is based respectively around Wroughton (WltWGN-IC1) and Goldbury Hill, West Hendred (BrkWHD-MC1). Finally a less clearly defined area covers the Darenth Valley (KntDRH-IC1) across to Croydon (SryCYN-MC1). Several 'dead zones' are also generated here from the presence of cemetery communities poor in copper alloy terms. These are western Surrey around Shepperton, Esher and Fetcham; the western Holmesdale through to the Weald; western Sussex and the South Downs through to Winchester, though with a slightly higher point of consumption around Droxford in the Meon valley (HtsSBT-IC1); and the entire western section of the study region. In Phase A, these 'dead' areas might be considered either as peripheral to the main concentrations of settlement wealth or else as buffer zones between them.

If the major source of copper alloy was from recycled Roman artefacts, it can be inferred that these items were most probably scavenged from deserted and derelict Roman sites in the vicinity. This proposition has been tested by overlaying the Roman sites onto the GDC/IDW Phase A map (Figure 40). There is a striking overlap between some of the 'dead zones' of copper alloy

*9. A Restricted Wealth in Copper Alloys?*

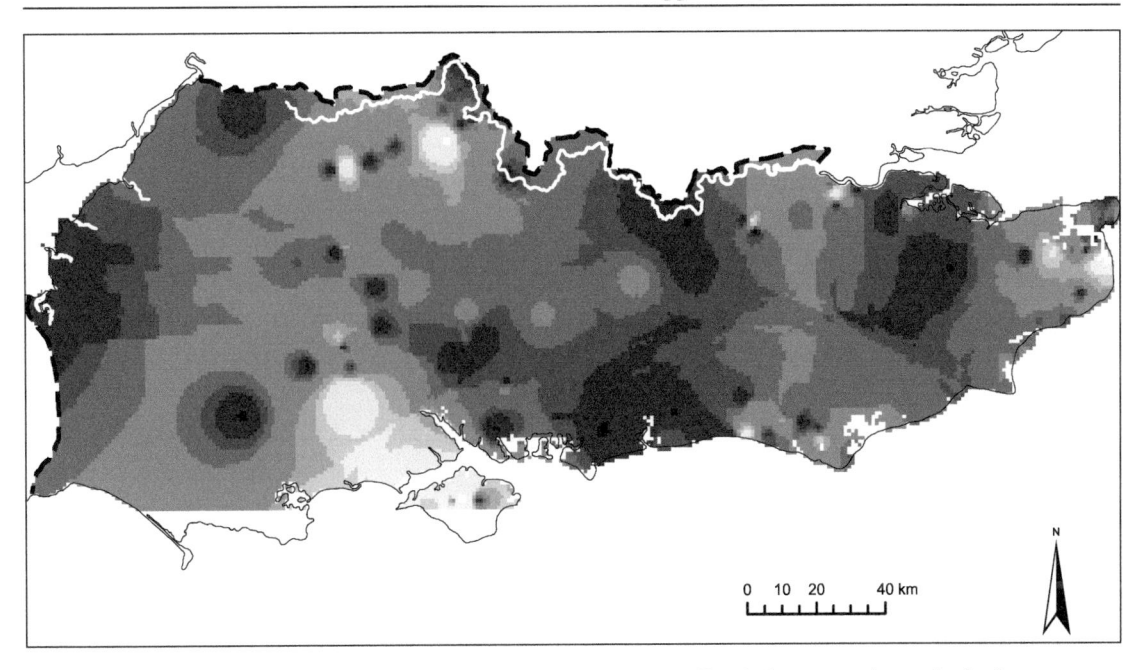

*Figure 39. Inverse distance weightings concentrations of copper alloy (white areas have the highest concentrations) in Phase A*

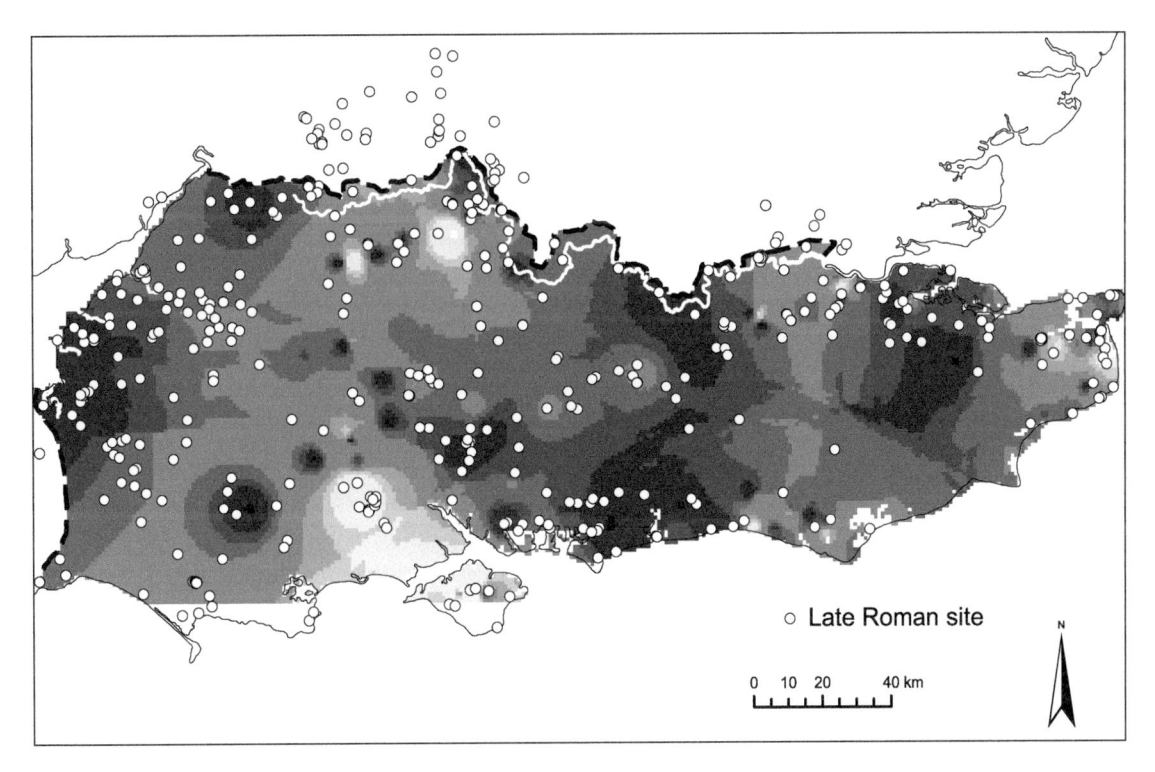

*Figure 40. Phase A copper alloy concentrations and Late Roman sites*

143

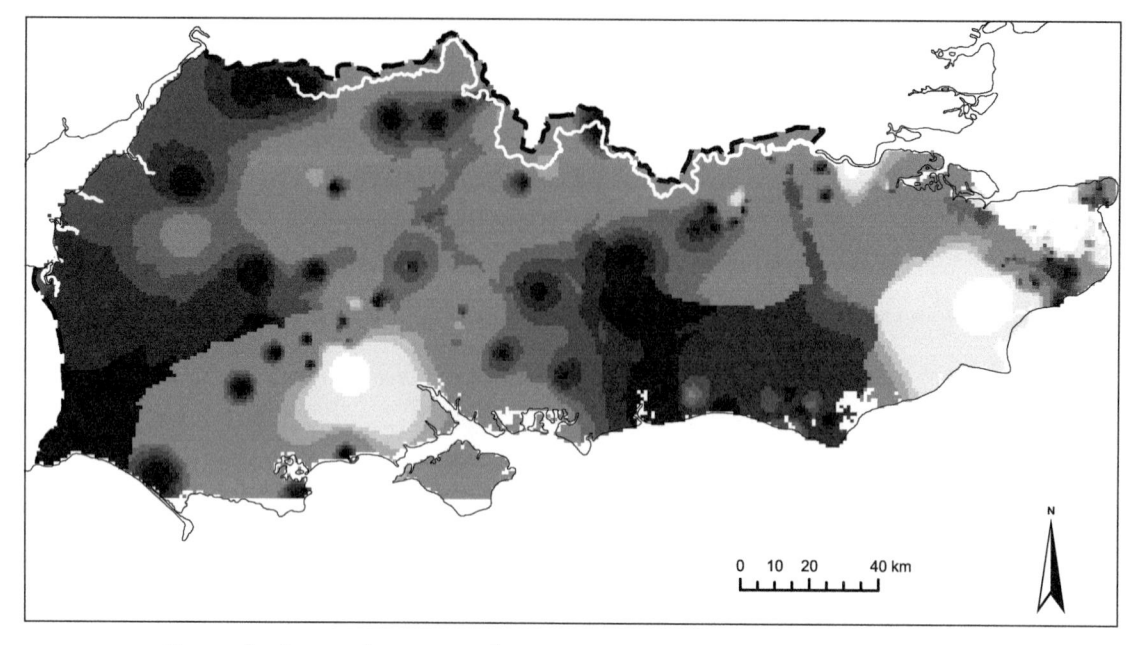

*Figure 41. Inverse distance weightings concentrations of copper alloy in Phase B*

usage and the densest concentrations of whole-period Roman sites. These occur in western Sussex, western Surrey, a south-western sector of the study region to the west beyond Hampshire, the territory enclosing Winchester and the western part of the Vale of Holmesdale. The coincidence of early Anglo-Saxon copper alloy wealth with Roman sites open to potential scavenging really only occurs in north Wiltshire. On this basis, it might be suggested that proximity to deserted sites may not have been the principal means by which Anglo-Saxon communities directly accessed scrap for recycling.

### Phase B comparative study
In Phase B (Figure 41), a period of diminished general use of copper alloy and thus inferred reduced availability, the concentration of wealth in east Kent and the Holmesdale is based primarily on imported artefacts. The cemetery at Breamore in Hampshire continues to dominate the western distribution, whilst Beddington, Surrey still maintains a profile. The region-wide pattern is one of reduced access to this material, as the range of weights is negligible everywhere. As no discernable relationship to Roman sites could be deduced from this distribution, that information is not presented here in map form.

### Phase C comparative study
Moving on to Phase C, there is a general smoothing away of access to what is now a scarce material. The only high spots are ones that would have been barely visible in Phase A. These are

## 9. A Restricted Wealth in Copper Alloys?

located at Basingstoke, at Gally Hills near Banstead and Buckland, Dover, all by virtue of copper alloy bowls recorded within cemeteries of more than two inhumations. Once again Roman sites cannot be demonstrated by proximity to contribute to this pattern (this data is not presented here in map form).

### Copper alloy case study 1: buckle loops and plates

Given Kent's wealth in iron, we might expect it to be relatively wealthy in copper alloy in comparison to the rest of the study area. Problematically, however, Faversham, which is by far the best-endowed site in Kent in terms of metalwork, does not appear as a hot spot for copper alloy wealth throughout the three phases. This is solely due to the fact that there are very few individual recorded grave groups available for analysis here, due to the circumstances of its discovery during the nineteenth century – found when a cutting was put through to level off the terrain for the railway and much of the material sold off to collectors. Over 41% of its finds (156 out of the 376 uncontexted items archived in the British Museum) are made of copper alloy, however, which suggests ease of access to the constituent raw materials, whether from its hinterland or through trade or gift exchange with Frisia or *Francia*, in common with other east Kentish communities. Given the overlying and statistically-skewing presence of heavy, imported copper alloy bowls in east Kent, the issue of general trends in wealth in copper alloy can be best addressed through contextual and morphological comparisons of buckles as an artefact type that reflects better the overall wealth positions of cemetery communities.

*Figure 42. A copper alloy buckle loop*

*Figure 43. A copper alloy and garnet inlaid buckle loop and belt plate*

Table 42. *Copper alloy buckle weights and provenances in Kent and the Saxon area by phase*

| Ae buckle provenances | Phase A | Phase B | Phase C |
|---|---|---|---|
| Kent regional | 15.75g | 13.7g | 4.3g |
| Saxon regional | 12.5g | 12g | 4g |
| Kent Imported and K/F | 18.75g | 22.2g | 7.6g |
| Saxon Imported and K/F | 22.4g | 11g | 18g |

Table 43. *Copper alloy buckles by percentage of population*

| Phase | Kent population as % of total | % of Ae buckles total | Saxon population as % of total | % of Ae buckles total | Total Ae buckles |
|---|---|---|---|---|---|
| A | 26% | 59% | 74% | 41% | 351 |
| B | 52% | 84% | 48% | 16% | 200 |
| C | 60% | 77% | 40% | 23% | 145 |

The term buckle is used here to include both simple buckle loops (Marzinzik type I series) and those combined with a fixed or hinge-attached plate (Marzinzik type II series). It excludes from the analysis, however, copper alloy studs and rivets. Copper alloy (Ae) buckles make up 37% of all buckles recorded in individual grave groups, excluding those from separate findspots and unassociated material within cemeteries. The comparison made here is again between Kentish-located buckles (from both west and east Kent) and those found elsewhere within the study region (termed for convenience as Saxon). It uses the attributes of weight, count and provenance. The buckles were divided into three main provenance categories. The first are *regional*, which covers many of the utilitarian forms that fall within Marzinzik's (2003) typology, but are without any clear geographical associations and are assumed therefore to be of indigenous manufacture. Secondly there are *Kentish/Frankish* (K/F) buckles, which are more esoteric objects that share stylistic associations with northern European types but may still have been manufactured in Kent. Finally we have the *Imported* buckles, probably not manufactured in Britain and strongly associated with either *Francia* or Byzantium and the Mediterranean basin.

Comparison of the weights of differently-provenanced copper alloy buckles, shown in Table 42, serves to demonstrate that, in Phase A, the more common *regional* buckles are slighter heavier in Kent. The more esoteric, imported and Frankish-influenced versions are slightly heavier outside of Kent, although this group includes objects that may well have been manufactured in Kent. Thus we are led to conclude that objects travelling outside of their proposed zone of manufacture are a little more substantial than those retained for local Kentish use. In Phase B, the *regional* types are similar everywhere in terms of weight, but the weightier imported items are retained for use in Kent. The imported copper alloy buckles available outside of Kent in Phase B are slight by comparison and suggest that Kent is restricting the flow of these buckle types outside its sphere of influence. By Phase C, the *regional* copper alloy buckles are small and lightweight, with the Kent *imported* items slightly heavier. The apparent anomaly of substantially heavier *imported* items in

## 9. A Restricted Wealth in Copper Alloys?

Table 44. Numbers of copper alloy buckles by provenance in Kent and elsewhere in Phase A

| Provenance | Kent | Saxon | Total |
|---|---|---|---|
| Regional | 88 | 112 | 200 |
| Kentish/Frankish | 107 | 17 | 124 |
| Imported | 7 | 7 | 14 |
| Other | 4 | 8 | 13 |
| Totals | 206 | 144 | 351 |

Table 45. Numbers of copper alloy buckles by provenance in Kent and elsewhere in Phase B

| Provenance | Kent | Saxon | Total |
|---|---|---|---|
| Regional | 93 | 29 | 122 |
| Kentish/Frankish | 68 | 2 | 70 |
| Imported | 6 | 0 | 6 |
| Other | 1 | 1 | 2 |
| Totals | 168 | 32 | 200 |

the non-Kent area in Phase C is a result of the weights of just three buckles, all of which appear to have been curated as 'heirlooms' from an earlier period until their eventual deposition.

The copper alloy buckles are numerically unevenly spread across the phases, as shown in Table 43, with 351 recorded for Phase A, 200 for Phase B and 145 for Phase C, thus reflecting the general decline in the presence of copper alloy artefacts over time in grave assemblages. On the other hand, Kent actually increases its proportion of the available copper alloy buckles over time. This suggests that, although copper alloy was less readily available or less frequently used, Kent's population was able to access a greater proportion of what was available. Such a result is not a direct reflection of the greater relative number of burials in Kent, as a simple correlate of more people equating with more buckles, for the proportions of population to buckles are as follows:

The deployment of copper alloy buckles appears then to be a distinctive trait of Kentish culture from Phase A onwards. Consideration of the provenances of these buckles shows that there was differential access to different types across time and space, however, as can be seen from Table 44.

The *regional*-type buckles in Phase A are widespread in their distribution, with Kent having the single greatest total (88), followed by Sussex with 46. The remaining counties have produced no more than nineteen each. Clearly Kent also has by far the most of those types provenanced as being *Kentish/Frankish* (107), but the remaining 17 buckles have a distinct distribution, in Sussex, on the Isle of Wight and in Hampshire at Breamore, and also at Mitcham in Surrey.

There is only one example from an area further away from Kent and that occurs in Oxfordshire. Of the *imported* items, all from *Francia*, the seven that were not found within Kent, are distributed along the south coast. There are two in Sussex, four on the Isle of Wight and just one from Hampshire at Andover. The 'Other' category here is populated by Curated/Roman buckles, with four in Kent and the remaining eight elsewhere, although surprisingly none from sites in Wiltshire.

Table 45 illustrates that in phase B Kent continues to lead numerically in its access to the *regional* types (93), with Sussex again the next in line with ten out of twenty nine. Kent wholly dominates in the *Kentish/Frankish* category (68), with the remaining two being from Surrey (Mitcham) and East Sussex (Selmeston), again well within the Kentish sphere of influence. All six of the distinctively *Imported* Frankish buckles were located unsurprisingly in Kent.

In Phase C Kent appears to have retained its dominance in the acquisition of copper alloy buckles,

*Table 46. Numbers of copper alloy buckles by provenance in Kent and the Saxon area in Phase C*

| Provenance | Kent | Saxon | Total |
| --- | --- | --- | --- |
| Regional | 91 | 30 | 121 |
| Kentish/Frankish | 7 | 1 | 8 |
| Imported | 14 | 2 | 16 |
| Other | 0 | 0 | 0 |
| Totals | 113 | 32 | 145 |

as shown in Table 46. It has most of the *regional* types (91), with eleven of the remaining thirty coming from Hampshire, including a clutch of four from Snell's Corner near Horndean. Kent has virtually all of those available of its own types, apart from a singleton from Wiltshire. Kent also enjoys a near monopoly over the *imported* types, retaining two of the three Frankish artefacts, the other occurring in Southampton at *Hamwic* (St Mary's Stadium site). There are twelve buckles of the new openwork types (Marzinzik type II.26) from the eastern Mediterranean, but the only outlier is recorded from the Butler's Field, Lechlade cemetery in Gloucestershire.

Kentish dominance through all phases in the deployment of copper alloy buckles is the most obvious outcome of this exercise. As such it mirrors Marzinzik's identification of a Kentish-dominated buckle 'fashion zone' that included Sussex and the Isle of Wight (Marzinzik 2003, 88). Unfortunately, metallurgical analyses of copper alloy buckles are rare events, but it is helpful to consider the implications of investigations into the corpus of finds from the Mill Hill, Deal, Kent cemetery (Halliwell 1997a, 261–266) for the use of copper alloy within the study region as a whole. It can be considered probable, for this artefact type if not for others, that the main supply source of scrap was from the near continent across the Dover Straits. If so, then any disruption to supply from within and throughout the rest of the study region, as seems to be indicated from Phase B onwards, does not seem to have unduly affected Kentish manufacture and usage of copper alloy. Kent may well have directly imported finished objects from the continent through all periods.

There is an anomaly in that those areas within the study region with the highest densities of Roman sites, which might be viewed as putative sources of copper alloy scrap, do not appear to have been able to mobilise these resources in order to manufacture their own buckles. This could have been the result of insufficient numbers of specialist metalworkers, or restricted access to the sources of scrap that were available, or a preference to convert the available copper alloy material into different artefact types, such as brooches. If copper alloy scrap became an important medium for exchange transactions, then those areas best able to scavenge this material may have traded it on, rather than seeking to re-cycle it into non-essential, or perhaps culturally less-significant, artefacts.

## Copper alloy case study 2: bowls and escutcheons

The complete and fragmentary copper alloy bowls deposited throughout the study period were in all probability imported into the study region as finished artefacts, albeit repaired locally when necessary. The bowl from Grave 91 at Mill Hill, Deal (KntGMM-IC1), although a rare find, "had been cheaply produced from a series of mis-matched spare components" (Halliwell 1997b, 245).

The database lists 107 copper alloy bowls, although only 66 are recorded within datable graves. A selection of the items from individual findspots were also broadly datable and have been included in the analysis here, providing 33 in Phase A, 32 in Phase B and seven in Phase C (total 72). Also included in our study are 42 examples of escutcheons from 'Celtic' hanging-bowls, from both burials and findspots. Excluded are those other receptacles or vessels for which there are only one or two examples, such as the bowls and skillet from Chessell Down, Isle of Wight and the Glastonbury, Somerset censer, which are *Imported/Byzantine* in origin. The focus of analysis is on the collective and typological distributions of bowls over time and space and their locational relationship to major routes. The buckles must be considered as personal dress items whereas the bowls are perceived to have a more visible gift-exchange status. Thus, an overview of their relationship to route ways may indicate extended networks and patterns of association.

The main types of copper alloy bowl present between AD 400 and 700 are curated Roman artefacts, 'Celtic' hanging-bowls, imported Byzantine bowls, Gotland and Vestland-type cauldrons, omega drop-handled bowls and bossed-rim bowls. In general terms, the imported Byzantine cast bowls are considerably heavier than all other types, the weighed items registering in excess of 2,000 grams. The Wilton 'Celtic' hanging-bowl, which is the most complete of the extant examples within the study region, together with its escutcheons, weighs 890 grams. The omega drop-handled bowls imported from the Rhineland weigh 727 grams, whilst the complete bossed-rim bowls from the same region are lighter, between 418 and 647 grams. The Gotland and Vestland cauldrons are lighter again at between 130 to 336 grams. All these Figures are based on actual weights and proportional estimates from fragmentary examples. Some bowls were clearly in a well-used state when deposited, so that their original weights when new may well have been greater to an unknown degree. Nevertheless, bowls are the heaviest copper alloy objects present and as noted, it appears that none were manufactured within the study region.

*Phase A distribution of copper alloy bowls (Figure 44)*
Two distinct groupings of bowls are evident in Phase A. The eastern group is centred on east Kent and extends with gaps along the south coast via East Sussex (the Ouse/Cuckmere site-complex) to the Isle of Wight, while a second strand runs along the north Kentish coast and on into eastern Surrey. Mortimer (2006: 381) in comparing the two Phase A copper alloy bowls from Finglesham (KntNBN-IC1), found that the compositional variability between them did not preclude a similar area and period of production. All contemporary imported bowl types are represented in this eastern group, although the only 'Celtic' hanging bowl from this group occurs at its westernmost point at Chessell Down on the Isle of Wight (Bruce-Mitford 2005, 154–6, no. 32). The unassociated hanging-bowl from Faversham in Kent has been considered to originate from a Late Roman or sub-Roman context rather than the Anglo-Saxon cemetery there (Bruce-Mitford 2005, 165–7, no. 38). Continuity of production from the Roman period is indicated, albeit probably imported into Kent through trade or dynastic intermarriage (*ibid.*, 40, contra Brenan 1991). A very recent metal-detected find of a Gotland-type cauldron from an inhumation context on the east side of the Ouse Valley in East Sussex (Martin Welch, pers. comm.) strengthens this distribution

pattern here. The grave probably belongs with others to a sector of the Beddingham cemetery first recorded in the nineteenth century. It is located significantly at the intersection of a Roman road and a tidal inlet.

The second grouping is focused on the Upper Thames Valley, from Berkshire's Long Wittenham (BrkLWM-MC1) to Gloucestershire's Fairford (GlsFFD-MC1), but the distribution appears to be more closely related to the Roman road network than to riverine connections. So perhaps these relate to continuing links to areas beyond the study region to the north and west using the Fosse Way (Margary number 5). Once again, all imported contemporary types are represented, although the unassociated Wilton bowl (Bruce-Mitford 2005, 291–3 no. 97) stands out as the isolated example of a Celtic hanging bowl in this second group, located along a major Roman road to the west. Its early dating might be contested, however, as it would coalesce more readily with the phase B examples and distribution. The absence of copper alloy vessels from the central part of the study region underlines the distinctiveness of the two groupings.

### *Phase B distribution of copper alloy bowls (Figure 44)*
The east-Kent cluster is the most dominant numerically in Phase B, with 23 bowls, including two 'Celtic' hanging-bowls and seven imported 'Byzantine' bowls, but no Gotland or Vestland-type cauldrons. The distribution in east Kent now extends over the North Downs into the Vale of Holmesdale, but the southern coastal distribution has disappeared and there is a more diffuse distribution elsewhere in the study region. The westernmost 'Byzantine' bowl appears in the 'Princely' barrow chamber at Taplow overlooking the Thames. Increasingly such bowls are present in high-status isolated burials dominating the landscape rather than within communal cemeteries. The 'Celtic' bowls show a relationship with major routes for this very reason. As a whole, the distribution of imported 'Byzantine' bowls in Britain is centred on Kent and the eastern seaboard of East Anglia and is principally limited here to just one of the vessel types available in the broader European context. This is the B1 bowl, which is also a widespread find in the cemeteries of the Middle Rhineland region (Harris 2003, 67).

### *Phase C distribution of copper alloy bowls (Figure 44)*
Of the seven bowls from this phase, one is a 'curated' Roman item, two are unidentified and the remainder are 'Celtic' hanging-bowls. The Kentish near monopoly in the possession of copper alloy vessels has all but disappeared. The association with major inland routes as opposed to coastal or riverine ones appears to be firmly established, particularly along the Roman road into and from Somerset (Margary number 45).

### *Sheet vessel fragments*
A number of objects in the 'unidentified artefact' category of the database may also actually represent fragments of copper alloy bowls, or other vessels such as stave buckets or pails with copper alloy fittings and bindings. These items are not included in the discussion here, but some observations about them are pertinent now. Each fragment or group of fragments from a burial,

## 9. A Restricted Wealth in Copper Alloys?

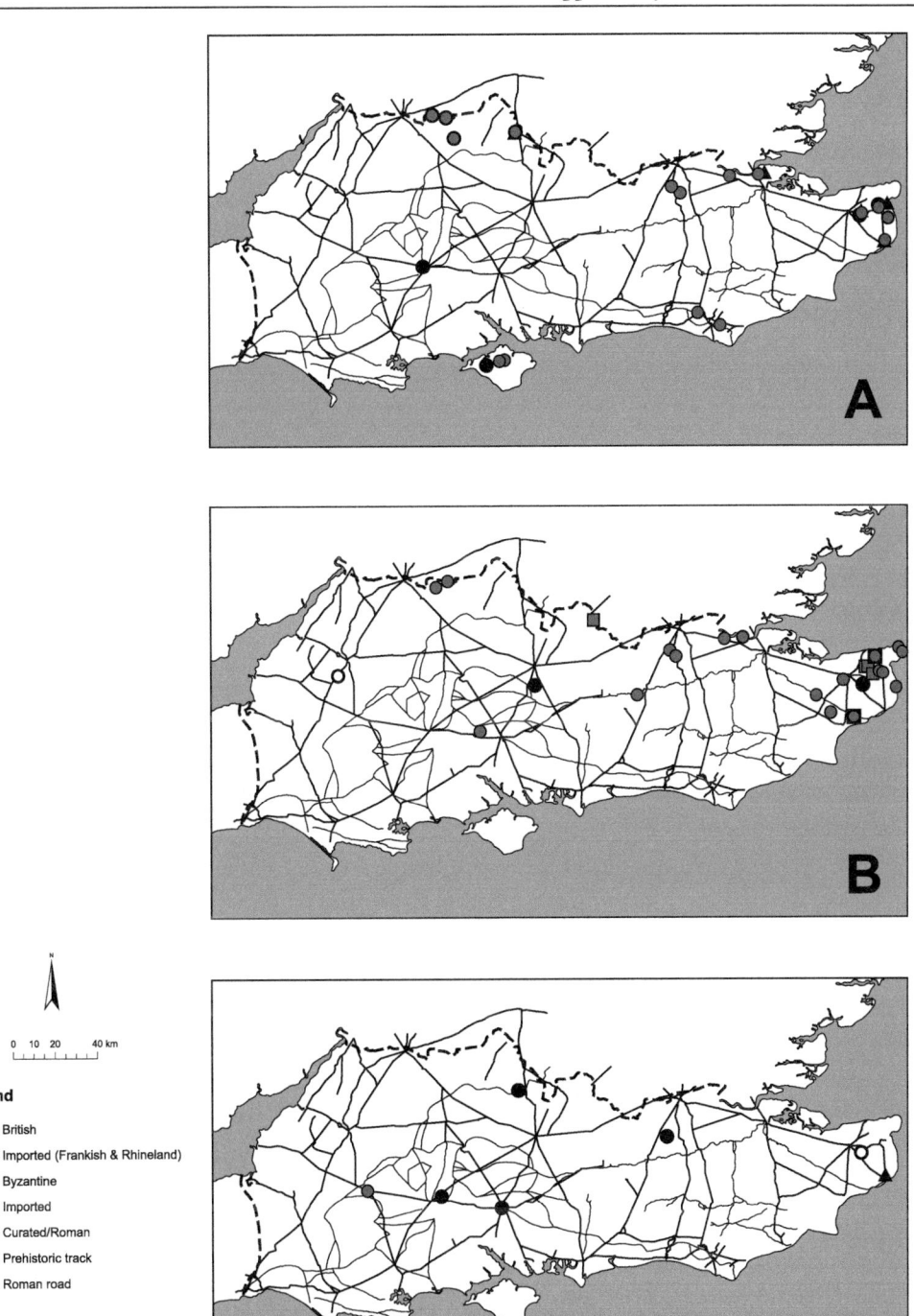

*Figure 44. The distribution of all copper alloy bowl types in three phases*

*Table 47. Copper alloy fragments in burials*

| Phase | No. of fragments |
|---|---|
| A | 99 |
| B | 52 |
| C | 41 |

when variously described as sheet, rim, plate or binding, typically weighed less than five grams. The main question here is whether the presence of these fragments represented an intention to deposit a complete vessel, without actually having sufficient material to do so, and thus is evidence of a stress on available resources reflected over time. As Table 47 illustrates, the rate of fall-off over time for this artefact category is no different to that outlined for complete copper alloy objects, but does in itself suggest that copper alloy may have had a variable availability for particular communities at different times.

### *Escutcheons (Figure 45)*

The majority of the 'Celtic' hanging-bowl escutcheons and mounts occur as poorly dated individual findspots and so these are best considered as a group. What this artefact type actually represents is unclear for they might be treated as an artefact type in their own right with a particular value to their owner. Alternatively they might simply be the relicts of complete bowls that were no longer extant, perhaps the product of grave-robbing or else unburied items intended to be converted as scrap into other artefacts. Their geographical distribution does fall within two distinct regional frameworks, however, and where datable they appear to be present in both zones from Phase A. The western group of escutcheons is located primarily in northwest Wiltshire and Somerset, however, with a central cluster that appears to follow the line of the Ridgeway, a prehistoric trackway. Others here are located on or near the major Roman roads. The eastern group is Kentish dominated, with 24 examples, including seven from Faversham and with a spread over sites open to Kentish influence, from Surrey round to south Hampshire. The conjunction of their findspots with Roman and prehistoric routes leading into and away from the core area of eastern Kent provides a consistent pattern here. The find from Kemsing in west Kent illustrates this point. Although this is an unassociated object, there is quite possibly an early Anglo-Saxon cemetery in its vicinity, as evidenced by two inhumations, one orientated east-west, the other west-east, discovered together with a spearhead in the 1880s (Kent HER TQ 55 NW 16). Another potential cemetery, possibly practising mixed burial rites, lies close by at Otford near the river Darent. A Roman villa evidenced by a detached bathhouse excavated in the 1940s lies further down the slope to the south. The North Downs east-west trackway runs near the Kemsing escutcheon findspot and the site is adjacent to the Darent valley that runs north to join the Thames near Dartford. It is also situated above a trackway crossing point for the river. The junction with a major north-south trackway leading into the Weald is located just to the east of the findspot. A further single escutcheon find from Hayes in Kent shares a similar landscape situation with a Roman road and routeway providing access through the North Downs.

## 9. A Restricted Wealth in Copper Alloys?

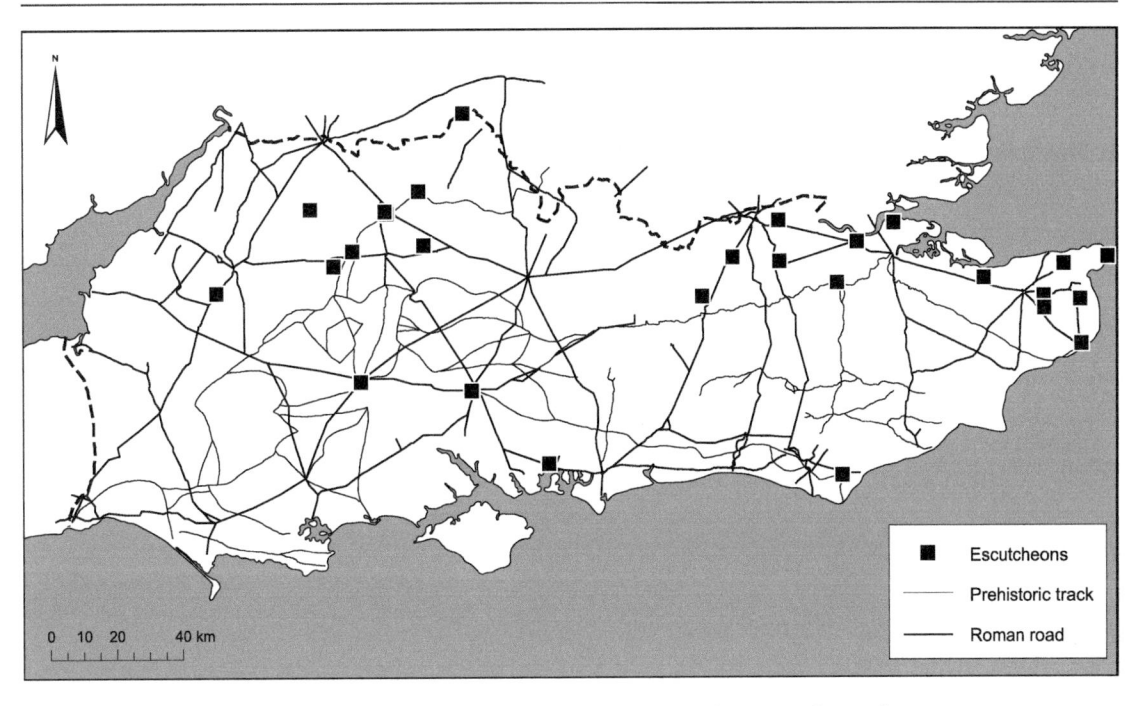

*Figure 45. The distribution of hanging bowl escutcheons in the study region*

*Figure 46. An example of a hanging bowl escutcheon*

## Conclusions on copper alloy bowl distributions

Whether the actual type of bowl was an important factor in its inclusion in a burial assemblage is uncertain. It may simply be that a large receptacle was appropriate for inclusion as a symbol of elevated status. Fortunately, the distribution of the bowls illustrates an inter-linkage of trading, exchange or booty networks from east and west across the study region. The match between copper alloy bowls or their escutcheons with major routes is amply demonstrated here and forms a consistent feature of their distribution from Phase A onwards. By Phase C the Celtic West appears to be the sole source for this artefact type, although some curation of heirlooms from Phase B, when such bowls were most common, cannot be discounted.

# 10. Esoteric Materials: Amber, Amethyst, Gold and Silver

**Case study: amber beads** *(Figure 47)*

The major distribution areas for amber beads lie beyond the study area, occupying a broad swathe of territory to the north and west of the Icknield Way across the Midlands and East Anglia (Huggett 1988). The greatest number from any single site has been given as the 981 from Sleaford in Lincolnshire, followed by Bergh Apton in Norfolk with 517 beads. Within the study region, the main concentrations occurred in Kent and across a broad band running through Hampshire and Wiltshire (Huggett 1988, 64). Nevertheless, there were three sites within the study area in Berkshire and Wiltshire, which contained relatively high numbers of beads per site as recorded nationally in 1988. These were the Saxton Road, Abingdon cemetery (BrkABD-MC1) with 386, Collingbourne Ducis (WltCBD-IC1) with 340 and Long Wittenham (BrkLWM-MC1) with 339. Unusually, on the evidence presented by Huggett, Kent appears to have played only a minor role in the importation and distribution of this particular raw material. Amber has been designated as an imported material, traded from the Baltic region and as yet no significant exploitation of amber washed up on Britain's east coast has been demonstrated for this period.

The national pattern for their deposition in burials revealed an average of between one and twenty amber beads per grave. A few burials contained very large numbers, but contemporaries in the same cemetery possessing markedly fewer frequently offset this. Huggett interprets this as suggesting differential access within communities to the supply of amber beads (*ibid.*, 66). Various other explanatory inferences might be added here, however. For example, it might represent a practice of curation of beads by a kin group, which were eventually deposited as heirlooms with a single individual. Alternatively there might be changing trends over time in the kinds of material deposited and the reasons behind the selection of certain materials (due to their colour or amuletic value, for example). Then there might also be changes in the regional mechanisms for the supply and distribution of amber beads.

The database records the presence of amber in burials mostly as beads, but they are also occasionally designated as spindle-whorls or sword-beads. Estimates of actual numbers of beads in a burial are uncertain, unless precisely and accurately recorded in a cemetery publication. In

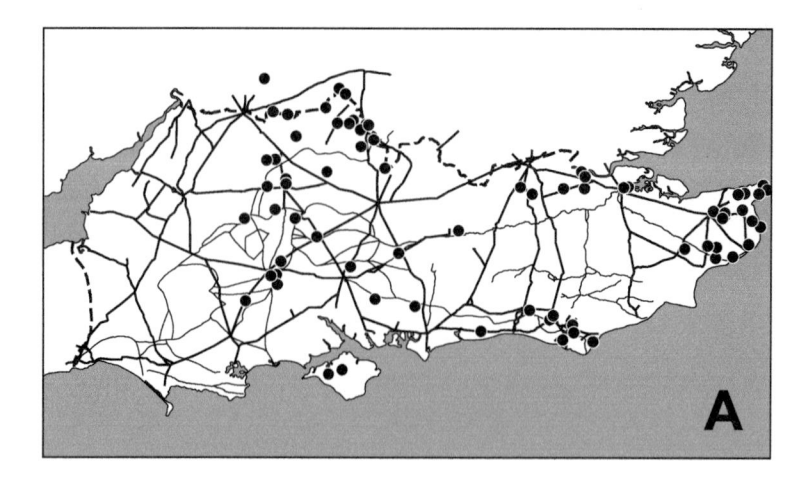

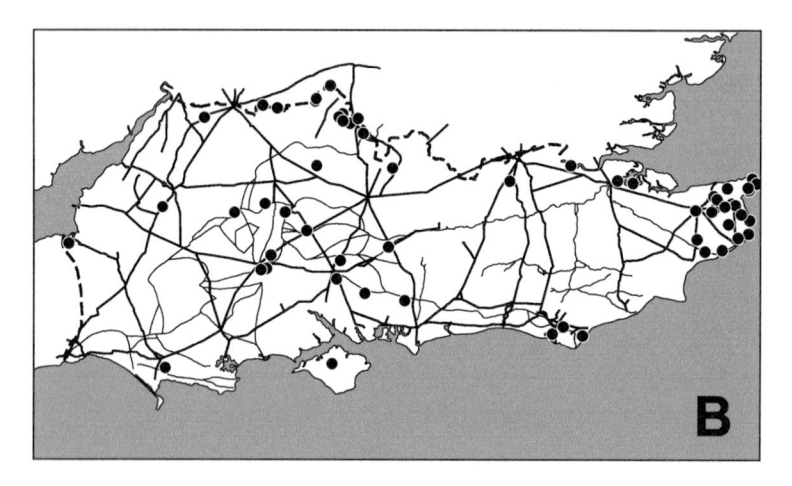

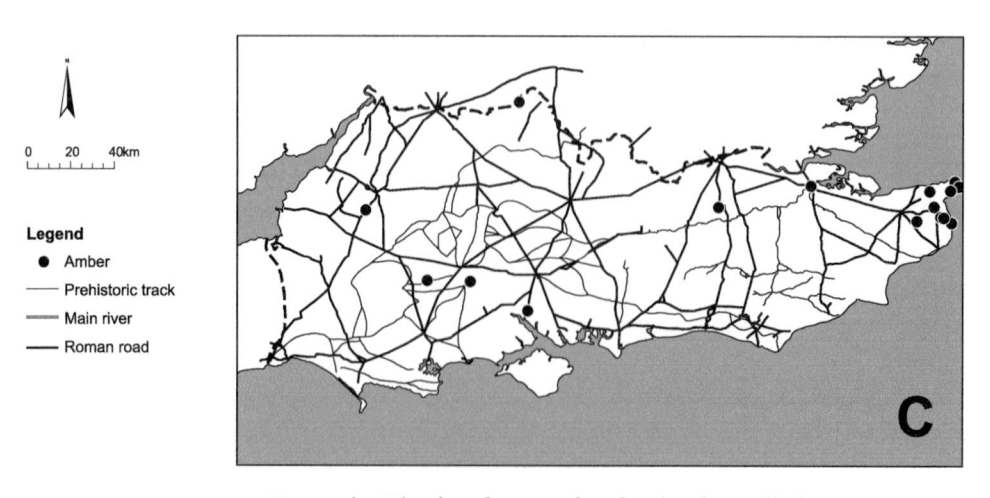

*Figure 47. The distribution of amber beads in all phases*

## 10. Esoteric Materials: Amber, Amethyst, Gold and Silver

many instances, an accurate count of beads per grave has not been determinable whether from antiquarian or indeed some later excavated material held in museum archives. That there might be considerable discrepancies in the numbers of amber beads reported to have been in circulation and used for statistical analyses is a point that emerged from the excavation report of the cemetery at Butler's Field, Lechlade. When entered into the database, this report provided an accurate total of 1,476 amber beads spread across two phases and divided between 47 burials, with Grave 10 containing 307 beads. This placed this 'Saxon' site on a par with contemporary 'Anglian' cemeteries in eastern England. By counting total numbers as the basis for analysis, however, we ignore the fact that amber beads are highly variable in both size and weight and therefore did not necessarily represent an equivalent value with each other. Unfortunately, the weighing of individual beads in museum archives proved in many cases to be completely impractical. This is due to the friable nature of the material, occasional museum practices of re-stringing sets of now de-contextualised beads from separate grave assemblages for display purposes, as well as the time constraints on unpacking individual beads in museum stores and the very large numbers of amber beads that weighed only fractions of a gram. Where weighing could be carried out, it was established, for example, that a single bead of 10 grams (the heaviest weighed) was the equivalent of over 50 much smaller beads. This leads to a sense of uncertainty as to whether count or weight can provide a meaningful statistical component in these analyses. For the bead strings from Lechlade Grave 10 (GlsLLe-MC1), Collingbourne Ducis Grave 31 (WltCBD-IC1) and Long Wittenham Grave 71 (BrkLWM-MC1), the average weight per bead was less than a gram, although each string included both very large and very small beads. The shape and form in which the amber arrived in these communities is unknown, but it may have been already prepared into beads, so at this point the count of beads presumably reflects on an unknown gift-exchange or trade-transaction event. Alternatively a substantial weighted lump of amber, as the product of such an exchange, might be converted into innumerable beads through the application of the simple lathe-turning and drilling techniques required in bead production.

The mapped distributions of amber (Figure 47) illustrate its very general spread throughout the study region in Phase A, with no significant spatial gap present apart from the unoccupied territories of the Weald. Its westernmost limit might be taken to coincide with the furthest reach of early Anglo-Saxon activity, be it through exchange or settlement. The Phase B distribution is not substantially different, apart from a further westwards extension and the beginnings of a central zone devoid of amber extending through much of Sussex, Hampshire, Surrey and Berkshire. The amber beads mapped in Phase C are few in number and are interpreted here as primarily curated items, with Kentish cemeteries giving the strongest representation.

The extent to which Kent was actually deficient in amber can be questioned. The actual number of beads from the Bifrons cemetery (KntPXB-IC1), including the nineteenth-century unassociated finds gathered up by the Marquis of Conyngham's gardener and held in Maidstone Museum, together with those from Brent's excavations, totals 835 items (Hawkes 2000). This makes it easily comparable in numbers to those from 'Anglian' cemeteries. Yet, the recently excavated cemeteries at Saltwood (KntSWD-IC1) conform more readily to Huggett's pattern, indicating differential access to amber. Here there are fourteen burials with a total of 310 beads. One grave contained 161, ten burials had fewer than twelve beads and the remainder contained 26, 31 and 61 respectively. Conversely, the Mill Hill, Deal community (KntGMM-IC1) produced 698 beads rather more equitably spread amongst 25 burials. Of these, three contained over 90 beads each (94, 106 and 107 beads), five had over twenty and two over fifty. The unassociated material from Faversham includes a mere 52 amber beads, although these are of substantial size (though unweighed), hinting that many more must have been discarded by collectors or lost from the site during its excavation. The Isle of Wight, which matches contemporary Kentish material culture in most respects, has produced only four amber-bearing graves however.

The major Kentish cemetery at Buckland, Dover (KntBLD-IC1) offered, from its first excavation in the 1950s, only twenty amber-bead graves. The second excavation in 1994 has produced (based on data in the public domain, although not yet available in full publication) an estimated further 47 such graves. This provides a site amber total in the region of 1150 beads, with approximately 900 in Phase A and over 200 in Phase B. The spread pattern in numbers of beads between graves in Phase A here is similar to that recorded for the Mill Hill, Deal cemetery. The Buckland, Dover Phase A amber-bead graves contained between 1 and 125 beads, but only half of these burials have seven or fewer beads, with the remaining half producing incrementally increasing numbers of beads. In Phase B there is much more of a split in the range of one to 70 beads, with two-thirds of the burials having fewer than seven. Grave 38 with its 70 beads is probably datable to *c.*590 at the latest, leaving the next Phase B burial containing only 44 beads. Apparently no Phase C amber-bead graves are recorded from this cemetery, although they do occur elsewhere within the study region.

Huggett's assertion regarding the extremes of differential access to amber beads was tested here using the available data of counts of amber beads in burials. County datasets were prepared and no division was made by phase here, in order to identify whether there were broad geographical differences in the range of numbers of beads that were deposited with women and to account in part for the issue of amber curation. The results are shown in Table 48, being expressed as the percentage of the total number of graves analysed that fell within each number range. The highest number of amber beads in a grave within each county is also shown here.

It emerges that the majority of women accompanied by amber beads possessed only ten or fewer. Regionally these account for two-thirds of all amber burials. The differentiation noted by Huggett, in which one or two burials occur with an abnormally large number of beads and the remainder have far fewer, is by and large supported by the data in this table. The major difference revealed, however, is that in Kent there are more burials with beads within the 31–100 range. Elsewhere within the study region, this pattern is only replicated in Wiltshire, thus mirroring the early regional patterning also observed in iron deposition. Sussex, which might have been expected to have access to an overflow or trickle-down of wealth from Kent along its south coast and to deploy this wealth in a similar manner, actually has relatively few amber beads. The greatest number is present at Alfriston (SsxALF-IC2) with just 57 beads.

The flow of amber beads into lowland Britain seems then to have been focused on the eastern seaboard and routes inland from there, but this extended only as far south as Kent and not

## 10. Esoteric Materials: Amber, Amethyst, Gold and Silver

*Table 48. Percentage of graves in a county with the number of beads in that range*

|  | Amber graves | 1–10 | 11–20 | 21–30 | 31–40 | 41–50 | 51–60 | 61–70 | 71–100 | 101+ | Most |
|---|---|---|---|---|---|---|---|---|---|---|---|
| Berks | 77 | 65% | 13% | 10% | 3% | 1% | 0% | 1% | 3% | 4% | 281 |
| Dorset | 2 | 100% | 0% | 0% | 0% | 0% | 0% | 0% | 0% | 0% | 7 |
| Glos | 53 | 60% | 13% | 8% | 4% | 0% | 4% | 0% | 2% | 9% | 307 |
| Hants | 46 | 70% | 17% | 2% | 7% | 0% | 0% | 0% | 2% | 2% | 139 |
| IOW | 3 | 67% | 0% | 0% | 33% | 0% | 0% | 0% | 0% | 0% | 34 |
| Kent | 256 | 64% | 14% | 8% | 4% | 2% | 2% | 2% | 3% | 2% | 161 |
| Oxon | 41 | 68% | 17% | 5% | 2% | 2% | 0% | 0% | 2% | 2% | 105 |
| Somerset | 4 | 100% | 0% | 0% | 0% | 0% | 0% | 0% | 0% | 0% | 2 |
| Surrey | 8 | 100% | 0% | 0% | 0% | 0% | 0% | 0% | 0% | 0% | 9 |
| Sussex | 73 | 78% | 12% | 1% | 5% | 1% | 1% | 0% | 0% | 0% | 57 |
| Wilts | 76 | 64% | 14% | 3% | 7% | 3% | 3% | 3% | 3% | 1% | 216 |

significantly beyond. The ability of communities in Kent and Wiltshire to spread their amber resources in greater numbers amongst more women might indicate differing societal structures for their territories in contrast to those where greater extremes in deposition numbers were present. We might contrast this perception as one between areas with a tiered society above a base (indicated by gradation of bead numbers) and areas where more clearly demarcated and hierarchically opposed structures were the norm (marked by extremes of bead numbers). These comments pertain primarily to Phase A, perhaps indicating the very early process of disjunction of society into different patterns over geographical space.

### Case study: amethyst beads *(Figure 48)*

Little has changed regarding our knowledge of the frequency and distribution of amethyst beads in the study region since 1988. Probably sourced from India via the eastern Mediterranean and *Francia*, they occur either as single pendants or drops, or else in groups strung on a necklace, usually with other beads and pendants. E. T. Leeds's observation that they may have been re-cycled from Frankish looting of Roman sites does not necessarily explain their appearance on the Continent in the late sixth century and concerted usage late into the seventh century (Leeds 1913, 131–2; see also Koch 1977). Alternatively, and more likely, they may be linked to the same patterns of gift-exchange or trade which brought the Byzantine cast bowls to Kent towards the end of the sixth century.

The total numbers in Kent have been added to lately by the second excavation in 1994 at Buckland, Dover and by other occasional items from the series of recently discovered and excavated cemeteries that appear so regularly in Kent. Regardless of that factor, Kent and in particular east

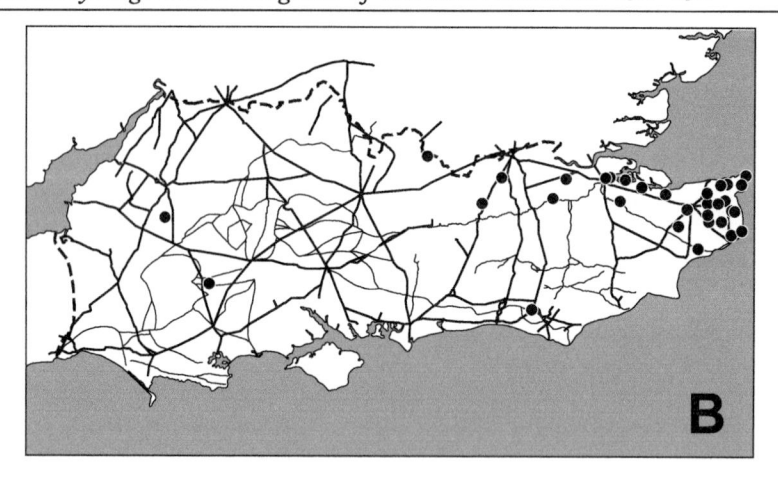

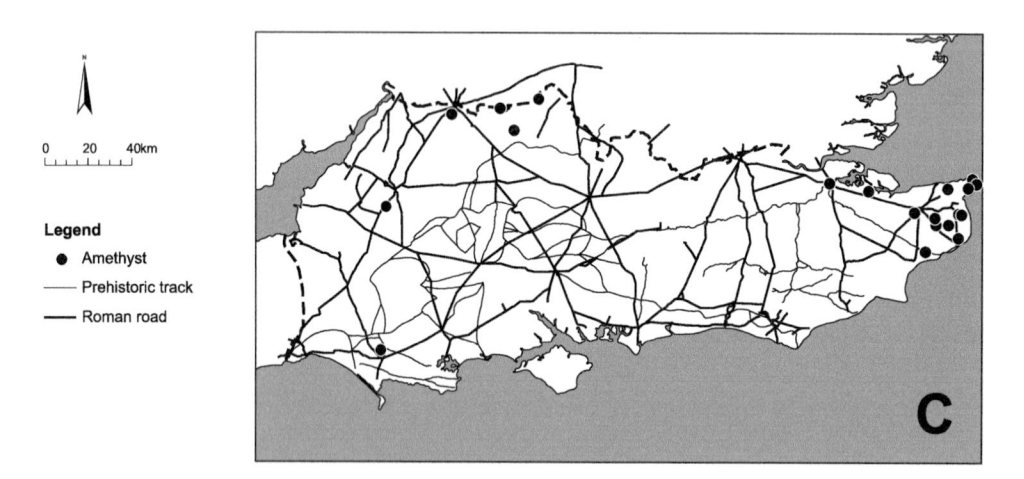

*Figure 48. The distribution of amethyst beads in Phases B and C*

Kent dominates the distribution of this object type. Thus of the 132 database entries for amethyst beads, only 12 are not from Kent. Amethysts make a marginal appearance in west Kent, as at Horton Kirby, Riseley (KntHKY-MC1) and Polhill (KntOTF-IC1), both in the Darent valley. Outside of Kent, as noted by Huggett, two amethyst beads is still the upper benchmark for a burial context. Within the rest of the study region, only five burials contain more than one amethyst bead. One occurs in Grave 172/2 at Butler's Field, Lechlade (GlsLLE-MC1) accompanying a female gendered child in a double inhumation with an older spear-and-seax male burial. Her neck adornments also included a Kentish/Frankish cabochon garnet pendant. It is tempting here to suggest a role for exogamous marriage of females from Kent into the husbands' households in facilitating the spread and maintenance of Kentish influence in the Upper Thames Valley. Another instance is from an isolated burial at Longcot in Berkshire (BrkLCT-BI1) within a sparse assemblage that included a penannular brooch. Further afield, the Somerset cemetery of Buckland Dinham (SmtBDM-IC1) also includes a female with two beads. Of the non-Kentish burials accompanied by a single amethyst, none occur in Hampshire or on the Isle of Wight.

The amethysts share a uniformity of shape, although not size, which suggests a common manufacturing procedure, probably outside Britain. There are variations in their weights, however, ranging between 1g and 11g, of those weighed in museum archives, with the median being at 2.3g. Of the seven weighed sets of amethysts from outside of Kent, all bar one ranged above this median weight. Kentish sites with larger numbers of amethysts, such as Sarre, tend to have a greater number of the lighter-weight beads.

The Phase B distribution is dominated by Kentish cemeteries and also extends into Sussex and Surrey. The sole Sussex example is from an antiquarian-dug and imprecisely located cemetery in the vicinity of Lewes, standing out as an extremely rare indication of a significant seventh-century female-gendered burial in that area. The two westernmost finds in Phase B seem to be unrelated to the Kentish corpus. This is a point reinforced by the Phase C distribution pattern. Two discrete distributions can be noted in Phase C. There is the ubiquitous Kentish group, which is numerically greater, and a western group, well spaced and running from the upper reaches of the Thames valley south down through to Dorset. The latter example is from an unpublished site at Bradford Peverell, whose cemetery dominates the Roman road running northwest from Dorchester and the ford across the river Frome here (see Figure 19). The absence of amethysts from much of Hampshire, Wiltshire and Berkshire substantiates the division between the western and Kentish groups. To date no amethysts have been forthcoming from the seventh-century St Mary's Stadium cemetery associated with the precursor to the major *emporium* at *Hamwic*, nor indeed from the contemporary burials associated with *Lundenwic* with the exception of a recently excavated female grave at St Martin-in-the-Fields at its western edge (pers. comm. Lyn Blackmore).

## Conclusions concerning amber and amethyst bead usage and distribution

Amber and amethyst beads present a series of contrasts through their patterns of usage within early Anglo-Saxon society. The numerical abundance of amber in the sixth century is replaced by the relative scarcity and esoteric nature of amethyst in the following century. Amber has a variable usage over space, in that it was either gradated through a society as an exhibition of wealth for all, or it was restricted, with most women having access to very little and just a few women having lots, thus underlining the hierarchy within that society. The gradation for all is reflected in a spatial pattern centred on east Kent and Wiltshire as the focal areas of two distribution networks within the study region. The Kentish domination of amethyst distribution calls into question the means by which the few sites further to the west might have acquired them. Reference to Huggett's map (1988, fig. 2), confirms the existence of a parallel distribution extending from Anglia and Mercia through into the study region in the west. Mercian expansion along the Thames and to its south seems to be reflected here.

## The role of precious metals: gold and silver

During the fifth and sixth centuries, access in Britain to new supplies of gold and silver were limited and certainly not available on the scale of consumption by contemporary Merovingian kingdoms, as evidenced in the descriptions by Gregory of Tours of sumptuous and weighty treasures. Within continental Europe there is some archaeological evidence to suggest continuity of precious-metal production based on coin finds related to known mining complexes. Examples have been cited of late sixth-century coins at Roman tin mines in the Loire Atlantique region and of Visigothic coins in Iberian silver mines (La Salvia 2007, 75). Additionally, both Frankish and Visigothic mints tend to be located in mining regions known from the Roman period. Nevertheless, much of the treasure circulating on the Continent took the form of booty, including plate and coins and of subsidies paid by the eastern Roman Empire in particular. Some of this could have trickled into lowland Britain, most probably through Kent, in the form of diplomatic and other reciprocal gifts. Precious metal for recycling was certainly available in post-Roman Britain. It is evidenced by a gold and silver hoard dated to the late 460s from Patching in West Sussex (White 1998), although this is an isolated example within the study region. Some of its silver pieces appear to relate to a weights system and two of the gold pieces are conspicuously pure, perhaps derived from Visigothic mined sources (*ibid.*).

Silver relief-decorated brooches of Scandinavian type and gold disc pendants also of Scandinavian origin referred to as bracteates feature in the wealthiest burials in Kent in the early sixth century (Axboe 1999; Hines 1984 and 1997). Indeed silver continues to be used on a substantial scale in brooch production within Kent through the remainder of the sixth century (Leigh 1980; Avent 1975). But gold and silver are rare materials in Anglo-Saxon burial assemblages outside Kent (Webster 2000, 54). It is in Kent that a regular supply of Byzantine gold *solidi* and plate appears to have been arriving as diplomatic gifts, in other exchanges and perhaps in the form of marriage dowries, some of which percolated through into burial assemblages here. Many of the other exotic and esoteric raw materials present in Kentish burials, such as cowrie shells, ivory items and garnets, probably arrived through the same route (Huggett 1988). Increased Byzantine gold subsidies to the Franks from the mid sixth century may have benefited Kent as it became "awash with the new gold filigree and Style II jewellery" (Webster 2000, 54). Any gold that arrived in the early seventh century in the form of East-Roman and Frankish gold coinage was treated as bullion to be used to produce jewellery fitted with imported garnets and other semi-precious stones, or else with coloured glass settings. The Kentish kingdom moved towards a coin- and market-based economy, first minting gold coins in the first half of the seventh century until available supplies of gold *solidi* and *trientes* ceased (Williams 1999). By the late seventh century they were minting silver pennies, better known as sceattas, in Kent and elsewhere in southeast England. The distribution of the earliest sceattas indicates that Kent had developed trade links with both Frisia and *Francia* (Metcalf 1993, 174–183).

In national terms, the archaeological and metallurgical evidence for the working of precious metals is meagre at best. Settlement sites have sometimes produced a few crucibles, but these are small, handmade cups with a capacity of about 20ml. Although a few of these can be dated before *c*.700, none of those listed occur within the study region (Bayley 1991, 117). Burials that contain artefacts described as either a bell or a crucible appear on closer inspection to be a bell in every case (*e.g.* Grave 259 at Sarre: KntSAR-IC1). *Hamwic* is the only Middle-Saxon manufacturing site to have produced a concentration of crucibles, which have been used in casting silver and a range of copper alloys, but all of these dated to the eighth or early ninth centuries (ibid). Beyond the study region, contemporary evidence for the working of precious metals has been found at Dinas Powys in south Wales, on the Isle of Man and at various sites in Scotland and Ireland. In contrast extremely rich evidence for metalworking in precious metals has been excavated from contemporary Scandinavian settlement sites, most notably at Helgö in the Malär region of central Sweden (Hovén *et al.* 1986; Lundström 1988). These have produced a wide range of material, including workshops, firing pits, casting moulds and crucibles, but nothing in terms of crude raw materials, rather accumulations of scrap in hoards.

The geographical distribution of small balances and weights deposited in Anglo-Saxon burials has not been extended significantly since Christopher Scull's reviews (Scull 1991 and 1992). The only new set within the study region comes from the second excavation at Buckland, Dover, in a sword-burial context at present only broadly dated to the sixth century. So, they remain centred on two areas, in east Kent and the Upper Thames Valley. Touchstones, which were used to assess the purity of precious metals, are restricted to coastal communities in Kent, although unfortunately none of these burials can be dated precisely. If, as Scull suggested, the balances and weights were used to effect bullion transactions within a non-monetary economy, although one based on the standards of contemporary gold coinages elsewhere in Europe, then we might expect to find the Upper Thames Valley, as well as Kent, to be a major area for finds of gold and silver. This is not the case, however. Scull contextualised the finds of these balances as occurring within essentially agrarian societies, whose elite members were engaged in inter-regional or even long-distance trade, in order to acquire prestige items, through the use of agents or officials (the balance-set owners), who dealt with their foreign equivalents (Scull 1991, 202). What goods were used to balance the exchange remains unknown. An alternative use or additional use of balance sets and bullion was the payment of fines or compensation to mitigate socially-disruptive feuds, as indicated in the earliest law codes of Kent and Wessex (Attenborough 1922).

The presence of small and very lightweight caches of garnet gemstones sharing much the same distribution pattern as the balances and weights, from Butler's Field, Lechlade in the Upper Thames region and both Buckland, Dover and St Peter's, Broadstairs indicates an extension to the types of material that may have had a marketable weight value. Both amber and glass beads have similar characteristics in terms of their value to size-and-weight ratios. Here it is tempting to also insert copper alloy scrap as a further possibility. It is the only other material that appears to have possessed a high value and yet be relatively light in weight, although it was both more common and widespread than true bullion. This last suggestion introduces the idea of a more purposeful and worthwhile acquisition of scrap material. If indeed there were real differences in the sophistication of monetary and value transactions between Kent together with the Upper

Thames Valley and elsewhere within the study region then here we might have another indicator of geographically varied complexities of social organisation within the pathways leading to the formation of the earliest kingdoms.

## Gold

Whilst there are some gold deposits in western and northern Britain, there is little evidence for their exploitation within the study period. Such indigenous gold working as may have been carried out in the British Isles early in the study period, for example on Pictish monastic sites, probably exploited re-cycled Roman antiquities (Spall 2006, 44). By the mid-sixth century, however, the gold that was available in southern Britain has been determined by X-ray fluorescent analysis to be derived from imported Late Roman and Byzantine *solidi* and from related Merovingian coins imitating Byzantine issues (Hawkes *et al.* 1966; Hawkes and Pollard 1981). Goldsmiths are elusive in the archaeological record, although the evidence of jeweller's rouge adhering to the edge of a fifth century Visigothic gold coin from the Marlowe's Car Park excavation in Canterbury, might indicate a workshop in the vicinity, as might the copper alloy die for making decorative gold foil mounts found at Rochester (Coatsworth and Pinder 2002, 21). Indeed, the Tattershall Thorpe itinerant smith may have been skilled in working a range of metals that included gold.

In Phase A the principal manufactured gold objects present in Anglo-Saxon burial assemblages are south Scandinavian-type gold bracteates (die-stamped disc pendants with looped mounts) (Figure 49). Their ornamentation imitates images found on fourth-century Imperial Roman medallions and coins and their iconography has been interpreted as depicting a Germanic deity, in particular Woden (Axboe 2007). As both these bracteates and Roman and Merovingian coins were commonly incorporated into bead strings and necklaces, their significance was non-monetary, but not necessarily non-economic. They can be seen as a medium for both creating and maintaining social and political relations through personal gift-giving and have been characterised as special-purpose money used to indicate linkages between the many small kingdoms within Scandinavia and beyond. This particular use of coins and bracteates appears to represent a translation of Roman customs and means of exchange (Gaimster 1992).

Within Kent and East Anglia, their main distribution centres in England, these bracteates appear in burial assemblages from the early sixth century (Axboe 1999). Very few Anglo-Saxon bracteates are the products of precisely the same die. Multiple types can appear on the same necklace, perhaps indicating that accumulation processes were taking place. The question arises as to whether any other categories of artefacts, such as beads, might also be considered as forms of special money, to be collected through particular social interactions. Within Kent, no Class C bracteate is known, and the only recorded Class B bracteate from the study area comes from Bifrons Grave 29 (with the only other example nationally from Norfolk – pers. comm. Charlotte Behr). Kent produced what some scholars have identified as insular copies of south Scandinavian D bracteates, with the production of new types continuing into the seventh century (Hines 1984; Hawkes and Pollard 1981; Arnold 1997). Die links exist between the bracteates found in Bifrons graves 29 and 64

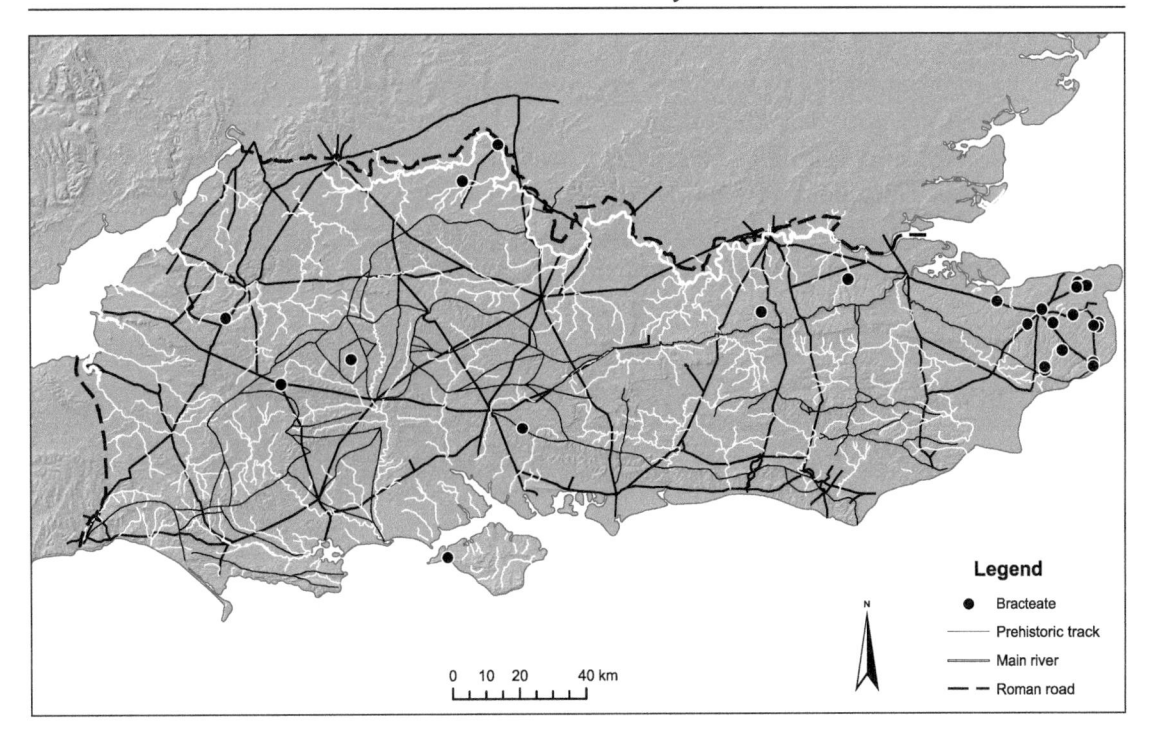

*Figure 49. The distribution of gold bracteates*

and in Lyminge Grave 16, which form a group, and similarly between the four fine-quality items from Finglesham graves D3 and 203. Whether the English-provenanced bracteates originated from a batch production carried out at a single point of origin, whether locally or in Scandinavia, and were retained as heirlooms over time with sequential deposition in graves as indicated at Finglesham, or were the products of curated dies and were manufactured sequentially remains a matter for conjecture. A copper alloy die for the production of D bracteates has been reported as a metal-detector find in northwest Essex (Axboe 2007, 15, fig. 4, IK609).

An interpretation of bracteates as having a significant role in the "reproduction of regional social structures and hierarchies" (Gaimster 1992, 21) suggests a context in which commodity and gift-exchange may have existed simultaneously. Their distribution across the study region serves to highlight the Kentish density of finds, although modern metal-detecting is beginning to produce isolated finds considerably further to the west, for example in Wiltshire at Kingston Deverell (WltKDV-IC1). The new finds might well be explained in the context of other Kentish and pseudo-Kentish material which is located along the southern inland strand of the study region in the sixth century, highlighting both the reach of Kentish contacts and the value of emulating access to Kentish material culture at this time.

The seventh-century process of the monetarisation of the economy of northwestern Europe was probably neither uniform nor necessarily coherent. The laws attributed to Æthelbert, ostensibly dated to the first two decades of the seventh century is a text that may well have been subject to later insertions and alterations. It required financial compensation for offences in terms of *scillings*, despite the fact that no coinage is evident here much before *c*.625. Any system of bullion equivalencies operating in the late sixth century might have been indicated by reference to weights, hence perhaps the incidence of balances and weights within Kentish graves and those in cemeteries within the Upper Thames valley. Indeed Scull (1992) has noted the equivalence between the balance weights found in these two areas and the bullion standards of contemporary continental and Byzantine finds.

A greater amount of gold may have become available in the later sixth century, as more of it began to be used for decorated metalwork (Mortimer 1990, 297), although gold coins continued to be used as ornaments on necklaces (Gannon 2003, 8). It has been demonstrated that in east Kent the average weight of gold deposited per individual remained fairly static from the later sixth century until the debasement of the Merovingian coinage over the course of the greater part of the seventh century (Brookes 2007, 118), with the wider Anglo-Saxon consumption of gold running in parallel with seventh-century Continental inflation. A change in the distribution of gold coins to include most Anglo-Saxon areas of Britain after *c*.625 is perhaps a result of a geographical change in the Continental source mints, involving a shift from those in southern *Francia* and the Mediterranean region to mints in the Meuse and Moselle valleys (Blackburn and Grierson 1986, 108–9). The point at which debasement of the Merovingian gold coinage occurred is reflected in the emergence of Anglo-Saxon gold coins, although Gannon (2003, 10) attributed this to the demand for coinage outstripping the metal supply. Brookes (2007, 119) concluded that Anglo-Saxon exchange rates for gold and silver were directly tied to an international balance of trade and, therefore, that changes in consumption patterns of these materials were economically-driven rather than fashion-led.

In essence the study region database records gold in two forms: as solid objects or as a major raw-material component in artefacts and as a minor raw-material component, for example as gilding on a decorated surface. The second minor component element is of limited relevance in statistical terms, neither is it viable outside of Kent (although it was included in Brookes' calculations for Kent). Therefore consideration is given here solely to solid gold artefacts, with other raw materials included as minor components, and their distribution over time and space. The central issue is the extent to which areas outside of Kent were included or excluded in terms of access to this precious metal, when it is assumed that Kent mediated any such access through its close Continental contacts. There is also a clear gender component in the gathering of certain raw materials into burial assemblages. Hence we find sumptuous collections of diverse materials including gold bracteates, woven gold braids and gold pendants associated with certain women and girls. These are particularly visible in sixth-century cemeteries in Kent and in the series of high-status isolated female burials belonging to the later seventh century. Their deposition into female burials of the sixth century points to the importance of exogamous marriage and female cross-channel mobility in the forming of political alliances in this period (Harrington 2011).

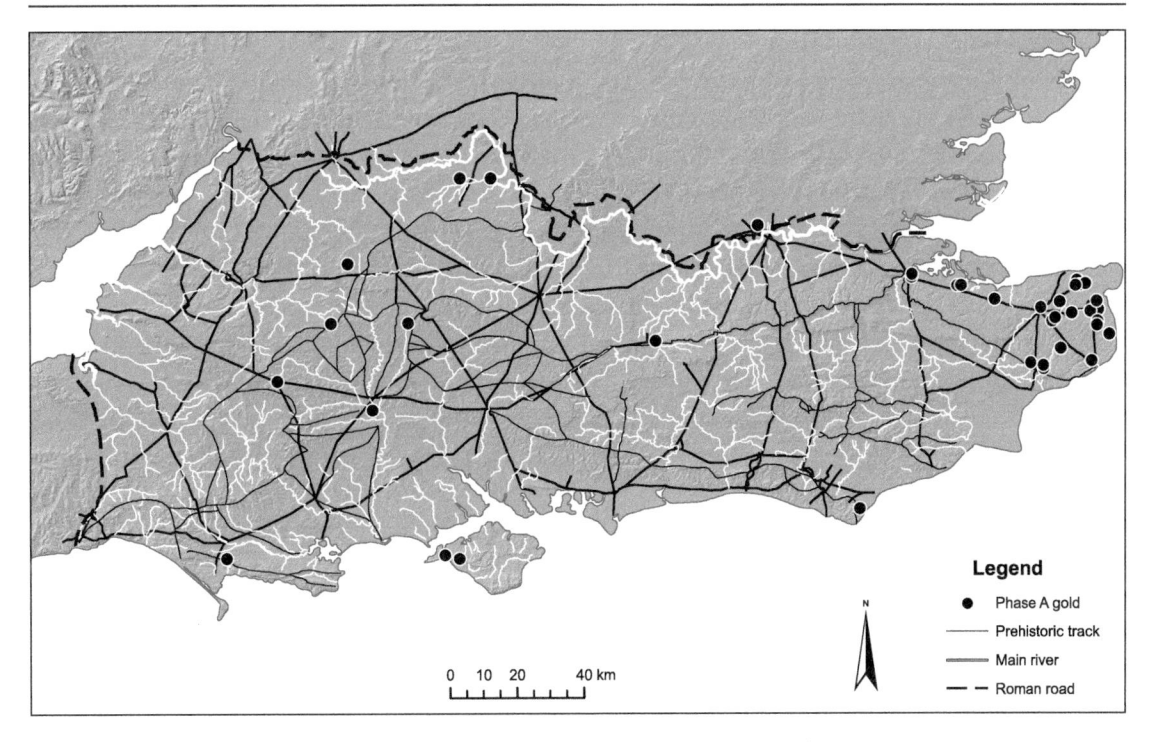

*Figure 50. The distribution of gold artefacts in Phase A*

## Phase A gold distribution (Figure 50)

Kent dominates in both the number and weights of predominantly gold artefacts in all phases, although the relatively small total number at 255 objects from burials and other findspots emphasises the rarity of its actual use. Apart from the occasional coin on a necklace, there is only one definitely identified curated Roman object – is an intaglio finger-ring from Milton Regis in east Kent. In Phase A Kent has 86% of the 79 gold objects. The list mainly comprises *Imported/Jutlandic bracteates* (each of which weighs only 2g–6g) and gold braid (left unweighed but probably not exceeding the gold weight of any other object). Beyond Kent the eleven listed artefacts consist of beads, finger-rings (some possibly Roman) and more bracteates. The distribution reveals a spatial division between a Kentish/South Coast zone, which now includes the site at St Ann's Road, Eastbourne ASE, forthcoming), and a western zone running obliquely north-eastwards from Dorset up through Wiltshire to Berkshire and presumably further on into the Midlands (and the future kingdom of Mercia). The gold bead from Grave 78 at Guildown in Surrey (SryGDN-MC1) is therefore unusually placed between these two zones. The female was buried additionally with a disc fitting from a Late Roman military belt set, so perhaps again this gold bead might represent a curated item.

## Phases B and C gold distribution

The Phase B regional profile is slightly different. Its 109 artefact entries are dominated numerically by the Kentish jewelled disc brooches and filigree pendants, as might be expected. Yet the Saxon area now contains 20% of the finds, which is mainly due to the widespread distribution of findspots of gold sword fittings, with seven of the eight listed. Several of these have garnet inlays with gold-foil reflectors similar to those from Sutton Hoo mound 1. There is only one sword fitting from Kent and that is an uncertainly located find from 'near Maidstone'. Once again, metal detection is generating new finds of this type, the furthest west example coming from Dorset at a potentially strategically important location at the junction of a Roman road out of central Wiltshire continuing to the southwest (Margary 4e) and a network of prehistoric trackways. This particular findspot is probably of similar importance to the contemporary site at Bradford Peverell in both its visual and actual domination of traffic through its area. The Kent/South Coast axis for the distribution of gold artefacts is maintained in Phase B, although the western region pattern appears to have become more diffuse. Also a new central area for finds distribution is now visible in Hampshire. By Phase C, however, there are still fewer artefacts (67), but then 37% of them (25 items) are from outside of Kent. A very similar range of artefact types, mainly consisting of pendants, is evident across the whole study region by this time.

## Silver

The only workable deposits of silver within the study region lie in the Mendip Hills. Although lower yielding than elsewhere in the Roman Empire, silver and lead production provided some prosperity and economic stability for the area, to judge by the large quantities of late fourth-century silver coins found there (Frere 1967, 286). Although half of the proceeds from such activities accrued to the state, the remainder circulated within the general economy, and in all probability mining and metal production continued after the official end of Roman administration in the early fifth century (*ibid.*, 291). Production was probably primarily organised under local enterprise, de-centralised arrangements, such as are widespread within cottage industries (Ellis 1992, 32–34). Additionally these mines may have been a focus for post-Roman trade routes and commodity exchange. The post-Roman earthwork enclosure at Charterhouse, northwest of Cheddar is possibly of fifth or sixth-century construction. It was built perhaps under the authority of a local lord with his power derived from control of the mines and their output (*ibid.*). In Europe, the main contemporary sources of silver were in the Harz Mountains of the Thuringian region, Saxony, Bohemia and Austria, areas much in evidence as resources for Carolingian and later medieval coin production. Other silver deposits are noted in Ireland, Sweden, Finland and Norway – the latter having a wide spectrum of mineral resources that include iron, tin, nickel, copper, lead and molybdenum. (Bowie *et al.* 1978). In contrast, Denmark has only iron and manganese, suggesting that its early silver brooch forms were more likely to have been made from re-cycled Roman coin.

Although very little metallurgical work has been carried out on silver artefacts from early Anglo-Saxon burial contexts, the general assumption is that the major source for this material was

## 10. Esoteric Materials: Amber, Amethyst, Gold and Silver

scrap, primarily recycling Roman coins as bullion. It is noted here that the six instances of pierced Roman silver coins in burial contexts in the database all occur in Kentish river-based and coastal communities, with further examples amongst the unassociated finds in the Upper Thames Valley cemetery at Wally Corner, Berinsfield near Dorchester-on-Thames (Oxfordshire). The hoard at Patching in West Sussex contained over 300g of high-purity silver, roughly equivalent in weight to a Roman pound (Johns 1999, 312). It also included a Continental silver scabbard-chape fitting datable to the second half of the fifth century (Webster in White *et al.* 1999, 312–3). In northern Britain in the fifth century silver was clearly available to the Picts, as evidenced by the hoards at Traprain Law, dated from after AD 395, and at Norrie's Law in Fifeshire, both probably acquired via raiding territory to the south of Hadrian's Wall (Hinton 2005, 43). The overall usage pattern for silver is that it was only rarely used for casting decorative artefacts. For example, only five out of the 28 complete quoit brooches recorded were in silver. The complete brooches occurred in Kent (two – Sarre and Howletts, with another fragmentary brooch there), Sussex (two – Alfriston and Highdown) and Hampshire (one – from the second excavation at Mount Pleasant, Alton, 1992). Indeed only 8% of all brooches recorded were cast in silver (167 out of 2073).

It was proposed in the early 1990s that further research was needed into the debased silver alloys used to cast selected 'Anglian'-type great square-headed brooches, together with other contemporary artefacts that were also common in Scandinavia, such as scutiform pendants and wrist clasps, in order to establish whether standard alloys were being used (Brownsword and Hines 1993, 9). It was suggested that immigrant Scandinavian craftsmen were attempting to maintain their craft in a new context in eastern Britain, but with only limited success, due to a scarcity of silver here other than in southeast England. In the late seventh century Merovingian realms the minting of gold coin ceased in favour of silver issues, a process broadly contemporary with the devaluation of the gold alloy used in the production of Anglo-Saxon jewellery and other fine metalwork and the transition from 'pale gold' coins to silver pennies (the sceattas). There appear to be very few Continental silver coins in England in the last quarter of the seventh century, but by the early eighth century a huge influx of coins from Frisia presumably implied intensifying trade links, presumably underpinned by an expansion of mining activities in the Harz Mountains of northern Germany. The expansion of coin circulation led to more widespread minting activity, however, including for Wessex the 'secondary phase' of silver sceatta coinage (Gannon 2003, 11). However, numismatic evidence 'provides no suggestion of the use of newly-mined English silver, with a large proportion of the metal being channelled to the country by way of the Rhine valley' (pers. comm. Peter Claughton)

The distribution of silver artefacts throughout the whole study period is overwhelmingly focused on Kent (see Figure 51 for all phases), making the absence of comparative metallurgical studies with northern Frankish material an issue, particularly if we wish to accept the assertion that much of Kent's wealth in this material will have been derived from *Francia*. Nevertheless, reflection on the types of artefact manufactured in silver and their distribution patterns, however limited throughout the study region, serve to contextualise Kentish wealth and its geographical networks.

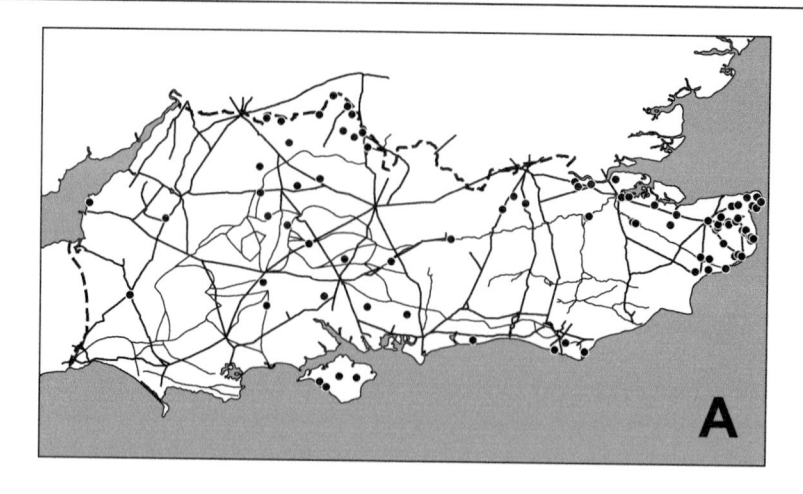

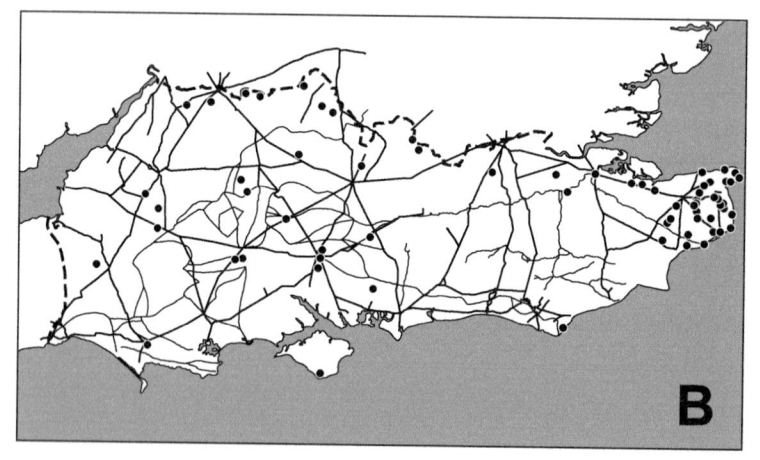

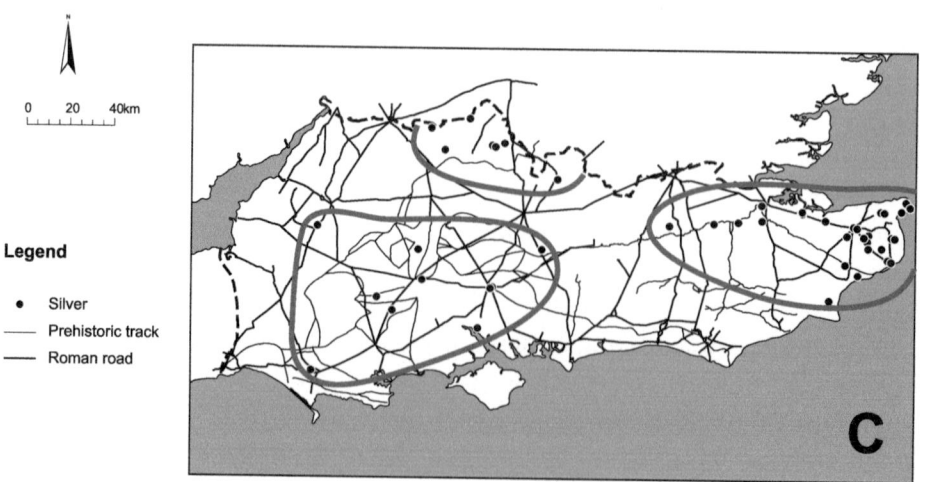

*Figure 51. The distribution of silver artefacts all phases*

## 10. Esoteric Materials: Amber, Amethyst, Gold and Silver

### Phase A silver distributions

The database holds records for 349 primarily silver artefacts from burials and individual findspots for Phase A. Kent has 234 (67%) of these objects rising to 77% (a further 35 items) if the Isle of Wight is included as effectively Kentish. Certainly the Isle of Wight appears to possess a disproportionate amount of silver in relation to other raw materials with 7% of all its finds in this precious material. Of course this feature may be primarily a function of the nineteenth-century excavation and the archiving history of most of the cemetery sites here. Imported items, mainly from *Francia*, but including isolated examples of Jutlandic and Thuringian brooch types, account for 20% of the total (72) in the study region. Given the presence of silver within Thuringia, from which the four known brooches may have been manufactured, it is significant to note that these brooches are not distributed further inland than the east Kent coast. A further 29 items are designated here as culturally wholly Kentish or Kentish/Frankish in style.

It is difficult to group the distributions into coherent units. Kent extending on into Surrey, but also along the south coast to the Isle of Wight forms a readily determinable unit. We might include additionally finds from eastern Hampshire and West Sussex opposite the Isle of Wight. Examples are the Jutlandic relief-decorated bow brooch from Apple Down Grave 14 and a Kentish small square-headed brooch from Highdown. Three items, all from individual findspots, might be argued similarly to demonstrate Kentish influence. There is an Avent Class 3.1 keystone-garnet disc brooch from Ampfield in Hampshire (HtsAMP-FS1) to the west of Winchester. Further west still there is a small square-headed brooch from Breamore (HtsBMR-FS5) and another from Ilchester (SmtICR-FS4), although the latter is an uncertainly provenanced, nineteenth-century find. A northern Wiltshire and Berkshire grouping is also proposed here, but with the majority of items coming from sites in the Upper Thames Valley.

The objects vary in weight, but the heaviest items are mostly curated bow brooches from southern Scandinavia, together with the stylistically early great square-headed brooch at 30g from Grave 225 at Mitcham in Surrey (SryMHM-IC1), or else perforated spoons designated as Kentish/Frankish (five items weighing between 30g and 94g). Brooches comprise the largest category of silver finds, with 145 items (41% of the total) and most of them weigh between six and ten grams. The types of finds that occur outside of the Kentish zone are all relatively lightweight, i.e. under six grams in weight. These include beads, pendants, finger-rings and various unidentifiable fragments of silver sheet and wire. In Phase A silver finger-rings represent the single most numerous artefact type with 76 (22%) of all recorded items, but only 39 or roughly half of these are from sites in Kent. Elsewhere they have a very widespread distribution that would merit further research, particularly if viewed as a special category of gift-given artefact that might relate to allegiances, royal contacts and possibly an indicator of status within hierarchical land-holding arrangements.

### Phase B silver distributions

Phase B offers only 185 silver objects, generally less substantial in weight than earlier, ranging between 1g and 28g for those items weighed in museum archives. Kent again contains the heaviest objects; in this case the range of jewelled and plated disc brooches. Outside Kent, the heaviest artefacts are a composite-jewelled disc brooch (28g) from Milton in Berkshire (BrkMTN-IC2) and a large triangular-plated buckle (10g) from Alton in Hampshire (HtsALT-MC1). A case can be made for both of these items being Kentish in manufacture and origin, as the same can be claimed for the drinking horn mounts (10g estimated) from the 'Princely' barrow at Taplow in Buckinghamshire (BckTPW-BI1).

There is a degree of overlap with the object types found in Phase A. Kent maintains its overwhelming proportion of the number of finds with 139 items (75% of those discovered). In general the same areas possessed silver artefacts as in Phase A, although there is precious little in both Sussex and Surrey. Further west and closer to the Mendip mines, rather more objects are in evidence, but yet again these are neither weighty nor substantial items, mainly consisting of wire rings, pins and earrings. A new artefact-type in silver emerges with sword pyramid mounts. There are four such metal-detected findspot examples with one each from Kent, the Isle of Wight, Somerset and Wiltshire. The Isle of Wight find represents the only silver artefact there in Phase B and, in contrast to Phase A, is located on the southern side of the island (IoWNAW-FS2). Significantly both the Wiltshire and Somerset finds were uncovered in the vicinity of a major Roman road or prehistoric trackway, in common with their gold counterparts.

## *Phase C silver distributions*

The Phase C distribution of silver artefacts presents three clear geographical groupings: Kent extending into Surrey; the Upper Thames Valley; a more diffuse distribution covering Wiltshire, Somerset and Dorset. Of the 181 entries for silver in Phase C, Kent has 131 (72%). The weight range of items is mainly between 1g and 12g, but most of them, the pendants, rings and pins, weigh less than two grams. The heaviest items all come from Wiltshire sites. There are the seax-scabbard fittings (30g) from a barrow at Ford near Laverstock (WltLVK-BI2) and the combined weight of a spoon and safety-pin brooches (36g) accompanying the woman in the Swallowcliffe Down secondary-barrow bed-burial (WltASY-BI1). This last assemblage shares clear affiliations with Kentish material. Within the study region the only other recorded safety-pin brooches are those from Grave 205 at Kingston Down (KntKSN-IC1). There is also a similar spoon at Broome Park near Barham (KntBHM-FS1), which was dated by G. Baldwin Brown (1915) as c.500 representing a development from Late Roman type spoons, but has been attributed instead to the seventh century by George Speake (1989, 46). Given the limited range of weights for silver objects in this period, it is tempting to favour an interpretation of these two spoons as curated Roman-manufactured items. Sixteen burials in Phase C contained silver sceatta coins. Of these, however, only one did not occur in Kent. This was the woman in Grave 4202 from the St Mary's Stadium cemetery (HtsSTN-MC1) near *Hamwic* whose burial contained three Series B sceattas and an imported Frisian gold pendant.

## Conclusions

Kent and in particular its eastern half stands out throughout all three phases as very much wealthier than its neighbours across southern Britain. Whether in terms of the numbers of items buried with each individual or the variety of their material content, there is no doubting the reality of the situation here. Further wealth is relatively evenly distributed through the burial population. The extremes with just a few richer grave assemblages accompanied by mostly fairly basically furnished burials typical of much of the overall study region was not a feature here. Thus copper alloy access as represented in Kent consisted of Frankish buckle and belt-set types, many of them imports, or else bowls and other vessels, particularly in phases A and B. Silver and gold were also available in much greater quantities than elsewhere, again particularly in Phase B. There are obvious changes to the availability of all raw materials over time, but Kent was never disadvantaged and continued to percolate wealth down through and within its communities. Elsewhere, apart from the north-Wiltshire area, a restricted access to all materials has facilitated, it is argued, a more hierarchical societal structure within the burial communities – a situation that was in place in phase A and not a consequence of phase A developments.

# 11. External Forces? A Review of the Frankish Influence within Southern Britain

Although our key research interests are concerned with the mechanisms of the internal processes within the societies of lowland southern Britain, we cannot ignore and therefore must assess the potential influence of external polities on these societies and nascent polities (see Figure 52, a general map of northern Europe). The Merovingian Frankish realms (Neustria, Austrasia, Burgundy *etc*.), often referred to collectively as *Francia*, were the most immediate and powerful neighbours of populations in the hinterlands of the British south coast (Wood 1983; 1994). Thus, it is important to establish the extent of Frankish imports and influences on the material culture of insular Anglo-Saxon populations (Welch 2002). Next we must consider whether the distribution of Frankish objects in Phase A is related to pre-existing Late Roman settlement patterns and landscape structures. In assessing whether Frankish influences might have acted as an external driver for economic and political change in southern Britain, we need to evaluate whether an established complex society in northern Gaul, utilising Roman administrative systems through a Roman aristocratic landowning elite, could provide a model for social change in southern Britain, where no such elite survived within the Anglo-Saxon settlement zones. We must consider to what extent such a process would have resulted from the extension of Frankish interests into such peripheral territories as southern Britain and Frisia. If Frankish interests were channelled through particular territories in southern Britain, then we need to establish whether archaeological evidence of Frankish imports and cultural influence coincided with the territories or wider zones of influence of individual Anglo-Saxon kingdoms.

We can then discuss whether *Francia* possessed an independent range of interests that interacted with a number of emerging polities across lowland Britain in the sixth to seventh centuries. Certainly, the formation of the Kentish kingdom within the sixth century has been linked consistently over time, by historians and other modern researchers, to the expansionist policies of *Francia* (*e.g.* Brooks 1989; Yorke 1990). More recently it has been demonstrated for the economic development in eastern Kent that communities in certain areas with unevenly spread resources and populations actually shaped the history of an entire region by stimulating change in their neighbouring communities (Brookes 2007). We need to establish what Frankish elite had to gain

*11. External Forces?*

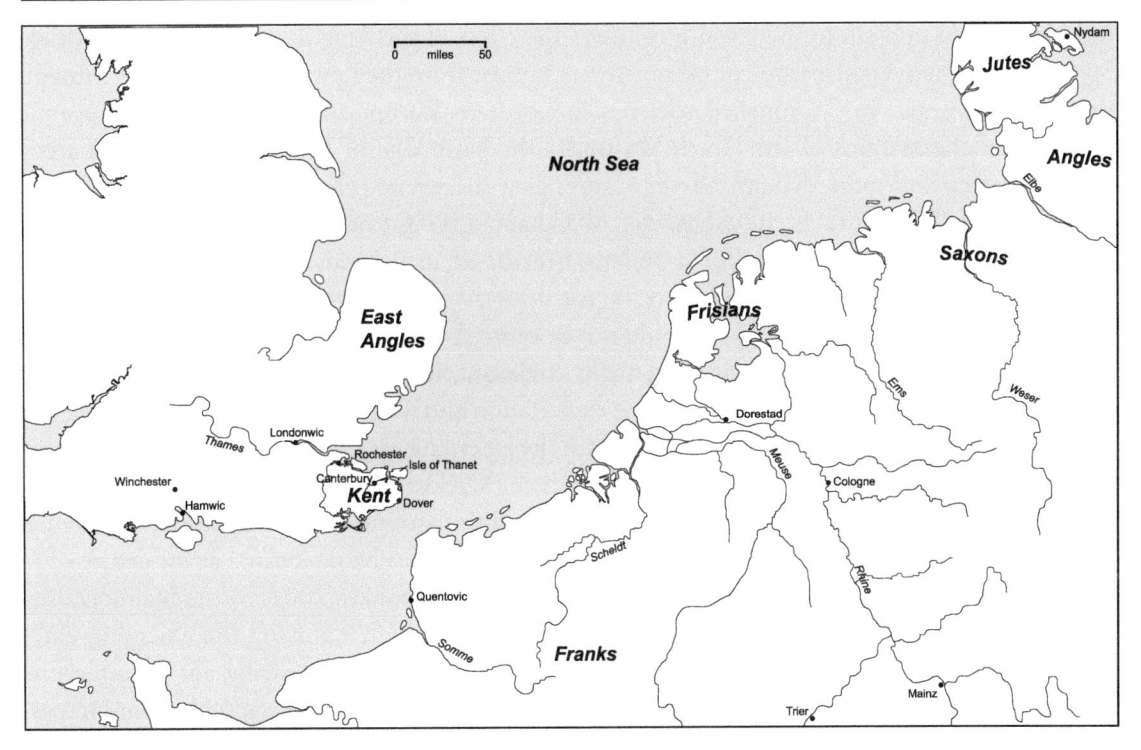

*Figure 52. Northern Europe around the North Sea*

from interactions with southern Britain. Freedom from fear of piratical raids on the exposed coastline of northern Gaul is one possibility that has been mentioned (Wood 1992). Another is that the Franks, by developing a coherent polity in Kent, could obtain access to particular resources that they could not supply in abundance for themselves, though it is difficult to determine directly from the archaeological evidence what those would be. If *Francia* acted as a catalyst for change with its neighbours, both within and beyond mainland Europe, then it may have stimulated change through Kent and beyond it to the rest of southern and eastern Britain. Here the key issue for us to consider is the spatial range and nature of links that *Francia* may have utilised within the study region independently of those it had clearly made with Kent. If we can postulate unequal links between the external superpower and its clients, whether in cultural, social, economic or political terms, we can query whether the formation of kingdoms within the study region was a uniform and coherent process over time and space. To what extent is it even realistic to postulate that kingdoms can be formed without the influence of external models? Thus we can explore the role *Francia* might have played in the development of hierarchically structured societies across Wessex and in Sussex and whether this involvement occurred contemporaneously with Frankish interaction with Kent and was in any way different from it.

Following the influential theories of Pirenne (1937), it has long been argued that Roman economic institutions were still effective within the former Empire until the impact of Islamic expansion on

175

the Mediterranean basin in the seventh century. The effect of the Arab invasions of North Africa, Spain and southern Gaul was to cut off northwest Europe from the flow of prestige goods through the Mediterranean. This compelled societies in northern Europe to develop a new economic area around the margins of the North Sea under the patronage of the Merovingian monarchy and aristocracy and more dynamically its Carolingian successors (Hodges 1982, 7; Hodges and Whitehouse 1983). More recently, however, Wickham, amongst others, has robustly questioned the value of Pirenne's thesis, despite, or perhaps because of, its deceptively attractive contribution to a trajectorial meta-narrative leading to the medieval ascendancy of northwest Europe. He has argued that the focus for explanation should not be centred on long-distance trading relationships, which he sees as rather superficial and essentially irrelevant. Instead he has placed his emphasis on the internal mechanisms of demand, resource exploitation and wealth accumulation within regions across mainland Europe. He used these to explain the emerging economic and cultural complexity of the early medieval period across Europe as a whole (Wickham 2005, 821–2).

Initially, however, it would appear that the communities around the North Sea were marginal to Frankish concerns, although *Francia* has been characterised as being located at the centre of "a diffusionary pattern of social and economic developments" (Brookes 2007, 8). Its highly crafted and standardised material culture was regarded enviously as high status by the emerging elites settled around its periphery, including those of Kent. If we compare visually, for example, the extraordinary range and sophistication of the artefacts recovered from grave assemblages at Herpes-en-Charente in the Saintonge with those from Faversham, the greater wealth of the continental site is immediately obvious. While Faversham is relatively rich in the context of Kent and southern Britain, it appears relatively meagre in both range and content by comparison. This particular evaluation is based on a visual inspection made in 2008 of the material from both sites in the public displays and the reserve collections of the Sturge basement in the British Museum. Wickham has cautioned that in considering luxury goods, for example wine, fine cloth and jewellery, we are not of necessity examining the economies of consuming communities, although such items can be instrumental in providing markers of contact and influence (Wickham 2005, 701). Rather the crucial component of regional economic systems was the demand for bulk goods that were internally distributed. Thus the scale of bulk exchange provides the principal marker of economic complexity. It underpinned the wealth of the landowning aristocracy, who both created demand and used demand to create their wealth through taxation (*ibid.*, 819). The earlier structures of developed Frankish economic activity should be seen as responsible for all the bulk production identified to date then and also for exchange mechanisms across northwest Europe, at least until the early eighth century AD. Goods that were sent across the Channel and around the North Sea in all likelihood formed only a small part of total Frankish production. They may well have been used to enhance Frankish political and diplomatic contacts and prestige in local contexts, through gift-exchange processes.

Nevertheless we still need to determine whether the artefacts recovered in the archaeological record were traded or exchanged goods *per se*, rather than the personal effects of individual 'Franks' who possessed some local influence within the study region and went on to die and be buried here.

## 11. External Forces?

What, if anything, did the Franks in northern Gaul get in return for the prestige items that were shipped across the Channel? It is widely accepted that Frankish material culture was influential in southern Britain throughout the study period (Welch 1991, 261). On the other hand, the precise and changing natures of that influence and the contingent impacts requires further research elucidation. Frankish relationships with Kent, as the major point of contact, are well established archaeologically from the fifth century onwards. If *Francia* did exercise influence over Kent, we should ask as a corollary to what extent in turn did Kentish influence extend spatially within the study region. Did the Kentish elite deploy particular aspects of their relationship to Frankish culture in order to enhance their regional status? Were the two in competition with one another for control of key resources over time and space and did this struggle give an impetus towards independence for the local Germanic polities? Additionally, can we observe evidence of direct Frankish influence further westwards into the study region beyond Kent?

Although most evident through the wide range of high-status and exotic traded goods that may have percolated through the economies of the Kentish coastal communities into the wider region of southern Britain, more substantially, although less readily detectable, there might have been a range of social connections that promoted the relationships between the earliest Anglo-Saxon kingdoms on the periphery and their powerful, if only marginally interested, continental neighbours at the centre. The Merovingian hegemony over Britain, though actual, appears to have been both 'vague and inconstant' over time, however (Wood 1992, 241). A contemporary Mediterranean written source, the Greek secretary and historian Procopius, provided apparent evidence for a claim of authority over *Brittia*, probably part of southern Britain, as exercised by Theudebert early in the 550s. This revolved around an alleged reverse Germanic migration from Britain to the continent, involving the settlement of Angles in *Francia*, bringing with them their title to their previous domicile (Procopius, *History of the Gothic Wars*). Intermarriage, primarily exogamous, involving females from *Francia* can be detected in the archaeological record of southern Britain. In all likelihood these were not women of the highest status within the royal court, however, as the evidence involves the presence of relatively ordinary sixth-century artefacts, such as gold-braided headbands and matched pairs of both miniature and radiate-headed bow brooches (Crowfoot and Hawkes 1967; Brugmann 1999). Nevertheless the physical and notional content of the associated dowries can only be conjectured. It may have comprised esoteric personal artefacts and perhaps entitlements to land in Britain and wealth in terms of treasure.

Intermarriage may have been something of a one-way street, however, as it has been suggested that "Saxon women brought no prestige to Merovingian men" (Wood 1992, 240). On the other hand, a Saxon slave could become a queen and queen regent in the seventh century, as apparently might be the case with Bathild (Nelson 1978). In any case, at the local level, the relative political values of ethnically different potential spouses may have been more nuanced. We could conjecture a strategy involving Kentish women marrying Saxon men or *vice versa* to achieve or cement local political alliances within southern Britain. Even the much-heralded alliance between Bertha, the daughter of a deceased Merovingian king of Paris, and the Kentish prince and heir to the throne Æthelbert in the later sixth century involved the cementing of bonds between dynasties of unequal status. There are hints that it occurred within a sequence of events that saw Æthelbert's father use a Frankish form for his name as Irminric and Æthelbert's son and successor Eadbald's subsequent marriage to another Frank Ymme (Welch 2007, 190–1). It has also been noted that the Frankish authorities were concerned to achieve the return of errant slaves in the Salic Law Code. This reference possibly relates to east Kent and in particular both Thanet and the Wantsum channel. It seems that there was an expectation that Frankish law codes could be enforced beyond the formal limits of their territories. There is also evident interest taken by the Franks in the Christian conversion of the Anglo-Saxons. This involved the activities of Frankish missionaries amongst the Angles and also the Saxons of the *Gewissae* from the late sixth century onwards (Mayr-Harting 1991; Yorke 2006). There was also their role in the Augustinian mission of AD 597 to Kent. Overall, the cultural impact of the triumvirate of marriage, law and Christian religion may have been impossible for the nascent elites of the study region to withstand. Indeed these events may also have had direct economic consequences.

Although Hines (1994), amongst others, has rightly stressed the continuing relevance of the Scandinavian heritage in the material culture of the Anglo-Saxons in the late fifth and sixth centuries, nevertheless the impact of explicitly Frankish material culture, both in terms of form and raw material content, had a culturally transformational effect. Its most direct effect was the evolution of distinctively Kentish styles. We need to establish whether Kent was falling under an irresistible influence from *Francia* or was merely assimilating current continental styles which were to be adapted and utilised by association in order to enhance its own status as a regional power. It has been suggested by Welch (1991, 267) that the Frankish-Kentish monopoly over cross-channel trade may have developed from Kentish acceptance of Merovingian overlordship. Then we might conjecture that a formal marriage treaty with the Merovingian royal houses might actually have signalled a move towards greater independence and regional standing on the part of Kent. We must also consider the issues of exchange between a lesser and a greater power, overlying a presumed network of various minor and localised movements of food rents, goods, gifts and labour obligations within and across the study region. There is no clear evidence of enforced obligations in the form of tribute payments made on behalf of Kent, at least, towards *Francia*, but the flow of goods that brought Merovingian culture to Britain must have been offset in the other direction and probably in a greater abundance of value.

This raises the crucial question of what lowland Britain could provide that would have prompted the development of exchange mechanisms with its continental neighbours and thus dramatically enhance the wealth of Kentish communities? Additionally what form did the exercise of Kentish and Frankish interests take within the study region of southern Britain? At certain stages in our period we may conjecture roles for Frankish and Kentish entrepreneurs as trading with Saxon communities west of Kent. They might also have operated as landowners or military overlords protecting their economic interests. We are already able to suggest that certain raw materials utilised within the study region, such as iron with its status as a valuable bulk good and its visibility in the archaeological record of contemporary burial, notwithstanding the potentially large scale ore resources in the Weald, together with other rarer metals, might have been derived mainly from

Continental sources. This certainly could have been the case in the coastal areas, removing the need for wholesale scavenging from minor Roman sites, other than for very limited domestic purposes. Evaluations of documentary sources have suggested that cloth, fur, hides, hunting dogs and slaves may have had a role to play in the other direction (Hinton 1990, 23). Certainly cloth, hides and slaves might be considered as bulk goods, whilst other organic products, such as cereal grain, may also have fallen into the equation. Surplus production of cereals is probably impossible to determine from the currently available archaeological evidence from burial and settlement sites, however, although the landscape placement of early sites and the productive capacity of the associated soils plays a major part in exploring such issues further.

Although contacts with Merovingian society at the highest levels of insular Anglo-Saxon society might fluctuate with the twists and turns of internal politics within the regional superpower, more basic links between broader layers of society might have continued uninterrupted. For example, in the sixth-century Kentish material in *Francia*, extending as far south as the dozen or more Anglo-Saxon burials recorded at the cemetery of Herpes-en-Charente, near the Atlantic seaboard in southwest France (Haith 1988), and including many other sites along the northern Channel coast might have represented trading enclaves (Welch 1991, 263–4). An alternative interpretation is that families or households linked to other traders by marriage were 'striking up private arrangements' (Hawkes 1982, 72). The settlement of successive groups of Saxons from lowland Britain along the northern coast of Gaul from the mid fifth century onwards might have enhanced such exchanges or facilitated specific links, within a complex of interactions. A hiatus in the sequence of objects present is noted from sites along the northern Gallic coast between *c.*AD 450 and 475. Prior to this time slot, Saxon cultural material is present, but it was derived directly from the northwest German homelands. After this date, however, the material is culturally Anglo-Saxon, being manufactured in Britain (Soulat 2009, 7). Again, explanations which suggest either the arrival of dress fittings as traded goods or alternatively as components relating to exogamous marriage between communities in southern Britain and culturally similar communities in northern France might be equally valid in this context (Welch 1991, 265). The geographical locations from which settlers moved into northern *Francia* included east and south Kent and the Hampshire/Isle of Wight region, but excluded West Sussex. This left a significant gap in evidence for the sector of northern France, known today as Upper Normandy, that lay directly across the Channel from West Sussex (Soulat 2009, figs 6 and 7). Whilst the identification of distinctively Jutish burials in Kent to match those recorded in the Jutland peninsular of Denmark has defeated modern researchers (Sørensen 1997; Welch 2007), it has been possible to identify continental Saxon and Anglo-Saxon burials within the cemeteries along the Frankish Channel coastline, including urned and unurned cremations (Soulat 2009, figs 86–89, 123).

Equally it has been argued that the presence of Frankish cultural material from burial sites along the southern coast of Britain, for example at Alfriston and Highdown in Sussex, might been a result of Kentish hegemony here, rather than an indication of direct contacts with *Francia* (Welch 1991, 268). The apparent breakdown of a Kentish trading monopoly during the seventh century took place at a time of emerging new patterns of trade within the study region. Particularly important here was the late seventh-century foundation of *Hamwic* by the West Saxons, which provided direct access to the northern French *emporia* of Quentovic on the Canche and Rouen on the Seine. Equally important was East Saxon control over London or *Lundenwic*, a trading place acquired by the Mercians relatively late in the seventh century, and the Mercian efforts to control access to Kent during the eighth century.

There is an issue as to how far back we should go in exploring the presence of continental artefacts and especially dress fittings in burials within lowland Britain. Furnished burials datable to the end of the fourth century and the first half of the fifth century that contained military-style belt sets might indicate the presence of federate troops of the Roman army. These will have been transferred from Gaul, most probably from the Rhineland frontier zone or else from northeastern France and Belgium. Such individuals should not be confused with persons buried within a 'Frankish Phase' of influence attributed to the later fifth and early sixth century period (Hawkes 1982, 72–4). Certainly the material culture of the earlier group has clear connections with that of northern Gaul. It must be recognised, however, that distribution maps of Late Roman 'military' fittings do not necessarily equate with the postings of military units, as belt sets may well have been worn as symbols of office by civil administrators in imperial service bearing quasi-military ranks (Böhme 1974, 1986 and 1987; Welch 1993, 270). Additionally large quantities of such fittings were deposited in graves in the Saxon homelands of northwest Germany and particularly between the Weser and Elbe estuaries. Warriors may have brought similar belt sets direct to Britain from the north German region that had previously been in Roman service (Welch 1993).

For burials with belt fittings in Late Roman cemeteries in lowland Britain, it cannot be assumed that all of them were actually of north German origin. For example, the case made for 'Saxons' being buried in the Lankhills extramural cemetery at Winchester (*Venta Belgarum*) remains far from convincing (*pace* Clarke 1979) and study of teeth from more recently excavated inhumations there seems to indicate that some of those buried with imported metal fittings had spent their childhood in southern Britain, whereas others buried with Romano-British fittings had been born outside Britain (Evans *et al.* 2006; Eckhardt *et al.* 2009). The case made from the same cemetery for Sarmatians recruited in Pannonia being stationed at Winchester remains plausible, however, though they may well have intermarried with other Roman and British communities whilst based there (Baldwin 1985). Confirmation of a Gothic origin for the man buried with a 'east Germanic' silver belt set at Kingsholm near Gloucester (*Glevum*) has also come from the dental evidence (*Current Archaeology* 2009). More probably of north German origin is the weapon burial containing a sword, spear, shield and a pewter bowl from an extramural site by the coastal fort at Richborough in Kent. Taken together with other weaponry recovered from this fort, there is a clear suggestion of a Saxon or Frankish component to the final garrison here (Böhme 1986; Welch 1993, 270). On the other hand, there is no secure archaeological evidence to support the suggestion that this garrison remained there throughout the first half of the fifth century and gradually developed into a settler community.

Further, an updated listing of artefacts from Late Roman 'military' type belt sets that includes metal-detected findspots confirms the distributions as presented *c.*1960 (Hawkes and Dunning

1961). There is a clear focus on east Kent and the Watling Street route to London as well as the Upper Thames Valley (*ibid.* fig. 4). Although the finds from sites in Surrey at Croydon, Wallington and Guildown would appear to be set away from this major routeway, nevertheless all of them were adjacent to Roman roads and the cemetery communities in which they appear may have exercised explicit control over these roads. A strategic positioning of military capacity offers the best explanation for their distribution and further finds from similar locations may be forthcoming in the future.

Large-scale invasion and settlement are unlikely to be represented by the relatively few burials containing fifth-century Frankish material. Vera Evison's attempt in the 1960s to relate their distribution to the 'origin myth' entries preserved in the *Anglo-Saxon Chronicle* seems extremely dated now (Evison 1965, 79). Her subsequent discussions of Frankish material in Anglo-Saxon period burials across the study region published since the 1970s sought deliberately to place this material as early as possible within the fifth century. This had the effect of conflating it with and viewing it as a direct temporal continuation of Late Roman 'military' type fittings. In turn this supported a particular view of invasion and settlement. As we will argue below, however, much of this material need not be dated so early. Indeed some of it first appears in the burial record within the last quarter of the fifth century. For example, there is no evidence to suggest that Kent ever received large-scale settlement directly from *Francia* itself. Individual weapon assemblages (Evison 1987, 134–6) or female dress combinations (Brugmann 1999) have been attributed to migrants, but these are relatively few in number.

On the other hand, Frankish influence in the mobilisation of migrant peoples around its borders and margins cannot be discounted. Indeed, an early connection between the 'Jutes' of Kent and the 'Franks' of the Rhineland has been claimed in the past (for example Leeds 1936; Stenton 1943, 14–15). Likewise it has been disputed at different times whether the 'Jutes' of southern Britain came directly from southern Scandinavia (Jutland). Stenton's preferred route for these migrants was via the mouth of the Rhine (ibid.). This point is reinforced by the close parallels between the Jutlandic square-headed plate brooch from grave 14 at Apple Down (SsxCPT-MC1) and its equivalent from grave 10 at Tournai Saint-Brice in Belgium (Brulet 1990; Down and Welch 1990). As mentioned earlier, a recent review of the burial evidence from the fifth to sixth centuries in east Kent and the Jutland peninsular has made it clear that entire communities from mainland Denmark were not transplanted to Kent with their burial practices unchanged (Sørensen 1997). Rather, the available evidence suggests that the Jutes of Kent may have been resident in Frisia or northern Gaul for more than one generation before they moved to Britain (Welch 2007).

On the issue of reverse migrations in the sixth century, presumably implying conflicts within southern Britain that encouraged less successful Germanic groups to return to mainland Europe, Stenton found support in the writings of Procopius for his suggestion that "the Franks planted the immigrants in the more deserted parts of their own territory" (Stenton 1943, 7). This would suggest that the Franks were well versed in the colonising techniques previously used by the Romans, and later adopted on a global scale in the later British Empire, of transplanting ethnic groups between territories, even whole continents, for economic gain.

The approach rather then is to focus on those individual burials that can be clearly identified, according to specific criteria, as sharing close affinities with the cemetery material culture of *Francia*. The Frankish Phase was a term adopted by E. T. Leeds in order to explore the presence of Frankish artefacts within burial sites in Kent and to a lesser extent elsewhere in lowland Britain (Leeds 1936, 44–58). His terminology for the Kentish sequence has continued in use following on from the initial Jutish phase of settlement and developing into the floruit of Kentish styles. Discussions of this Frankish Phase have tended to concentrate on stylistic issues and their impact on high-status craft production with access to significant quantities of silver and garnet being seen as an adjunct of trade (Hawkes 1982, 72–4). The project database records only 30 artefacts as Imported/Frankish within burials dated to the fifth century, with a geographical distribution that encompasses the entire study region and, most significantly, with only two items in Kent. The artefact types are mainly weaponry and dress fitments. The caveat here is the research history of the region that may have dated burials, in the Upper Thames Valley particularly, into a continuity phase from the Roman period. They may present themselves as deceptively early. Nevertheless, the Frankish material culture is spatially coherent and is not evidence of a fall-off from the supposed nearest point of contact in East Kent. Numbers of Frankish artefacts increase as the sixth century progressed, but imports of brooches in particular tail off during the second half of the sixth century and they become relatively rare after *c.*575. Thus the majority of Frankish imports belong within our project Phase A. So, it is necessary to establish whether Frankish interest in southern Britain abruptly changed at this juncture of *c.*575 or whether its involvement was displayed thereafter in other ways.

It has been suggested (Wood 1992, 237) that there was a consistency in the exercise of Merovingian regional hegemony in the late sixth to the mid seventh centuries, taking in lowland Britain's Phase B. If that was the case, however, we might have expected to see more evidence for the presence of 'Frankish' individuals through the later burial records. Admittedly Anglo-Saxon belt fittings and buckles in the seventh century continue to be heavily influenced by Frankish forms (Marzinzik 2003) and the range of iron buckles with triangular plates inlaid with silver from the coastal region of Kent in phase B may signal continuing Frankish influence (Hawkes 1979). Likewise imports of continental wheel thrown pottery first appear in quantity around the end of the sixth century (Evison, 1979). Earlier Frankish material culture does not appear to have enjoyed the same cultural caché accorded to Scandinavian-influenced material, however. Thus it is rarely curated beyond its main circulation and immediate date range, in the manner of, for example, the 'Finglesham Man' buckle (Hawkes *et al.* 1965) or indeed the Roman objects that recur in some seventh-century assemblages.

# 12. The Frankish Data Examined

## Research questions

A series of queries were posited for the data and map resources, in order to track where the Frankish material was located, to examine the types of site where it has been recorded and to infer some preferences with regard to their positioning in the landscape. A central concern was to establish whether Frankish material was restricted to the wealthiest sites in southern Britain, or whether it was the presence of Frankish material that made a site wealthy. Conversely for those cemeteries that produced no Frankish finds, did they also lack any significant material wealth as a result? In particular, two datasets were mapped. The first recorded Frankish objects across all three phases and the second the location of spear burials in which the spearhead occupied a reversed position point down by the feet, which was a recognisably Frankish trait.

The initial problem was to define those artefact types that are unambiguously Frankish in manufacture and can contribute to an analysis of the geographical spread of any possible direct Frankish influence on the study region. Underlying this task, and recognisably untested, is the assumption that certain artefacts can be taken to equate with individual agents, against the background noise of artefacts arriving from *Francia* via Kent and being utilised within predominantly Saxon communities. Only those objects that fell within the *weaponry* and *personal effects* categories of the database were considered. These were seen as most likely to reflect personal contacts with *Francia*, through gift exchange, trade or marriage, even if, certainly in the case of some brooches, they were not positioned in their traditional Frankish manner in the burial (Brugmann, 1999). As a basis for selection, the phased artefact groupings for the French regions between the Channel coast and Lorraine (Legoux *et al.* 2004) were used to produce lists of relevant, culturally Frankish artefacts. Phase A objects which are equivalent to French pre-Merovingian and Merovingian phases PM, MA1, MA2 dated up to *c.*570 consist of francisca-type axeheads, S-shaped brooches, buckles of iron and silver, spindle whorls of black and white glass or facetted rock crystal, pursemounts of iron with silver inlays, selected buckle types, earrings, bird brooches, radiate-headed brooches, garnet disc and rosette brooches, garnet inlaid pins, spearheads of Swanton classes A1 and B2, crystal balls and perforated spoons, as well as selected swords. The Phase B objects equivalent to phases MA3 and MR1 up to *c.*640, are seaxes, certain buckle types, wheel ornaments, inlaid sword

Table 49. Number of personal artefacts and weapons from Frankia and Kent by phase

| Phase | Imported Frankish | Kentish/Frankish | Kentish |
|---|---|---|---|
| A | 409 | 409 | 352 |
| B | 67 | 195 | 285 |
| C | 23 | 53 | 126 |

pommels, triangular silver inlaid buckles plates and any of the earlier personal items or weapons which continued into this phase. The Phase C objects, equivalent to phases MR2 and MR3 up to *c*.710, are anseate brooches, buckles with multiple long plates and any of the earlier personal items or weapons also dated to this phase.

It can be questioned whether Swanton Series A throwing spears are Frankish imports, but they certainly reflect a Frankish mode of warfare and this will be discussed further below in relation to spear positions in burials. A proportion of the background material recorded in the database was designated as *Kentish/Frankish* particularly buckle loops. These might be seen as a secondary diffusion of continental styles throughout the Anglo-Saxon littoral region via Kent. A further group were clearly *Kentish* in manufacture. The collected types provide the principal context for the deployment of the primary Frankish material throughout the study region, in order to test the hypothesis that Frankish and Kentish influence was synonymous over time and space. Marzinzik has listed types of buckle loop with or without plates and these can be designated as most probably of Frankish manufacture, when compared to the northern French chronology. Essentially these are the buckles with wire inlay (Marzinzik types I.7a; II.4; II.5; II.8; II.9; II.10; II.11a; II.11b; II.12; II.13). More culturally widespread types here designated as *Kentish/Frankish* coincide with other Marzinzik types (I.2, I.3, I.4, I.5, I.6a, I.7b and c, I.9). Distinctively or most probably *Kentish* types are all provided with a fixed plate (Marzinzik II.15a and b, II.23).

The total numbers of personal and weapon artefacts falling within the designated provenances and used for mapping across the study region are presented in Table 49. The items include all contexted and unassociated burial material and all relevant findspot artefacts.

A control group of Imported/Frankish items that fell outside of the main categories was also mapped by phase. These were glass vessels, although it is accepted that a proportion of these may have been manufactured in lowland Britain before the seventh century (Evison 2008), and also wheel thrown pottery vessels, possibly with the same caveat (Evison 1979). In neither case has direct evidence for vessel production been recovered from archaeological sites of this period within the study region.

## Phase A Frankish data

Of 247 excavated cemetery and burial sites with a presence in Phase A, only 43 (17%) present Imported/Frankish artefacts. The total number of locations of this type of material is actually greater than this, however, due to the number of metal-detected findspots. As each findspot may

## 12. The Frankish Data Examined

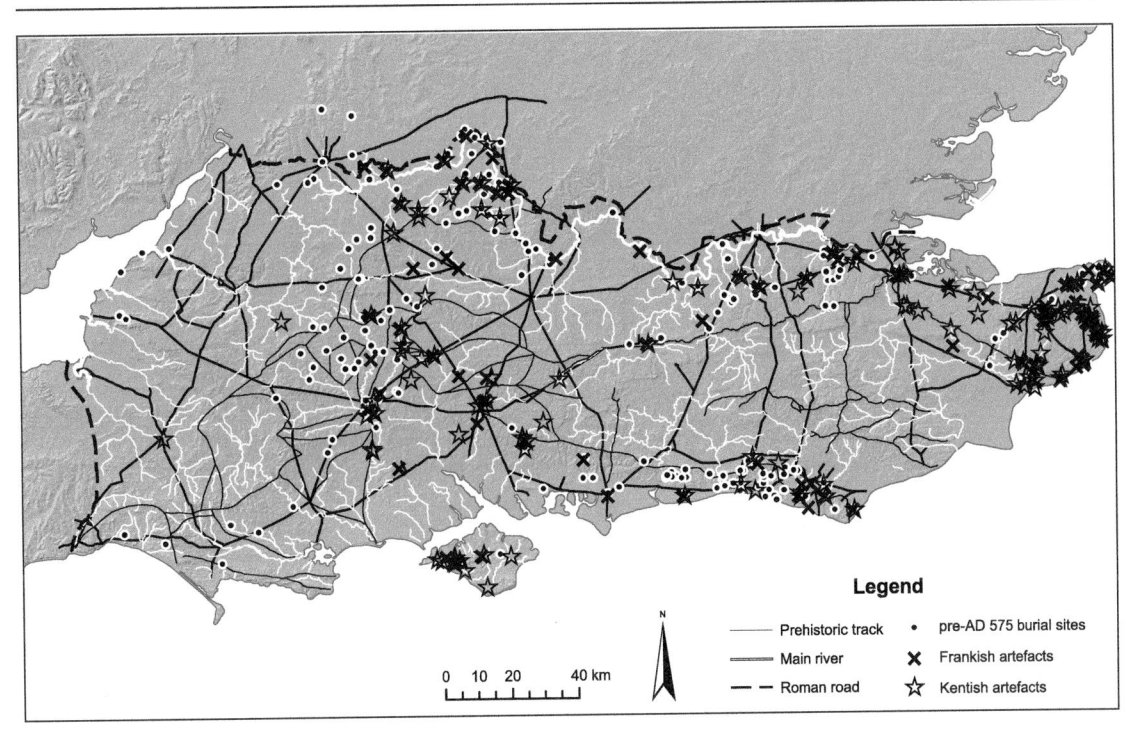

*Figure 53. An overview of the distribution Frankish material in the study region*

represent a larger burial context, it is merely chance that has revealed Frankish artefacts for the present distribution pattern and only time will tell whether some of these will develop into more significant sites upon further investigation. Taking an overview of the entire study region, it can be observed that there are five major clusters of Frankish material (Figure 53). These are: the coast of east Kent through to east Surrey: the Upper Thames Valley; central Wiltshire and the uplands of the Salisbury Plain; westwards from the east Sussex coast; the Isle of Wight, which on this particular distribution appears rather isolated. Each area exhibits different characteristics regarding the presence and absence of the Frankish and Kentish artefacts, either in combination or separately. Also within each spatial cluster there are sites in which neither type of material is present.

Outside of Kent, there are 62 burial sites (that is, excluding individual findspots) that have Frankish or Kentish material present. Of these, 27 sites possess both types of material, 20 sites have Kentish material, but no Frankish items and 15 sites have Frankish material, but no Kentish finds (Figure 54). Many of these sites occur in the same geographical districts within the Saxon littoral and they are assumed to be broadly contemporary. The westward reach of all this material merits some comment as two notional extents can be traced on the map. The Frankish material does not extend westwards beyond a south-north line extending essentially from the Avon on the south coast, through Salisbury and on up to Fairford and Lechlade in south Gloucestershire. The principal sites along this western edge are in Wiltshire at Winterbourne Gunner, Petersfinger and

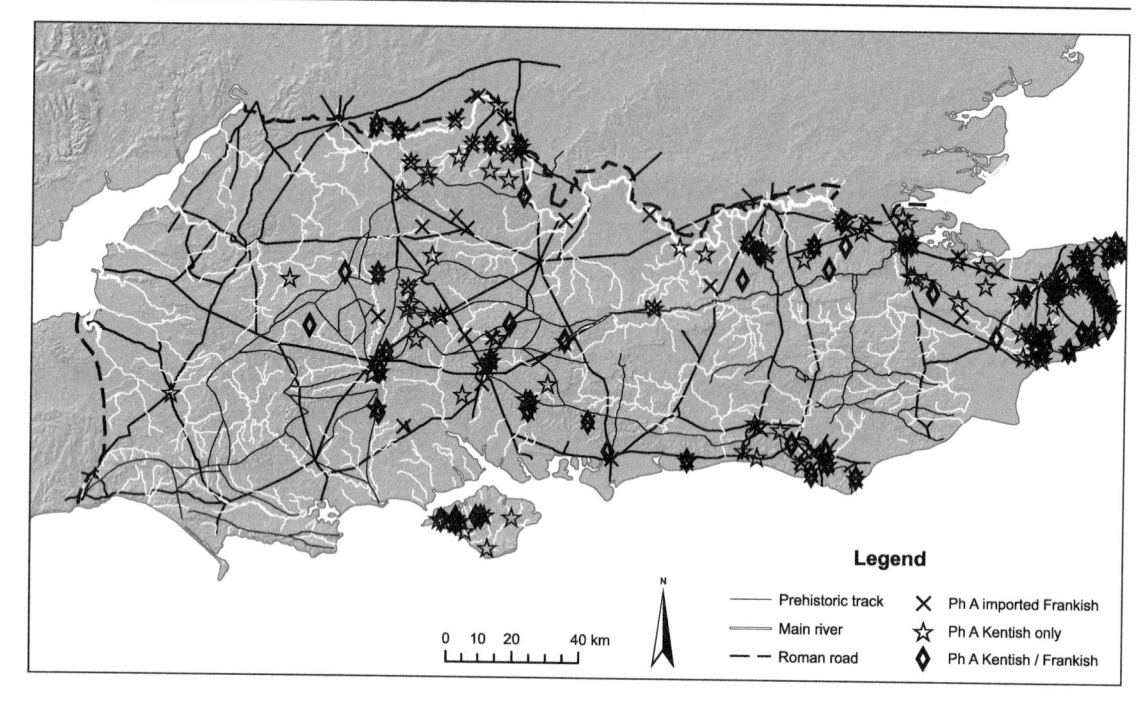

*Figure 54. The distribution Frankish and Kentish finds in Phase A*

Pewsey, each of which contained a francisca-type throwing axe. Another such axe is recorded at a findspot in North Bentley Wood, Hampshire near the junction of two Roman roads (Margary 1973, 422 and 424). It is tempting therefore to see this north-south line as marking a significant frontier. Overall the distribution of franciscas is limited to this western line, the east Kent coast and the easternmost part of the east Sussex down lands. Nevertheless, further to the west of this notional frontier across central Wiltshire there are other relevant finds. These are Kentish in character, however, and not Frankish, consisting of a keystone garnet disc brooch and a small square-headed brooch and significantly they are of a distinctly non-military nature. There are also two further finds in this western zone of Kentish/Frankish buckles.

Axeheads appear in northern-French burials throughout the period AD 440 to 610 (Legoux *et al.* 2004), and in the main can only be attributed to Phase A in our study region. The examples from Alfriston in East Sussex, including a prestigious axe hammer, are typologically early, however (Evison 1965; Welch 1983; Böhme 1986). They also include one associated with a sword and appear to represent fifth-century males of equal importance to those deposited in the sixth century with swords. Several of the corpus of 35 examples in the database have not been matched into a typology and many are from poorly-dated contexts. Where identifications of the axehead type can be made, however, they are all consistent with Frankish types (25 out of the 35). Thus, there does not appear to have been an indigenous axe type, although the place of manufacture using Frankish prototypes could conceivably have been within the study area. Nevertheless, given

## 12. The Frankish Data Examined

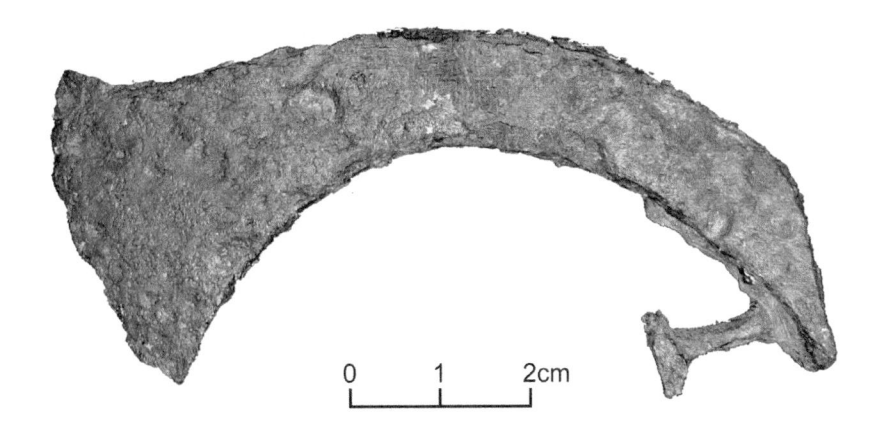

Figure 55. An example of a francisca

the considerable quantity of iron that they represent, it is reasonable to look critically at their provenances. With an average weight of 557 grams (with a range of 317 to 810 grams from 15 weighed examples), these are substantial weapons. Their raw material content by weight is well in excess of that for shield bosses and is only outstripped by long swords. The weight range is comparable to that for contemporary continental finds, with six examples being in excess of 700 grams, though the British corpus does not contain any examples comparable to the very heaviest continental axes (Hübener 1981).

Although Hübener identified regional differences in the distribution of axe weights in the regions of the Lower Rhine and northern France, this information does not readily transpose to the study region, due to a much smaller sample size. The bearded axe from an unknown context at Hardown Hill, Dorset may well fit with the francisca group in being an import, as its closest comparator is from grave 1 at Welschbillig in the Trier region (Böhner 1958, Tafel 33:1; Evison 1968, 236) and it is unduly heavy at 740g. If correct, this find adds an irregular zone of Frankish association through north Dorset to the identified south Wiltshire pattern. So, assuming that all axeheads in the study region are of Frankish origin and were meaningful as an expression of Frankish identity, their distribution as a group adds to the developing pattern of Frankish influence in Phase A (Figure 56). Unfortunately axes do not extend into Phase B within the current dating scheme, being replaced as a secondary prestige weapon in the warrior repertoire by seaxes from the late sixth century onwards (Härke 1992; Hübener1981, 89–90). It is their distribution around the edge of the study region in Phase A that appears key, focussing on the two major coastal access points in East Kent and East Sussex (Ouse-Cuckmere region) as well as the dominant fluvial network of the Thames. Taken together with the western boundary cutting through Wiltshire, their distribution appears to delineate an entire territory. In particular they enclose an interior landscape within which this weapon form is entirely absent. By contrast more personal kinds of material culture are present within that enclosed region, perhaps implying a settled territory with naturalised social reproduction amongst varied cultural groupings. Presumably these axe burials looked outwards to impress territories beyond their bounds, rather than inwards over less individualistic weaponed

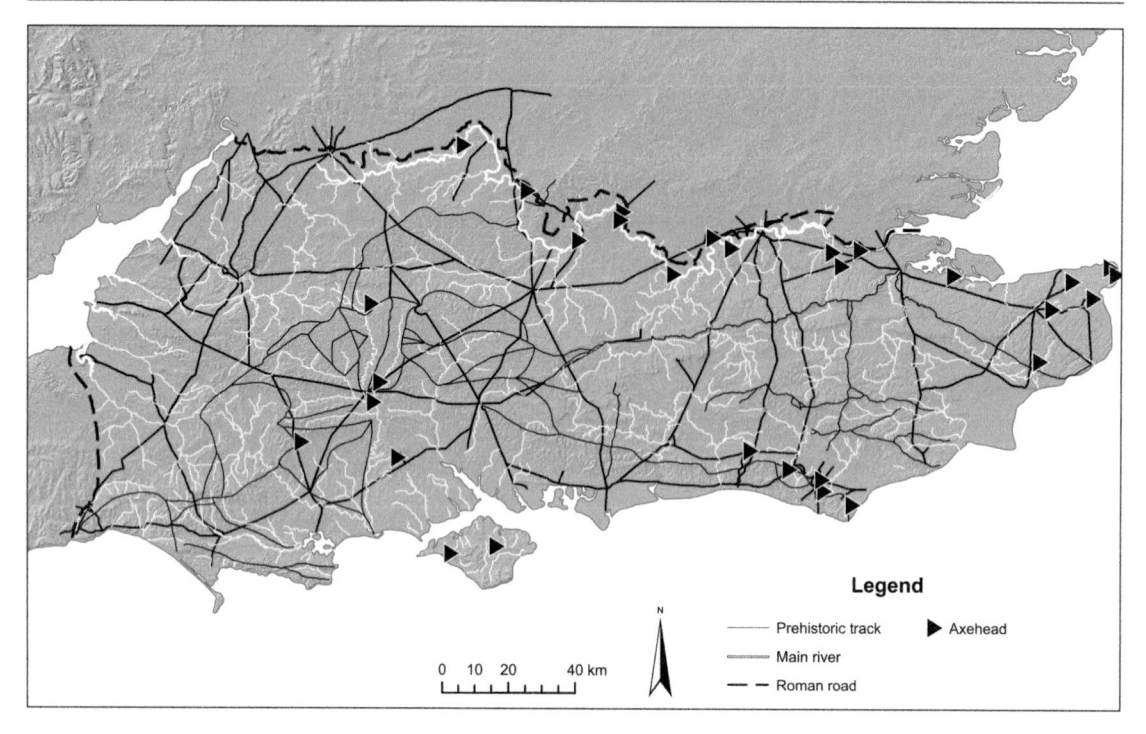

*Figure 56. The distribution of franciscas in the study region*

communities. Those territories would of necessity include those across the Channel, but also any existing polities to the west. The notional coherence of delineation by these artefacts with the Late Roman territory of Britannia Prima to the west may have some currency in this instance.

It is tempting, therefore, to invoke a centre-periphery relationship in which those occupying a marginal territory used public deposition of key artefacts, in this case symbolic weaponry, to reinforce the perception that they as individuals exercised real authority, when in reality their hold on power and their ability to pass on their control of land and other resources to the next generation was perhaps far from secure. A parallel is perhaps provided by the distribution of helmets in sixth to seventh-century burials across *Francia*, lowland Britain and Scandinavia (Hedeager 1992b). The absence of helmet burials in the heartland of the Neustrian kingdom within northern France and again in Denmark with only a single helmet from Jutland (pers. comm. J. Ljungkvist) contrasts with their deposition within the Rhineland and south-west Germany and in both Norway and Sweden. The few seventh-century helmets recorded within the territories of Anglo-Saxon kingdoms imply that their rulers exercised a similarly insecure, ephemeral and peripheral authority on the margins of two continental superpowers (*Francia* and Denmark). In addition to the Sutton Hoo helmet, these are represented by the boar figurine from Guilden Morden in Cambridgeshire, the Wollaston helmet in Northamptonshire and the Benty Grange example from the Derbyshire Peak District, to which the parts of helmet fittings present in the 2009 Staffordshire hoard can now be

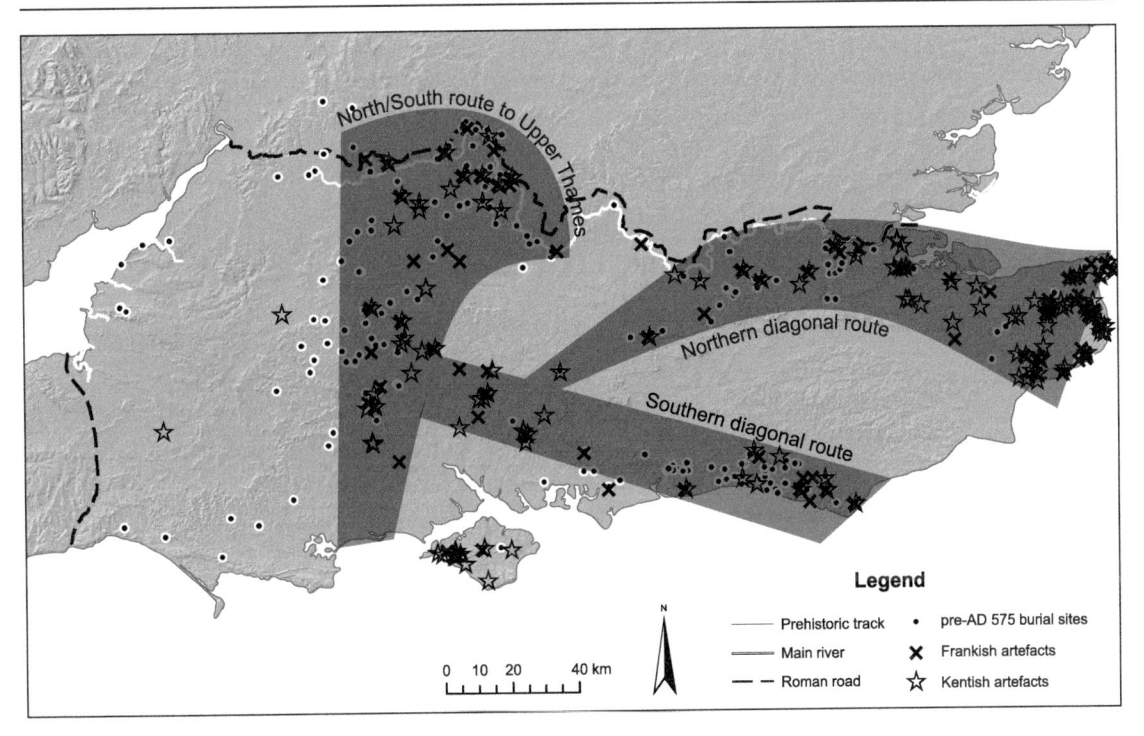

*Figure 57. Activity corridors through the study region*

added. The recent metal-detected find of a Frankish-style helmet in a weapon burial at Shorwell on the Isle of Wight confirms the peripheral location of such finds (Hood *et al.* 2012). This example is clearly dated to the early to mid sixth century and speaks to the particular role of the Isle of Wight as a gateway community at the interface with the British West at this time.

It is possible to define three major routeways or corridors of activity through the study region (Figure 57):

- A northern diagonal route from east Kent through to the Upper Thames Valley, utilising a combination of coastal routes, transhipment points on the north Kent coast, Roman roads and the River Thames;
- A parallel diagonal route to the south of the Weald, from the East Sussex coast overland via high-level routeways to Winchester and beyond, but not engaging with the West Sussex coastal area, though this route may be discontinuous;
- A minor linking avenue which joins the northern diagonal route to the southern diagonal route running between the North Downs and the Hampshire Downs via the Hog's Back in Surrey, based on a Roman road and prehistoric trackways;
- A broader route running south to north linking the sector of the south coast to the west of the Isle of Wight and the New Forest with the westernmost parts of the Upper Thames Valley.

The Frankish and Kentish material is buffered against these linear routes, spreading to both sides, yet retaining proximity and ease of access for trade and exchange. It is suggested here that we might have two potentially competing models to explain this pattern:

- A military encirclement of a large territory and subsequent infilling settlement, mediated through marriage treaties.
- Opportunistic trading by armed settlers using a network of links along the most viable routeways.

Frankish identity here may be piggy-backing on Kentish expansion along these routes, for the men of Kent could be demonstrating their Frankish connections in order to reinforce their own hegemony and cultural advancement within Saxon settlement contexts. Conversely, the men of Kent might be operating in the slipstream of Frankish activity, being dependent on Frankish control over the territory to enable them to act as middlemen with local producers in the exchange of goods. Nevertheless independent contact between local Saxons and the Franks, without any Kentish involvement, cannot be ruled out. The reach of Frankish and Kentish influence into central Wiltshire, and also far into the Upper Thames Valley suggests a need to access goods and staple materials that were not being produced, certainly in sufficient quantity, in the hinterland of their base in coastal east Kent. This is evidenced more clearly in Phase B by the distribution of Celtic hanging bowls and escutcheons in the eastern part of the study region (Figures 44 and 45). The spatial pattern for Phase A swords follows broadly similar lines, with coastal, riverine and western concentrations, although the provenance of these artefacts as specifically Kentish, Frankish or Saxon is uncertain.

Wheelthrown pots that can be assigned within Phase A are few in number (just five) and restricted to east Kent, the Isle of Wight and the Upper Thames Valley. Glass vessels are much more in evidence, but their Phase A distribution is clustered around three principal areas on the south coast of east Kent, Sussex and the Isle of Wight. They are also found inland along some, but by no means all of the major Roman and riverine routeways, and unlike other Frankish material, do not extend into Hampshire and Wiltshire. More helpfully, another artefact type in the form of gold braid reveals a very distinctive distribution throughout Phase A. The published 1960s listing (Crowfoot and Hawkes, 1967) can be added to with further finds from Kent and an extension of the range into Sussex. This brings the total (at 2007) within the study region to 25 examples. Gold-threaded braided textile borders to female head-dresses and edgings to the garments of both men and women have been found in continental Germanic graves between the late fifth to early sixth centuries and on into the eighth century. Their distribution in burials was centred in *Francia*, including the Lower and Middle Rhine regions, Thuringia, and both Alamannic and Lombardic graves either side of the Alps. Gold-brocaded garments had been worn by the wealthier classes of Roman and Byzantine society between the fourth and sixth centuries, as exemplified by a fourth-century female grave from Spitalfields in London excavated in 1999 (Wild, unpublished). It seems likely that the Merovingian Franks adopted the use of gold-threaded cloth as a consequence of their occupation of northern Roman Gaul. Whether there was continuity of Roman craft production into the Merovingian period or whether skilled Germanic craftswomen imitated this technique has yet to be determined, but the former seems probable. There is a significant degree of similarity between Kentish and continental braids, in which the braid had its surface brocaded with flat gold strip. Kentish production within the study region has yet to be demonstrated and no inference has been drawn here of the potential for continuity of Roman production within the British study region. Instead the assumption made is that these are imports of mostly female apparel.

The principal use of gold braids in the early Anglo-Saxon period appears to have been as a short brocaded fillet worn around the head as *vittae*, symbolic of betrothal and marriage. The relatively large numbers found in burial contexts indicate that women continued to wear them after marriage and on into the grave. That they could have a less restricted function in Kent than elsewhere in the Germanic continental world is suggested by two females with gold-brocaded wristlets (Chatham Lines grave 18; Sarre grave 4). This is a function for which there are no contemporary continental parallels, although they do occur in *Francia* as costume sleeve borders. The Anglo-Saxon burials have been interpreted as exogamous brides, cementing marriage links with local landholding families on behalf of the Kentish royal house and in the process emphasising their Frankish cultural and political links (Crowfoot and Hawkes 1967, 65). The Kentish females were all adults, young adults, or else juveniles.

The sole incidence of gold braid clearly associated with a man within the study region is from the early seventh-century burial at Taplow in Buckinghamshire. The braid here might have been used for a belt, a baldric, or more probably a jacket or cloak edging for the costume of a regional ruler or 'prince', whose isolated burial mound dominated river access to the Upper Thames Valley (Webster 1992; Rogers 2007, figure 5.64). Broadly contemporary is the narrow braid from Prittlewell princely burial within the Southend conurbation in Essex (Hirst 2004). The fragmentary example embedded in a sword scabbard from Faversham, Kent, may be earlier (Harrington, forthcoming). The earliest continental uses of gold braid in burials are also from high-status male graves, all probably datable before *c.*525, with the oldest being the Merovingian 'king' Childeric I who died in 481–2 and was interred under a great mound at St Brice across the river from Roman Tournai. Gold braid predominates in female graves of the sixth century, however, and Kent has approximately half of those recorded for that period, the remainder being distributed across *Francia* and the Middle Rhineland. By the end of the sixth century, gold braids have a much diminished presence in Kentish female cemeteries, but their use continues in the Frankish heartlands into the seventh century, as at St Denis near Paris, and in Langobardic graves in Italy. There is a perceptible shift from an association predominantly with women in the sixth century, most evident in east Kent, to a situation throughout the seventh century where men regained equal or indeed greater access to this high-status cultural symbol. The evidence from Taplow and Prittlewell therefore fits this continental pattern.

There are multiple occurrences of gold braid on just three Kentish sites with five examples from Bifrons and four each from Buckland near Dover and from Sarre. Each of these sites was adjacent to or located on a major element of the Kentish routeway network. Only two Kentish women can be argued to be buried as late as the early seventh century at Breach Downs grave 1 and Sarre grave 90. Within the Anglo-Saxon corpus of gold-braid burials, two of the non-Kentish examples (a child in grave 11 at Holywell Row, Suffolk, and an adult at Chessell Down, Isle of Wight grave

45), demonstrated through their attendant material culture to have had Kentish cultural links. The case for the Holywell Row example is assisted by the presence of a Kentish-type iron weaving beater, which is an artefact type shared with the Chessell Down grave, both burials being datable to the middle third of the sixth century. The Sussex example of gold braid from Eastbourne grave 655 is probably contemporary with these other outliers, if not slightly earlier, and is Kentish-associated through its small square-headed brooch.

### Frankish artefacts in Kent and Surrey

So far, little Frankish material has been recorded from the Holmesdale in Kent, apart from that area closest to the coast near Saltwood, excavated recently as a result of the Channel Tunnel rail-link (ADS Collection: 335. doi:10.5284/1000230). Most of the Kentish artefacts in the Upper Holmesdale have been metal detected and many of these stray finds may well prove to relate to more extensive burial and cemetery sites. Virtually nothing has been found along the major inland route of the North Downs Way, although Kentish cultural material is certainly present there. The stream of Frankish finds into eastern Surrey appears to coincide with the major Roman roads running south from London. We should note here the glass vessels recovered from isolated burials on the southern side of the North Downs at both Dorking and Bletchingley.

Major Kentish cemeteries on the coast, the Wantsum and also along Watling Street as far west as Dartford and the mouth of the river Darent have invariably produced Frankish material from excavation, but in the overall context, of 47 excavated sites with Phase A burials only 17 (36%) contained Frankish material. Therefore it is suggested that not every Phase A cemetery in east Kent will automatically produce Frankish material.

Many of the Surrey Frankish artefacts fall within the personal effects category, but the only specifically Frankish weaponry was recorded well to the west in the Guildown cemetery. This rather isolated site fits well as being located on an overland link between the main Kentish/Surrey cluster and the tranche of finds from sites extending through Sussex to Wiltshire. Its position at the nexus of a major route from the North Downs trackway where it meets the Roman road south to Chichester (Margary 1973, road 15), on a viable river route north to the Thames and at a gap through the Downs and the Greensand to the Weald, does imply an early and deliberate strategic location for this key community.

### Isle of Wight

The Phase A artefact provenances and raw material profiles of the Isle of Wight are directly comparable to those of east Kent. The presence of Kentish and Frankish material on the Isle of Wight, together with some Frisian material, highlights its extended links via maritime trade routes, despite its apparent isolated situation. The presence of franciscas and swords, together with the new helmet find, illustrates the defensive requirements of these communities. Although the principal cemeteries are located along the chalk spine of the island, their general positioning faces west-north-west, across the western approaches to the Solent and clearly they were visible from the opposed mainland shore.

On a mapped basis, the focus appears to lean towards the coastal access point of the identified major south-north routeway corridor, which would have been effectively accessed via Hengistbury Head and the Avon. The Wight cemeteries are positioned on the end of the island furthest from the sea-lanes linking it to Kent and Sussex, if such existed. Prevailing winds and tidal flows from the south-west may have precluded easy and predictable maritime movement in either direction along the Channel coast, however. Additional sites on the eastern half of the island around Carisbrooke and the harbour at Bembridge are indicated by findspots of further material. For the Middle Saxon period emphasis has been put on sites perhaps representing a central place in the Carisbrooke and Bowcombe valley area where the river Medina cuts through the main chalk ridge (Ulmschneider 1999, 2000, 48–50). Perhaps we can raise the possibility of the chalk spine providing a short overland route linking embarkation points at either end of the island providing equally short ship-based crossings to the mainland (illustrated by Ulmschneider 1999, fig.4). Such a route, extending perhaps from the east via Chichester or Portsmouth harbours, might provide long-distance access to the south-west of Britain without the need to travel across the Winchester area.

## Westwards from the East Sussex coast

The amount of sixth and seventh-century wealth and cemetery evidence in East Sussex, in contrast to the relatively meagre amounts in West Sussex, has been noted elsewhere (Harrington and Welch, 2010). In terms of both object numbers and burial count eastern Sussex outscores the western half by 2:1. The isolated cemetery at Highdown is the exception here (Welch 1983). Frankish material too is most frequent in the downlands between Eastbourne and the Ouse, particularly occurring in sites that can be argued to have a strategic location or at the very least are related to the main routeways. These are Rookery Hill in Bishopstone parish above the Ouse confluence with the Channel; Alfriston by the tidal head of the Cuckmere and adjacent to the main east-west Roman road; the coastal location of Eastbourne commanding perhaps a natural inlet providing safe access for coastal traffic; and various brooch finds along the tidal Lower Ouse valley, including a probable embarkation point onto the Roman road at Beddingham and Glynde. This eastern area is also characterised by a concentration of sword burials. It is noticeable that the upland cemetery communities here produce neither Frankish not Kentish artefacts, particularly those sites located to the west of the main group beyond the Ouse valley.

Kentish artefacts are recorded along the two main routeways either side of the South Downs, whereas excavated cemeteries and burials along the top of the Downs and on the upper slopes above the rivers that intersecting the downland are more sparsely furnished, and thus poorly datable, although some weapons are present. In West Sussex, the Frankish finds from Highdown and Chichester can again be related to the Roman road skirting the southern edge of the Downs, but otherwise there is no density of finds at all in this area. Indeed there is virtually nothing that is distinctively Kentish until sites and other findspots become more frequent within the presumed zone of Jutish settlement situated between the Hampshire and Sussex boundary and the Meon Valley: the territory of the *Meanware*.

The area around Winchester might be seen as a logical extension of the East Sussex group, linked by the principal trackway along the ridge of the Downs, with a bridging community at Appledown with its early Jutlandic plate bow brooch and a Kentish/Frankish buckle loop. Kentish and Frankish finds are centred here not only along the trackway, but in the Meon and Itchen valleys advancing into the Dever valley. Once again the Frankish artefacts were associated with both male and female burials. Nevertheless, further to the north-west by the Roman road running from Portchester through Winchester to Mildenhall, near Marlborough, Wiltshire (Margary 1973, 420 and 43) is a potentially large cemetery site at Barton Stacey in Chilbolton parish, Hampshire. The key finds here are a Frankish B2 spearhead, a Saxon class K1 spearhead and a Saxon cast five-spiral saucer brooch. The distribution of Frankish finds here extends in a more westerly direction than the Kentish artefacts that centre on Winchester.

### *Central Wiltshire and the Salisbury Plain*

The westernmost distribution of Frankish material presents a more coherent pattern in relation to those excavated sites with neither Frankish nor Kentish material. The main focus is on sites around Old Sarum and the confluences of the rivers Avon, Wylye, Nadder and Bourne together with the principal Roman road from Winchester (Margary 1973, road 45). Excavated burials that lack either Kentish or Frankish material on the upland area to the north west of Old Sarum are mainly isolated graves. The majority of these burials are men equipped with spearhead and shield, together with just three sword burials that form an outer perimeter at the junction of trackways with river headwaters along the western scarp. Other poorly furnished excavated cemeteries in this Wiltshire landscape belong to what might be best characterised as ordinary rural communities. An example is the contemporary cemetery and settlement at Market Lavington. There are also three Frankish brooches recorded as individual findspots on the adjacent Berkshire Downs, but with little Kentish material present in the vicinity.

### *Upper Thames Valley*

This is the only sub-region in which a definite spatial separation between Frankish and Kentish artefact types can be established, though this may well be the overall pattern across the study region as a whole. The Frankish finds are mainly distributed along river-valley sites, but while Kentish artefacts are present there too, they also occur towards the upland scarp away from the river, whereas no Frankish material is recorded there. Interspersed with these sites are Saxon cemeteries with neither Frankish nor Kentish-provenanced material. The westernmost limit of Frankish material coincides with the Kentish finds recorded at Fairford and Lechlade in south Gloucestershire and also at the nearby partially excavated cemetery in Oxfordshire at Watchfield. Here the Frankish element is represented by a silver decorated buckle set in grave 67, significantly associated with a set of scales and weights and also with what appears to be a Kentish-type Group 3 shield boss. Again, individual findspots have revealed a significant number of Frankish brooches from sites close to the Thames. The recent metal-detected find of a composite jewelled disc brooch near the Roman road at Milton in Berkshire can be linked to an earlier find of a Kentish small square-headed brooch in the same complex of fields. Together they suggest a substantial cemetery and an enduring Kentish presence in this area between the sixth and seventh centuries.

Finally, perhaps, we can observe a possible relationship between the deposition of Frankish artefacts and a high individual consumption of iron and copper alloy. In the case of copper alloys, no determining relationship could be established as cemetery communities with a full range of copper alloy wealth do not appear to have been dependent on the presence of Frankish copper alloy artefacts to constitute that wealth. Of course such Frankish copper alloy artefacts might indeed be present, but such items tended to belong to the same artefact categories of brooches and buckles that did constitute metal wealth. The situation regarding iron consumption distributions and the presence or absence of Frankish and indeed Kentish artefacts is, however, a little more complex. Areas of high iron consumption throughout the study region tend to coincide with the presence of Kentish artefacts, but in many instances the Kentish items fall within the weaponry category. The key exception is an area of high iron consumption in which neither Frankish nor Kentish material is present. This is located to the west and north of their furthest reach in the study region, around the cemeteries of Bassett Down and Overton Hill in northern Wiltshire.

*Conclusions relating to Phase A*

To summarise, once away from the coast of Kent, where the overlap between Frankish and Kentish material is commonplace, we begin to observe a spatial separation in their distributions. They are not indivisibly linked, suggesting that some Saxon communities may have possessed their own direct links with *Francia*, unmediated by Kentish, Frankish or Frisian traders. It is possible that we are seeing evidence of very localised distributions that do not readily transpose into regional patterns, however. A core and periphery pattern can be proposed, with Kentish and or Frankish artefacts found on sites surrounded by other contemporaries that contained no such material. The focus on nodal points on the routeways through the study region suggests the early formation of localised central places. One notable feature is the number of findspots of Frankish material occurring at a considerable distance from their presumed point of origin. This is particularly the case on the central uplands and western part of the study region.

Elsewhere the coincidence of Frankish artefacts with Roman roads and major riverine networks is clearly demonstrable. Both male and female associated artefacts are present at such sites, but with different overall distribution patterns. Whether there is sufficient material to reconstruct patterns of landholding and intermarriage within Saxon communities at such an early stage seems unlikely. Where neither Frankish nor Kentish material occurs, we can suggest that these are tracts of landscape that presented no special attraction for either traders or landholders. Examples are the south Hampshire coastlands opposite the Isle of Wight and the landscape enclosing Silchester (*Calleva Atrebatum*), although the low level of modern archaeological activity has also been noted for these areas. The primary mechanism for the movement of these artefacts is considered to be human agents transporting personal items rather than merchants delivering traded goods. Thus people were moving across the study region for specific purposes rather than undertaking an organic, cost-benefit settlement pattern of activity.

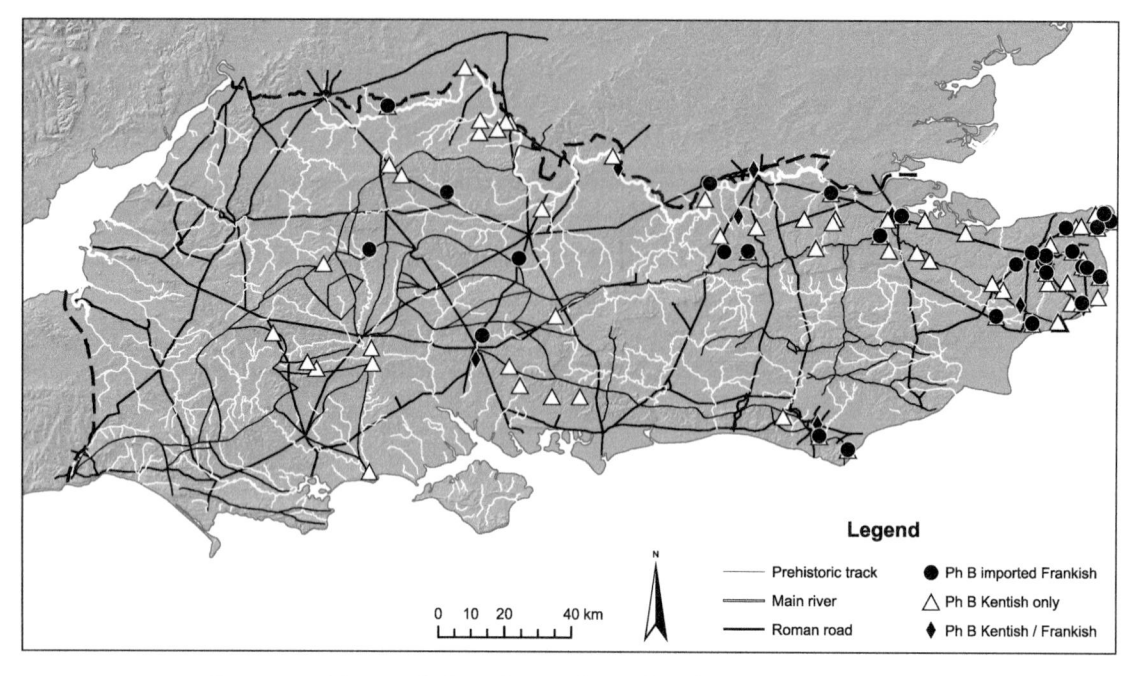

*Figure 58. The Frankish and Kentish artefact distributions in Phase B*

## Phase B Frankish data

The Phase B distribution map (Figure 58) reveals a spatial contraction of the Frankish material. Although still much in evidence in east Kent between the coast and Canterbury, it no longer extends west much beyond Winchester in Hampshire. In any case, it could be argued that the Frankish items present occur only early in Phase B rather than later or else represent artefacts curated from Phase A. The reach of the Kentish finds matches the same overall extent into the periphery of the western sector of the study region, although with nothing present within the middle sector. Frankish material is noticeably absent in the Upper Thames Valley, although the Kentish cluster around Abingdon and Milton merits some comment in the light of the probable high-status hall-based settlement at Drayton/Sutton Courtenay identified from aerial photographs (Benson and Miles 1974) and the princely assemblage at Taplow further downstream in Buckinghamshire. Perhaps here we can see evidence of a Kentish displacement of previous Frankish interests in the Upper Thames region.

Also altered from the Phase A situation is the distribution pattern along the South Downs. While Frankish and Kentish material is still present between Eastbourne and the Ouse estuary, notably at the Saxonbury (Kingston) cemetery on the western edge of Lewes that is on the approaches to a high-level trackway, there is little further along this downland scarp for some considerable distance. Otherwise we have to wait until we reach the West Sussex border with Hampshire and the sequence of Kentish-type weaponry at Apple Down, Horndean and Droxford, as well as the Kentish-type gold bracteate from an isolated burial at Exton in Hampshire. Yet there are substantial numbers of excavated and contemporary cemeteries occupying the intervening landscape. This evidence may provide an explanation for the continued presence of Kentish artefacts at Alton, Hampshire in Phase B, principally evidenced by a seventh-century triangular plated gold and garnet buckle. If the Meon area had been separated from the main Kentish lands by the Saxon cemetery communities to their east, then the obvious alternative route would use the combined Roman and prehistoric routeways between Winchester and Guildown in Surrey This passed through Alton on its way north and then skirted the Weald using the North Downs trackway, continuing thence to the north Kent coast.

There is no relationship at all in Phase B between areas of high consumption in iron and copper alloy and the presence of Kentish and Frankish artefacts. Outside of Kent, the most significant find of a Frankish artefact is a silver-inlaid iron buckle loop and plate dated *c.*570–610, from Manor Farm, Monk Sherborne. This was located near the Roman road from Winchester to Silchester (Margary 1973, road 42a), but formed part of a hoard rather than an internment. Once again, this may be indicative of a reduction and retraction of access to high-status Frankish material from this area. Its value lay as scrap, rather than as a symbol of continuing and meaningful social contact. Wheel thrown imported pottery is present within the main areas of Kent and also in the communities along its northern coastal inlets, but inland does not extend further west than Stane Street in Surrey. The glass vessels possess the same overall distribution as before, though now they extend for the first time up the Hampshire/Wiltshire Avon routeway with a palm cup from Shallows Farm, Breamore, Hampshire dated to the second half of the sixth century and a further palm cup recovered with a cone beaker from the isolated weapon burial on Salisbury Racecourse at Coombe Bissett in Wiltshire. The latter grave may belong a generation or more later, however, in the second quarter of the seventh century.

## Phase C Frankish data

The distribution evidence for Frankish contacts in Phase C (Figure 59) has been compared here with the distribution of early continental and regionally manufactured coins, which offer a context to the burial and other findspot data (Figure 60). Taking only the Frankish and Kentish artefacts, three main yet spatially constricted groupings emerge. An eastern group is present between the coast of Kent and Stane Street in Surrey to the west. Two main concentrations are identifiable here. One is based on Thanet and on the Downs between the coast and the Roman road to the southwest of Canterbury. The other is centred on Rochester between Watling Street and the North Downs trackway where both routes cross the Medway. The westernmost artefact is a B1 spearhead from a weapon assemblage at Banstead in Surrey. Wheel thrown pots occur in the same areas, as do most of the contemporary glass vessels. Thus we have a relatively homogenous zone of activity in Kent that still extends into eastern Surrey.

A second grouping appears in the Upper Thames Valley beyond Reading, with two female-associated Frankish artefacts present in the cemeteries to the west beyond Oxford. A B1 spearhead and three Group 7 shield bosses are present in the cemeteries on the scarp of the uplands overlooking the Thames further downstream, although whether these weapons can be claimed to be truly

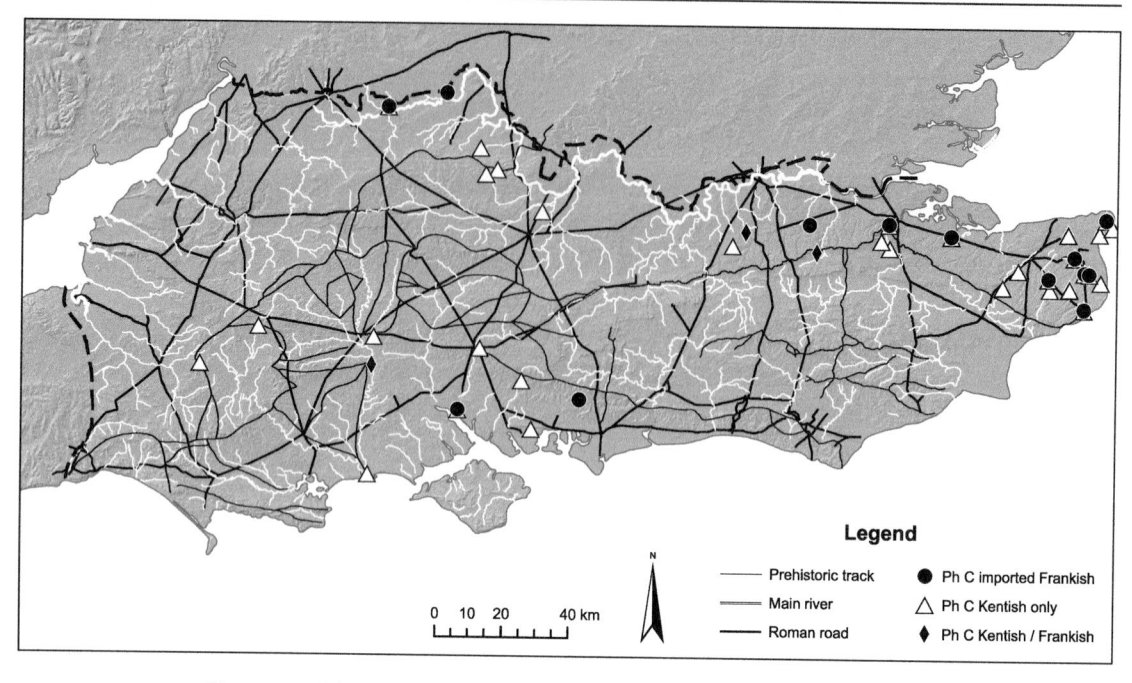

*Figure 59. The Frankish and Kentish artefact distributions in Phase C*

diagnostic of Kentish identity is a moot point, as Group 7 bosses are the most common of seventh-century shield types. The third grouping pivots around Southampton (*Hamwic*), again with a B2 spearhead at its eastern limit, in the cemetery at Appledown. This last area does not extend any further north than Winchester (the location of a jewel plated disc brooch), but it does bulge out to the west to include a Group 7 shield boss context at Hicknell Slait. Indeed there is a recorded sword burial at Queen Camel still further to the west. Only three glass vessels occur outside of Kent within the study region proper. All of them are palm cups that might be of Frankish manufacture, namely a pair from the female bed burial on Swallowcliffe Down (Speake 1989, 81) and a single unassociated find from *Hamwic* (the Golden Grove, Southampton excavations: Morton 1992, 194). To these can be added the older and the modern finds of palm cups from a site peripheral to the study area, the seventh-century cemetery by the London church of St Martins-in-the-Fields on the western edge of *Lundenwic*. Such a distribution around the south coast and its hinterland might suggest a bounded territory here or at least one with clear cultural limits. Again the absence of Frankish and Kentish material in Sussex between Chichester and Eastbourne is noted (unless the B2 spearhead from the Brighton cemetery belongs to this period: Welch 1983, 127, fig. 76a). There is a similar absence for west Surrey, although there are excavated cemeteries in both Sussex and Surrey. On this basis there would appear to be an overall contraction and localisation of both Frankish and Kentish material culture in Phase C.

Coinage presents a rather different picture, however (Figure 60). Kentish and other Anglo-Saxon Regional coins (including some from West Saxon and Anglian mints) are broadly spread

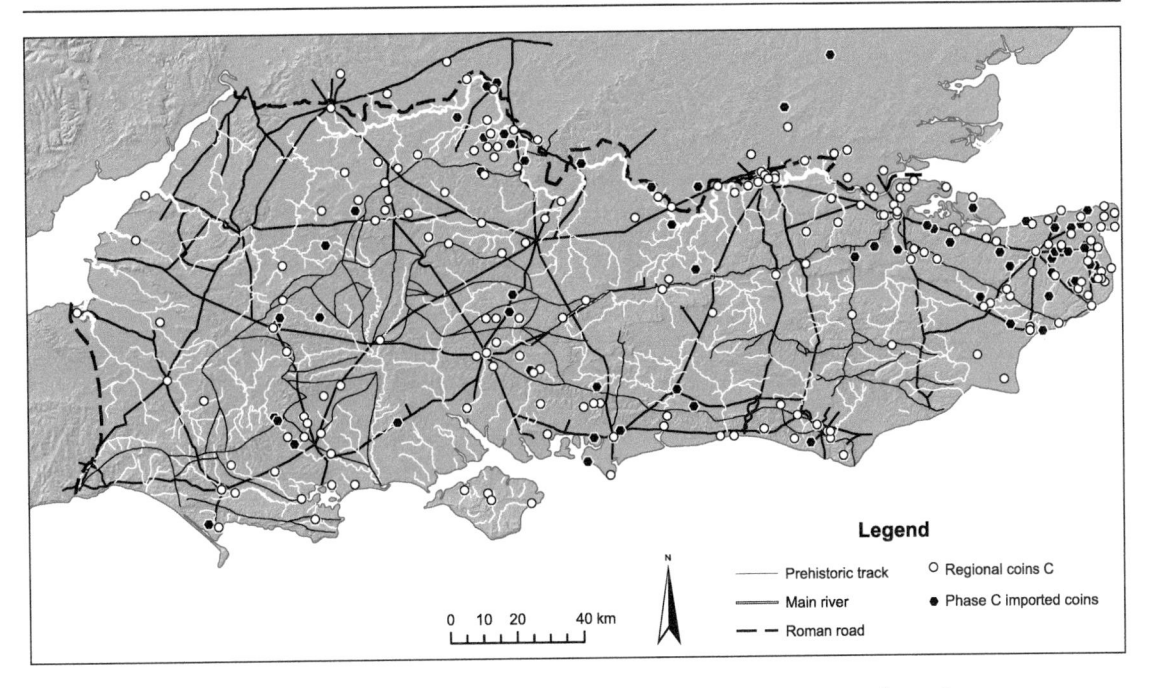

*Figure 60. The distributions of imported and regional coins in Phase C*

throughout the study region. Indeed they are now to be found in western coastal districts, for example at Cannington, Somerset. They also occur in the Kentish Weald, although not in the Sussex sector of the Weald, recorded along the main Roman and prehistoric trackways, indicating more securely the exploitation of its resources of seasonal grazing, timber and iron by the second half of the seventh century. The previously void area around Silchester has produced coins along its major arterial roads. Perhaps this supports the case for continuity of recovered scrap resource exploitation of the former *civitas* that can be dated through as late as the seventh century. What had appeared to be inland routeways previously unused for the movement of distinctively Frankish and Kentish artefacts based on the Phase C cemetery evidence now provide linear findspots along their lengths. An exception is the area around east-central Wiltshire and northwest Hampshire, despite the presence of excavated cemeteries and isolated burials there. Again, concentrations of finds occur in the Upper Thames Valley around Abingdon and Milton and also in the area of north Wiltshire bounded by the Ridgeway trackway to the west and the intersection of the main Roman roads passing through. Strikingly, the adjacent area further to the south has no such material present. The importance of trading locales such as *Lundenwic* and the Isle of Wight are evidenced by concentrations of these coins. On the basis of this distribution, the main riverine and routeway communities of Sussex are also included in the network of Kentish coinage, despite the absence of well-dated contemporary mortuary material.

The Early Continental coinage adds a further layer of complexity throughout the study region in Phase C, although its distribution broadly mirrors the spatial patterning of the indigenous

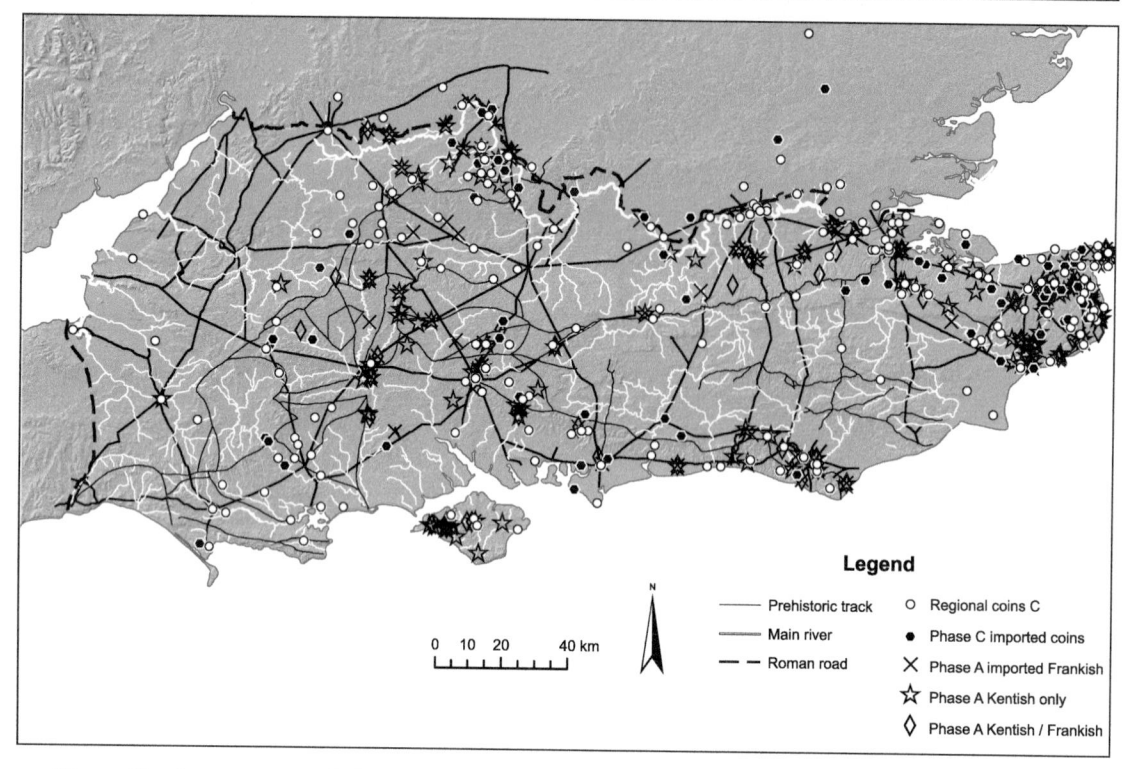

*Figure 61. A comparison of Phase A Frankish and Kentish artefacts with Phase C coin distributions*

coinage, except in two respects. As Figure 60 reveals, to date no Early Continental coins have been found beyond the Holmesdale extending into the Weald. More significantly, the western reach of the Early Continental coinage is not found beyond an arc running from Oxford, along the line of the Ridgeway through to the Dorset coast at Chickerell near Weymouth. The Regional coinage extends well to the west of this arc, in a manner redolent of the relative distributions of Kentish and Frankish material in Phase A. There are also no Early Continental coins in the void zone for Regional coins of central Wiltshire and northwest Hampshire. There are a mere two examples in the area to its north dominated by the Regional coins. In the Upper Thames Valley these coins are only found to the south of Oxford, mainly along the course of the Thames and clustering with the Regional coinage in the Abingdon and Milton district. Once again, Sussex produces a good representation of these coins.

As a test of the trajectorial nature of the data organisation, the Phase A Kentish and imported Frankish artefacts have been mapped against the Phase C coin distributions (Figure 61). Without the insertion of Phase B, which appears to show a contraction of Kentish and Frankish interest beyond Kent, this new map would only show a sequential movement of activity to the west in Phase C. Here the western limit of the Frankish material moves from the routeway through the Avon to the Upper Thames Valley to the western edge of the Wiltshire uplands. In advance of it is the Kentish material, which offers a pattern that the Frankish coinage appears to consolidate behind this advance guard. Do changes in burial practice in Phase B show a reality that the coins attributed here to Phase C conceal?

## Frankish weapon burials

Whilst gold braid acts as a useful indicator of the possible presence of female Franks married exogamously into Kentish families in the sixth century, for male Franks the most practical and convincing identifier is the spearhead position in the burial. Although a positioning of a spearhead with its point upwards near the skull is not unknown in continental cemeteries, there is a preference in others for the spearhead to point downwards and be placed close to the feet.

As has been pointed out long ago, no true *angon* of Frankish manufacture with a pyramidal barbed head has ever been recovered from an Anglo-Saxon grave (Schnurbein, 1974; Welch 1983). However, where the spearhead position is known for the Swanton-type A1 and A2 barb-headed equivalents of the Frankish throwing spear (five examples), the orientation of the head is consistently downwards to the feet. It can be asserted, therefore, that all 14 examples of this spear type should be included in the analysis of the spatial distribution of this particular cultural trait. The orientation evidence calls further into question whether any examples of this spear type are of local Kentish manufacture, although they could have been made there to the specification of a Frankish client. Another 24 spearheads of other and varying types were placed in the downward position within the study region. They include examples of Swanton's C, E, F, G and H series, together with a single B1, all types for which the normal orientation is upwards by the head.

The date range for burials with downward placed spears can only be conjectural. Where dates have been ascribed to the A series throwing-spear burial assemblages, many of the Kentish examples have been placed within Phase B. The remainder there and elsewhere have generally been attributed to within the date range of an entire cemetery spanning both phases A and B, given the absence of other datable artefacts within the particular burials. We can tentatively suggest that this throwing spear type is more likely to have been in use in Phase B, but probably not much earlier. As throwing spears go out of fashion entirely in *Francia* in the early seventh century (Härke 1990) it is almost certain that they ceased to be buried in Anglo-Saxon contexts after Phase B. For mapping purposes, however, the previously attributed phase of the constituent burials for throwing spears has been adhered to in the present exercise.

Of the remaining downward pointing spearhead burials, the earliest is most probably the child buried in grave 93 at Long Wittenham (BrkLWM-MC1). An E1 spearhead was found here with two imported containers. One was a copper alloy *Vestlandkessel* and the other a fifth-century Christian stoup, reminiscent of the Lavoye grave 319 pouring jug (Joffroy 1974). This assemblage has been dated to the second half of the fifth century (Dickinson 1976, 2, 161) and the boy child identified as an immigrant from the Namur region (Evison 1965, 32, 42) or at least from northeast Gaul. On the other hand, this is the only example in the corpus of a very early dating given to an E1 spearhead. Others fall within the sixth century and deposition can extend on late into the seventh century. Thus the copper alloy 'cauldron' and the sheet-metal decorated stoup provide the main dating determinates for this burial. Both are products of the fifth century and the greatest concentration of the angular cauldron within the study region occurs around Long Wittenham and the Upper Thames Valley (Dickinson 1976 1, 364–5, 367). It is questioned here, however, whether this burial is quite as early as the late fifth century. Both the stoup and the cauldron may well have been treasured status items and accompanied a child rather than an adult. A dating in the first half of the sixth century is favoured here, although clearly this burial still falls firmly within Phase A.

Overall there are few closely datable burials with the reversed spear position, indicating the frequent absence of other diagnostic and higher-status artefacts within these particular burials from which to derive a dating assessment. Some twenty examples plausibly fall within Phase B, with four more that were clearly deposited after *c*.650 in Phase C. Of the twenty Phase B spears, only eight may have shared a dating footprint with Phase A. A few burials had mismatched pairs of spears placed with the heads orientated towards the feet of the interred. In Phase A there is one such example from Saxton Road, Abingdon, Berkshire, grave 69, dated *c*.525–600 but nevertheless placed here in Phase A. The weapon set consisting of A1 and A2 throwing spears included a Group 3 shield boss, identified in the project database corpus as a primarily Kentish type. Thus this example might well fit better with the Kentish Phase B throwing-spear grouping. This would place this particular Abingdon burial as a broadly contemporary adjunct of the Taplow burial further downstream and evidence for continuing Kentish influence in the Upper Thames Valley. The Taplow burial itself contained a throwing spear in the 'Frankish' reversed position, perhaps placed on top of the burial chamber that may in turn have contained a bed or bier covered in textile and other furnishings. Two other spears were present here, which on visual inspection in the British Museum appear to be fragmentary G1/2 types. The extensive weapon assemblage include two Group 6 shield bosses and part of a third, as well as a sword with Frankish style fine braiding bound around the scabbard mouth (Cameron 2000).

Two other males with multiple spears in the reversed position are recorded in the corpus from the east Kentish cemetery in the Holmesdale at Saltwood. The male in C6653 had multiple weapons, including three shield bosses, G2 and A1 spearheads, a sword and appropriately a high-status object in the form of a copper alloy bowl, as indeed can be matched by the Taplow male. Another male in C1048, possibly buried a generation earlier within Phase B, has the same spear-type combination, multiple Kentish-type shield bosses, a sword, a copper alloy bowl and a gaming piece. Thus demonstrable similarities are shared by these three high-status weapon burials from Saltwood and Taplow and it is tempting to suggest that at least one of these individuals was a Frank rather than a man of Kent adopting continental fashions in spear positions. It has been argued, however, that the Taplow burial represents an exclusively Kentish assemblage drawn from over two generations of acquisition including heirlooms such as the drinking horns (Webster 1992). The key point here, however, is that there is nothing to suggest the Taplow barrow contained a high-status Saxon burial that related to the antecedents of its surrounding communities.

The spatial distribution of reversed spear burials, grouped by the attributed phases is presented in Figure 62. In Phase A (14 examples) these only occur on sites where both Frankish and Kentish

## 12. The Frankish Data Examined

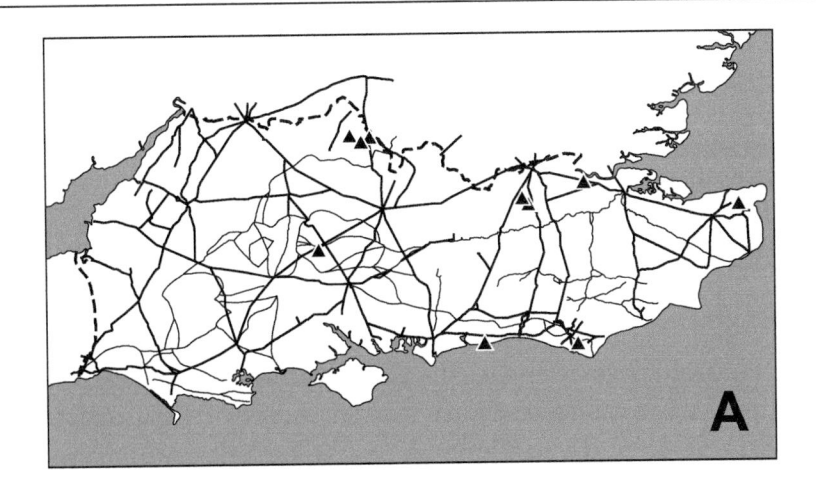

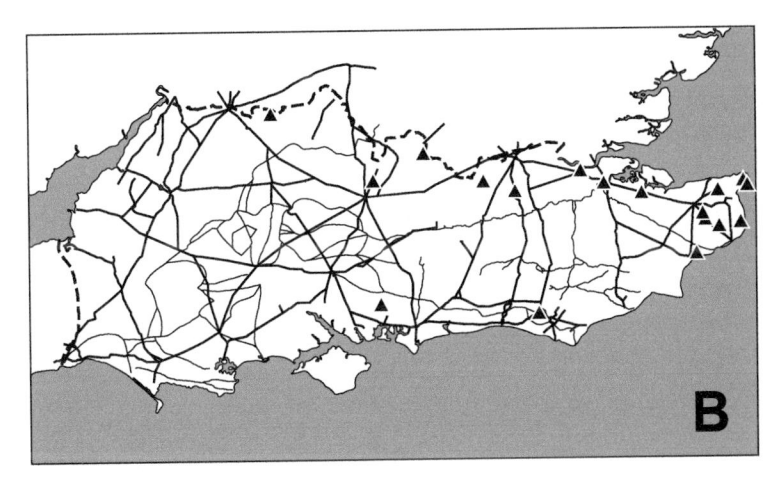

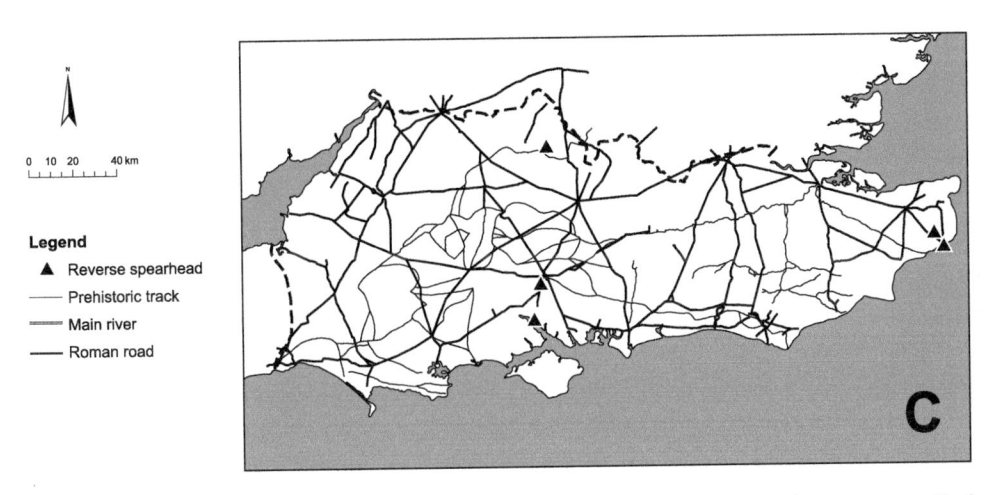

*Figure 62. The distribution of burials with spears in the reversed position in all phases*

artefacts are also present. Surprisingly there is only one of these relatively early examples from east Kent, though small clusters occur around the east Surrey/west Kent area and in the Upper Thames Valley (from Long Wittenham as discussed above as well as Abingdon and Berinsfield). A couple are recorded from Sussex, while the furthest west such burial is that from grave 15 at Andover in northern Hampshire. Phase B is more fully populated with reversed spear burials (25 examples), which are most frequent in east Kent. Their clearest association throughout the study region is their presence in cemeteries with Kentish finds, but no Frankish material. This is most markedly so in the 'princely' assemblage at Taplow commanding riverine access to the Upper Thames Valley. This is matched also in the otherwise unremarkable grave 146 at Burghfield in Berkshire on the Roman road between the Thames at Reading and Silchester (Margary 1973, road 4a). The most westerly outlier is by the Thames at grave 191 in Lechlade. Once again this is a poorly dated assemblage, although probably belonging in Phase B or later. One reversed spear burial also occurs at grave 14 in Snells Corner, Horndean in the proposed district for Kentish settlement, whilst further to the east in Sussex an unprovenanced findspot of a throwing spear is located in the environs of Lewes.

The five examples from Phase C offer no opportunity for the spatial analysis of meaningful distributions, nor of exploring associations with regional and imported coinages. Nevertheless, certain observations can be made regarding unusual features of these five broadly contemporary burials. They represent a more diverse group than the earlier individuals and were associated with a wide range of esoteric material. The two examples with F2 reversed spearheads from Sibertswold (graves 176 and 150) were each accompanied by an imported Byzantine buckle indicating continental and long-distance trading associations. The male from grave 114 at Buckland, Dover also had a lyre. The crouched burial from Harwell, Berkshire was otherwise poorly furnished, but the two Hampshire burials, in a county that produced none in the previous phases merit further comment. The Oliver's Battery isolated burial overlooked the Roman road south from Winchester (Margary 1973, road 42b) contained a Celtic hanging bowl and a seax as well. The *Hamwic* burial (from the St Mary's Stadium, Southampton cemetery) produced nothing else of note, but there is an inference to be drawn regarding the likely presence of other buried individuals with Frankish associations there. The seax from grave F183 is a Frankish object, the female in grave 4202 had two Series B sceattas and the seax scabbard with one of the males in the double burial grave 3520 has distinctive Frankish affinities (Loader *et al.* 2005, 59–60). All of these can be dated in the late seventh or early eighth century.

## Conclusions

The above discussion is in the main predicated on the assumption that Frankish-type artefacts within the weaponry and personal effects categories would most likely represent people with a vested interest in expressing that particular cultural contact, whatever their ethnic identity. Whilst there is a large degree of overlap between Kentish and Frankish material culture for a number of sites, most evident in the east Kent area, the two types do not invariably coincide.

## 12. The Frankish Data Examined

This distribution pattern points to differing spatial relationships with Saxon cultural groupings beyond the bounds of the early Kentish kingdom. The geography of Frankish contacts changed over the three phases. In Phase A there was an early focus on the perimeters of the study region exploiting well-defined corridors of activity to access the westernmost part of the Anglo-Saxon settled areas and by inference the contact zone with the British West. Within Phase A and each successive phase, we can also identify contemporary sites that had no access to this imported cultural material and in the case of West Sussex there was a whole district that failed to obtain a significant quantity of such material. Phase B appears to demonstrate a spatial retraction of the Frankish material, together with a consolidation of the Kentish finds, particularly in the Upper Thames Valley. Yet it is at this point in the study period that we can point more clearly towards weapon-bearing men making a concerted appearance around east-Kent coastal sites. In Phase C, although there were fewer objects, there appears to be direct contact with the Frankish continent, in particular through *Hamwic*. The range of evidence over the three phases of the study period appears to demonstrate the sustained presence of a small number of Frankish people, whose societal roles in Britain can only be conjectured. They seem to appear as spouses, as free weapon-bearers, in some cases as probable lords (whether as warlords or as landowners) and perhaps even as entrepreneurs and traders. Their societal relationship to their Kentish contemporaries may have been a source of conflict, with competition for access to the resources, products and tribute that gave enhanced status.

# 13. Synthesis: Beneath the *Tribal Hidage*

If we consider the *Tribal Hidage* document as the embellishing veneer over the sturdy carcase of the archaeological evidence, then any relationship between the two can be characterised as one placed upon the other to enhance the status of the whole, but also effectively disguising the complex framework of what lay beneath. By being derived from different sources, for example a mahogany veneer onto a complex jointed carcase of English oak and Scandinavian softwood to produce a piece of now antique furniture, each component has a different narrative to deploy in the construction of the whole. So, it is important to consider the narrative of the archaeological carcase without reference to its later embellishments in order to understand its construction.

The first objective of the project was to gather together into a coherent framework as much as possible of the available data. This data is expanding annually and the location of further sites may in the longer term become predictable and quantifiable. There appears to have been landscape syntax in use, from the fifth century onwards, with common approaches to site location and control of movement along extant routeways from the earliest appearances of Germanic material into the archaeological record of burial. It is argued essentially that the range of choices was predicated on existing topography already laid down across the physical geography and geology of southern Britain south of the Thames. The ability to support wealth-producing activities was undiminished, particularly as widespread woodland regeneration is no longer seen as a basic tenet of the fifth century landscape context.

The key finding of this project is that the deployment of Germanic material in Phase A, regardless of whether it is interpreted as indicative of agents of North European origin or as an inscribed acculturation of material culture onto extant communities, very quickly encompasses the entire study region. It does not appear as an organic movement, rather as a strategic annexation of the productive chalklands that stopped short of the Jurassic landscapes of the British West, with subsequent in filling. Soils *per se* are not now seen, in this study, as a determinant for occupation, rather it is the transportation nodal points that come to the fore. Such nodal points would include a riverine and a land route conjunction, highlighted through the placement of cemeteries to mark their presence from a distance. Certainly, such nodal points had a relationship to the better soil types, but they are not placed directly onto these. It is therefore tempting to suggest that any movement of surplus resources from these productive areas would of necessity encounter the nodal points, perhaps therefore fulfilling a function as central places for the extraction of surplus for tribute. Such a characterisation of the landscape structure would also suggest that the persons so encountered were acting as agents and were not themselves the producers – a kind of entrepreneurial middle class within a network of local, regional and international associations. This of course assumes that economic, particularly agricultural activity was ongoing throughout the fifth century at a level above that of subsistence.

The geography of the study region presents variable distributions of raw materials, all of which were exploited during the Roman period. Mining could have continued into the post Roman period, as it was in part a decentralised entrepreneur-led activity in its latter stages. Given the range of potential scrap and mining resources in the study region, is it feasible to suggest that all raw materials were imported from mainland Europe and mediated through Kent, apart from a specific and exceptional material such as amber? But, is scrap in itself a viable basis for a society that has such a display of metalwork in the burial as well as furnishing social replication in the everyday? Rather, is scarcity of resources the real issue, leading to selective and controlled deployment from the fifth century onwards?

We propose that different layers of circulation existed geographically for iron and copper alloy, which did not of necessity overlap. Evidence for iron smithing on settlement sites presents it as a local activity for the production of domestic wares, tools and agricultural implements. The iron requirements for warfare perhaps operated within a different sphere of circulation, given the need to accumulate larger amounts of raw materials for their manufacture and the metallurgical evidence that has identified the constituent raw material as composites. The fact of regional types of shield fittings and spearheads, particularly with standardised format, if irregular shaping, such as the H series, would suggest that a common template was used in their manufacture, rather than reliance on the occasional activities of the multi-skilled farmer.

Indeed, despite the documentary sources indicating their activities, there is, in the archaeological record, no substantial evidence for itinerant smiths. Rather we are seeing more evidence, in the form of scales, for agents for the exchange of copper alloy, bullion and other lightweight, but valuable goods such as semi-precious stones. This then leaves a problem of explaining the mechanisms for the production of culturally specific dress fitments such as brooches and buckles. Perhaps these should not be considered as the result of a single mechanism, in that the cruder iron buckles may have been locally produced. The more complex artefacts requiring a range of technical skills including casting and gilding would suggest manufacture by craftsmen in a central place, converting raw and re-cycled materials, brought to them for a specific purpose. It is argued that the production of brooches in particular was an adjunct of gift exchange relating to exogamous marriage (Harrington 2011), resulting in the commissioning of specific items.

The mechanisms that can be proposed for the control or access to supplies of copper alloy include scavenging for personal use, although those cemeteries with copper alloy wealth are not located within the densest zones of relict Roman sites. Perhaps we can suggest scavenging for the exchange value of the metal retaining only a portion of the metal objects for their own use, which in turn might lead to purposeful asset stripping/recycling from derelict Roman sites, much as has been proposed for iron working in Silchester in the post Roman period. Finally we might suggest that copper alloy objects in particular may have been still active in cultural usage, obtained by Anglo-Saxon peoples through exchange (or theft) from the post-Roman British population but also acknowledging an Imperial past.

A centralised manufacture of high-status items and of standard fittings, such as brooches on the Helgö model (Hovén *et al.* 1986), appears to be indicated. Here Faversham readily presents itself as a central place for these activities. The temporal framework within which centralisation of production might occur is conjectural, but its effects are visible in the distribution pattern of high-status material occurring on nodal points in the landscape. Therefore one must suppose that power may have come from the ability to dominate the layers of circulation and manipulate distribution. If itinerance of craft metalworkers was a factor in production, this may have been occurred around the upper echelons of society rather than across all communities.

The consumption pattern based on wealth production and intra-regional networking, that operates at its most obvious and widespread *after c.*525 was already in place within the second half of the fifth century, but apparently not before then, based on current dating schema. Already the amount of copper alloy in circulation by the later fifth century suggests a boom in its availability. Perhaps we can assume therefore that iron working, be it as a result of iron mining, smelting and forging, or simply the recycling of scrap from derelict Roman sites, had also become a necessary and more intensive activity in the second half of the fifth century. Perhaps this was when many of the Roman objects available hitherto became no longer usable and needed replacing. Clearly, much more iron was needed to furnish the proliferation of weapons visible in burial assemblages, particularly if those arms imported by migrants had already been consigned to grave. There could have been competition now for these vital source materials, in the process enhancing their value as commodities and offering the potential for wealth enhancement for those able to control the supply. The accumulation of metalwork raw material as an integral part of exchange and tribute systems from the fifth century onwards is inferred. Shifts in the availability of these key resources are evidenced in the late fifth to early sixth centuries and again in the interface between phases A and B at the end of the sixth century.

Within the study region it is clear that there was continuity with late Roman landscape structures as an overall framework, although with variability within the region. Although the vast majority of sites from late Roman Britain end well before *c.*400 and only a few can be demonstrated to be still viable in the fifth century, the relationship of sites on Roman road junctions, or road and track way junctions, or road and waterway junctions to later successors is demonstrated. This is not to suggest a direct re-occupation of sites, rather locations in proximity to their precursors, and determined by the topography of the transport network. The use of the Roman road network in particular was crucial in the dissemination of Frankish influence and access of its material culture to certain areas. The establishment of new routeways is not apparent on a region-wide scale.

Differential access to and production of wealth is readily demonstrated within and across communities, but in what ways does this evidence contribute to understanding of state formation processes in the sixth century? Conspicuously wealthy communities are evidenced amongst the chronologically earlier furnished graves. Such groups may have benefited from a commercial environment, such as existed along the east coast of Kent with links to *Francia* and beyond. Yet they are also evident at a distance from the coast, in the Upper Thames Valley and in Wiltshire, reinforcing the perception that the study region should be considered as a whole formed by that Frankish influence. If anything there is an upsurge of Frankish military interest in Kent in the latter part of the sixth century and the early seventh, perhaps to protect their economic and political interests. Clearly the establishment of the international trading emporia at *Hamwic* on the south coast by the expansionist kingdom of Wessex in the seventh century was a means of superseding any remaining Kentish monopoly of those contacts. This would suggest that in the fifth and sixth centuries any successful kingdom was a client component part of the larger whole. Yet, the analysis of the data presented in this text does not supply us with three centres of wealth that reflect the named kingdoms of Kent, Wessex and Sussex. Whilst a royal presence is expected at Canterbury, the centre of wealth appears to have been at Lyminge, for example. There are intra-regional hot spots that changed location over time.

To what extent can the scale of these early kingdoms be discerned through analysis of the data? Given the distribution of Kentish material it is tempting to identify the whole of the study region as being within the ambit of Kentish influence, with various sub groups of Saxons settling the landscape for productive purposes. A real problem is the idea that these early kingdoms were bounded entities, as on present analysis there are no sharp edges to be found. If anything we may point to occupied and perhaps militarised centres of productive importance with diffuse territories surrounding and rights to unoccupied areas such as the Weald and the forests.

State formation theories might suggest that where there were unevenly spread resources in a region, then certain communities would have the ability to shape the history of their region by expanding and stimulating change in their neighbours, for example the expansion onto the Downlands of Kent from the coastal fringes in the seventh century and the acquisition of West Kent in the fifth or sixth centuries. This was certainly a proposition that was considered within the project. Yet, it would appear that core areas rather than central places were instrumental in underpinning emergent hierarchies. The uniformity and coherence of these changes could not be determined, however, indicating a far more nuanced and subtle system of processes was at play.

It became apparent that, whilst one might attempt to explain the formation of the early Anglo-Saxon kingdoms as an insular and bottom-up process, it could equally be argued that external forces had had a major impact on the situation. If *Francia* did indeed drive the economic exploitation of lowland Britain by annexing the eastern tranche of Roman Britain, it may have imposed a hierarchical structure through the deployment of displaced North European groups over and amongst the indigenous population to act as their agents. The necessity for the Germanic communities to manage these up and down relationships, intermingling through marriage with both, may have been the impetus towards independence and the inevitable conflicts over resources with others in the same situation.

This first tranche of Germanic settlement buffered against the British West, again an entity of unknown complexity. Yet, there do not appear to have been fixed boundaries despite the delineations by Frankish and Kentish material discussed above. The interdigitation of Germanic and British material culture is evident from the earliest phase. Additionally, one might propose that in the sixth century the British West mediated access to cultural trade material from the western seaboard of Gaul and beyond from the Mediterranean. On present evidence, this material reaches the Isle of Wight and West Sussex in the sixth century but does not reach further east until the early seventh century. One might also argue that the value of southern Britain to *Francia* was that it enabled Frankish traders to leapfrog across to the communities further west with their attendant resources, hence the wealth of northwest Wiltshire and of the furthermost fringes of the Upper Thames Valley.

In conclusion, the creation of kingdoms in southern Britain by the seventh century remains a matter of the greatest conjecture. The archaeological narrative is pointedly open to various interpretations of which the above is but one and is inevitably determined by one's theoretical standpoint on the politics of empire and the mechanics of wealth acquisition. Clearly southern Britain had a wealth creating potential that was exploited in the aftermath of the vacuum created by the breakdown of Roman administration in the early fifth century. The *Tribal Hidage* document shows to archaeology that the myriad activities and processes of the fifth and sixth centuries had been written into the landscape and had value that could be quantified.

# Bibliography

Alcock, L. (1981) Quantity or quality, the Anglian graves of Bernicia. In V. Evison, (ed.), *Angles, Saxons and Jutes. Essays presented to J. N. L. Myres*, 168–186. Oxford, Clarendon Press.

Allen, M. J. and Gardiner, J. (2000) *Our Changing Coast. A survey of the intertidal archaeology of Langstone Harbour, Hampshire*. CBA Research Report 124. York, Council for British Archaeology.

Allen, M. J. and Gardiner, J. (2006) Rhythms of Change, a Region of Contrasts. In B. Cunliffe, *England's Landscape. The West*, 13–34. English Heritage vol. 4. London, Collins.

Anderson. T. and Andrews, J. (1997) The human skeletons. In K. Parfitt, and B. Brugmann, *The Anglo-Saxon Cemetery on Mill Hill, Deal, Kent*, 214–239. The Society for Medieval Archaeology monograph series no. 14. London, The Society for Medieval Archaeology.

Andrews, P. *et al.* (2009) *Kentish Sites and Sites of Kent. A miscellany of four archaeological excavations*. Salisbury, Wessex Archaeology.

Annable, F. K. and Eagles, B. N. (2010) *The Anglo-Saxon Cemetery at Blacknall Field, Pewsey, Wiltshire*. Devizes, Wiltshire Archaeological and Natural History Society.

Applebaum, S. (1972) Roman Britain. In H. P. R. Finberg (ed.), *The Agrarian History of England and Wales*, I.ii, 3–277. Cambridge, Cambridge University Press.

Applebaum, S. (1975) Some observations on the economy of the Roman villa at Bignor, Sussex. *Britannia* 6, 118–32.

Arnold, C. J. (1997) *An Archaeology of the Early Anglo-Saxon Kingdoms* (2nd edn) London, Routledge.

Arnold, C. J. and Wardle, P. (1981) Early medieval settlement patterns in England. *Medieval Archaeology* 25, 145–149.

Attenborough, F. (1922) *The Laws of the Earliest English Kings*. Cambridge, Cambridge University Press.

Avent, R. (1975) *Anglo-Saxon Garnet Inlaid Disc and Composite Brooches*, BAR British Series 11. Oxford, Archaeopress.

Axboe, M. (1999) The chronology of the Scandinavian gold bracteates. In J. Hines, K. Høilund Nielsen and F. Siegmund (eds), *The Pace of Change. Studies in medieval chronology*, 126–47. Oxford, Oxbow Books.

Axboe, M. (2007) Brakteatstudier, Nordiske Fortidsminder, Serie B, Band 25. Copenhagen, Kongelige Nordiske oldskriftselskab.

Baldwin, R. (1985) Intrusive burial groups in the Late Roman cemetery at Lankhills, Winchester: a reassessment of the evidence, *Oxford Journal of Archaeology* 4, 93–104.

Baldwin Brown, G. 1915. *Saxon Art and Industry in the Pagan Period*. London, J. Murray

Banham, D. (2010) 'In the sweat of thy Brow Shalt thou eat Bread', cereals and cereal production in the Anglo-Saxon landscape. In N. Higham and M. Ryan (eds), *The Landscape Archaeology of Anglo-Saxon England*, 175–92. Woodbridge, The Boydell Press.

Barnes, G. and Williamson, T. (2006) *Hedgerow History. Ecology, history and landscape character*. Oxford, Windgather Press.

Barnetson, L. (2007) Faunal remains. In R. Chambers and E. McAdam *Excavations at Radley Barrow Hills, Radley, Oxfordshire*. vol. 2, 263–290. Thames Valley Landscapes Monograph 25. Oxford, Oxford University School of Archaeology for Oxford Archaeology.

Bassett, S. (ed.) (1989) *The Origins of Anglo-Saxon Kingdoms*. Leicester, Leicester University Press.

Bayley, J. (1991) Anglo-Saxon non-ferrous metalworking, a survey. *World Archaeology* 23 (1), 115–130.

Bayley, J. (1998) Metals and metalworking in the first millennium AD. In J. Bayley (ed.), *Science in Archaeology. An agenda for the future*, 161–168. London, English Heritage.

Beechey, F. W. (1850) Report of Further Observations Made upon the Tidal Streams of the English Channel and German Ocean, under the Authority of the Admiralty, in 1849 and 1850. In *Abstracts of the Papers Communicated to the Royal Society of London*, vol. 6, (1850–1854), 68–70. London, The Royal Society.

Bell, M. (1977) Excavations at Bishopstone. *Sussex Archaeological Collections* 115, 1–291.

Bell, M. (1981) Valley Sediments and Environmental Change. In M. Jones and G. Dimbleby (eds), *The Environment of Man. The Iron Age to the Anglo-Saxon Period*, BAR British Series 87, 75–91. Oxford, Archaeopress.

Bell, M. (1983) Valley sediments as evidence of prehistoric land-use on the South Downs, *Proceedings of the Prehistoric Society* 49, 119–50.

Benson, D. and Miles, D. (1974) Aerial photos from Sutton Courtenay and Drayton. *Antiquity* 48, 223–6.

Birch, T. (2001) Living on the edge, making and moving iron from the 'outside' in Anglo-Saxon England. *Landscape History* 31, 1, 5–23.

Blackburn, M. and Grierson, P. (1986) *Medieval European Coinage*, vol. 1. *The Early Middle Ages*. Cambridge, Cambridge University Press.

Blair, J. (1989) Frithuwold's kingdom and the origins of Surrey. In S. Bassett, *The Origins of Anglo-Saxon Kingdoms*, 97–107. Leicester, Leicester University Press.

Blair, J. (1991) *Early Medieval Surrey. Landholding, church and settlement before 1300*. Stroud, Sutton Publishing Ltd.

Blair, J. (2005) *The Church in Anglo-Saxon Society*. Oxford, Oxford University Press.

Böhme, H. W. (1974) *Germanische Grabfunde des 4. bis 5. Jahrhunderts zwischen unterer Elbe und Loire, Studien zur Chronologie und Bevölkerungsgeschichte*. Munich, Beck.

Böhme, H. W. (1986) Das Ende der Römerherrschaft in Britannien und die angelsächsische Besiedlung Englands im 5. Jahrhundert. *Jahrbuch des Römisch-Germanisches Zentralmuseum Mainz* 33, 469–574.

Böhme, H. W. (1987) Gallien in der Spätantike. *Jahrbuch des Römisch-Germanischen Zentralmuseums Mainz* 34, 770–773.

Böhner, K. (1958) *Die fränkischen Alterthümer des Trierer Landes*. Berlin, Verlag. Gebr. Mann.

Bond, J. (2006) A Kaleidoscope of Regions. In B. Cunliffe, *England's Landscape. The West*, 117–34. English Heritage vol. 4. London, Collins.

Bonney, D. (1976) Early boundaries and estates in southern England. In P. Sawyer, *Medieval Settlement: Continuity and change*, 72–82. London, Edward Arnold.

Boon, G. C. (1974) *Silchester, the Roman town of Calleva*. Revised edn. London, David and Charles.

Booth, P., Dodd, A., Robinson, M. and Smith, A. (2007) *The Thames through Time. The archaeology of the gravel terraces of the Upper and Middle Thames – the early historical period, AD 1–1000*. Thames Valley Landscape Monograph no. 27. Oxford, Oxford University School of Archaeology for Oxford Archaeology.

Bourdillon, J. (2006) Animal bones. In P. Williams and R. Newman, *Market Lavington, Wiltshire: An Anglo-Saxon cemetery and settlement, excavations at Grove Farm, 1986–90*, 150–169. Wessex Archaeology Report no. 19. Salisbury, Wessex Archaeology Ltd.

Bowie, S., Kvalheim, A. and Haslam, H. (1978) *Mineral Deposits of Europe*, vol. 1. London, The Institute of Mining and Metallurgy and The Mineralogical Society.

Boyle, A. *et al.* (1998) *The Anglo-Saxon Cemetery at Butler's Field, Lechlade, Gloucestershire*. Oxford, Oxford Archaeological Unit.

Bradshaw, J. (1970) Ashford area, Westwell. *Archaeologia Cantiana*, 85, 179–80.

Brenan, J. (1991) *Hanging Bowls and their Contexts. An archaeological survey of their socio-economic significance from the fifth to seventh centuries AD*. BAR British Series 220. Oxford, Tempus Reparatum.

Brookes, S. (2007) *Economics and Social Change in Anglo-Saxon Kent AD 400–900. Landscapes, communities and exchange*. BAR British Series 431. Oxford, Archaeopress.

Brookes, S. and Harrington, S. (2010) *The Kingdom and People of Kent AD 400–1066: Their history and archaeology*. Stroud, The History Press.

Brooks, C. E. P. and Glasspoole, J. (1928) *British Floods and Droughts*. London, Benn.

Brooks, N. (1989) The creation and early structure of the kingdom of Kent. In S. Bassett (ed.), *The Origins of Anglo-Saxon Kingdoms*, 55–74. Leicester, Leicester University Press.

Brown, A. G. (1997) *Alluvial Geoarchaeology, Floodplain Archaeology and Environmental Change*. Cambridge, Cambridge University Press.

Brownsword, R. and Hines, J. (1993) The alloys of a sample of Anglo-Saxon great square headed brooches. *Antiquaries Journal* 73, 1–11.

Bruce-Mitford, R. (2005) *A Corpus of Late Celtic Hanging-Bowls*. Oxford, Oxford University Press.

Brugmann, B. (1999) The role of Continental artefact-types in sixth-century Kentish chronology. In J. Hines, J. Høilund Nielsen and F. Siegmund (eds), *The Pace of Change. Studies in medieval chronology*, 37–64. Oxford, Oxbow Books.

Brugmann, B. (2004) *Glass Beads from Early Anglo-Saxon Graves*. Oxford, Oxbow Books.

Brulet, R. (1990) *Les fouilles du quartier Saint-Brice à Tournai, l'environnement funéraire de la sépulture de Childéric*. Louvain-la-Neuve, Département d'Archéologie et d'Histoire de l'Art.

Butler. C. (2000) *Saxon settlement and earlier remains at Friars Oak, Hassocks, West Sussex*. BAR British Series 295. Oxford, Archaeopress.

Cameron, E. (2000) *Sheaths and Scabbards in England AD 400–1000*. BAR British Series 301. Oxford, Archaeopress.

Cameron, K. (1979–80) The meaning and significance of Old English *walh* in English Place-Names. *Journal of the English Place-Name Society* 12, 1–53.

Campbell, J. (1982) *The Anglo-Saxons*. London, Harmondsworth.

Campbell, J. (1986) *Essays in Anglo-Saxon History*. London, Hambledon Press.

Carruthers, W. (1991) The plant remains. In P. Fasham, and R. Whinney, *Archaeology and the M3*, 67–75. Winchester, Hampshire Field Club and the Trust for Wessex Archaeology.

Chatwin, D. and Gardiner, M. (2005) Rethinkng the early medieval settlement of woodlands, evidence from the western Sussex Weald. *Landscape History* 27, 31–49.

Chester-Kadwell, M. (2009) *Early Anglo-Saxon Communities in the Landscape of Norfolk*. BAR British Series 481. Oxford, Archaeopress.

Clarke, G. (1979) *The Roman Cemetery at Lankhills*. Winchester Studies 3, part II. Oxford, The Clarendon Press.

Cleere, H. (1975) The Roman Iron Industry of the Weald. *Archaeological Journal* 131, 171–199.

Cleere, H. (1981) *The Iron Industry of Roman Britain*. Unpublished PhD thesis. University College London.

Cleere, H. (1984) Ironmaking in the economy of the ancient world, the potential of archaeometallurgy. In B. G. Scott and H. Cleere (eds), *The Crafts of the Blacksmith*, 1–6. Belfast, USIPP Comité pour la Siderurgie Ancienne.

Cleere, H. and Crossley, D. (1985) *The Iron Industry of the Weald*. Leicester, Leicester University Press.

Coatsworth, E. and Pinder, M. (2002) *The Art of the Anglo-Saxon Goldsmith*. Woodbridge, The Boydell Press.

Collard, R. (1988) *The Physical Geography of Landscape*. London, Collins Educational.

Costen, M. (2011) *Anglo-Saxon Somerset*. Oxford, Oxbow Books.

Cowie, R. and Blackmore, L. (2008) *Early and Middle Saxon Rural Settlement in the London Region*. MoLAS monograph 41. London, Museum of London Archaeology Service.

Cox, B. (1975–6) The place-names of the earliest English records. *Journal of the English Place-Name Society* 8, 12–66.

Coy, J. and Maltby, M. (1987) Archaeozoology in

Wessex. In H. C. M. Keeley (ed.), *Environmental Archaeology. A regional review* vol. II, 204–251. London, English Heritage.

Crabtree, P. J. (1989) *West Stow, Suffolk, Early Anglo-Saxon Animal Husbandry*, East Anglian Archaeology 47. Ipswich, Suffolk County Planning Department.

Cracknell, B. E. (2005) *'Outrageous Waves'. Global Warming and Coastal Change in Britain through Two Thousand Years*. Chichester, Phillimore and Co Ltd.

Cresswell, R. K. (1959) *The Physical Geography of Beaches and Coastlines*. London, Hulton Educational Publishers.

Crowfoot, E. and Hawkes, S. C. (1967) Early Anglo-Saxon gold braids, *Medieval Archaeology* 11, 42–86.

Cunliffe, B. (1980) The evolution of Romney Marsh, a preliminary statement. In F. Thompson (ed.), *Archaeology and Coastal Change*, 37–55. London, Society of Antiquaries of London.

Cunliffe, B. (1993) *Wessex to AD 1000*. London, Longman.

Dark, K. and Dark, P. (1997) *The Landscape of Roman Britain*. Stroud, Sutton Publishers.

Dark, P. (2000) *The Environment of Britain in the First Millenium AD*. London, Duckworth.

Davidson, H. E. (1962) *The Sword in Anglo-Saxon England*. Paperback edn (1998) Woodbridge, The Boydell Press.

Davidson, H. E. and Webster, L. (1967) The Anglo-Saxon burial at Coombe (Woodnesborough), Kent. *Medieval Archaeology* 11, 1–41.

Davies, H. (2002) *Roads in Roman Britain*. Stroud, Tempus Publishing.

Davies, W. and Vierck, H. (1972) The contexts of the Tribal Hidage, social aggregates and settlement patterns, *Frühmittelalterliche Studien* 8, 223–93.

De la Bédoyère, G. (1993) *Roman Villas and the Countryside*. London, B. T. Batsford/English Heritage.

Devoy, R. J. (1980) Post-Glacial Environmental Change and Man in the Thames Estuary, a Synopsis. In F. Thompson (ed.), *Archaeology and Coastal Change*, 134–48. London, Society of Antiquaries of London.

Dickinson, T. (1976) *The Anglo-Saxon Burial Sites of the Upper Thames Region, and their bearing on the history of Wessex, c.AD 400–700*. Unpublished Dphil thesis, University of Oxford.

Dickinson, T. (1993) Early Saxon saucer brooches; a preliminary overview. *Anglo-Saxon Studies in Archaeology and History* 6, 11–44.

Dickinson, T. and Härke, H. (1992) *Early Anglo-Saxon shields*. London, The Society of Antiquaries of London.

Dodgson, J. M. (1966) The significance of the distribution of the English place-name in -ingas, -inga- in South-east England. *Medieval Archaeology* 10, 1–29.

Dodgson, J. M. (1973) Place-names from *hām*, distinguished from *hamm* names, in relation to the settlement of Kent, Surrey and Sussex. *Anglo-Saxon England* 2, 1–50.

Down, A. and Welch, M. (1990) *Chichester Excavations VII: Apple Down and the Mardens*. Chichester, Phillimore and Co Ltd.

Draper, S. (2006) *Landscape, settlement and society in Roman and early medieval Wiltshire*. BAR British Series 419. Oxford, Archaeopress.

Drewett, P. (1978) Field systems and land allotment in Sussex 3rd millennium BC to 4th century AD. In H. Bowen and P. Fowler, *Early Land Allotment in the British Isles*, 67–80. BAR British Series 48. Oxford, Archaeopress.

Drewett, P. (1982) *The Archaeology of Bullock Down, Eastbourne, East Sussex. The development of a landscape*. Lewes, Sussex Archaeological Society.

Duhig, C. (unpublished) *Osteoarchaeological report on the skeletal material from the Anglo-Saxon cemetery at Broadstairs St Peter's Tip, Kent*.

Dumville, D. N. (1985) The West Saxon genealogical regnal list and the chronology of early Wessex, *Peritia* 4, 21–66.

Dumville, D. N. (1989) The Tribal Hidage, an introduction to its texts and their history In S. Bassett (ed.), *The Origins of Anglo-Saxon Kingdoms*, 225–30. Leicester, Leicester University Press.

Eagles, B. (1979) *The Anglo-Saxon Settlement of Humberside*. BAR British Series 68 (i). Oxford, Archaeopress.

Eagles, B. (1994) The archaeological evidence for

settlement in the fifth to seventh centuries AD. In M. Aston and C. Lewis (eds), *The Medieval Landscape of Wessex*, 13–32. Oxbow Monograph 46. Oxford, Oxbow Books.

Eagles, B. (2001) Anglo-Saxon presence and culture in Wiltshire c.AD 450–c.675. In P. Ellis (ed.), *Roman Wiltshire and After. Papers in honour of Ken Annable*, 199–233. Devizes, Wiltshire Archaeological and Natural History Society.

Eagles, B. (2004) Britons and Saxons on the eastern boundary of the Civitas Durotigum. *Britannia*, 35, 234–240.

Eckhardt, H., Chenery, C., Booth, P., Evans, J. A., Lamb, A. and Müldner, G. (2009) Oxygen and strontium isotope evidence for mobility in Roman Winchester, *Journal of Archaeological Science* 36, 2816–2825.

Edmondson, J. (1989) Mining in the Later Roman Empire and beyond, continuity or disruption? *Journal of Roman Studies* 79, 84–102.

Edwards, J. F. and Hindle, B. P. (1991) The transportation systems of medieval England and Wales. *Journal of Historical Geography*, vol. 17, issue 2, April, 124–134.

Ellis, P. (1992) *Mendip Hills. An archaeological survey of an Area of Outstanding Natural Beauty*. Taunton, English Heritage and Somerset County Council.

Ellison, A. and Harriss, J. (1972) Settlement and land use in the prehistory and early history or southern England, a study based on locational models. In D. Clarke (ed.), *Models in Archaeology*. London, Methuen.

Evans, J., Stoodley, N. and Chenery, C. (2006) A strontium and oxygen assessment of a possible fourth century immigrant population in a Hampshire cemetery, southern England, *Journal of Archaeological Science* 33, 265–72.

Everard, C. E. (1980) On Sea-Level Changes. In F. H. Thompson *Archaeology and Coastal Change*, 1–23. London, The Society of Antiquaries of London.

Everitt, A. (1986) *Continuity and Colonization. The evolution of Kentish settlement*. Leicester, Leicester University Press.

Evison, V. (1956) An Anglo-Saxon cemetery at Holborough. *Archaeologia Cantiana* 70, 84–141.

Evison, V. I. (1965) *Fifth-Century Invasions South of the Thames*. London, University of London, The Athlone Press.

Evison, V. I. (1968) The Anglo-Saxon finds from Hardown Hill. *Proceedings of the Dorset Natural History and Archaeological Society* 90, 232–240.

Evison, V. I. (1979) *A corpus of wheel-thrown pottery in Anglo-Saxon graves*. London, Royal Archaeological Institute.

Evison, V. I. (1987) *Dover, the Buckland Anglo-Saxon Cemetery*. London, Historic Buildings and Monuments Commission.

Evison, V. I. (2008) *Catalogue of Anglo-Saxon Glass in the British Museum*. London, The British Museum.

Faussett, B., edited by Smith, C. R. (1856) *Inventorium Sepulchrale*. London: printed for subscribers.

Fells, S. (1980) Section 8, possible sources of iron ore. In J. Haslam, A middle Saxon iron smelting site at Ramsbury, Wiltshire. *Medieval Archaeology* 25, 55–56.

Fern, C. (2005) The archaeological evidence for equestrianism in early Anglo-Saxon England, c.450–700. In A. Pluskowski (ed.), *Just Skin and Bones? New perspectives on human-animal relations in the historical past*, 43–71. BAR International Series 1410. Oxford, Archaeopress.

Finberg, H. P. R. (1972) Anglo-Saxon England to 1042. In H. P. R. Finberg (ed.), *The Agrarian History of England and Wales*, I.ii, 385–525. Cambridge, Cambridge University Press.

Fowler, P. (2000) *Landscape Plotted and Pieced. Landscape history and local archaeology in Fyfield and Overton, Wiltshire*. London, Society of Antiquaries of London.

Fowler, P. (2002) *Farming in the First Millennium AD*. Cambridge, Cambridge University Press.

Frere, S. (1967) *Britannia*. London, Routledge and Kegan Paul.

Fulford, M. (2006) Discussion and synthesis. In M. Fulford, A. Clarke, and H. Eckardt, *Life and Labour in Late Roman Silchester*, 249–285. Britannia Monograph series 22. London, Society for the Promotion of Roman Studies.

Fulford, M. and Timby, J. (2000) *Late Iron Age and Roman Silchester*. Britannia Monograph Series no. 15. London, Society for the Promotion of Roman Studies.

Gaffney, V. and Tingle, M. (1989) *The Maddle Farm Project. An integrated survey of prehistoric and Roman landscapes on the Berkshire Downs*. BAR British Series 200. Oxford, Archaeopress.

Gaimster, M. (1992) Scandinavian Gold Bracteates in Britain: money and media in the Dark Ages. *Medieval Archaeology* 36, 1–28.

Gannon, A. (2003) *The Iconography of Early Anglo-Saxon Coinage, Sixth to Eighth Centuries*. Oxford, Oxford University Press.

Gardiner, M. (1984) Saxon settlement and land division in the Western Weald. *Sussex Archaeological Collections* 122, 75–84.

Gardiner, M. (2003) Economy and landscape change in Post-Roman and Early Medieval Sussex, 450–1175. In D. Rudling (ed.), *The Archaeology of Sussex to AD 2000*. King's Lynn, Heritage Marketing and Publications Ltd on behalf of CCC University of Sussex.

Gardiner, M. *et al.* (2001) Continental trade and non-urban ports in Mid-Anglo-Saxon England, Excavations at Sandtun, West Hythe, Kent. *Archaeological Journal* 158, 161–290.

Geake, H. (1997) *The Use of Grave-Goods in Conversion-Period England, c.600–c.850*. BAR British Series 261. Oxford, John and Erica Hedges.

Geological Survey of Great Britain. (1935) *Map of the Iron Ores of England and Wales*. Southampton, Director General of the Ordnance Survey.

Gerrard, S. (2000) *The Early British Tin Industry*. Stroud, Tempus Books.

Gibson-Hill, J. and Worrsam, B. C. (1976) Analyses of Wealden iron ores and their archaeological significance. *Bulletin of the Institute of Archaeology* 13, 247–263.

Gingell, C. J. (1978) The excavation of an early Anglo-Saxon cemetery at Collingbourne Ducis. *Wiltshire Archaeological and Natural History Magazine* 70–1, 61–98.

Goodier, A. (1984) The formation of boundaries in Anglo-Saxon England, a statistical study. *Medieval Archaeology* 28, 1–21.

Goudie, A. S. and Brunsden, D. (1994) *The Environment of the British Isles: An atlas*. Oxford, Clarendon Press.

Green, F. J. (1994) Cereals and plant food, a reassessment of the Saxon economic evidence from Wessex. In J. Rackham (ed.), *Environment and Economy in Anglo-Saxon England*, 83–88. CBA Research Report 89. York, Council for British Archaeology.

Gregory of Tours. *The History of the Franks*. Penguin edition 1974.

Grocock, C. (2010) Barriers to knowledge, coppicing and landscape usage. In N. Higham and M. Ryan (eds), *Landscape Archaeology of Anglo-Saxon England*, 23–37. Publications of the Manchester Centre for Anglo-Saxon Studies vol. 9. Woodbridge, Boydell Press.

Haaland, R. (2004) Technology, transformation and Symbolism, ethnographic perspectives on European iron working. *Norwegian Archaeological Review* 37 no. 1, 1–19.

Haith, C. (1988) Un nouveau regard sur le cimetière d'Herpes (Charente), *Revue Archéologique de Picardi* 3–4, 71–80.

Hall, T. (2000) *Minster Churches in the Dorset Landscape*. BAR British Series. Oxford, Archaeopress.

Halliwell, M. (1997a) Metal analysis of the copper-alloy buckles. In K. Parfitt and B. Brugmann, *The Anglo-Saxon Cemetery on Mill Hill, Deal, Kent*, 261–266. The Society for Medieval Archaeology monograph series no. 14. London, The Society for Medieval Archaeology.

Halliwell, M. (1997b) The bronze bowl from grave 91 (f). In K. Parfitt and B. Brugmann, *The Anglo-Saxon Cemetery on Mill Hill, Deal, Kent*, 245. The Society for Medieval Archaeology monograph series no. 14. London, The Society for Medieval Archaeology.

Hamerow, H. (1992) Settlement on the gravels in the Anglo-Saxon period. In M. Fulford and E. Nichols (eds), *Developing Landscapes of Lowland Britain. The archaeology of the British gravels, a review*, 39–46. London, The Society of Antiquaries of London.

Hamerow, H. (1993) *Excavations at Mucking* vol. 2. *The Anglo-Saxon settlement*. London, British Museum Press.

Hamerow, H. (2002) *Early Medieval Settlements. The archaeology of rural communities in North-West Europe 400–900*. Oxford, Oxford University Press.

Hansen, I. L. and Wickham, C. (eds) (2000) *The Long Eighth Century*. Leiden, Brill.

Harding, A. (1982) Climatic change and archaeology. In A. Harding (ed.), *Climatic Change in Later Prehistory*, 1–10. Edinburgh, Edinburgh University Press.

Härke, H. (1990) Warrior Graves? The background of the Anglo-Saxon weapon burial rite. *Past and Present* 126, 22–43.

Härke, H. (1992) *Angelsächsische Waffengräber des 5. bis 7. Jahrhunderts*. Zeitschrift für Archaeologie der Mittelalters 6. Bonn.

Harman, M. (1990) The human remains. In A. Down and M. Welch, *Chichester Excavations 7, Apple Down and the Mardens*, 183–194. Chichester, Chichester District Council.

Harman, M. (1998) The human remains. In A. Boyle et al., *The Anglo-Saxon Cemetery at Butler's Field, Lechlade, Gloucestershire*. vol. 1, 43–52. Thames Valley Landscape Monographs no. 10. Oxford, Oxford University Committee for Archaeology for Oxford Archaeological Unit.

Harrington, S. (2003) *Aspects of Gender and Craft Production in Early Anglo-Saxon England, with particular reference to the kingdom of Kent*. Unpublished PhD thesis. University College London.

Harrington, S. (2004) *A Study in Woodlands Archaeology, Cudham, North Downs*. BAR British Series 368. Oxford, John and Erica Hedges.

Harrington, S. (2008) *Aspects of Gender and Craft Production in the European Migration Period: Iron weaving beaters and associated textile making tools from England, Norway and Alamannia*. BAR International Series 1797. Oxford, John and Erica Hedges Ltd.

Harrington, S. (2011) Beyond exogamy. In S. Brookes, S. Harrington and A. Reynolds (eds), *Studies in art and archaeology: papers in honour of Martin G. Welch*, 88–97. BAR British Series 527. Oxford, Archaeopress.

Harrington, S. and Welch, M. (2010) Beyond the Tribal Hidage, using portable antiquities to explore early Anglo-Saxon kingdoms in southern England. In S. Worrell, G. Egan, J. Naylor, K. Leahy and M. Lewis (eds), *A Decade of Discovery: Proceedings of the Portable Antiquities Scheme conference 2007*, 167–173. British Archaeological Reports British Series 520. Oxford, Archaeopress.

Harris, A. Q. (2003) *Byzantium, Britain and the West, the archaeology of cultural identity*. Stroud, Tempus Publishing Ltd.

Haslam, J. (1980) A middle Saxon iron smelting site at Ramsbury, Wiltshire. *Medieval Archaeology* 25, 1–68.

Hawkes, S. C. (1979) Eastry in Anglo-Saxon England Kent, its importance, and a newly-found grave, *Anglo-Saxon Studies in Archaeology and History* 1, 81–113.

Hawkes, S. C. (1981) Recent finds of inlaid iron buckles and belt plated from seventh century Kent. *Anglo-Saxon studies in Archaeology and History* 2, 49–70.

Hawkes, S. C. (1982) Anglo-Saxon Kent c.425–725. In P. E. Leach (ed.), *Archaeology in Kent to AD1500*, 64–78. London, CBA Research Reports 48.

Hawkes, S. C. (2000) (Cameron, E. and Hamerow, H. eds) The Anglo-Saxon cemetery at Bifrons in the parish of Patrixbourne. In D. Griffiths (ed.), *Anglo-Saxon Studies in Archaeology and History*, 1–94. Oxford: Oxford University School of Archaeology.

Hawkes, S. C. and Grainger, G. (2006) *The Anglo-Saxon cemetery at Finglesham, Kent*. Oxford University School of Archaeology Monograph 64. Oxford, OUSA.

Hawkes, S. C. and Dunning, G. (1961) A catalogue of animal-ornamented buckles and related belt fittings. *Medieval Archaeology* 5, 1–70.

Hawkes, S. C. and Pollard, A. (1981) The gold bracteates from sixth century Anglo-Saxon graves in Kent, in light of a new find from Finglesham. *Frühmittelalterliche Studien* 15, 316–70.

Hawkes, S. C., Merrick, J. and Metcalf, D. (1966) X-ray fluorescent analysis of some Dark Age coins and jewellery. *Archaeometry* 9, 98–138.

Hawkes, S. C., Ellis Davidson H. and Hawkes, C. (1965) The Finglesham Man. *Antiquity* 39, 17–32.

Haywood, J. (1991) *Dark Age Naval Power. A reassessment of Frankish and Anglo-Saxon activity*. London, Routledge.

Heaton, M. (1993) Two Mid-Saxon grain-driers and Later Medieval features at Chantry Fields, Gillingham, Dorset. *Proceedings of the Dorset*

*Natural History and Archaeological Society* 114, 97–126.

Hedeager, L. (1992a) *Iron-Age Societies*. Oxford, Blackwell Publishers.

Hedeager, L. (1992b) Kingdoms, ethnicity and material culture: Denmark in a European perspective. In M. O. H. Carver (ed.), *The Age of Sutton Hoo. The seventh century in north-western Europe*, 279–300. Woodbridge, Boydell Press.

Heidinga, A. (1987) *Medieval Settlement and Economy North of the Lower Rhine*. Assen/Maastricht, Van Gorcum.

Higham, N. (ed.) (2007) *Britons in Anglo-Saxon England*. Woodbridge, The Boydell Press.

Hill, D. (1981) *An Atlas of Anglo-Saxon England*. Oxford, Basil Blackwell.

Hill, D. (2000) *Sulh* – the Anglo-Saxon plough *c.*1000 AD. *Landscape History* 22, 5–19.

Hills, C. (2009) Anglo-Saxon DNA? In D. Sayer and H. Williams (eds), *Mortuary Practices and Social Identities in the Middle Ages. Essays in honour of Heinrich Härke*, 123–40 . Exeter, Exeter University Press.

Hills, C. M. and O'Connell, T. C. (2009) New light on the Anglo-Saxon succession, two cemeteries and their dates, *Antiquity* 83, 1096–1108.

Hindle, B. P. (1993) *Roads, Tracks and their Interpretation*. London, B. T. Batsford Ltd.

Hines, J. (1984) *The Scandinavian Character of Anglian England in the pre-Viking period*. BAR British Series 124. Oxford, Archaeopress.

Hines, J. (1994) The becoming of the English, identity, material culture and language in early Anglo-Saxon England. *Anglo-Saxon Studies in Archaeology and History* 7, 49–59.

Hines, J. (1997) *A New Corpus of Anglo-Saxon Great Square-headed Brooches*. Woodbridge, The Boydell Press.

Hines, J. (2004) *Sūpre-gē*: the foundations of Surrey. In J. Cotton, G. Crocker and A. Graham, *Aspects of Archaeology and History in Surrey, towards a research framework for the county*, 91–102. Guildford, Surrey Archaeological Society.

Hines, J. and Høiland Nielsen, K. (1999) Synopsis of discussion. In J. Hines, K. H. Nielsen and F. Siegmund (eds), *The Pace of Change. Studies in Early-Medieval Chronology,* 89. Oxford, Oxbow Books.

Hinton, D. (1990) *Archaeology, Economy and Society. England from the fifth to the fifteenth century*. London, Seaby.

Hinton, D. (2000) *A Smith in Lindsey. The Anglo-Saxon Grave at Tattershall Thorpe, Lincolnshire*. Society for Medieval Archaeology monograph series no. 16. Leeds, Maney Publishing.

Hinton, D. (2005) *Gold and Gilt, Pots and Pins*. Oxford, Oxford University Press.

Hippisley Cox, R. (1973) *The Green Roads of England*. Facsimile of 2nd edn. London, Garnstone Press.

Hirst, S. (2004) *The Prittlewell Prince. The discovery of a rich Anglo-Saxon burial in Essex*. London, Museum of London Archaeology Service.

Hirst, S. M. and Clark, D. (2009) *Excavations at Mucking, vol. 3. The Anglo-Saxon Cemeteries*. London, Museum of London Archaeology.

Hodges, H. (1989) *Artifacts. An introduction to early materials and technology*. London, Duckworth.

Hodges, R. (1982) *Dark-Age Economics. The origins of towns and trade AD 600–1000*. London, Duckworth.

Hodges, R. and Whitehouse, D. (1983) *Mohammed, Charlemagne and the Origins of Europe*. London, Duckworth.

Hodgkinson, J. (2000) Slag and evidence for ironworking. In C. Butler, *Saxon Settlement and Earlier Remains at Friars Oak, Hassocks, West Sussex*, 41–2. BAR British Series 295. Oxford, Archaeopress.

Hodgkinson, J. (2008) *The Wealden Iron Industry*. Stroud, The History Press.

Hood, J, Ager, B, Williams, C, Harrington, S and Cartwright, C. (2012) Investigating and interpreting an early-to-mid sixth century Frankish style helmet. *British Museum Technical Research Bulletin* 6, 83–96.

Hooke, D. (1985) *The Anglo-Saxon Landscape. The kingdom of the Hwicce*. Manchester, University Press.

Hooke, D. (1988) Regional variation in southern and Central England in the Anglo-Saxon period and its relationshipto land units and setlement. In D. Hooke (ed.), *Anglo-Saxon settlements*, 123–151. Oxford, Basil Blackwell.

Hoskins, W. G. (1955) *The Making of the English*

*Landscape*. (1985 reprint). Harmondsworth, Penguin Books.

Hovén, B. *et al.* (1986) Excavations at Helgö 10: Coins, iron and gold. Stockholm, Kungliga Vitterhets Historie och Antikvitets Akademien.

Hübener, W. (1981) Eine Studie zu den Beilwaffen der Merowingerzeit. *Zeitschrift für Archäologie des Mittelalters* 8, 65–127.

Huggett, J. (1988) Imported grave goods and the Early Anglo-Saxon economy. *Medieval Archaeology* 32, 63–96.

Ilkjær, J. (2001) *Illerup Ådal. Archaeology as a magical mirror*. Aarhus, Moesgård Museum.

James, D. (2010) Settlement in the hinterland of *Sorviodunum*, a review. *Wiltshire Archaeological and Natural History Magazine* 103, 51–89.

Johns, C. (1999) The silver bullion. In S. White, J. Manley, R. Jones, J. Orna-Ornstein, C. John and L. Webster, A mid-fifth century hoard of Roman and Pseudo-Roman material from Patching, West Sussex, *Britannia* 30, 312.

Joffroy, R. (1974) *Le cimetière de Lavoye (Meuse): nécropole mérovingienne*. Paris, Picard.

Jones, E. T. (2000) River navigation in medieval England. *Journal of Historical Geography*, 26, issue 1, January, 60–75.

Jones, G. (1976) Multiple estates and early settlement. In P. Sawyer (ed.), *Medieval Settlement, Continuity and Change*, 15–40. London, Edward Arnold.

Jones, J. and Straker, V. (2002) Macroscopic plant remains. In S. M. Davies, P. S. Bellamy, M. J. Heaton and P. J. Woodward, *Excavations at Alington Avenue, Fordington, Dorchester, Dorset, 1984–87*, 118–121. Dorchester, Dorset Natural History and Archaeological Society.

Jones, M. (1981) The development of crop husbandry. In M. Jones and G. Dimbleby (eds), *The Environment of Man. The Iron Age to the Anglo-Saxon Period*, BAR British Series 87, 95–127. Oxford, Archaeopress.

Jones, M. E. (1996) *The End of Roman Britain*. London, Cornell University Press.

Joosten, I. (2004) *Technology of Early Historical Iron Production in the Netherlands*. Geoarchaeological and Bioarchaeological Studies 2. Amsterdam, Vrije Universiteit.

Kain, R. and Oliver, R. (2001) *Historic Parishes of England and Wales. An electronic map of boundaries before 1850 with a gazetteer and metadata*. CD Rom. Colchester, History Data Service of the UK Data Archive at the University of Essex.

Kendall, J. D. (1893) *The Iron Ore Deposits of Great Britain and Ireland*. (Ulan Press).

Kirk, S. (1971–2) A distribution pattern, *-ingas* in Kent. *Journal of the English Place-Name Society*, 4, 37–59.

Koch, U. (1977) *Das Reihengraberfeld bei Schretzheim*. Berlin, Gebr. Mann Verlag.

La Salvia, V. (2007) *Iron making during the Migration Period*. BAR International Series 1715. Oxford, Archaeopress.

Lamb, H. H. (1981) Climate from 1000 BC to 1000 AD. In M. Jones and G. Dimbleby (eds), *The Environment of Man, the Iron Age to the Anglo-Saxon Period*, 53–65. BAR British Series 87, Oxford, Archaeopress.

Lambrick, G. (1992) Alluvial Archaeology of the Holocene in the Upper Thames. In S. Needham and M. G. Macklin (eds), *Alluvial Archaeology in Britain*, 209–226. Oxbow Monograph 27. Oxford, Oxbow Books.

Lawrence, E. (ed.) (1995) *Henderson's Dictionary of Biological Terms*, 11th edn. Harlow, Longman Scientific and Technical.

Leahy, K. (2003) *Anglo-Saxon Crafts*. Stroud, Tempus Publishing Ltd.

Leeds, E. T. (1913) *An Archaeology of the Anglo-Saxon settlements*. Oxford, Clarendon Press.

Leeds, E. T. (1936) *Early Anglo-Saxon Art and Archaeology*. Oxford, The Clarendon Press.

Legoux, R., Périn, P. and Vallet, F. (2004) *Chronologie normalisée du mobilier funéraire mérovingien entre Manche et Lorraine*. Paris, AFAM.

Leigh, D. (1980) *The Square-Headed Brooches of Sixth-Century Kent*, unpublished PhD thesis, University College Cardiff.

Lewit, T. (1991) *Agricultural Production in the Roman Economy AD 200–400*. BAR International Series 568. Oxford, Tempus Reparatum.

Loader, E. *et al.* (2005) Grave goods from the inhumation burials. In V. Birbeck, *The Origins of Mid-Saxon Southampton*, 53–73. Salisbury, Wessex Archaeology Ltd.

Long, A., Hipkin, S. and Clarke, H. (eds) (2002) *Romney Marsh: Coastal and landscape change through the ages*. Oxford, University of Oxford, School of Archaeology.

Loveluck, C. (1996) The development of the Anglo-Saxon landscape, economy and society 'On Driffield', East Yorkshire, 400–750 AD. *Anglo-Saxon Studies in Archaeology and History* 9, 25–48.

Lundström, A. (1988) *Thirteen Studies on Helgo*. Stockholm, Statens Historiska Museum.

Lyngstrøm, H. (2003) Farmers, smelters and smiths. In L. C. Nørbach (ed.), *Prehistoric and Medieval Direct Iron Smelting in Scandinavia and France*, 21–26. Aarhus, Aarhus University Press.

Maclean, L. and Richardson, A. (2010) Early Anglo-Saxon brooches in southern England. The contribution of the Portable Antiquities Scheme. In S. Worrell, G. Egan, J. Naylor, K. Leahy and M. Lewis (eds), *A Decade of Discovery: Proceedings of the Portable Antiquities Scheme conference 2007*. British Archaeological Reports British Series 520, 156–466. Oxford, Archaeopress

Macphail, R. and Scaife, R. (1987) The geographical and environmental background. In J. Bird and D. Bird (eds), *The Archaeology of Surrey to 1540*, 31–51. Guildford, Surrey Archaeological Society.

Malcolm, G., Bowsher, D. and Cowie, R. (2003) *Middle Saxon London. Excavations at the Royal Opera House 1989–99*. MoLAS Monograph 15. London, Museum of London Archaeology Service.

Manning, W. H. (1985) *Catalogue of the Romano-British Iron Tools, Fittings and Weapons in the British Museum*. London, British Museum Publications Ltd.

Margary, I. D. (1973) *Roman Roads in Britain*. 3rd edition. London, John Baker.

Margary, I. D. (1965) *Roman Ways in the Weald*. London, Phoenix House.

Marlow, C. A. (1993) Human bone from 1989. In C. Scull, Excavation and survey at Watchfield, Oxfordshire, 1983–92, 215–221. *The Archaeological Journal* 149, 124–281.

Marzinzik, S. (2003) *Early Anglo-Saxon Belt Buckles (late 5th to early 8th centuries AD), their Classification and Context*. BAR British Series 357. Oxford, Archaeopress.

Mayr-Harting, H. (1991) *The Coming of Christianity to Anglo-Saxon England*. London, Batsford.

McCormick, M. (2001) *Origins of the European Economy, Communications and Commerce, AD 300–900*. Cambridge, Cambridge University Press.

McDonnell, G. (1989) Iron and its alloys in the fifth to eleventh centuries AD in England. *World Archaeology* 20.3, 373–381.

McDonnell, G. (1993) Slags and ironworking residues. In H. Hamerow, *Excavations at Mucking*, vol. 2, *the Anglo-Saxon settlement*, 82–3. London, Museum of London Archaeology.

Meaney, A. (1964) *A Gazetteer of Early Anglo-Saxon Burial Sites*. London, Allen and Unwin.

Metcalf, D. (1993) *Thrymsas and Sceattas on the Ashmolean Museum, Oxford*. London, Royal Numismatic Society and Ashmolean Museum.

Miles, D. (1974) Abingdon and Region: early Anglo-Saxon settlement evidence. In T. Rowley (ed.), *Anglo-Saxon Settlement and Landscape*, 36–41. British Archaeological Reports 6. Oxford, Oxford University Department for External Studies.

Miles, D. (1978) The Upper Thames Valley. In H. Bowen and P. Fowler (eds), *Early Land Allotment in the British Isles: A survey of recent work*, 81–88. BAR British Series 48. Oxford, Archaeopress.

Miles, D. (ed.) (1986) *Archaeology at Barton Court Farm, Abingdon, Oxon*. Oxford Archaeological Unit Report 3. CBA Research Report 50. Oxford, Oxford Archaeological Unit and the Council for British Archaeology.

Millett, M. (1990) *The Romanization of Britain. An essay in archaeological interpretation* Cambridge, Cambridge University Press.

Milne, G. (2003) *The Port of Medieval London*. London, Stroud.

Montague, R. (2006) Metalwork. In P. Williams and R. Newman, *Market Lavington, Wiltshire, and Anglo-Saxon Cemetery and Settlement*, 72–86. Wessex Archaeology Report no. 19. Salisbury, Wessex Archaeology Ltd.

Moreland, J. (2000) The significance of production in eighth century England. In I. L. Hansen, and C. Wickham (eds), *The Long Eighth Century*, 69–104. Leiden, Brill.

Mortimer, C. (1988) Anglo-Saxon copper alloys from Lechlade, Gloucestershire. *Oxford Journal of Archaeology* 7(2), 227–233.

# Bibliography

Mortimer, C. (1990) *Some Aspects of the Early Medieval Copper Alloy Technology, as illustrated by a study of the Anglian cruciform brooch*. Unpublished PhD thesis, University of Oxford.

Mortimer, C. (1991) Northern European metalworking traditions in the fifth and sixth centuries AD. In P. Budd, B, Chapman, C. Jackson, R. Janaway and B. Ottaway (eds), *Archaeological Sciences 1989*, 162–168.

Mortimer, C. (1993) Chemical composition of Anglo-Saxon brooches in the Ashmolean Collections. In A. MacGregor, and E. Bolick, *A Summary Catalogue of the Anglo-Saxon collections (non-ferrous metals)*, 27–30. British Archaeological Reports British Series 230. Oxford, Tempus Reparatum.

Mortimer, C. (1999) Technical analysis of the cruciform brooch. In U. v. Freeden, U. Koch, and A. Wieczorek (eds), *Völker an Nord- und Ostsee und die Franken*, 83–90. Bonn, Dr. Rudolf Habelt GmbH.

Mortimer, C. (2006) X-ray fluorescence analysis of two copper alloy bowls from graves 203 and 204. In S. C. Hawkes and G. Grainger, *An Anglo-Saxon Cemetery at Finglesham, Kent*, 381. Oxford University School of Archaeology, monograph 64. Oxford, OUSA.

Mortimer, C. (2007) Compositional analysis of non-ferrous metalwork. http://ads.ahds.ac.uk/catalogue/archive/wasperton_eh_2008/downloads.cfm

Morton, A. D. (1992) *Excavations at Hamwic* vol. 1. *Excavations 1948–83 excluding Six Dials and Melbourne Street*. CBA Research Report 84. London, Council for British Archaeology.

Muir, R. (2000) Conceptualising landscape. *Landscapes* 1, 4–21.

Müller-Wille, M. (1999) Settlement and Non-Agrarian Production from the High Mountain Region to the Shoreline. An Introduction. In C. Fabech and J. Ringtved (eds), *Settlement and Landscape*, 205–211. Proceedings of a conference in Århus, Denmark, May 4–7, 1998. Aarhus, Jutland Archaeological Society.

Murphy, P. (2007) *Managing the Coastal Environment*. Kent Coastal Conference.

Myhre, B. (1987) Chieftains' graves and chiefdom territories in South Norway in the Migration Period. *Studien zur Sachsenforschung* 6, 169–188.

Myres, J. N. L. (1969) *Anglo-Saxon Pottery and the Settlement of England*. Oxford, Clarendon Press.

Nelson, J. (1978) Queens as Jezebels, the careers of Brunhild and Bathild in Merovingien History. In D. Baker (ed.), Medieval Women, 31–77. Oxford, Blackwell for the Ecclesiastical History Society.

Nielsen, K. Høiland (1997) The schism of Anglo-Saxon chronology. In C. K. Jensen and K. Høiland Nielsen (eds), *Burial and Society: The chronological and social analysis of archaeological burial data*, 71–99. Aarhus, Aarhus University Press.

Oddy, W.A. (1980) Gilding and tinning in Anglo-Saxon England. In W. A. Oddy (ed.), *Aspects of Early Metallurgy*, 129–134. British Museum Occasional Paper 17. London, British Museum.

Oddy, W.A. (1996) Fire-gilding in early medieval Europe. In D. Hinton, *The Gold, Silver and other Non-Ferrous Alloy Objects from Hamwic*, 81–2. Southampton Finds vol. 2. Southampton, Alan Sutton Publishing.

Oliver, L. (2002) *The Beginnings of English Law*. Toronto, University of Toronto Press.

Parfitt, K. and Brugmann, B. (1997) *The Anglo-Saxon Cemetery on Mill Hill, Deal, Kent*. The Society for Medieval Archaeology monograph series no. 14. London, The Society for Medieval Archaeology.

Parfitt, K. and Haith, C. (1995) Buckland Saxon cemetery. *Current Archaeology* 144, 459–64.

Parry, M. (1978) *Climatic Change, Agriculture and Settlement*. Folkestone, W. M. Dawson and Sons Ltd.

Pelling, R. (2003) Early Saxon cultivation of Emmer wheat in the Thames Valley and its cultural implications. In K. Robson-Brown (ed.), *Archaeological Sciences 1999*, 103–109. BAR International Series 1111. Oxford, Archaeopress.

Philp, B. (1973) *Excavations in West Kent 1960–1970*. Dover, Kent Archaeological Rescue Unit.

Philp, B. and Hawkes, S. C. (1973) The Anglo-Saxon cemetery at Polhill. In B. Philp (ed.), *Excavations in West Kent 1960–1970*, 164–221. Dover, Kent Archaeological Rescue Unit.

Pirenne, H. (1937) *Economic and Social History of Medieval Europe*. New York, Harcourt Brace.

Pleiner, R. (2000) *Iron in Archaeology: The European bloomery smelters*. Prague, Archeologický ústav AV ČR Praha.

Procopius (1989) *History of the Gothic Wars*. Project Gutenberg

Rackham, O. (1993) *Trees and Woodland in the British Landscape*. Revised edition. London, Weidenfeld and Nicolson.

Rackham, O. (1995) *The History of the Countryside*. London, Weidenfeld and Nicolson.

Rahtz, P. and Fowler, P. Somerset AD 400–700. In P. J. Fowler (ed.), *Archaeology and the Landscape*, 187–221. London, John Baker.

Ravn, M. (2003) *Death Ritual and Germanic Social Structure (c.AD 200–600)*. BAR International Series 1164. Oxford, Archaeopress

Richards, J. (1978) *The archaeology of the Berkshire Downs, an introductory survey*. Reading, Berkshire Archaeological Committee publication no. 3

Richards, J. D. (1987) *The significance of form and decoration of Anglo-Saxon cremation urns*. BAR British Series 166. Oxford, Archaeopress.

Richardson, A. (2005) *The Anglo-Saxon Cemeteries of Kent*. BAR British Series 391. Oxford, John and Erica Hedges.

Rippon, S. (2000) *The Transformation of the Coastal Wetlands*. Oxford, Oxford University Press for The British Academy.

Rippon, S. (2006) *Landscape, Community and Colonisation. The North Somerset Levels during the 1st and 2nd millennia AD*. CBA Research Report 152. York, Council for British Archaeology.

Rippon, S. (2007) Emerging regional variation in historic landscape character, the possible significance of the 'long eighth century'. In M. Gardiner, S. Rippon and C. Dyer (eds), *Medieval Landscapes: Landscape history after Hoskins*, vol. 2, 105–121. Oxford, Windgather Press.

Roberts, B. and Wrathmell, S. (2000) *An Atlas of Rural Settlement in England*. London, English Heritage.

Robinson, M. (1981) The Iron Age to early Saxon environment of the Upper Thames terraces. In M. Jones and G. Dimbleby (eds), *The Environment of Man, the Iron Age to the Anglo-Saxon Period*, BAR British Series 87, 251–286. Oxford, Archaeopress.

Robinson, M. (1992) Environment, archaeology and alluvium of the South Midlands. In S. Needham and M. G. Macklin (eds), *Alluvial Archaeology in Britain*, 197–208. Oxbow Monograph 27. Oxford, Oxbow Books.

Rogers, P. W. (2007) *Cloth and Clothing in Early Anglo-Saxon England, AD 450–700*. CBA Research Report 145. York, Council for British Archaeology.

Rowley, T. (ed.) (1974) Anglo-Saxon settlement and landscape. British Archaeological reports 6. Oxford, Oxford University Department for External Studies.

Russel, V. (2002) Anglo-Saxon. In N. Stoodley (ed.), *The Millennium Publication. A review of archaeology in Hampshire 1980–(2000)*, 20–26. Winchester, Hampshire Field Club and Archaeological Society.

Ryder, M. (1981) Fleece changes in sheep. In M. Jones and G. Dimbleby (eds), *The Environment of Man. The Iron Age to the Anglo-Saxon Period*, 215–229. BAR British Series 87. Oxford, Archaeopress.

Salter, C. (2007) Slag. In R. Chambers and E. McAdam, *Excavations at Radley Barrow Hills, Radley, Oxfordshire*, vol. 2, *the Romano-British cemetery and Anglo-Saxon settlement*, 259–262. Thames Valley Landscape Monograph no. 25. Oxford, Oxford University School of Archaeology for Oxford Archaeology.

Sandon, F. (1975) Tides of the British Seas. *Physics Education* June, 262–6.

Sawyer, P. H. (1968) *Anglo-Saxon Charters*. London, Royal Historical Society.

Scaife, R. (1987) A review of Later Quaternary Plant Microfossil and Macrofossil Research in Southern England. In H. C. M. Keeley (ed.), *Environmental Archaeology, a Regional Review* vol. II, 125–159. London, English Heritage.

Scaife, R. G. and Burrin, P. J. (1992) Archaeological inferences from alluvial sediments, some findings from southern England. In S. Needham and M. G. Macklin (eds), *Alluvial Archaeology in Britain*, 75–92. Oxbow Monograph 27. Oxford, Oxbow Books.

Schnurbein, S. (1974) Zum Ango. In G. Kossack and G. Ulbert (eds), *Studien zur vor- und frühgeschichtlichen Archäologie : Festschrift f. Joachim Werner z. 65 Geburtstag*, 411–433. München, Beck.

Schubert, H. R. (1957) *History of the British Iron and Steel Industry from c.450 BC to AD 1775*. London, Routledge and Kegan Paul.

Scull, C. (1991) Scales and weights in early Anglo-Saxon England. *Archaeological Journal* 147, 183–215.

Scull, C. (1992) Excavation and survey at Watchfield, Oxon., 1983–1992. *Archaeological Journal* 149, 124–281.

Scull, C. (1999) Social archaeology and kingdom origins. In T. M. Dickinson and D. Griffiths (eds), The Making of Kingdoms. *Anglo-Saxon Studies in Archaeology and History* 10, 7–24.

Semple, S. (1998) A fear of the past, the place of the prehistoric burial mound in the ideology of middle and later Anglo-Saxon England. *World Archaeology* 30(1), 109–126.

Semple, S. (2003) Burials and political boundaries in the Avebury region, North Wiltshire. In D. Griffiths, A. Reynolds and S. Semple (eds), Boundaries in Early Medieval Britain. *Anglo-Saxon Studies in Archaeology and History* 12, 72–91.

Semple, S. (2008) Polities and Princes AD 400–800, new perspectives on the funerary landscape of the South Saxon Kingdom. *Oxford Journal of Archaeology* 27, 407–29

Semple, S. (2009) Recycling the Past, Ancient Monuments and Changing Meanings in Early Medieval Britain. In M. Aldrich and R. J. Wallis, *Antiquaries and Archaists. The Past in the Past, the Past in the Present*, 29–45. Reading, Spire Books Ltd.

Shephard, J. (1979) *Anglo-Saxon Barrow Burials of the Later Sixth and Seventh Centuries AD*. Unpublished PhD thesis. University of Cambridge.

Short, B. (2006) *England's Landscape. The South East*. London, English Heritage/Collins.

Sims-Williams, P. (1983) The settlement of England in Bede and the 'Chronicle'. *Anglo-Saxon England* 12, 1–41.

Somerville, E. (2000) The environmental background, a brief synthesis. In C. Butler, *Saxon Settlement and Earlier Remains at Friars Oak, Hassocks, West Sussex*, 47. BAR British Series 295. Oxford, Archaeopress.

Sørensen, P. (1997) Jutes in Kent? Consideration of the problem of ethnicity in southern Scandinavia and Kent in the Migration Period. In G. De Boe,. and F. Verhaege (eds), *Method and Theory in Historical Archaeology (Papers of the 'Medieval Europe Brugge 1997' Conference)*, 65–73. Zellik, Instituut voor het Archeologisch Patrimonium.

Soulat, J. (2009) *Le matériel archéologique de type Saxon et Anglo-Saxon en Gaule Mérovingienne*. Paris, Tome XX des Mémoires publiés par l'Association française d'Archéologie mérovingienne.

Spall, C. (2006) All that glitters, the case for goldworking at the early medieval monastery at Portmahomack. *Historical Metallurgy* 40(1), 42–48.

Speake, G. (1989) *A Saxon Bed Burial on Swallowcliffe Down*. London, Historic Buildings and Monuments Commission for England.

Spurrell, F (1883) Tumuli and pits in Westwood, Lyminge. *The Archaeological Journal* 40, 292.

Stenton, F. (1943) *Anglo-Saxon England*. Oxford, Clarendon Press.

Stenvik, L. (1997) Iron production in Mid-Norway, an answer to local demand? *Studien zur Sachsenforschung* 10, 253–263.

Straker, V. (2006) Charred, mineralised and waterlogged plant macrofossils. In P. Williams and R. Newman, *Market Lavington, Wiltshire, an Anglo-Saxon cemetery and settlement, excavations at Grove Farm, 1986–90*, 137–149. Wessex Archaeology Report no. 19. Salisbury, Wessex Archaeology Ltd.

Swanton, M. J. (1973) *The Spearheads of the Anglo-Saxon Settlements*. London, The Royal Archaeological Institute.

Swanton, M. (1974) *A Corpus of Anglo-Saxon Spear types*. BAR British Series 7. Oxford, Archaeopress.

Taylor, C. (1974) The Anglo-Saxon countryside. In T. Rowley (ed.), *Anglo-Saxon Settlement and Landscape*, 5–15. British Archaeological reports 6. Oxford, Oxford University Department for External Studies.

Taylor, C. (1979) *Roads and Tracks of Britain*. London, J. M. Dent and Sons Ltd.

Taylor, C. (1997) Dorset and beyond. In K. Barker and T. Darvill (eds), *Making English Landscapes*, 9–25. Oxbow Monograph 93. Oxford, Oxbow Books.

Tebbutt, C. F. (1973) The problem of bloomery sites. *Wealden Iron Research* VI:8, 8–10.

Tebbutt, C. F. (1980) A Saxon iron working site at Buriton, Hants. *Wealden Iron* no. 17, 15–16.

Tebbutt, C. F. (1981) Wealden bloomery iron-smelting furnaces. *Sussex Archaeological Collections* 119, 57–64.

Tebbutt, C. F. (1982) A Middle Saxon iron smelting site at Millbrook, Ashdown Forest, Sussex. *Sussex Archaeological Collections* 120, 19–35.

Thirsk, J. (1987) *Agricultural Regions and Agrarian History in England, 1500–1750*. Economic History Society. Basingstoke, Macmillan Education.

Thomas, M. G., Stumpf, M. P. and Härke, H. (2006) Evidence for an apartheid-like social structure in early Anglo-Saxon England. *Proceedings of the Royal Society, Biological Sciences* 273, 2651–7.

Tootell, K. (2006) Ironmaking and ironworking, the archaeological context. In Fulford, M., Clarke, A. and Eckardt, H., *Life and Labour in Late Roman Silchester*, 145–159. Britannia Monograph series 22. London, Society for the Promotion of Roman Studies.

Tubbs, C. (1978) An ecological appraisal of the Itchen Valley flood plain. *Hampshire Studies* 34, 5–22.

Turner, J. (1981) The vegetation. In M. Jones and G. Dimbleby (eds), *The Environment of Man. The Iron Age to the Anglo-Saxon Period*, 67–73. BAR British Series 87. Oxford, Archaeopress.

Tyers, I., Hillam, J. and Groves, C. (1994) Trees and woodland in the Saxon period, the dendrochronological evidence. In J. Rackham (ed.), *Environment and Economy in Anglo-Saxon England*, 12–22. CBA Research Report 89. York, Council for British Archaeology.

Tylecote, R. (1987) *The Early History of Metallurgy in Europe*. London, Longman.

Tylecote, R. (1992) *A History of Metallurgy*. 2nd edn. London, Institute of Materials.

Tylecote, R. and Gilmour, B. (1986) *The Metallography of Early Ferrous Edge Tools and Edged Weapons*. BAR British Series 155. Oxford, Archaeopress.

Ulmschneider, K. (1999) Archaeology, history and the Isle of Wight in the Middle Saxon period. *Medieval Archaeology* 43, 19–44.

Ulmschneider, K. (2000) *Markets, Minsters, and Metal-Detectors: The archaeology of Middle Saxon Lincolnshire and Hampshire compared*. BAR British Series 307. Oxford, Archaeopress.

Veeck, W. (1926) Der Reihengräberfriedhof von Holzgerlingen. *Fundberichte aus Swaben n.F.* 3, 154–201.

Vierck, H. (1977) Zur relativen und absoluten Chronologie die anglischen Grabfunde in England. In G. Kossack and J. Reichstein, *Archäologische Beiträge zur Chronologie der Völkerwanderungszeit*, 42–52.

Waller, M. and Schofield, J. (2007) Mid to late Holocene vegetation and land use history in the Weald of south-eastern England, multiple pollen profiles from the Rye area. *Vegetation History and Archaeobotany* 16, 367–384.

Watts, V. (ed.) (2004) *The Cambridge Dictionary of English Place-Names, based on the collections of the English Place-Name Society*. Cambridge, Cambridge University Press.

Webster, L. (1992) Death's diplomacy, Sutton Hoo in the light of other male princely burials. In R. Farrell, and C. Neumann de Vegvar (eds), *Sutton Hoo, Fifty Years After*, 75–81. Oxford, Ohio, American Early Medieval Studies.

Webster, L. (2000) Versions of treasure in the Early Anglo-Saxon world. In E. Tyler (ed.), *Treasure in the Medieval West*, 49–59. York, York Medieval Press.

Welch, M. (1983) *Early Anglo-Saxon Sussex*. BAR British Series 112. Oxford, Archaeopress.

Welch, M. (1985) Rural settlement patterns in the Early and Middle Anglo-Saxon periods. *Landscape History* 7, 13–26.

Welch, M. (1991) Contacts across the Channel between the Fifth and Seventh Centuries, a review of the archaeological evidence. *Studien zur Sachsenforschung* 7, 261–269.

Welch, M. (1993) The archaeological evidence for federated settlement in Britain in the fifth century. In F. Vallet and M. Kazanski (eds), *L'armée romaine et les barbares du IIIe au VIIe siécle*, 269–78. Mémoires AFAM 5. Paris, Association Française d'Archéologie Mérovingienne.

Welch, M. (1999) Relating Anglo-Saxon chronology to Continental chronologies in the fifth century AD. In U. von Freeden, U. Koch und A. Wieczorek (eds), *Völker an Nord- und Ostsee und die Franken, Akten des 48. Sachsensymposiums in Mannheim vom 7. bis 11. September 1997*, 31–8. Bonn, Habelt.

Welch, M. (2002) Cross-Channel contacts between Anglo-Saxon England and Merovingian Francia. In S. Lucy and A. Reynolds (eds), *Burial in Early Medieval England and Wales*, 122–31. London, Society for Medieval Archaeology.

Welch, M. (2007) Anglo-Saxon Kent to AD 800. In J. H. Williams (ed.), *The Archaeology of Kent to AD 800*, 187–248. Woodbridge, The Boydell Press.

Whaley, R, (2007) *Roman Road Reports*. Farnborough, NEHAS.

White, G. (1934) A settlement of the South Saxons. *Antiquaries Journal* 14, 393–400.

White, R. (2007) *Britannia Prima, Britain's Last Roman province*. Stroud, Tempus Pubs.

White, S. (1998) The Patching Hoard. *Medieval Archaeology* 42, 88–93.

White, S., Manley, J., Jones, R., Orna-Ornstein, J., Johns, C. and Webster, L., (1999) A mid-fifth century hoard of Roman and Pseudo-Roman material from Patching, West Sussex. *Britannia* 30, 301–15.

Wickham, C. (2005) *Framing the Early Middle Ages. Europe and the Mediterranean, 400–800*. Oxford, Oxford University Press.

Wild, J. P. (unpublished report) *Spitalfields, the Textiles*. London, Museum of London Archaeology.

Wilkinson, K., Barber, L. and Bennell, M. (2002) The examination of six dry valleys in the Brighton area. In D. Rudling (ed.), *Downland Settlement and Land-Use. The archaeology of the Brighton bypass*, 203–238. London, Archetype Publications with English Heritage.

Williams, G. (1999) The gold coinage of Eadbald of Kent (AD 616–40). *British Numismatic Journal* 68, 137–40.

Williamson, T. (1988) Explaining Regional Landscapes: woodland and champion in Southern and Eastern England. *Landscape History* 10, 5–13.

Williamson, T. (2003) *Shaping Medieval Landscapes. Settlement, society, environment*. Oxford, Windgather Press.

Williamson, T. (2007) The distribution of Woodland and Champion landscapes in medieval England. In M. Gardiner and S. Rippon (eds), *Medieval Landscapes: Landscape history after Hoskins*, vol. 2, 89–104. Oxford, Windgather Press.

Wilson, D. M. (1962) Anglo-Saxon rural economy. *Agricultural History Review* 10.2, 65–79.

Wiltshire, P. (2006) Palynological analysis of the palaeochannel sediments. In P. Williams and R. Newman (eds), *Market Lavington, Wiltshire: An Anglo-Saxon cemetery and settlement, excavations at Grove Farm, 1986–90*, 121–137. Wessex Archaeology Report no. 19. Salisbury, Wessex Archaeology Ltd.

Witney, K. P. (1976) *The Jutish Forest. A study of the Weald of Kent from 450 to 1380 AD*. London, Athlone Press.

Wood, I. N. (1983) *The Merovingian North Sea*. Alingsås, Viktoria Bokförlag.

Wood, I. N. (1990) The Channel from the 4th to the 7th centuries AD. In S. McGrail (ed.), *Maritime Celts, Frisians and Saxons*, 93–7. London, Council for British Archaeology.

Wood, I. N. (1992) Frankish hegemony in England. In M. O. H. Carver (ed.), *The Age of Sutton Hoo: The seventh century in north-western Europe*, 235–241. Woodbridge, The Boydell Press.

Wood, I. N. (1994) *The Merovingian Kingdoms, 450–751*. London, Longman Pubs.

Woolf, A. (2007) Apartheid and economics in Anglo-Saxon England. In N. Higham (ed.), *Britons in Anglo-Saxon England*, 115–29. Woodbridge, The Boydell Press.

Wright, D. (2010) Tasting misery among snakes, the situation of smiths in Anglo-Saxon settlements. *Papers of the Institute of Archaeology* 20, 131–136.

Yorke, B. A. E. (1983) Joint kingship in Kent, c.560–785. *Archaeologia Cantiana* 99, 1–20.

Yorke, B. A. E. (1989) The Jutes of Hampshire and Wight and the origins of Wessex. In S. Bassett (ed.), *The Origins of Anglo-Saxon Kingdoms*, 84–96. Leicester, Leicester University Press.

Yorke, B. A. E. (1990) *Kings and Kingdoms of Early Anglo-Saxon England*. London, Seaby.

Yorke, B. A. E. (2006) *The Conversion of Britain 600–800*. London, Longman Pubs.

Yorke, B. A. E. (2009) The *bretwaldas* and the origins of overlordship in Anglo-Saxon England. In S. Baxter, C. E. Karkov, J. L. Nelson and D. Pelteret (eds), *Early Medieval Studies in Memory of Patrick Wormald*, 81–95. Farnham, Ashgate.

## Primary Sources

ASC: *Anglo-Saxon Chronicle*, ed. and transl. M. J. Swanton (London 1996)

Asser, *Life of King Alfred*, ed. and transl. S. Keynes and M. Lapidge (Harmondsworth 1983)

Beowulf: *Beowulf and the Fight at Finnsburg*, F. Klaeber (3rd edn. 1950)

Gildas, *The Ruin of Britain and other works*, ed. and transl. M. Winterbottom (Chichester 1978)

HB: Nennius, *Historia Brittonum*, ed. and transl. J. Morris (Chichester 1980)

HE: Bede, *Historia Ecclesiastica Gentis Anglorum*, ed. and transl. B. Colgrave and R. A. B. Mynors (Oxford 1969)

Jordanes: *Getica*

*Life of Saint Bonface*

*Tribal Hidage*

VW: *The Life of St Wilfrid*, by Eddius Stephanus, B. Colgrave (ed. and trans.) (Cambridge 1927)

# Index

Page numbers in italics are illustrations; with Pl are plates; with 't' are tables.

Abbots Worthy (Hants) 71, 85t
Abbotsbury (Dorset) 106, *106*
Abingdon (Berks/Oxon) 70, 81, 196
   coins 199, 200
   Saxton Road 26t, *81*, 85t, 89, 155, 202
Ælle of the South Saxons 1, 5
Æthelbert 5, 6, 7, 165–6, 177–8
Æthelwalh of the South Saxons 5
Agilbert 6
agriculture 66–9, 71, 73, 81, 207
   *see also* soil/soil types
Alcock, L. 10
Alfriston (Sussex) 17, 142, 158, 169, 179, 186, 193
Alton (Hants) 133, 169, 172, 197
amber 12, 155–9, *156*, 159t, 161, 163, 207
amethyst 12, 159–61, *160*
Ampfield (Hants) 171
Andover (Hants) 147, 204
*Anglo-Saxon Chronicle* 4, 5, 6, 181
Anglo-Saxon Kent Electronic Database (ASKED) 13, 16, 18, 34
Anglo-Saxon Regional coins 198–9, *199*, 200, *200*, 204
animal husbandry 67, 69–70, 71, 81, 82
Apple Down (Sussex) Pl4, Pl7, 88, *92*, 93, 132, 171, 181, 196, 198
Applebaum, S. 67
artefacts 30, 30t
   beads 29
      amber 155–9, *156*, 159t, 163
      glass 18, 33, 34, 163
      gold 167
   belts/fittings 180–1, 182
      *see also* buckles
   and the database 29–36
   Frankish 147, 148t, 171, 176–7, 182, 183–92, 194, 204–5
      up to AD 575 184–95, 184t, *185–9*
      AD 575–650 196–7, *196*
      AD 650–750 197–201, *198–200*, 204
      weapon burials 201–4
   gold 12, 162–8, *165*, *167*
   hoards
      gold and silver 162, 169
      iron 120
   iron 116–17
      knives 29, 31, 36t, 117, 125–6, *125*, 125t, 126t
      shield bosses 123, *123*, 123t, 197–8, 202
      swords 116–17, *124*, 124, 124t
   Kentish 184–6, 184t, *185–6*, *189*, 196–7, *196*
   pottery 34, 36t, 38, 190, 197
   Roman, 32, 34t 100, 117, 137–8, 137t, 142, 167, 180–1
   shield bosses 123, *123*, 123t, 197–8, 202
   silver 12, 162–4, 168–72, *170*
   spoons 171, 172, 183
   tools 36t, 38, 117, 118
   *see also* brooches; coins; copper alloy; Surrey, archaeological evidence; weaponry
Axe (river) 13
axes/axeheads 30, 36t, 38, 186–8
   axe hammer 186
   bearded 187
   francisca-type 183, 186, *187*, *188*

Baldwin Brown, G. 172
Banham, Debbie 69
Banstead (Surrey) 102, 134, 145, 197
Bargates, Christchurch (Dorset) 106, *106*, 132, 132t
Barham (Kent) 172
Barrow Hills, Radley (Berks/Oxon) 71, 85t, 119
Barton Court Farm, Abingdon (Berks) 56, 67
Barton Stacey (Hants) 194
Basingstoke (Hants) 19t, 145
Bassett Down (Wilts) 130, 195
Bathild 177
beads 29
   amethyst 159–61, *160*
   glass 18, 34, 163
   gold 167
   weights 35

# Index

beakers 197
Beakesbourne (Kent) 142
Beckford (Herefs and Worcs) 80
Beddington (Surrey) 130, 133, 133t, 144
Bede 6, 7, 95
   *Historia Ecclesiastica* 5, 62
beech (Fagus) 57
Bell, Martin 72
belts/fittings 180–1
Berkshire 22t, *81*, 196, 204
   artefacts
      amber 155, 157, 159t
      amethyst 160
      bowls 150
      brooches 171, 172, 194
      coins 199, 200
      Frankish 194, 196, 197
      personal effects 38
   cemeteries/burials 23t, 24t, 25, 28, 28t, 82, 84, 85t, 89, 201–2, 204
   copper alloy 142, 150
   iron 105, 119, 134
   pastoral practices 70
   settlements 82, 84
Bertha (daughter of Charibert) 5, 6, 177
*Beyond the Tribal Hidage* project 2
Bickton (Hants) 85t
Bifrons cemetery (Kent) 157, 164, 191
Birch, T. 118
bishops 6, 63, 95
Bishopstone (Sussex) 119
Black Patch, Pewsey (Wilts) 24, 130
Blackmore, L. 118
Blair, John 77–8, 116
Bletchingly (Surrey) 192
Blunsdon St Andrew (Wilts) 134
boats 63, 108, 116
bone, animal 30, 31, 56
Bonney, D. 75
Boon, G. C. 67
Booth, P. 70
boundaries, parish Pl3, 20, 77–8, 95, 102
bowls, copper alloy 38, 141, 145, 148–52, *151*, 153, 190, 202
bracteates 162, 164–5, *165*, 166, 167, 196
Bradford Peverell (Dorset) *93*, 161, 168
Breamore (Hants) 130, 132, 133t, 144, 147, 171, 197
Brighthampton (Oxon) 85t
Brighton (Sussex) 88, 130t, 142, 198
Britannia Prima 7, 9
British 1, *4*, 7, 7–8, 9, 33, 34t
Broadstairs, St Peter's Tip (Kent) 16, 26t, 163
brooches 37–8, 37t, 207, 208
   annular Pl6
   anseate 184
   bow 171, 177, 194
   button 37, 37t
   cruciform 37–8, 37t, 103, 138–9
   disc 32, 37t, 38, 103, 140, 168, 171–2, 183, 186, 194, 198
   pennanular 161
   quoit 169
   relief-decorated 162

   S-shaped 183
   safety-pin 172
   saucer 17, 32, 37t, 38, 140, 194
   square-headed 17, 32, 37t, 139, *140*, 169, 171, 181, 186, 195
Brookes, Stuart 10, 13, 34, 42, 60, 74, 78–9, 140, 166, 176
Brown, A. G. 55
Brownsword, R. 139
Brugmann, Birte 16, 18
Buckinghamshire 22t, 23t, 24t, 172, 191
Buckland Dinham (Somerset) 80, 161
Buckland, Dover (Kent) 16, 24, 25, 26t, 141, 145, 158, 159, 163, 191, 204
buckles 145–8, *145*, 146t, 147t, 148t, 172, 207
   Frankish 182, 183, 184, 186, 194, 197
   Kentish 197
Bullock Down (Sussex) 70, 83
burials *see* cemeteries/burials; reversed spear burials
butchery 69
Butler's Field, Lechlade (Glos) 13, 25, 85t, 134, 148, 157, 160, 163
Byzantium 113, 159, 204
   copper alloy 146, 149, 150, *151*, 159
   gold 162, 164, 166, 190

Caedwalla 5
Cambridge Dictionary of English Place Names (Watts) 40
Cameron, K. 40
Camerton (Somerset) *42*
Cannington (Somerset) 199
Canterbury (Kent) 164
*Cantwarena* 1, 96
Cassington Enclosure (Oxon) 85t
Cassini Old Series of Historical Maps 42, 43
cauldrons 149, 150, 201, 202
Ceawlin, king of the West Saxons 5
cemeteries/burials Pl7, 9, 21t, 22–9, 22t, 23t, 24t, 25t, 26t, 27t
   and artefacts 87–8
      *see also* iron
   dating framework 15–16, 28–9
   and findspots 38
   location 41, 54
   and settlements 74, 75, 84–7, 85t, 88–9, 89t, 93–4
   site types 20, 21t
   soil types 90–1, 91t
ceramic 34
Cerdic 7
cereals *see* crops
Chalton/Chalton Peak (Hants) 70, 72, 77, 84, 85t
Chantry Fields, Gillingham (Dorset) 73
charcoal 30–1, 71–2, 107, 108
Charibert (Frankish king) 5
Charterhouse, Cheddar (Somerset) 168
Chatham Lines (Kent) 54–5, *55*, 191
Chertsey (Surrey) 95, 96
Chessell Down (Isle of Wight) 130, 149, 191–2
Chester-Kadwell, Mary 94
child burial 201–2
Childeric I 191
Christianity/Church 6, 7–8, 15, 178
Cirencester (Glos) 82
Cleere, H. 109, 116

228

# Index

climate 52–3, 66–9, 73
coastlines 58–60
   changes to 60–3
codes, site 19, 19t
coins 14, 36t, 162, 166
   Anglo-Saxon Regional 198–9, *199*, 200, *200*, 204
   bracteates 164, 166
   Early Continental 199–200
   gold 162
   Kentish 198–9, *199*
   silver 169, 172
   Surrey *102*, 103
Collingbourne Ducis (Wilts) 24, 25, 85t, 155, 157
Coln House School (Glos) 85t
Coombe Bissett (Wilts) 197
Coombe Woodnesborough (Kent) 38
copper alloy Pl6, 34, 35, 36t, 117, 137–8, 137t, 141–5, 142t, *143–4*, 207, 208
   artefacts
      bowls 38, 141, 145, 148–52, *151*, *153*, 154, 190, 202
      buckle loops and plates 145–8, *145*, 146t, 147t, 148t
      cauldrons 149, 150, 201, 202
      escutcheons 152, *153*
      'unknown' 150, 152, 152t
      weights 140–1, 141t
   British production 138–40
   European production 138
   Frankish 195, 201
corn driers 69, 73
Cornwall 139
Corporation Farm (Berks) 85t
Cowie, R. 118
Cox, B. 40
Coy, J. 69
Cracknell, B. E. 52
cremations 17, 21t, 24, 25, 26, 26t, 30, 35, 38, 77, 93, 101, 179
crops 67–9, 68t, 71, 72, 73, 179
Croydon (Surrey) 99, 101, 130, 133, 133t, 142, 181
Cunliffe, Barry 79–80, 83
Cuxton (Kent) 54, *54*
Cyprus 138

Darenth Valley (Kent) 41, 48, 98, 132, 142
Dark, P. 56
Dartford (Kent) 92, 95, 192
data-quality assessment 14–15
database 14–19
   artefacts 29–39
   cemeteries/burials 22–9
   findspots 36–9
   other datasets used 39–40
   sites 19–22
dating framework 15–19, 18t
dendrochronology 57
Denmark 111, 113, 168, 188
Devon 80
Dickinson, Tania 13, 123
diet 71
Dodgson, John McNeal 40
Dolland's Moor (Kent) 85t

Dorking (Surrey) 100, 101, 192
Dorset *3*
   artefacts
      amber 159t
      amethyst 161
      gold 168
      silver 172
   cemeteries/burials 23t, 24t, 25, 28, 28t, *93*
   corn driers 73
   iron 106, 127, 132, 132t, 133, 133t
   place-names 92
   settlements 80
   site types 22t
Draper, Simon 13, 82
dress fittings 32, 33, 34, 36, 36t, 38, 171, 179, 180, 182, 207
droveways 64
Droxford (Hants) 88, 142, 196

Eadbald 178
Eagles, Bruce 77, 80
Early Continental coinage 199–200
Early Medieval Coin Corpus (EMCC) 14
East Ilsley (Berks) 134
East Saxons 5
East Sussex *see* Sussex
Eastbourne (Sussex) 26t, 62, 72, 83, 129–30, 192, 193, 196
Eccles (Kent) 26t
economies 8, 78–83
edaphic units Pl1–3, 51, 90
Ellison, A. 76
English Heritage 18, 46
environmental contexts 9, 11, 41–2
   central chalk lands to the south coast 71
   climate 52–3
   eastern area of the Thames, Weald, coast 71–3
   geology 43–5
   land use 48–50, 70–3
   landscape units 45–7, 50–1
   mapping the evidence 42–3
   palaeo-environment 56
   rivers/floodplains 53–6
   Upper Thames Valley and chalklands to the south 70–1
   western area 73
   woodlands 56–7
Eorcenwald 95
escutcheons, copper alloy 152, *153*
Esher (Surrey) 130, 142
Essex 22t, 23t, 24t, 56, 84, 95, 113, 119, 165, 191
Europe 110–13, 138, 168
   see also *individual countries*
Everitt, Alan 42, 46, 51
Evison, Vera 16, 31, 181
Ewell (Surrey) 99, 102, 130
Exton (Hants) 196
Eynsham (Oxon) 85t

Fairford (Glos) 150, 194
Farthingdown (Surrey) 101, 102, 126, 134
Faversham (Kent) 32, 88, 108, 129, 132, 133, 145, 149, 152, 158, 176, 191, 208

# Index

fertility *see* soil types
Fetcham (Surrey) 142
Finberg, H. P. R 67
finds *see* artefacts
findspots 15, 16, 20, 22, 36–9, 36t
Finglesham (Kent) 26t, 142, 149, 165, 182
'Finglesham Man' buckle 182
floodplains 53–6
Fordcroft Roman villa 99
fords 62, 87, 161
Fosse Way 150
Fowler, P. 67, 82
*Francia* 6, 8, 9, 12, 174–82, *175*, 209
   *see also* artefacts, Frankish
francisca-type axes 183, 186, *187*, *188*
Frankish Phase 15, 182
Frere, Shepherd 76
Friar's Oak (Sussex) 72, 114
Frisia 53, 77, 136, 139, 145, 162, 169, 172, 174, *175*, 181, 195
   *see also* Germany; Netherlands
Frithuwold 95–6
Fulford, M. 120
furnished burial 2, 15, 18, 124, 126, 134

Gally Hills, Banstead (Surrey) 102, 134, 145
Gannon, A. 166
Gardiner, Mark 42, 70, 83
garnets 104, *145*, 160, 163, 168, 171, 182, 183, 186, 197
Geake, Helen 15
geology 43–5, *44*, 207
Germany 110, 112, 113
*Gewissae* 5
Gildas 1, 8
gilding 32, 34, 139, 166, 207
Gillingham (Dorset) 73
Gilmour, B. 116
glass 34
   beads 18, 33, 34, 163
   spindle whorls 183
   vessels 38, 184, 190, 192, 197, 198
Gloucester (Glos) *3*, 180
Gloucestershire *3*, 22t, 82
   artefacts
      amber 157, 159t
      amethyst 160
      belt sets 180
      copper alloy 148, 150
      Kentish 194
   cemeteries/burials 23t, 24t, 25, 28, 28t, 85t
   iron 105, 134
Godalming (Surrey) 95
gold 12, 162–8, *165*, *167*
   beads 167
   bracteates 162, 164–5, *165*, 166, 167, 196
   braid 166, 167, 190–2
   gilding 32, 34, 139, 166, 207
   pendants 172
Goldbury Hill, West Hendred (Berks) 142
grave equipment 30, 30t
Gregory of Tours 52, 162

*Ten books of History, The* 5
Grocock, C. 57
Grove Farm, Market Lavington (Wilts) 71, 80, 85t, 118, 194
Guildown (Surrey) 100, *100*, 167, 192

Halliwell, M. 139
Hamerow, Helena 48
Hampshire/Isle of Wight 3, *3*, 6, 20, 112, *131*
   agriculture/land use 67, 68, 70, 71, 72, 81
   artefacts
      amber 155, 157, 159t
      coins 199
      copper alloy Pl6, 145, 147, 148, 152
      Frankish 196, 198
      glass vessels 197
      silver 169, 171, 172
      spears 193–4
   cemeteries/burials 23t, 24t, 25, 28, 28t, 84, 85t, 88, 204
   coastline 62
   copper alloy 142, 144
   environmental evidence 56
   metalworking 163
      iron 105, 114, 120, 127, 130, 130t, 132, 133, 133t, 135
   site types 20, 22, 22t
   trade 180, 209
      shield bosses 198
*Hamwic see* Southampton (*Hamwic*) (Hants)
hanging bowl escutcheons 39
Hangleton (Sussex) 89
Hardown Hill (Dorset) 80, 187
Härke, H. 10, 123
Harriss, J. 76
Hawkes, Sonia Chadwick 31
Heidinga, A. 76
helmets 188–9
Herpes-en-Charente (France) 179
hides 5, 77, 96
Highdown Hill (Sussex) *61*, 85t, 88, 89, 169
Hill, D. 53
Hines, John 97, 139, 178
Hippisley Cox, R. 64
*Historia Ecclesiastica* (Bede) 5, 6, 62
hoards 36, 82, 88, 120, 141, 162, 163, 169, 188, 197
Holborough (Kent) 54
Holywell Row (Suffolk) 191–2
Hooke, Della 78
Horndean (Hants) 132, 148, 196, 204
horse harnesses 30, 36
Horton Kirby, Risley (Kent) 160
Hoskins, W. G. 65–6
Howletts (Kent) 169
Hübener, W. 187
Huckles Bridge (Hants) 85t
Huggett, Jeremy 8, 137, 155, 157, 158, 160
hunting 69
*Hwicce* 78

Ilchester (Somerset) 171
Ine of Wessex, King 7
intermarriage 177–8, 191, 207

# Index

invasion see migration
iron 34, 104–5, 122, 178, 195, 207, 208
    artefacts 116–17, 123–6
    Europe 110–13
    ore deposits 105–6, *106*
    processing 106–7
    in Roman Britain 105, 107–9, 120, 130, *131*, *135*
    in southern Britain 113–16, *115*, 116–21, 126–36, *128*, *129*, 130t, *131*, *132*, 133t, *134*, *135*
    in Western Roman Empire 109–10
Islamic expansion 175–6
Isle of Wight 3, 5, 6, 62
    amber 158, 159t
    cemeteries/burials 22t, 23t, 24t, 25, 87, *87*
    copper alloy 142, 147, 148, 149
    Frankish/Kentish influence 179, 185, 189, 190, 191, 192, 199, 210
    iron 105, 106, 130, 130t, 136
    silver 171, 172
Italy, iron working 112–13
Itchen Abbas (Hants) 130

jewellery
    bracteates 162, 164–5, *165*, 166, 167, 196
    pendants 159, 160, 162, 164, 166, 168, 169, 171, 172
    rings 167
    see also brooches
Jones, G. 83
Jones, M. E. 56
Jutes 3, 6, 181

Kemsing (Kent) 152
Kent 13, 20, 22t, *43*, 55
    artefacts 34, 38, 173, 184t, 185
        amber 155, 157–8, 159–60, 159t
        amethyst 159
        copper alloy 141, 145–8, 146t, 147t, 148t, 149, 150, 152, 173
        Frankish 192
        gold 162, 163–4, 165, 167, 168, 173, 191
        knives 125–6, *125*, 125t
        lyre 204
        shield bosses 123, *123*, 123t
        silver 169, *170*, 171, 172, 173
        spears 204
        swords 124, *124*, 124t
    cemeteries/burials 23, 23t, 24, 24t, 25, 26t, 28t, 85t, 89, 95
    coastlines 58, 60, 61
    copper alloy 139, 142, 144, 145, 148, 149, 152
    droveways 64
    environmental evidence 41, *47*, 48, 50–1, 52, 54–5, 94
    and *Francia* 174–80, 181–2, 184t, 190, 191, 192, 197
    in historical sources 3, *3*, 5, 6
    iron 105, 106, 108, 116, 127, 129, 130t, 132, 133, 133t, 134, *134*
    land use 67, 69
    place-names 91, 92
    settlements 74, 78–9
    soil types *47*, 50–1, 94
    see also artefacts, Kentish
Kent Road, Nos. 10–20 (Kent) 85t
Keymer (Sussex) 130

kings 1, 5
Kingston Deverell (Wilts) 165
Kingston Down (Kent) 26t, *43*, 79, 172
Kirk, S. 40
knives 29, 31, 36t, 117, 125–6, *125*, 125t, 126t

La Salvia, V. 113
Lamb, H. H. 52
Lambrick, G. 55–6
land use 48–50, 70–3
    see also agriculture; pastoral practices
landscape units 45–7, 50–1, 83
Laverstock (Wilts) 142, 172
laws 7, 163, 178
Lechlade (Glos) 13, 25, 85t, 134, 148, 157, 160, 163, 194
Leeds, E. T. 159, 182
Leuthere 6
Leverhulme Trust 2
Lewes (Sussex) Pl9, 61–2, 63, 83, 87, 89, 130, 133, 161, 196, 204
*Limenwara* 1
Liudhard 6
livestock see animal husbandry
London (*Lundenwic*) 13, 14, 180, 198
    Basin 44–5, *44*
    iron working 118–19
    pollen analysis 72
Long Gill, Mayfield (Sussex) 113
Long Wittenham (Berks) 26t, 82, 84, 150, 155, 157, 201–2, 204
Longcot (Berks) 160
loomweights 37t, 38
Loveluck, Chris 10, 105
Low Field (Wilts) 85t
Lower Warbank, Keston (Kent) 89, 100
*Lundenwic* see London (*Lundenwic*)
Lyminge (Kent) 67, 69, 116, 165
Lympne (Kent) 42, 52, 61

Maclean, L. 37
Malling Estate, Lewes (Sussex) 83, 87
Maltby, M. 69
Manning, W. H. 117
Margary, I. D. 63–4
marine resources 31, 71
Market Lavington (Wilts) 71, 80, 118, 194
Market Place, Romsey (Hants) 114
Marzinzik, S. 146, 148, 184
Meaney, Audrey 13, 14
*Meonware* 1, 5, 6, 193
mercenaries 1, 8, 80
Mercia 1, 3, 96
mercury 140
Merovingians 162, 174, 176–9, 182
    artefacts 68, 183
        coins 164, 166, 169
        gold 190–1
metal working 12, 31
    see also copper alloy; gold; iron; silver
methodology 10–11
Mid Saxon Shuffle 2
Middle Street Meadow (Wilts) 85t

231

# Index

Middlesex 22t, 23t, 24t
migration 1, 2, 15, 52, 76, 77, 80, 177, 181
Migration Period 15
Mill Hill, Deal (Kent) 16, 139, 142, 148, 158
Millbrook, Ashdown Forest (Sussex) 112, 113, 115
Milton (Berks) 172, 194, 196, 199, 200
Milton Regis (Kent) 167
Mitcham (Surrey) 25, 26t, 97, 101, 133, 147, 171
mixed-rite cemeteries 25, 26t
Mortimer, C. 139
mounts 172
Mucking, Essex 13, 84, 95, 113, 119
Müller-Wille, M. 76
Myhre, B. 10
Myres, J. N. L. 81

National Monuments Records 39
Netherlands 112, 138
New Wintles Farm (Oxon) 84, 85t
No-Man's Lands 8–9
North Bentley Wood (Hants) 186
Northbrook (Hants) 85t
Northern European Barbaricum, and iron working 110–13
Northfleet (Kent) 95
Norway 111, 112, 168

Old Sarum (Wilts) 142, 194
Oliver's Battery (Hants) 204
Ordnance Survey One-Inch Old Series 42
organic materials, in burials 31, 35
Orpington (Kent) 95, 99
Otford (Kent) 152
Ouse (river) 85, *86*, 87
Overton Hill (Wilts) 130, 195
Oxfordshire 22t, *81*
    artefacts
        amber 155, 159t
        coins 199, 200
        Kentish 194, 196
    cemeteries/burials 23t, 24t, 26t, 28, 28t, 85t, 89, 202
    iron-wealth 133t
    land use 70, 71, 84
Ozengell (Kent) 16, 25, 26t

palaeo-environmental evidence 56
Parfitt, K. 16
pastoral practices 69–70
Patching (Sussex) 162, 169
*pays* 42, 46, *47*, 51
Pelling, R. 69
pendants 159, 160, 162, 164, 166, 168, 169, 171, 172
personal effects 30, 30t, 36t, 37
   Frankish 183, 184t, 204
Pewsey (Wilts) 24, 44, 46, 130, 130t, 186
Pirenne, H. 175
place-names 6, 9, 40, 57, 76, 80, 91–2, 108
ploughs 67, 69
Polhill (Kent) 16, 41, 160
pollen analyses 55, 56–7
pommels, sword 183–4

'Port Ways' 64
Portable Antiquities Scheme (PAS) 14, 38
pottery 34, 36t, 38, 89, 190, 197
Poverest Road (Kent) 85t
prehistoric monuments 74
Prittlewell (Essex) 191
Procopius 177, 181
provenance, terms of 31–3, 34t
Purley, Surrey 134
Purton (Wiltshire) 134
Purwell Farm (Oxon) 85t

quern stones 38

Rackham, Oliver 46, 108
Ramsbury (Wiltshire) 114
Ravn, Mads 10
raw materials 12
receptacles 30, 30t, 36t, 38, 149
recycling
   metal 118, 121, 139, 142, *143*, 144, 207–8
   Roman antiquities 164, 169
region of study *3*, *4*, 13
*regiones* 5, 77
reversed spear burials 202, *203*, 204
Richards, Julian 83
Richardson, Andrew 13, 16, 37
Ridgeway (trackway) 152, 199, 200
Rippon, S. 81
ritual deposits 38, 39
rivers 53–6, *53*, 195
   Avon 54, 194
   Axe 13
   Bourne 194
   Darenth/Darent 51, 152
   Frome *93*
   Itchen 54
   Kennet 54
   Medway *54*, *55*, 134, 197
   Nadder 194
   Ock 89
   Ouse 62
   Parrett 13, 54, 62
   Ravensbourne 72
   Rother 54
   Stour 54
   Swale 129, 134
   Test 54
   Thames 13, 45, 52, *53*, 54, 60, 89, 197
   Wey 54
   Wylye 194
roads, Roman Pl2, *42*, *43*, 63–5, *65*, 87, *97*, 152, 186, 194, 195, 208
   Fosse Way 150
   Stane Street 65, 100, 101, 102, 197
   Watling Street 109, 127, 133, 181, 192, 197
Robinson, M. 56
Rochester (Kent) 197
Roman, curated artefacts 33, 150, *151*, 167
Roman Britain 1, 7, 9, 73, 94, 208
   agriculture 66, 67, 77, 81

232

# Index

artefacts 32, 34t, 100, 117, 142, 167, 180–1
  copper alloy 139, 141, 142, *143*, 144, 145, 149
  gold 164, 167
  iron 105, 107–9, 120, 130, *131*, *135*
  sites 14, 39–40, 39t, 40t, 60
  soil types 90, 98–9, *98*
  taxation 66
  villas 61, 66, 67, 76, 82, 85t, *98*, 99, 99t, 101, 152
Romano-British Transgression (RBT) 52
Romney Marsh (Kent) 61
Rookery Hill (Sussex) 62, 75, 84, 85t, 89, 119, 193
routes 11–12, 86, 88–9, 89t

St Ann's Road, Eastbourne (Sussex) 26t, 167
St Giles Hill (Hants) 130, *131*
St Peter's Tip, Broadstairs (Kent) 16, 26t, 163
Salic Law Code 178
Saltwood, Stone Farm (Kent) 26t, 85t, 157–8, 192, 202
Sandown Park, Esher (Surrey) 130
Sarmatians 180
Sarre (Kent) 26t, 60, 161, 163, 169, 191
'Saxon Shore' forts 60, 62
Saxons 1–2, 6, 32, 80, *175*, 178, 179, 180, 209
Saxton Road, Abingdon (Berks/Oxon) 26t, *81*, 85t, 89, 155, 202
scales 163, 166, 207
Schleswig-Holstein 110, 112, 113
Schubert, H. R. 107
Scull, Christopher 163, 166
seaxes 38, 117, 183, 204
Selmeston (Sussex) Pl8, 147
Selsey Bill (Sussex) 60, 62, 92
semi-precious stones *see* amber; amethyst; garnet
Semple, Sarah 82, 83
settlements 84
  and cemeteries/burials 74, 75, 84–7, 85t, 88–9, 89t, 93–4
  and iron ore deposits 105–6, *106*
  patterns 65, 75–8
  place names 91–2
  soil types 90–1, 91t
  and wealth 78–83
Shavard's Farm (Hants) 85t, 133
Shephard, John 16
Shepperton (Surrey) 101, 130, 142
Sherbourne House (Glos) 85t
shield bosses 123, *123*, 123t, 197–8, 202, 207
shields 38
Sibertswold (Kent) Pl10, 118, 204
Silchester (Hants) 67, 81, 120, 135, 195, 199
silver 12, 162–4, 168–72, *170*
sites in the study 19–22, 21t
slaves 179
smiths 111, 121, 164, 207
Smith's Pitt II (Oxon) 85t
social structure 1, 11, 74, 159
soil/soil types Pl1, 9, 12, 48–51, *49*, 49t, 50t, *51*, 90–1, 90t, 206
  Surrey Pl3, 98–9, *98*, 103
Somerset 3, 22t, *42*
  artefacts
    amber 159t
    amethyst 161

    coins 199
    copper alloy 152
    Frankish 198
    silver 171, 172
  cemeteries/burials 23t, 24t, 28, 28t
  iron, and wealth 127, 133t
  place-names 92
  settlements 80–1
South Saxons *see* Sussex
Southampton (*Hamwic*) (Hants) 56, 112, 148, 163, 172, 180, 198, 204, 209
Southfleet (Kent) 85t
Speake, George 172
spears/spearheads 35, 38, 101, 117, 184, 207
  Frankish 197, 198, 201–4, *203*
spindle whorls 30, 33, 36t, 155, 183
spoons 171, 172, 183
Springhead (Kent) 85t
Staines (Surrey) 95
Stane Street 65, 100, 101, 102, 197
*Stæningas* 95
Stenton, F. 181
Stone Farm (Kent) 26t, 85t, 157
stoups 201–2
sunken-featured buildings (SFBs) 71, 72, 84, 113
*Supsexena* 1
Surrey Pl3, 12
  agriculture 66, 94, 98–9, *98*
  archaeological evidence 96–103, 96t, *97*, *98*, *99*, *101*, *102*
  artefacts
    amber 157, 159t
    amethyst 161
    coins *102*, 103
    copper alloy 145, 147, 152
    gold 167
    knives 126
    silver 171
  cemeteries/burials 23t, 24t, 25, 97, 101
  copper alloy working 142, 144, 147
  documentary sources 95–6
  Frankish influence 181, 192, 197
  in historical sources 3, *3*, 5
  iron 105, 130, 130t, 133, 133t, 134
  settlement/cemeteries 100–1, *101*
  site types 22t
Sussex Pl4, 3, 5, Pl8–9, 12, 13, 20, 22t
  artefacts 17
    amber 157, 158, 159t
    amethyst 161
    brooches 181
    copper alloy 147, 148, 149
    gold 162, 167, 192
    silver 162, 169, 171
    weaponry 186, 196
  cemeteries/burials Pl7, 23, 23t, 24t, 25, 26t, 28, 28t, 38, *61*, 92
  and settlements 75, 83, 84–7, *86*, 88–9, 91
  coastlines 60, 61–2
  copper alloy 142
  Frankish influence on *175*, 193–4, 196, 198
  in historical sources 3, *3*

233

Sussex *contd.*
   iron 105, 113, 114, 115, 119, 127, 129–30, 130t, 132, 133, 133t, 135
   land use 63, 70, 72
   place-names 91
   routeways 65
Sutton Courtenay (Berks) 82, 84, 196
Swallowcliffe Down (Wilts) 172
Swanage (Dorset) 126
Swanton, M. J. 31, 117
Sweden 112, 163
sword pyramid mounts 38
sword-beads 155
swords 30, 36t, 38, 116–17, 124, *124*, 124t, 186

Tanner's Field (Glos) 85t
Taplow (Bucks) 172
taxation 121, 176
Taylor, C. 77, 80
Tebbutt, C. F. 114
*Ten books of History, The* (Gregory of Tours) 5
Thames (river) 13, 45, 52, *53*, 54, 60, 89
Thanet (Kent) 197
Theudebert 177
Thirst, Joan 46
tide rotation 58, *59*
tinning 139
tools 30, 30t, 36t, 38, 117, 118
touchstones 163
trackways Pl2, 64, 87, 152, 199, 200
trade 76, 104, 107, 208
   amber 155
   amethyst 159
   copper alloy 145, 148, 149
   crops 67
   with *Francia* 178
   iron 104, 107, 111, 113, 136
   Kentish/Frankish 148–9, 182–3, 190, 192
   laws 7
   precious metals/semi-precious gems 157, 159, 162–3, 166, 168, 169
transhumance 57, 70, 115
transportation 55, 63, 104, 195, 206–7, 208
   *see also* boats; rivers; roads, Roman; trackways
*Tribal Hidage* 1, 3, 95, 96, 103
tribute 121, 208
Turner, J. 56
Turner's Hill (Sussex) 114
Tylecote, R. 108, 116
typologies, artefact 31, 35

Ulwell, Swanage (Dorset) 126

Vale of the White Horse (Berks/Oxon) 20, 70, 82
Veeck, W. 10
Vierck, Hayo 8, 9
villas, Roman 61, 66, 67, 76, 82, 85t, *98*, 99, 99t, 101, 152

Wallington (Surrey) 101, 181
Wanborough (Wilts) 130

war bands 8
Watchfield (Oxon) 194
Watling Street 109, 127, 133, 181, 192, 197
wave fetch 58, *59*
weaponry 30, 30t, 36t, 38, 122–6, 201–4
   Frankish 183, *186–8*, 186–8, 197–8
   and iron working 111, 116–17, 122–6
   seaxes 38, 117, 183
   in Surrey 101–2
   swords 30, 36t, 38, 116–17, 124, *124*, 124t, 183, 186
   *see also* axes; knives; shield bosses
weight of objects 11, 34–6
Welch, Martin 13, 14, 17, 71, 78, 83, 84, 178
Wessex (West Saxons) 12, 13, 17, 32, 96, 209
   and Frankish influence 175
   historical documents 3, 4–5, *4*, 7
   iron, and wealth 127, 132
   settlements and wealth 79–83
   *see also individual counties*
West Stow (Suffolk) 68, 69, 71
West Sussex *see* Sussex
Weston Colley (Hants) 85t
wheel ornaments 183
Wickham, Chris 104, 176
Wilfrid, Bishop 63
Williamson, T. 76–7
Wilton 'Celtic' hanging-bowl 149
Wiltshire *3*, 20, 22, 22t
   artefacts
      amber 155, 157, 159, 159t
      copper alloy 142, 147, 152
      Frankish 185, 194
      gold 165
      silver 171, 172
   cemeteries/burials 23, 23t, 24, 24t, 25, 28, 28t, 80, 85t
   copper alloy 142
   iron 105, 114, 118, 127, 130, 133–4, 133t
   place-names 92
   settlements 80, 82–3
Winchester (Hants) 130, *131*, 144, *175*, 180, 193–5
Wine (bishop) 6
Winterbourne Gunner (Wiltshire) 130, 130t, 185
*Woccingas* 95
Woking (Surrey) 95
women
   burials 11, 26, 117, 125
   and copper alloy artefacts 137
   Frankish family monasteries 6
   gold braid 166, 190–1
   intermarriage 177
   semi-precious gems 158–9, 160, 161
Wood, Ian 6
woodlands 56–7, 71, 72, 73
Worthy Park (Hants) 85t, 130
Wraysbury (Berkshire) 119
written sources, kingdoms 3–8
Wroughton (Wilts) 142
Wulfhere of Mercia, King 5, 96

Ymme 178

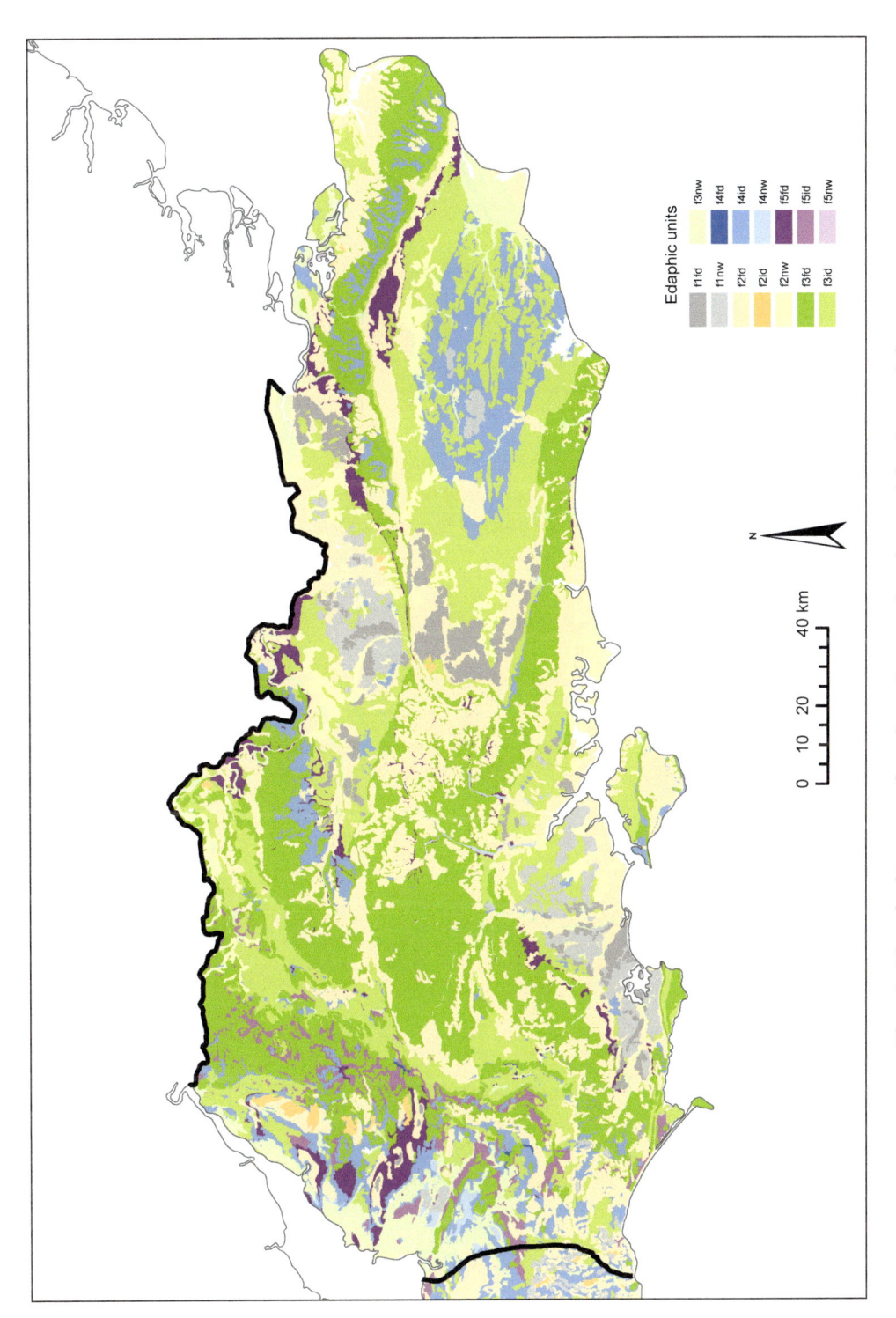

Plate 1. The edaphic units of southern Britain, based on soil fertility and drainage

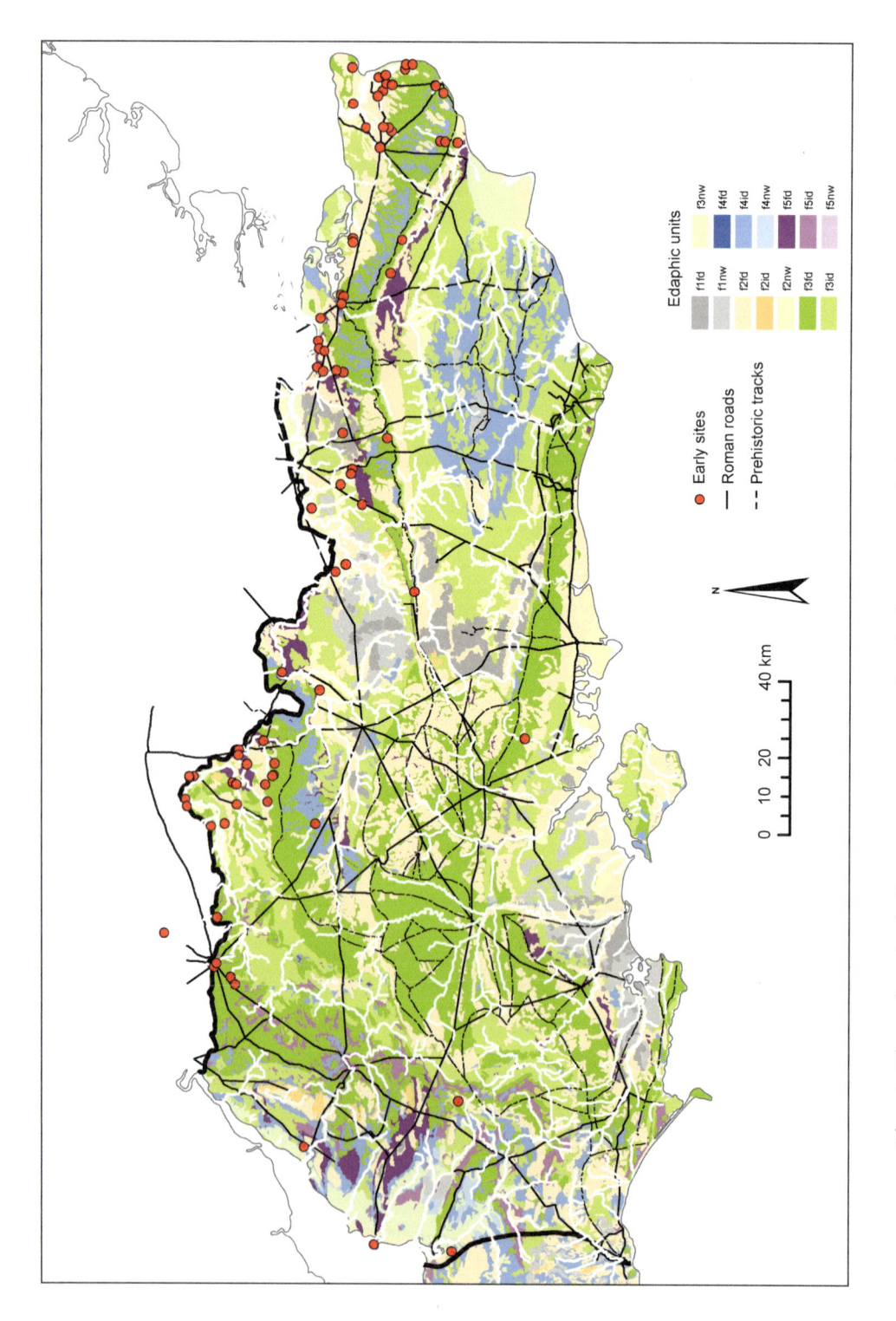

Plate 2. *The earliest Anglo-Saxon sites set against the edaphic units, with the Roman roads and trackways*

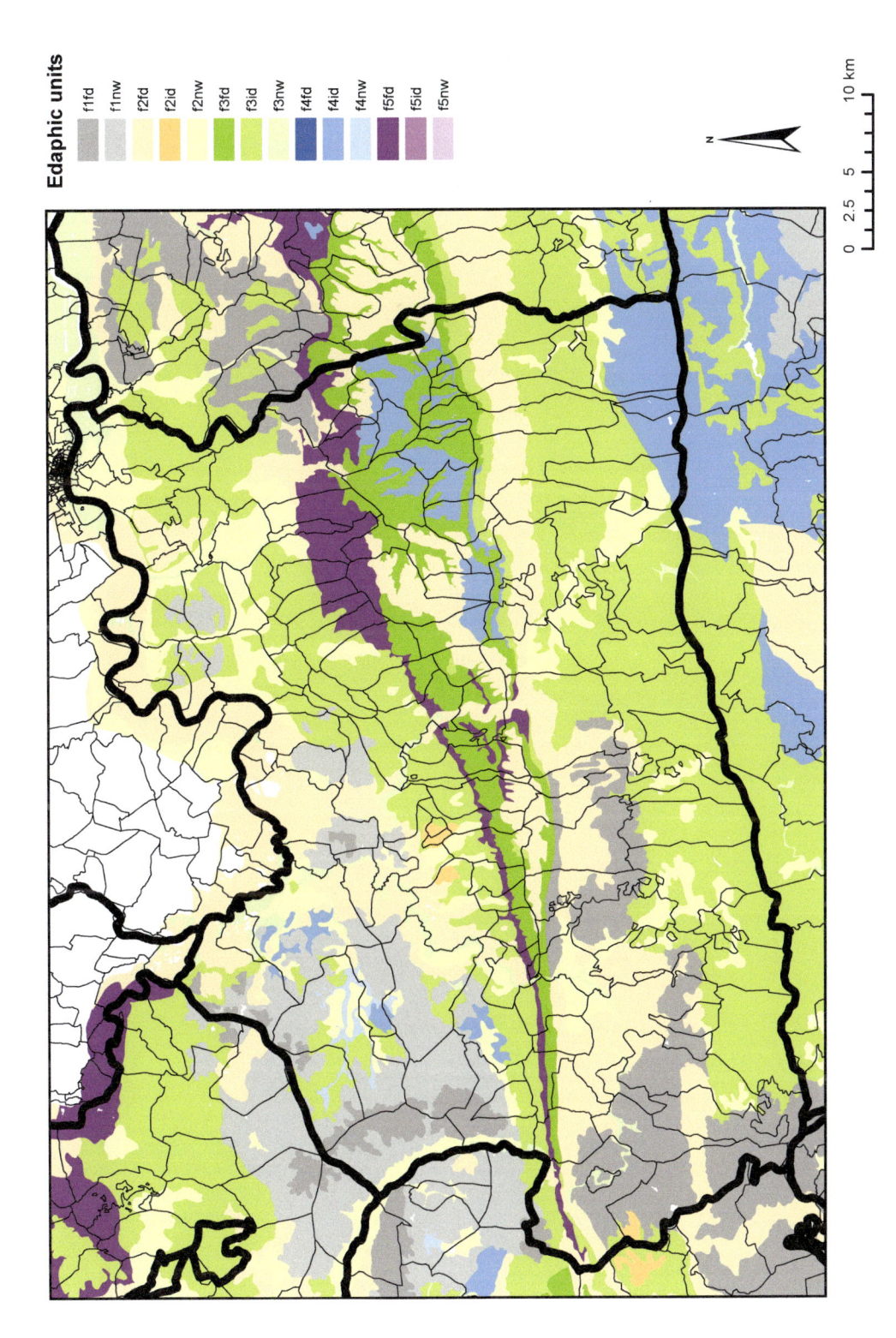

Plate 3. The Surrey parish boundaries set against the edaphic units

*Plate 4. Apple Down to Isle of Wight*

*Plate 5. Market Lavington from the edge of the site towards Salisbury Plain*

*Plate 6. Annular Brooch from Hampshire*

*Plate 7. Apple Down grave 56*

*Plate 8. Selmeston to Caburn*

*Plate 9. The Kingdom of the South Saxons across the River Ouse at Lewes*

Plate 10. Sibertswold to Barfreston